P9-DNO-314

Drug War Heresies

This book provides the first multidisciplinary and nonpartisan analysis of how the United States should decide on the legal status of cocaine, heroin, and marijuana. It draws on data about the experiences of Western European nations with less punitive drug policies as well as new analyses of America's experience with legal cocaine and heroin a century ago and of America's efforts to regulate gambling, prostitution, alcohol, and cigarettes. It offers projections on the likely consequences of a number of different legalization regimes and shows that the choice about how to regulate drugs involves complicated tradeoffs among goals and conflict among social groups. The book presents a sophisticated discussion of how society should deal with the uncertainty about the consequences of legal change. Finally, it explains, in terms of individual attitudes toward risk, why it is so difficult to accomplish substantial reform of drug policy in America.

Robert J. MacCoun, a psychologist, is Professor of Public Policy and Law at Goldman School of Public Policy and Boalt Hall School of Law, University of California, Berkeley. Previously, he was Behavioral Scientist at RAND from 1986 to 1993, where he is now a consultant. Professor MacCoun's work with Peter Reuter on street-level drug dealing in Washington, DC, European drug policies, harm reduction, and other drug policy topics has appeared in *Science*, *Psychological Bulletin*, *Journal of Policy Analysis and Management*, *Journal of Quantitative Criminology*, and *American Psychologist*. His research on jury decision making and civil litigation has appeared in *Science*, *Psychological Review*, *Journal of Personality and Social Psychology*, *Law and Society Review*, *Law and Human Behavior*, and *The Handbook of Psychology and Law*. Professor MacCoun's current work examines bias in the interpretation of research results (*Annual Review of Psychology*, 1998). He has testified before Congress and given policy briefings to many government officials in the United States and Europe and is a member of a National Academy of Sciences committee on drug policy research.

Peter Reuter, an economist, is Professor of Public Policy, School of Public Affairs and Department of Criminology, University of Maryland. He founded the RAND Drug Policy Research Center, directed it from 1989 to 1993, and continues to serve there as a consultant. Professor Reuter is currently editor of the *Journal of Policy Analysis and Management*. He is a member of the National Academy of Sciences' Committee on Law and Justice and has served on two Institute of Medicine panels. His early research focused on the organization of illegal markets and resulted in the publication of *Disorganized Crime: The Economics of the Visible Hand* (1983), which won the Leslie Wikins award as most outstanding book of the year in criminology and criminal justice. Recent papers have appeared in *Addiction*, *Journal of Quantitative Criminology*, *American Journal of Public Health*, *Journal of Policy Analysis and Management*, and *Science*. He testifies frequently before Congress and has addressed senior policy audiences in many countries, including Australia, Chile, Colombia, and Great Britain. He has served as a consultant to numerous government agencies.

RAND Studies in Policy Analysis

EDITOR: Charles Wolf, Jr., Series Economic Advisor and Corporate
Fellow in International Economics, RAND

Policy analysis is the application of scientific methods to develop
and test alternative ways of addressing social, economic, legal,
international, national security, and other problems. The RAND
Studies in Policy Analysis series aims to include several significant,
timely, and innovative works each year in this broad field. Selection
is guided by an editorial board consisting of Charles Wolf, Jr.
(editor), and David S. D. Chu, Paul K. Davis, and Lynn Karoly
(associate editors).

Also in the series:
David C. Gompert and F. Stephen Larrabee (eds.),
America and Europe: A Partnership for a New Era

John W. Peabody, M. Omar Rahman, Paul J. Gertler, Joyce Mann,
Donna O. Farley, Jeff Luck, David Robalino, and Grace M. Carter,
Policy and Health: Implications for Development in Asia

Samantha F. Ravich, *Marketization and Democracy:
East Asian Experiences*

Further Praise for *Drug War Heresies*

"Confronting the failure of our highly punitive prohibitionist policy, MacCoun and Reuter thoroughly examine the consequences of drug legalization in the United States. Marshaling the available empirical evidence, they provide an example of what a rational, sophisticated inquiry into U.S. drug policy ought to be. Works like *Drug War Heresies* are needed to shatter the current ideological barriers to vigorous public debate on alternatives to repression."

– Gerald M. Oppenheimer, *Columbia University*

"The authors have produced a clearly and well-written analysis of the complex and interconnected empirical and normative issues that make drug policy debate so contentious in the USA and elsewhere. Given the intellectual dominance of American research and thinking about drug policy in the international drug policy debate, the book has a significance that goes beyond the narrowly parochial context of the USA. The reputation and track record of the authors will guarantee the book a wide international readership."

– Wayne Hall, *University of New South Wales, Australia*

Drug War Heresies

Learning from Other Vices, Times, and Places

Robert J. MacCoun
University of California, Berkeley

Peter Reuter
University of Maryland

CAMBRIDGE
UNIVERSITY PRESS

AUSTIN COMMUNITY COLLEGE
LIBRARY SERVICES

PUBLISHED BY THE PRESS SYNDICATE OF THE UNIVERSITY OF CAMBRIDGE
The Pitt Building, Trumpington Street, Cambridge, United Kingdom

CAMBRIDGE UNIVERSITY PRESS
The Edinburgh Building, Cambridge CB2 2RU, UK
40 West 20th Street, New York, NY 10011-4211, USA
10 Stamford Road, Oakleigh, VIC 3166, Australia
Ruiz de Alarcón 13, 28014 Madrid, Spain
Dock House, The Waterfront, Cape Town 8001, South Africa

http://www.cambridge.org

© Robert J. MacCoun, Peter Reuter 2001

This book is in copyright. Subject to statutory exception
and to the provisions of relevant collective licensing agreements,
no reproduction of any part may take place without
the written permission of Cambridge University Press.

First published 2001

Printed in the United States of America

Typeface Times Roman 10.5/13 pt.   *System* QuarkXPress [BTS]

A catalog record for this book is available from the British Library.

Library of Congress Cataloging in Publication Data
MacCoun, Robert J.
    Drug war heresies: learning from other vices, times, and places / Robert J. MacCoun,
Peter Reuter.
        p. cm. – (RAND studies in policy analysis)
    Includes bibliographical references and index.
    ISBN 0-521-57263-0 (hb) – ISBN 0-521-79997-X (pb)
    1. Drug legalization – United States.   2. Narcotics, Control of – United States.
3. Narcotics, Control of – Cross-cultural studies.   4. Drug abuse – Government
policy – United States.   5. Drug abuse – Goverment policy – Cross-cultural studies.
I. Reuter, Peter, 1944– MacCoun, Robert, 1958–   II. Title.   III. Series.

HV5825 .M225 2001
364.1'77'0973–dc21   00-045451

ISBN   0 521 57263 0   hardback
ISBN   0 521 79997 X   paperback

AUSTIN COMMUNITY COLLEGE
LIBRARY SERVICES

For Madeline and Timothy

Contents

Figures and Tables

Figures

Tables

Acknowledgments

This book comes out of 10 years of research, time enough to accumulate a very long list of debts of various kinds – financial, intellectual, and personal. (We should mention that this wasn't *all* we did during the past decade – it just felt that way.)

More than perfunctory acknowledgment of foundation support, so utterly discretionary on the part of the officers, runs the risk of pandering. We gladly run that risk by expressing our gratitude to Ralph Gomory, president of the Alfred P. Sloan Foundation. The basic idea of this project, namely to provide a stronger analytic and empirical foundation for the drug legalization debate, was his. He provided a substantial enough grant to research the issue thoroughly. It was then his insistence that a series of academic articles were not enough, that the topic required a book, which led to this volume. Additional funding was provided by the Drug Policy Research Center at RAND, out of core funds from the Ford Foundation; and we thank Audrey Burnam and Martin Iguchi (the Center's Co-Directors) for that support. Barbara Williams, former Co-Director, helped in initiating the project.

Intellectually we owe a great deal to two long-term collaborators, Jonathan Caulkins and Mark Kleiman. Not only did they serve as sounding boards for many of the ideas here, but both also read the manuscript carefully and provided detailed comments. Wayne Hall's review of the manuscript was most helpful. Working with Tom Schelling, our co-author in a paper that provided an important analytic element of the book, was one of the pleasures of this whole enterprise. Joe Spillane contributed the original research reported in Chapter 9, under funding from the Sloan grant. We also benefited from collaborations early in the project with Jim Kahan and Karyn Model at RAND. Beau Kilmer joined us as a research assistant in 1997 and made a substantial contribution to the completion of a book that threatened to die a slow death of incomplete footnotes and references. Others who contributed invaluable research assistance during the project included Joel Feinleib, James Gillespie, Jeeyang Rhee, Aaron Saiger, Mark Sarney, Sue Schechter, and Heide Shockley-Phillips. Jeri Smith-Ready prepared the index.

For expert advice on our cross-national research, we thank Gabriel Bammer (Australia); Agner Skjodt, Axel Herlov, and Kavs Gravesen (Denmark); Patrick Mignon (France); Ernesto Savona, Luigi Solivetti, and Enrico Tempesta (Italy); Ed Leuw, Martin Grapendaal, Eddy Englesman, Arjan Sas, Peter Cohen, Marieke Langemeijer, and Wil de Zwart (The Netherlands); Ragnar Hauge, Ketil Beutzen, and Roger Adresen (Norway); Jodi Cami (Spain); Eckhart Kühlhorn, Orvar Olsson, and Rolf Löfstett (Sweden); Margret Rihs-Middel and Martin Gebhardt (Switzerland); and Michael Farrell and John Strang (The United Kingdom). We reserve their right to distance themselves from any egregious misunderstandings about their countries that we may have unwittingly perpetuated here.

Rob MacCoun would like to express his love and gratitude to Lori Dair, but her distaste for clichés makes this almost impossible. Nevertheless, she was a careful and thoughtful commentator, a generous (if sometimes ignored) arbiter of taste and style, a constant source of encouragement, and she resisted snide comments each time he announced that the book would be done in one more week.

1 Preface and Overview

PART I: OVERVIEW

Americans have long recognized that psychoactive drugs can create serious hazards for users and others. Yet some see the nation's principal drug problem not as the drugs themselves but rather prohibition and its enforcement. America's highly punitive version of prohibition is intrusive, divisive, and expensive and leaves the United States with a drug problem that is worse than that of any other wealthy nation. Notwithstanding a very substantial investment of resources and of public authority and rhetoric in drug control, there is little sign of major remission in America's drug problems.

It is not surprising then that some advocate a repeal of the prohibition of cocaine, heroin, and marijuana. Legalization has been a politically weak but intellectually powerful influence in American life for the last decade. Its criticism of the current regime has a great deal of truth in it. The most conspicuous harms of drugs currently are those caused by prohibition, namely crime, disorder, corruption, and the diseases related to injecting with dirty needles. From that critique, the legalizers conclude that elimination of prohibition is essential. They assert that legalization would reduce disease, crime, and human suffering.

Arrayed against them, but with a curiously weak representation in the academic and intellectual community, are all the forces of political power. Few basic American policy doctrines are more fervently and frequently affirmed by the President and major politicians of

1

both parties than that the nation must continue to enforce toughly prohibitions of cocaine, heroin, and marijuana as the principal means for reducing their use. No major political figure, and but a handful of lesser ones, has advocated legalization or even discussion of it. The dangers of any relaxation, summarized in the ubiquitous warning "sending the wrong signal," make legalization a taboo topic.

But given the pervasiveness of the American drug problem, and the many visible drawbacks of the punitive way the nation confronts it, many are curious to know whether a dramatically less invasive policy might be preferable.

This book assesses the likely effects of legalization. It reviews a wide variety of experiences and theories that have been used in the debates and some other experiences that could help inform those debates. We offer it as an honest guide for those who are curious about legalization but warn that it does not reach a strong conclusion about what should be done. Instead, we will attempt to review comprehensively what is and is not known; project the likely consequences of alternative regimes for cocaine, heroin, and marijuana; highlight the most important tradeoffs posed by these alternative regimes; and identify the policy and political implications of the uncertainty and complexity of the projections.

Chapter 2 describes current U.S. drug problems and policies. Though illicit drug use is much less common than in 1980, the severity of the drug problem in terms of addiction, crime, disorder, and disease is only somewhat moderated from its recent peaks.

By the late 1990s, 400,000 persons were imprisoned for drug offenses, compared to fewer than 50,000 in 1985. Blacks and Hispanics constitute three-quarters of those locked up for drug offenses, compared to half of total incarcerations for property and violent crimes. Drug testing and other searches have become ubiquitous features of many settings, such as schools and workplaces.

Notwithstanding all this, illicit drugs remain available and widely used by adolescents and young adults; more than half of high school seniors report having at least tried an illicit drug. The fraction who become frequent users of more dangerous drugs (cocaine, heroin, and methamphetamine) remains modest (indeed is declining), but these drugs continue to be available to large sectors of the population.

Illicit drugs are extraordinarily expensive compared to what they would cost if available legally. For example, cocaine sells for ten times the price of gold. Illicit drug markets generate earnings of about $50 billion in the United States and such large incomes in Colombia and Mexico that drug dealers threaten the stability of governments.

U.S. policy remains frozen in a punitive mode. Illicit drugs are perceived primarily as a crime problem rather than as a public health problem. The appropriate response then is seen as tough punishment and that has been the dominant element of policy since 1980.

PART II: THE ARGUMENTS

The basic philosophical arguments regarding prohibition have a long history, most famously in John Stuart Mill's *On Liberty*. What is new in the last decade is that they are being articulated more forcefully and that the anti-Prohibitionists have become more pragmatic. The first section of the book assesses the theoretical bases of prohibition and its critiques.

Chapter 3 describes the emergence of the modern American debate and its social and political context. Though sanctions for marijuana possession were hotly debated in the 1970s, there was little discussion of broader drug law reform till the late 1980s. An analysis of newspaper editorial and op-ed essays show a sudden upsurge in writing on this topic in 1988, just as public concern about the damage from drugs was reaching near panic levels. The debate has been essentially ideological, with bitter denunciations of motivation on both sides. Senior federal officials and politicians make frequent and shrill denunciations of the dangers even of discussion of legalization. The arguments are repetitious. In the absence of systematic empirical work, references to the failure of Prohibition and the success or failure of more-harm-reduction oriented Western European policies play an important role.

Since the late 1980s, the legalization movement has established a reasonably firm institutional base, but it remains politically marginal, unable to generate any increase in popular support. While propositions allowing the use of marijuana for medical purposes, laxly defined, have now passed in seven states, public opposition to legalization has remained stable for many years.

Chapter 4 examines a wide array of philosophical arguments about the moral basis for prohibition. None of them can resolve the matter

without complex empirical inquiry, unless one subscribes to a deontological position that moral obligations hold irrespective of empirical consequences. The deontological position for legalization is
libertarian – there is a natural right to use drugs. The deontological
position for prohibition is the "legal moralist" view that drug use is
intrinsically immoral and must be banned for that reason.

The classic liberal position, rooted in Mill, does not provide an
unequivocally libertarian conclusion about prohibition. Though there
is a strong presumption toward individual freedom in making choices,
negative consequences for others can override that. Yet another
philosophical position, legal paternalism, focuses on harms to self; it
asserts that prohibition may be invoked if to do so would reduce the
harms suffered by the users themselves, a proposition of considerable
plausibility given the pain that many suffer from addiction itself and
their claims of difficulty in controlling their conduct. On principled
grounds, citizens may differ on the relative weight they give to various
types of harms to users and nonusers and on whether fundamental
moral principles trump any consideration of empirical consequences
at all. While the remainder of the book is consequentialist in
approach, we do not contend that the drug control dilemma could be
"solved" purely by a technocratic algorithm or analysis, no matter
how complete the relevant data.

How might one predict the impact of lifting prohibitions on drug
use and drug-related harms (Chapters 5 and 6)? Formal prohibitions
can affect the decision to use drugs in at least seven different ways,
ranging from "forbidden fruit," whereby the very existence of a prohibition increases curiosity about drugs, to price mechanisms, where
the higher price under a toughly enforced prohibition reduces initiation. Almost nothing is known directly about the relative importance
of these individual mechanisms. Research on the effects of marijuana
depenalization (a term we prefer to the potentially misleading label
"decriminalization") provides the most direct evidence. Twelve states
depenalized marijuana possession in the 1970s; the change appears
to have had little or no impact on the prevalence of marijuana use
or on adolescents' attitudes and beliefs about marijuana use. The
experience is not conclusive because the policy difference between
low enforcement marijuana prohibition and depenalization turns out
to be surprisingly slight. But the American experience is mirrored
by similarly weak effects of depenalization in Australia in the 1990s

and the Netherlands between 1976 and the mid-1980s. (As discussed in Chapter 11, the Dutch system later evolved away from simple depenalization toward de facto legalization.)

Many laws are a product of social norms; for example, a popular social movement appears to be driving antitobacco legislation today. The law probably plays a reciprocal role in shaping and reinforcing informal norms and beliefs. If so, legalization (allowing sale and production as well as possession) might weaken existing social norms against drug use. Also, some of the informal sanctions that work as deterrence factors – the embarrassment and threat to relationships and opportunities that can result from being arrested – would no longer be operative in a legalization regime.

But the argument on prohibition is only partly about the prevalence of drug use. Prohibition brings a variety of harms (Chapter 6). Some arise from the extent of drug use (e.g., reduced commitment to education by adolescents); others are primarily driven by illegality per se (e.g., the creation of black markets and use of dangerous diluents); and yet others are principally a function of the stringency of enforcement (corruption and criminal incomes).

These harms are not evenly distributed in society. Much of the crime and violence associated with drugs comes from trafficking rather than consumption. The resulting harms are borne principally by the urban poor.

PART III: THE EVIDENCE

The United States has no experience in modern times with legal availability of these specific drugs, so the empirical argument has proceeded largely by analogy. Casual and sometimes careless references are made to other periods, other places, and other substances and behaviors to project the consequences of legalization.

We give particular attention to certain distinctive features of American society and law. The combination of First Amendment protections on commercial free speech and the political economy of taxation (e.g., large corporate campaign contributions) help generate low excise taxes and loose regulation. After a drug is legalized for any but medicinal purposes, its promotion and sale are likely to be subject to only modest regulations and taxes.

Other vices

Prostitution and gambling have, like heroin and cocaine, generated enormous illegal markets in the past, been the source of endless corruption, and the centerpiece of moralistic debates about prohibition (Chapter 7). Prostitution, little referred to in the current legalization debate, represents an illegal market subject to very light enforcement, aimed not so much at reducing the extent of prostitution as the disorder, incivility, and crime that can be associated with its unregulated operation. It is an illustration of harm-reduction-oriented enforcement; it has been successful enough that, notwithstanding a continuing flow of low-level corruption cases, a large illegal prostitution industry has not been seen as a major social problem.

Gambling represents the opposite policy dynamic. In one generation, the United States has shifted from an almost universal prohibition to almost universal availability of lotteries and casinos. The thirty-seven state-operated lotteries aggressively promote a product that is taxed much more heavily than any other precisely because it is still considered frivolous or harmful. Lottery sales are disproportionately to the poorest members of society, generating an extremely regressive tax collection. Lotteries illustrate the difficulty of restraining the production of a vice, even (perhaps *particularly*) when the state itself is the operator.

Tobacco and alcohol (Chapter 8) are closer to the central target, since both are substances with high dependency potential. Both were once illegal, cigarettes in only a few states and alcohol, more notoriously, for the entire nation from 1919 to 1933. Both are now massive industries selling products that give pleasure to vast numbers while shortening the lives of a significant fraction. Finally, both have been targeted for many years by public health activists who accept their legal status but have sought to restrict availability and promotion and to raise the price substantially. Outright prohibition is almost reflexively rejected, with references to the failure of the Prohibition era as apparently overwhelming evidence.

Tobacco is the most active policy battlefront. A continuing and extraordinarily prominent public health campaign has cut overall smoking rates by one-half in a generation, but high school senior rates of cigarette use have been stuck around 20 percent since 1982.

A wide array of civil restrictions on the convenience of smoking (e.g., broad workplace prohibitions), education programs, and increasing pressure from physicians have made smoking a stigmatized behavior in many communities and subcultures. Nonetheless, the industry has until recently defeated the imposition of much restriction on commercial promotion or of punitive taxes. The legal battles continue and may indeed eventually yield major victories. Nonetheless, it is striking that a generation after the nation became aware of the dangers of smoking, the industry has managed to retain and promote a mass legal market for a deadly product.

Alcohol regulation has been more restrictive. Repeal was a rejection of Prohibition but less than a ringing endorsement of unrestricted access to liquor. Since Repeal the restrictions have been gradually eroded, except for those governing the minimum legal drinking age. Efforts to restrict the promotion of alcohol have been squarely halted by the courts. Taxation is, by international and historical standards, very modest. Harm reduction programs, aimed particularly at youthful drinking and driving, along with other measures specifically aimed at reducing drunk driving, have had a substantial impact on youth road-fatality rates but not much on youth drinking itself. Alcohol consumption still leads to 100,000 excess deaths annually.

American society has shown little capacity to restrict the marketing of vices once they are legalized. If cocaine, heroin, or marijuana were legal, we assume controls and taxation would be light, unless distribution were left in the hands of doctors.

History

There were no prohibitions on cocaine or heroin until the 1914 Harrison Act (Chapter 9). Reference to the nation's "first cocaine epidemic" is a staple (though low-salience) item in the legalization debate.

Cocaine was a major addition to the small pharmacopoeia available to physicians in the late nineteenth century, but medical practice quickly turned away from a drug that generated addiction and violence in patients. Compared to the 1990s, cocaine use was no more than one-fifth as common, and it led to much less violent crime. Nonetheless, there was little hesitation about prohibiting cocaine in the Harrison Act of 1914 because it had become a recreational drug, mostly consumed by the unrespectable and with no substantial therapeutic base.

Was the legal cocaine regime a failure? Cocaine consumption and related problems apparently declined substantially following the Harrison Act and remained quite low for fifty years; to that extent prohibition looks successful. However, cocaine use was already declining before those prohibitions were introduced; as is often the case, the law ratified ongoing changes in social attitudes. Moreover, the severity of contemporary cocaine addiction problems is far greater than those in the earlier era of legal availability.

Western Europe

Chapters 10, 11, and 12 examine European drug control experiences over the last twenty years. It is well known that some Western European nations have adopted drug policies that seem much more tolerant than those in the United States.

Chapter 10 provides a broad overview of drug laws and policies in ten nations in Western Europe: Denmark, France, Germany, Italy, the Netherlands, Norway, Spain, Sweden, Switzerland, and the United Kingdom. All have a smaller drug problem than the United States, whether measured by drug use, addiction, or drug-related violence. No European nation has legalized any of the drugs prohibited in the United States – although the Dutch cannabis policy comes close. But two nations, Italy and Spain, depenalized the possession of drugs several decades ago, and all ten nations enforce their drug laws less aggressively than the United States. Consistent with theory and U.S. evidence cited in Chapter 5, the best available indicators of the stringency of drug law enforcement and the prevalence of cannabis and injection drug use suggest little apparent link between drug law enforcement and the prevalence of drug use. But for various reasons, these cross-national comparisons are problematic.

Chapter 11 examines the Dutch cannabis regime from 1976 to the present. Though cannabis remains illegal in the Netherlands, the Dutch have adopted an explicit, formal policy of nonenforcement for possession or sales of small quantities. The Dutch policy evolved from a depenalization regime (mid-1970s to mid-1980s) to a de facto legalization regime (since the mid-1980s); the distinctive character of the latter was the commercialization of cannabis via an expanding network of coffee shops, engaging in increasingly overt promotion. Depenalization, per se, had no detectable effect on cannabis use. However, data from the second decade suggest that the gradual commercialization of cannabis was associated with rising levels of use in the Netherlands, increases not seen elsewhere.

Chapter 12 examines how European nations have addressed the health consequences of heroin addiction. In the 1980s the emergence of the HIV/AIDS epidemic led many nations to reframe drugs as principally a public health problem. They saw drug enforcement as contributing to the spread of HIV, creating significant tensions between public health concerns and traditional police enforcement of drug laws. Cross-national differences in provision of clean needles and methadone (a heroin substitute) provide some indication that these interventions are associated with more modest health consequences (specifically, overdose deaths and HIV/AIDS among drug users). These comparisons are based on questionable data and support only weak inferences, but our conclusion is consistent with a growing body of more rigorous and focused program evaluation evidence.

Switzerland has tried to move beyond needle and methadone provision by implementing two novel variations on traditional heroin prohibition. One, a "zone of tolerance" at the so-called Needle Park in Zurich (the Platzspitz), allowed addicts to congregate and inject openly without fear of legal sanctions, facilitating contact with health services. By all accounts, the Platzspitz experiment was a failure, though a revealing one. The second innovation was a quasi-experimental study of governmental provision of heroin (heroin maintenance) and was judged to be a success, though a careful look suggests some important qualifications to that conclusion.

The experiences described in Chapters 7 to 12 suggest a number of propositions. The four principal propositions follow. First, the removal of criminal penalties for possession is unlikely to increase significantly the numbers who use drugs. Second, legalization is very likely to lead to commercialization of the product – lower prices, easier access, and heavy promotion. Third, commercialization will generate higher prevalence and consumption. Finally, prohibition is a major source of harms and yet legalized intoxicant use is far from harmless; there is no evidentiary or analytical basis for quantifying total harm under either type of regime.

PART IV: ASSESSING THE ALTERNATIVES

Projecting changes in total drug-related harm

Legalization is an intellectually serious alternative that merits close examination. The prohibition of psychoactive drugs cannot be justified through a cavalier assertion that they are dangerous, not in a nation that allows the promotion and distribution of cigarettes and alcohol and views its Prohibition era as an unmitigated failure of government intrusion into private conduct.

Legalization is a portmanteau term, encompassing a wide array of regimes that push criminal sanctions to the margin. These regimes can be evaluated by breaking up the damages caused by drug use into three components, as expressed in the following relationship:

$$\text{Total Harm} = \text{Number of Users} \times \text{Average Number of Doses/User} \times \text{Harm/Dose}$$

or more simply

$$\text{Total Harm} = \text{Prevalence} \times \text{Intensity} \times \text{Harmfulness}$$

Using the evidence and theory presented in earlier chapters, we make projections of the likelihood of significant increase or decrease in these three components, and their major elements, under various regime changes.

Cocaine or heroin adult legal market

If cocaine or heroin were to become available to adults generally, use and addiction would substantially increase. Some health and social costs, such as poor parenting, reduced treatment seeking, and workplace intoxication, would probably increase as a consequence. For heroin, that increase must be balanced against the large reductions in the immiserization of addicts, criminal justice costs, criminality, and AIDS transmission. Cocaine dependence poses greater risks to others through disinhibition (in the form of both accidents and violence), even though there would be quite limited gains from reduced AIDS transmission and deaths due to adulterants.

Heroin maintenance

Providing heroin to registered addicts poses little risk of adverse outcomes and may yield substantial gains, if the program diverts sufficient numbers from the street market. The only source of risk is increased prevalence of heroin use, which seems unlikely. The Swiss trials suggests that if a substantial percentage of current heroin addicts were to participate, heroin maintenance might result in large gains in health, social functioning, and criminal justice costs.

Cannabis

These projections are made with more confidence because more directly relevant evidence is available.

Depenalization of itself has minimal consequence for prevalence, either of marijuana or any other drug; increases no harms; and reduces criminal justice costs and infringements on liberty and privacy. Depenalization still leaves the black market untouched, indeed perhaps even slightly expanded if the duration of marijuana-using careers is extended by the reduction in stigma and legal risk.

Depenalization along with removal of sanctions for home production and gifts (within quantity limits – the model used in South Australia) should substantially weaken the black market and generate a much greater reduction in criminal justice costs, with at most a small effect on prevalence and intensity of use.

Full-scale legalization is much more likely to increase prevalence, and somewhat raise intensity, because promotion could not be controlled in the United States. Relative to depenalization with home production, there are no major additional gains to counterbalance the increase in prevalence.

Weighing the alternatives

How should the consequences of these regime changes be assessed? Such assessment is not simply a matter of adding up the gains and losses for three reasons.

1. The magnitudes of changes in prevalence of use, addiction, and related harms are extremely uncertain. Moreover, many of the harms, such as intrusiveness and sentencing inequity, do not lend themselves to quantification, let alone monetization.
2. The advantages and disadvantages of regime changes will be unevenly distributed across segments of society. Changes that promise substantial reduction in illegal sales confer large net benefits on urban minority communities that suffer so much from black markets and their accompanying crime and disorder, even if the changes may also increase the level of drug use and addiction in those communities. For the middle class, the benefits of eliminating the black market may look very small in comparison to the costs of increased risk of drug involvement of other family members, particularly adolescent children.
3. How one weights the changes depends on one's values and on the normative framework one applies. For legal moralists, the increase in drug use under most of these changes is, of itself, a major detriment to the changes. From a strict Millian perspective, harms borne by others are the only harms that should be weighed, whereas legal paternalists also give weight to those borne by the user. How does one trade off reductions in violence against potential increases in accidents and other behavioral risks of drug use? How much weight should be given to the harm caused by prohibiting any benefits of drug use, a factor resolutely ignored by most in the debate?

How strong is the case for each of these regime changes? That depends on the standard of proof that one applies. We suggest three relevant standards.

> ***The philosophical standard.*** If we were to start a society from scratch, the burden might well be placed on those who would prohibit drug use. If this standard were applied today, the current laws would be changed unless prohibiters could make a convincing case. Only libertarians believe this to be the applicable standard.

> ***The political standard.*** In the United States at the end of the twentieth century, public opinion and the almost complete absence of drug reform rhetoric among elected officials make it clear that the political burden lies on those who would advocate significant relaxations in our current drug laws. To carry the day politically, any projected net gains from

legal change must have a high certainty, and the projected changes should not offend fundamental values, such as substantially increasing the extent of intoxication or use, particularly among the young.

The policy analytic standard. There is an intermediate standard: a change in laws is justified if (a) theory and available evidence provide reasonable confidence that the change would yield (b) a net reduction in total drug-related harm (c) across all but the most extreme weightings of types of harm (morbidity vs. crime vs. lost liberty) and bearers (users vs. nonusers, the middle class vs. the urban poor).

We believe that heroin maintenance can meet the policy analytic standard but almost certainly not the political standard. The projections do not have sufficiently high credibility. Moreover, there is likely to be considerable public skepticism of the direct provision by the state of a drug that has been the source of so much actual damage (albeit much because of conditions created by policy). Cannabis depenalization can meet both standards; it generates important gains and no losses, unless one believes, against the weight of the evidence and the stronger theoretical arguments, that initiation of cannabis use will rise and that this will in turn lead to a higher prevalence of more dangerous drugs. Allowing home production and gifts may not meet the political standard, given that the Alaska data are weak and that there is a potential for increased consumption among users.

Sale of cocaine or heroin to adults can meet only extreme philosophical standards. There is clearly a substantial risk of increasing total harm to society, notwithstanding substantial reductions in crime-related harms.

Prospects for change

American policy seems paralyzed; on the basis of a false dichotomy between two extremes – a Bennett-style War on Drugs and a libertarian free market – more moderate alternatives to the status quo are either buried or crushed by the political mainstream. This is largely traceable to a sweeping but unreflective allegiance to "prevalence reduction" – the notion that the only defensible goal for drug policy is to reduce the number of users, hopefully to zero. Two other strategies seem equally important for rational drug control: quantity reduction (reducing the quantity consumed by those who won't quit using drugs) and harm reduction (reducing the harmful consequences of drug use when it occurs). There are tradeoffs among these strategies, but they are less severe than the ones implied by the sweeping cliché "would send the wrong message." An examination of the political psychology of attitudes toward drugs helps to explain the quagmire; it also suggests reasons why the public could shift views rapidly and unexpectedly.

We believe that our conclusions concerning the potential desirability of some major legal reforms have a reasonable empirical and ethical basis. To scorn discussion and analysis of major change, in light of the extraordinary problems associated with our current policies, is frivolous and uncaring.

2 Drug Prohibition: American Style

The legalization debate can be understood only in the context of existing American drug policies and the confusing debate about how poorly or successfully they have worked in recent years. This chapter attempts to provide a parsimonious description of both U.S. policies and their effects.

PATTERNS OF DRUG USE

Occasional drug use

Since the mid-1970s, drug use in the general population has been tracked through two regular surveys, one of the household population [the National Household Survey on Drug Abuse (NHSDA)] and the other of high school students [Monitoring the Future (MTF)]. The two surveys tell a consistent story, as illustrated in Figure 2.1.

Experimentation with drugs is a common experience among adolescents (Kandel, 1993; Shedler & Block, 1990). In most birth cohorts since 1960, over half have tried an illicit drug, marijuana being used far more commonly than the others. Taking out marijuana, the figure drops dramatically. Only 28 percent of high school seniors in 1994 reported trying some illicit drug other than marijuana; 38 percent had tried only marijuana. The birth cohorts coming to maturity in the late 1970s (i.e., born between 1957 and 1962) were much more involved with drugs than any other cohorts. The figures for high school seniors dropped dramatically in the 1980s. They have risen substantially and

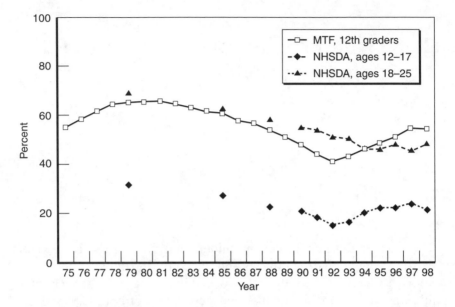

Figure 2.1 Percentage reporting use of illicit drug at least once in their lifetime, 1975–95

steadily since the early 1990s but remain well below the peak figures of the late 1970s (Johnston, O'Malley, & Bachman, 1997; Bachman, Johnston, & O'Malley, 1998).

Most who start using illicit drugs desist of their own volition, without treatment or coercion, within five years.[1] Indeed, even by age 18 most of those who have been daily users of marijuana have cut back from that rate[2]; most who try drugs, even a number of times, do not become dependent users. This represents a very different pattern from that for the legally available psychoactive drugs, alcohol, and cigarettes; most who use alcohol and tobacco even occasionally have lengthy careers, measured in terms of decades. In the case of cigarettes, users consume quite heavily (over half consume at least 15

---

1. Ebener et al. (1994) reported that in the NHSDA 60 percent of respondents report that they are no longer using within five years of initiation (p. A19).
2. *Monitoring the Future* included a question about whether the respondent has ever been a daily user of marijuana for at least one month. In 1994, 11.3 percent reported that they had been at some point; only 3.6 percent reported that they had used daily in the past 30 days (Johnston, O'Malley, & Bachman, 1995, p. 263).

cigarettes per day) throughout most of that career (Centers for Disease Control, 1994).

Why desistance comes so early and easily to most users of illicit drugs is an important question that has received almost no attention. There are references in the literature (Kandel & Chen, 1995) to "maturing out," particularly from marijuana use, which is a description rather than an explanation. There is evidence that moving from school and college settings, in which drugs are more readily accessible and more widely used, into adult communities and roles (especially parenthood) leads to desistance (Bachman et al., 1997). If so, the shortness of most drug-using careers can be marked up as a success of prohibition. However, it is also possible that these specific drugs are simply not so attractive over the long run, particularly as young people start to accept greater responsibilities in the form of marriage and child rearing (Kandel & Chen, 1995).

The patterns of drug use across socioeconomic and demographic groups have changed in interesting ways during the last twenty years. The increases in the late 1970s were quite uniform by education and across ethnic groups. The declines in the 1980s were not nearly so uniform. Whereas in 1985 for males there was only a very slight correlation between use of cocaine (as reported in the National Household Survey on Drug Abuse) and education, by 1990 the NHSDA found a strong negative correlation, a change that has also been observed, over a longer period, for cigarettes (Schelling, 1992). The educated may be much more sensitive to health (and other) messages about the dangers of drug use, including cigarettes. There has also been a much noted but unexplained differential in rates of drug use among African-American high school students; for marijuana only 26.2 percent report use in the past year in 1994, compared to 34.2 percent among white students.

Frequent use

These surveys rely on self-report by members of the household and high school populations. They probably capture the general trends in occasional drug use. They clearly do much less well in describing trends in dependent use, for at least three reasons: dependent users are (a) much more likely to be nonrespondents to these surveys because they lead more erratic lives, (b) less likely to provide truthful responses to survey questions, and (c) more likely to be found among nonhousehold populations (e.g., the homeless and incarcerated[3]). Indicative of this is the fact that the federal government did not produce official estimates of the size of the heroin-addicted population for almost twenty years and in doing so recently has relied primarily on data sources other than the household survey.

The best estimates (which are not very good) of the numbers dependent on expensive drugs (principally cocaine and heroin) suggest a pattern over time that is very different from that for occasional use. There was rapid recruitment into heroin use in the late 1960s and early 1970s, but this abruptly ended; by 1975 the number of new heroin initiates had dropped dramatically and has stayed low ever since.[4] However, heroin addiction (at least for those addicted in the United States rather than while with the military in Vietnam) has turned out to be a very long-lived condition; the addicts recruited between 1967 and 1973 were still mostly addicted in 1990, as revealed in a remarkable 24-year follow-up of a California sample. Hser, Anglin, and Powers (1993) found 28 percent had died after 24 years and that only 25 percent of the remainder tested negative for opiates at that point. It is now estimated that there are almost a million heroin addicts, not including those incarcerated, whether for drug offenses or some other crimes (Rhodes et al., 2000).

Cocaine dependence grew in the 1980s, as the pool of those who had experimented with the drug expanded. The probability that someone who experimented with cocaine became a dependent user was about 17 percent (Anthony, Warner, & Kessler, 1994). Rhodes

3. Official estimates of drug use omit the incarcerated, on the assumption that they do not continue to use drugs while in prison. The prevalence of drug use in prisons has been found relatively low (unpublished data from the Bureau of Prisons in Bureau of Justice Statistics, 1992, p. 198), and those who do use probably use small amounts because they have access to few funds. Nonetheless, since most drug addicts who are incarcerated return to frequent drug use on release, it is reasonable to include them in measures of the severity of the problem if one defines it as the number of persons whose lives are adversely affected by drug consumption.

4. There is a continuing claim of a new heroin epidemic (e.g., ONDCP, 1996), but none of the existing indicators (e.g., urinalysis of arrestees) shows any such epidemic (Reuter, 1999). Some observers claim that it is primarily among middle class young adults (e.g. Wren, 1999), which would explain it being missed by these indicators, but so far the evidence is only moderately convincing, consisting mainly of anecdotes of heroin overdoses among young adults in unexpected settings, such as Plano, Texas, a stable middle class community.

et al. (1997) estimated that the number of persons using cocaine weekly peaked about 1988 at 3.6 million, some of whom were also heroin dependent. By 1995 that figure may have declined to about 3.3 million, perhaps because so many were incarcerated. Whether dependence on a stimulant can be maintained as long as narcotic dependence is unclear, but there are certainly many cocaine users who have, over a ten-year period, maintained frequent use of the drug, albeit with less regularity than heroin addicts. Desistance early in a career of regular use seems to be strongly and positively associated with education; thus, those who have continued to be frequent cocaine users are less educated and more criminally active.

Cocaine dependence is heavily concentrated in inner-city minority communities. Though it is often, and correctly, asserted that rates of drug use are similar in the major ethnic communities of the United States (African-American, Hispanic, non-Hispanic white), a variety of imperfect data sources point to a dramatic concentration of frequent cocaine use among urban African-Americans and Hispanics. For example, research has shown that a high proportion of those arrested in large cities are dependent on cocaine and that they account for a large fraction of the total cocaine-dependent population (Wish, 1990–1). The arrested population is disproportionately drawn from young minority males. The same inference about the concentration of cocaine dependence can be drawn from data on the composition of the populations in treatment and those seeking help in emergency rooms for cocaine-related problems.[5]

Many more people are dependent on marijuana than on either cocaine or heroin. At least 2 million use the drug daily, indeed as frequently as three times per day. According to the NHSDA, of those who are dependent on illicit drugs, the majority are dependent only on marijuana (Ebener et al., 1994). The percentage of marijuana users diagnosed by the Diagnostic Interview Schedule as ever dependent is approximately 10 percent (Reilly et al., 1998). In Chapter 14, we suggest that cannabis dependence may be a different phenomenon than cocaine or heroin dependence. However, there is little research

5. Data from SAMHSA's Drug Abuse Warning Network (1997a) indicated that "in 1996, 66 percent of cocaine-related episodes occurred among males. By race/ethnicity, 52 percent occurred among blacks, 30 percent among whites, and 11 percent among Hispanics."

about these users and only a tiny fraction of them seek treatment each year.[6] It seems that though most of them would like to quit and have been unable to do so, this dependence does not produce great damage to them or to others (Kleiman, 1992a, Chapter 9). Whether these are five-year or fifteen-year dependence careers is difficult to determine, but the severity of addiction is modest enough that there is scarcely any research on treatment of marijuana dependence.

Drugs other than cocaine, heroin, and marijuana are widely used only in certain places or for limited periods of time in the United States. For example, amphetamines are prevalent in Dallas, San Diego, and a few other cities but almost unheard of in most of the country; for many years half of all deaths related to amphetamines were found in just five cities.[7] PCP (phencyclidine, a hallucinogen) was found in the urine of about half of all arrestees in Washington, DC, in 1987; in Baltimore, just 35 miles away, the figure was less than 5 percent. The fraction in Washington dropped rapidly and has remained below 10 percent since 1990.[8] More recently, there has been a sharp upsurge in the fraction of arrestees testing positive for methamphetamines in a number of Western and Midwestern cities, generating a concern about a new national epidemic in a cheap stimulant.

Expenditures on illicit drugs, one metric for the damage they do to society through crime and the generation of criminal incomes, are estimated to be close to $60 billion annually, roughly 1 percent of Personal Consumption Expenditures (Rhodes et al., 1997). It is likely that no other illicit market has ever generated such a large income to sellers.[9] Most of this money goes to those at the bottom of the dis-

6. There were approximately 190,000 treatment admissions in 1997 for which marijuana was the primary drug of abuse. It was listed as a secondary drug by a similar number of those admitted with some other primary drug of abuse. However, the user base (taking those who used in the last year) is about 20 million so that no more than 1 percent seek treatment. If one takes account of the estimates of marijuana dependence, the fraction rises to around 5 percent.
7. In 1994, Las Vegas, Los Angeles, Phoenix, San Diego, and San Francisco accounted for 414 of the recorded 492 deaths attributed to methamphetamine or speed in twenty-six metropolitan areas reporting to the Medical Examiner panel of the Drug Abuse Warning Network (DAWN).
8. Monthly data memorandum from the DC Pretrial Services Agency.
9. Systematic estimates of the scale of illegal markets are almost nonexistent. See Simon and Witte (1982) for a review of estimates at the end of the 1970s. Dertouzos, Larson, and Ebener (1999) provided a figure of $5 billion for stolen computer hardware in 1995, often alleged to be a very significant contemporary illegal market; most of that loss results from indirect economic effects rather than theft and resale itself.

tribution system,[10] who earn modest incomes. In Washington, DC, we estimated that in 1988 the average street dealer working four or five days a week earned about $25,000 per annum (Reuter et al., 1990). Studies for more recent years suggest a substantially lower figure (e.g., Bourgois, 1996) However, there are vast numbers of such sellers; nationally, if one includes marijuana, there are certainly more than 1 million.

DRUG-RELATED PROBLEMS

Under current conditions, many of the adverse effects associated with drug use in the United States are the crime and morbidity/mortality arising from prohibition or its enforcement. As already mentioned, a large share of those who commit crimes are frequent users of drugs, as revealed by the Drug Use Forecasting (DUF) system [now Arrestee Drug Abuse Monitoring (ADAM) system]; in most cities over half test positive for some drug other than marijuana, usually cocaine (National Institute of Justice, 1997). Nor is this simply a reflection of the expenditure preferences of the criminally active. Drug use exacerbates the criminal activity of those who are frequent users of expensive drugs; the same person may commit five times as many offenses when using drugs as when abstinent. For example, Ball et al. (1982) followed 243 Baltimore addicts for 11 years and found that they committed crimes on 248 days each year when using heroin and only on 41 days when abstinent. Moreover, there is a good basis for believing that a large fraction of those now dependent on cocaine and heroin are criminally active. An interesting way of expressing this is that over half of all cocaine and heroin is probably purchased by users who were formally under the control of the criminal justice system (i.e., on pretrial release, probation, or parole; Kleiman, 1997). Frequent use of marijuana, without involvement with cocaine or heroin, does not seem to be criminogenic itself, though it may be predictive, inasmuch as it increases the probability of involvement with cocaine and heroin.

10. The explanation for this statement, made in a much more definitive fashion than others in this chapter, is that the mark-ups at the low levels of the drug trade are so high, between 50 and 100 percent. If each of the last two mark-ups are two-thirds, then those two transactions account for 64 percent of the retail price. We are assuming, with some empirical basis, that this money goes to the agents at the retail and low wholesale level, rather than to higher level bosses.

The connections between expensive drug use and crime are multiple and complex. Most of the crimes seem to be the consequence of the extraordinary value of the drugs under a prohibition regime. A great deal of violence is generated by the markets, both directly and indirectly. For example, a careful study in New York City in 1988 (Goldstein, Brownstein, & Ryan, 1992) estimated that 53 percent of homicides were related to drug selling or use; of those, 14 percent were classified as psychopharmacological (68 percent involving alcohol), while 74 percent were classified as by-products of drug trafficking (88 percent involving crack or powder cocaine). The official figures from the FBI on the fraction of homicides that is drug related is much smaller, only about 6 percent; for technical reasons, this is probably a serious underestimate.[11]

We also note that drug selling has become a common activity among poor minority urban males. For Washington, DC, we estimated that nearly one-third of African-American males born in the 1960s were charged with drug selling between the ages of 18 and 24 (Saner, MacCoun, & Reuter, 1995). This represents a serious problem in many dimensions for the communities in which they live because drug selling itself generates high levels of violence and creates criminal records for those who participate at a young age. In addition, though most sellers make modest incomes, the potential for fabulous earnings probably reduces incentives for finishing high school and seeking legal work and contributes to the extraordinarily low workforce participation rates in so many center city poverty communities (Wilson, 1996).

The health consequences of illicit drugs are severe. The share of new AIDS cases that have a primary risk factor of intravenous drug use (IVDU) has now reached about 35 percent (Normand, Vlahov, & Moses, 1995). In some areas of the country, particularly around New York City with its large heroin addict population, the HIV rate among IVDUs is close to 50 percent. Hepatitis, both B and the more newly discovered C strain, is rampant among IVDUs.[12] Intoxication

---

11. The principal problem is that the data are generated by the Supplemental Homicide Report (SHR); the SHR allows only one reason to be provided for a homicide. If it were a dispute over money related to drugs, it might be recorded as robbery related rather than drug related.

12. Harwood, Fountain, & Livermore (1998) estimated that 12 percent of hepatitis B and 36 percent of hepatitis C infections were attributable to intravenous drug use. They

and the obsessive search for the money to purchase drugs leads to neglect of basic health; tuberculosis (TB) is now a major problem among the drug dependent who may also account for a significant fraction of that disease in the United States. Though the official estimates of deaths from illicit drugs are scarcely 14,000 per annum (Peters, Kochanek, & Murphy, 1998), representing a rate of barely one-half percent per annum for the severely addicted, cohort studies find rates closer to 1 to 2 percent per annum (e.g., Hser et al., 1993); the official aggregate figures represent only the deaths from direct acute, as opposed to chronic or indirect, effects. For example, the totals exclude homicides caused by drug dealing or by acquisitive crime by the drug dependent. Similarly, they omit deaths due to chronic heart disease that may be a consequence of frequent use of cocaine. Deaths attributable to AIDS in which intravenous drug use was the primary risk factor amounted to an additional 10,000 in 1992.

Compared to alcohol and tobacco, the number of deaths is small. Harwood et al. (1998) estimated that, including AIDS, deaths due to illicit drug use in 1992 totaled 25,000, compared to 107,000 for alcohol. For tobacco, the Centers for Disease Control (CDC) estimates 400,000 premature deaths.[13] The difference, as measured in terms of years of life lost, is less substantial because deaths from cocaine and the like occur at a substantially younger age.[14] The other aggregate health measure, morbidity, is also likely to be much smaller for illicit drugs. For example, Harwood et al. (1998) estimated that drug abuse led to 1.5 million days of hospitalization in 1992, compared to 2.7 million for alcohol. This reflects simply the small base of regular users.

regard these as conservative estimates because at least 30 percent of cases are of unknown origin (pp. 4–55).

13. Note though that the alcohol and cigarette numbers come from sophisticated epidemiological estimates that take account of differences in mortality among users and nonusers. The estimates for illicit drugs have no such comprehensive base. However, given the difference in the number of frequent users, it is highly unlikely that the total would get close to that for alcohol; there are fewer than 4 million frequent users of illicit drugs other than marijuana, compared to 11 million heavy drinkers and 40 million current daily smokers (SAMHSA, 1996).

14. It is estimated that each cigarette death represents 9 years of life lost (YLL), and each alcohol death, 26 YLL. The figure for illicit drugs is likely to be larger because 40 percent of the deaths occur between the ages of 30 and 39, but we have found no explicit YLL calculation. See Institute for Health Policy of Brandeis University (1993).

ENFORCEMENT

The most striking characteristics of the U.S. response to illicit drugs in the last decade have been its scale and its punitiveness. The federal government spends about $18 billion annually on drug control, carried out in almost all cabinet departments, ranging from the Department of Education to the Department of State.[15] State and local governments spend at least as much, though it is far more difficult to obtain good estimates of these expenditures on an annual basis.[16] Thus, drug control is a roughly $35 billion government program in the mid-1990s, massively up from $10 billion in the mid-1980s.

The punitiveness is reflected both in budgets and the extent of incarceration. At least three-quarters of the national U.S. drug control budget is spent on apprehending and punishing drug dealers and users, with treatment getting about two-thirds of the remainder. In terms of punishment, the U.S. imprisonment rate for drug offenses alone is much higher than that of most Western European nations for all crimes.

Stringency

The number of state and local arrests for drug offenses rose from 581,000 in 1980 to approximately 1,500,000 in 1996 (from 5.5 percent to 9.9 percent of total arrests). But this masks the real increase in punitiveness; understanding that requires an examination of the changing composition of the arrests. In 1980, arrests for drug offenses were predominantly for marijuana (70 percent); marijuana possession offenses alone accounted for 58 percent of the total. In 1996, heroin/cocaine arrests rivaled those for marijuana (40 percent versus 43 percent, respectively) and distribution arrests accounted for a

---

15. The figures for federal expenditures are of questionable accuracy because they come from a bizarre set of ex post calculations that are subject to no effective monitoring. The actual figure may be substantially less than $18 billion and may be even more enforcement-dominated than the current estimate. See Murphy (1994).
16. The only estimates are Census Bureau figures for 1990 and 1991 (ONDCP, 1993). The brief published description of the methodology used suggests that many figures come from judgments by individual enforcement agencies that were not given clear directions by the Census Bureau on how to develop estimates.

Table 2.1. *Trends in drug enforcement, 1981–96*

	1980	1985	1990	1994	1996
Drug arrests	581,000	811,000	1,090,000	1,350,000	1,506,000
Heroin and	70,000	240,000	590,000	635,000	602,400
cocaine only	(12%)	(30%)	(54%)	(47%)	(40%)
Distribution only	104,000	192,000	345,000	370,000	376,500
	(18%)	(30%)	(31%)	(27%)	(25%)
Currently incarcerated for drug offenses (one day count)					
(Total)	31,000	68,000	291,000	392,000	401,000
Local jails	7,000	19,000	111,000	137,000	112,000
State prisons	19,000	39,000	149,000	202,000	234,000
Federal prisons	4,900	9,500	30,500	51,800	55,200

Sources: FBI (annual); BJS (biannual); 1980–94 jail figures are authors' estimates, 1996 from BJS.

slightly higher share of the total (25 percent in 1996, compared to 18 percent in 1980).[17]

The total punishment levied for drug control purposes has increased massively since 1981, when the concern with cocaine became prominent (Table 2.1). The number of commitments to state and federal prison has risen over tenfold during the same time period. By 1996, there were over 400,000 people in prison or jail serving time for selling or using drugs; the comparable figure for 1980 was about 31,000. The percentage of felony drug trafficking convictions resulting in prison sentences has also risen; by 1996, the figure was 43 percent, compared to 37 percent in 1986. Felony drug possession convictions and prison commitments were also rising; in 1994, 136,000 persons were convicted of felony possession (which does not include possession with intent to distribute[18]), and 29 percent of these were sentenced to state prison. Federal incarcerations for drug offenses show similarly rapid increases in the same period as well, from 6,600 in 1986 to 18,000 in 1996. More remarkably, drug

17. Interestingly, marijuana possession arrests have risen much faster than others since 1991; they doubled between 1991 and 1996.
18. It includes an unknown number of persons who were originally charged with possession with intent to distribute but whose charges were bargained down.

commitments now represent over 50 percent of all those sent to federal prison.

Legislatures, led by Congress, passed statutes mandating longer sentences for drug offenders. For example, California has a mandatory minimum sentence of 1 year for possession of a small amount of crack cocaine. These statutes have led to a modest increase in time served at the state level. Maximum sentences are now on average 51 months, up from 48 months; over one-third of the sentence (41%) is served. The principal effect of the statutory changes has probably been to ensure that fewer low-level convictions result in sentences of probation. Only at the federal level has there been a rise both in the length of sentences (70 months in 1986 to 83 months in 1996) and in the share of those sentences actually served; by 1992 the fraction was 0.85, reflecting the combined impact of mandatory minimum sentencing statutes and the guidelines of the U.S. Sentencing Commission.

Sentencing figures are of themselves insufficient to show that enforcement has become more stringent; that depends on the ratio of convictions (or years of prison time) to offenses. Estimating the number of offenses (or at least the rate of change in that number) is itself a highly speculative task. We believe that the number of offenses might have risen as rapidly as arrests/sentences/years of prison time between 1980 and 1985 but from 1985 to 1995 it is very likely that the number of offenses and offenders (sales/sellers) was essentially flat and that the stringency of enforcement became much greater.

How risky is drug selling or drug possession? The aggregate data suggest that the 1996 risk of being arrested for marijuana possession was about 3 percent per annum[19] and for cocaine the figure was 6 percent. For drug selling we estimated that in 1988 street dealers of drugs in the District of Columbia faced about a 22 percent probability of imprisonment in the course of a year's part-time selling and that, given expected time served, they spent about one-third of their

19. In 1996, marijuana possession arrests totaled 547,000; the NHSDA, which undercounts marijuana use, estimated 18 million past year users. The marijuana possession arrests include an unknown fraction of arrests that posed no threat of criminal penalties because they were for first-time offenders in states that had decriminalized marijuana during the 1970s. For example, one-third of all California's marijuana possession arrests were under a statute that imposed only fines (unpublished data from the California Bureau of Criminal Justice). Some of those arrested were in fact marijuana sellers whom the police were unable to charge with any other offense. To that extent, the 3 percent figure overstates the risk for possession alone.

selling career in prison (Reuter et al., 1990). These figures are consistent with crude calculations at the national level, assuming that each cocaine seller has about ten customers.[20]

Does this make drug selling appropriately risky? One-third of a career in prison seems quite a lot. On the other hand, the risk per sale is very small indeed; a seller who works two days a week at this trade may make 1,000 transactions in the course of a year. His imprisonment risk per transaction is only about 1 in 4,500; by that metric it is a great deal less risky than, say, a burglary or robbery. Another way to consider the risk is to look at aggregate figures. It is estimated that American users consume 300 tons of pure cocaine per annum. If these are sold in units with 300 milligrams, then this represents 1 billion transactions. Since only about 100,000 persons receive prison sentences annually for cocaine selling, that generates a prison risk for a single cocaine sales transaction of about 1 in 10,000.[21]

Divisiveness

It is hard to analyze drug enforcement in contemporary America without reference to race (Tonry, 1995). Those arrested for drug selling are predominantly minority; that disproportion is even higher for prison sentences. In 1992, African-Americans constituted two-thirds of those admitted to state prison for drug offenses, compared to slightly less than one-half for all nondrug offenses; African-Americans constitute 12 percent of the general population. Hispanics (10.2 percent of the general population) accounted for 25 percent of commitments for drug offenses, compared to about 15 percent for nondrug offenses.

The disproportion in sentences for crack offenses, for which arrests are overwhelmingly of African-Americans and Hispanics, has been a major political issue. At the federal level, Congress in 1996 affirmed its views by decisively rejecting a possible downward revision in the 100 to 1 disparity in the amount of drug generating a five-year sentence for crack and for powdered cocaine, despite the

20. Given the implosion of the cocaine market since about 1985, so that most frequent users are occasionally sellers, these calculations have become extremely speculative.
21. In many ways these figures mirror the realities for property crimes as well. The probability of an individual robbery or burglary resulting in prison is slight, but offenders make it up in volume: most who commit these crimes regularly thus spend a substantial amount of time in prison.

recommendation by the Sentencing Commission, a body generally given to great sentencing severity, that the difference be substantially reduced. President Clinton also expressed his disagreement with the Sentencing Commission's recommendation. Though drug problems are disproportionately concentrated in minority urban communities, the sentencing disparities have also been highly divisive. Edsall and Edsall (1991, p. 237) reported that focus groups in the late 1980s found that many African-Americans believed that drug enforcement was part of an effort by the white community to oppress African-Americans.

Nor is this the only division in society arising from tough drug policies. For the young, the growing harshness of rhetoric and policy to marijuana, arrests for simple possession having doubled in the last five years, reduces the credibility of government generally. The claims about marijuana's dangers, both in public rhetoric and school prevention programs, seem grossly exaggerated and indeed lack much scientific basis (see Chapter 13). At least one senior Clinton administration official has equated marijuana and crack in dangerousness.

Intrusiveness

A whole array of legal innovations have been justified by the need to end the "scourge of drugs," to use President George Bush's memorable 1989 phrase. Drug dealer "profiling" by police has allowed police to undertake numerous searches with barely plausible cause; most of those searched are again either minority or young or both.[22] Drug testing of federal employees (such as those in the Executive Office of the President) for purely symbolic purposes has demeaned public service. Similarly, some states require that candidates for state office be drug tested; the Supreme Court in 1997 ruled (8–1) against a Georgia statute that required such testing and prohibited any candidate who tested positive from having his or her name on the ballot.[23] Preventive detention, a particularly chilling power, has been extended in the context of the Controlled Substances Act.

22. On these matters generally, see Rudovsky (1994).
23. In *Chandler v. Miller*, the Supreme Court found that this statute violated the Fourth Amendment's protection against unreasonable search and seizure.

Drug policy may be getting harsher in this respect. Some jurisdictions are contemplating testing welfare recipients for drug use and disqualifying those who cannot remain drug-free.[24] Abe Rosenthal (1996) of the *New York Times*, the most prominent of columnist drug hawks, quickly pounced on President Clinton's 1996 election campaign proposal that all teenage applicants for drivers licenses be subject to a drug test, suggesting that this was not nearly enough and that the logic and facts spoke to the need to do random tests of young adults as well, since they are the highest risk group.[25]

The punitive cycle

The response to emerging drug problems is invariably punitive: the first twitch is to raise the statutory penalty for some offense. This was true in 1996 when methamphetamine showed signs of moving out of its long-established base in San Diego, Dallas, and other Western cities. It has not yet happened for marijuana federally, somewhat surprisingly.[26] However, state legislatures are starting to take up the gauntlet. For example, in 1997 the Virginia Senate passed an increase in maximum sentences for marijuana possession offenses; a second conviction can result in a 4-year prison sentence.

This is truly a vicious cycle since the argument for raising the sentence for offenses involving a particular drug is mostly that the sentence is less than that for other drugs and hence encourages sellers to pick that drug. The result is to generate sentence inflation. Indeed, many in Congress responded to the claim of imbalance between crack and powder cocaine by suggesting dramatically increasing penalties for powder. In May 1997, the U.S. Sentencing Commission, defeated in its previous effort at reducing the use of crack-powder cocaine discrepancy by lowering the crack penalties, made recommmendations that would indeed increase the powder penalties,

---

24. The Legal Action Center (1997) identifies eight states as proposing such testing. As of two years later, an informal survey of state welfare offices suggested that they had not implemented testing but only much weaker screening procedures.
25. Curiously, the President's proposal was never heard of again. The Secretary of Transportation and Director of ONDCP were to report back to the President within 90 days as to the desirability of the change, but nothing further was ever heard, confirming the hypothesis that it was purely a campaign tactic, intended to appeal to the public mood.
26. Perhaps the relatively high fraction of marijuana arrestees who are middle class and white reduces the willingness to impose further criminal penalties.

while trying again to lower the discrepancy. At about the same time, Attorney General Reno and ONDCP Director McCaffrey recommended that the disparity be reduced, partly by raising the penalties for powder offenses and partly by reducing those for crack (Wren, 1997).

How successful has enforcement been?

Has the toughness been effective at least in decreasing drug use in the general population? The evidence is against this. Factors other than policy changes are probably more important, but tight evaluations of drug enforcement are almost impossible with current data sets. The most sensible approach would be to examine variation in the intensity of enforcement across cities or states and to see if that explains variations in drug problems. Unfortunately, there are no measures of the number of offenses (comparable to the reports of burglaries to the Uniform Crime Reports or in the National Crime Victimization Survey) so that it is not possible to estimate how stringency varies across cities or states for specific drugs. Nor is it clear just what is the right measures of offense levels; the total amount of drugs sold, the number of users, or the amount of violence and disorder that is generated by drug use and selling are all plausible candidates.

Price is the only outcome measure generally available at both the national and metropolitan-area level. Tougher enforcement should, in the short run, raise prices, assuming (as seems reasonable for a mature market) that demand, the relationship between the quantity sought by users and the price charged, remains stable (Reuter & Kleiman, 1986). What we observe (Figure 2.2[27]) is that during the period of increasingly tough enforcement, prices for cocaine and heroin have fallen steadily since 1981; by 1995, after adjusting for inflation, they were only about one-third of their 1981 levels. For marijuana, prices rose steadily and substantially from 1981 to 1992 and then fell in the next four years back close to their 1981 level. Even more surprising is the observation that crack cocaine, singled out for tough sentencing, both at the national level and in some major states

---

27. We owe the figure to Jonathan Caulkins, who first noted the striking parallel in the declines of the prices of the two drugs.

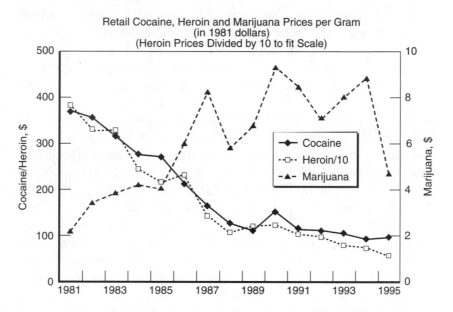

Figure 2.2 Price trends for cocaine, heroin, and marijuana, 1981–95

(e.g., California, where possession of small quantities is subject to mandatory state prison sentence), is no more expensive at the retail level than powder cocaine (Caulkins, 1997).

The decline in prices might be explained by a lower demand. It is difficult to assess whether this is a major factor but certainly estimated consumption has not declined substantially.[28] Occasional middle class use has dropped precipitously; this never constituted a large share of total consumption, but it is impossible to dismiss the possibility that it was important in determining measured prices.[29]

28. Systematic estimates cover the period 1988 to 1995. The cocaine series (developed by Rhodes et al., 1997) showed essentially no change from 1988 to 1992; there is then a one time drop of about one-third in 1993 and a flat trend thereafter. Such a one-time shift is implausible, particularly for 1992.
29. The logic here is that cocaine markets allow for ample discrimination among purchasers. High prices for some groups can coexist with lower prices for others. Assume that the middle class users were willing to pay more for convenience (delivery) and more assured quality. If the police sample from both high and low price markets in measuring prices, then the decline of the middle class market would have a greater effect than would be expected if one looked only at their contribution to the number of users.

If tough enforcement did not raise drug prices, then it might still have been successful if it lowered availability. The existing data, mostly from the annual survey of high school seniors, show no decrease. For example, the percentage of seniors reporting that cocaine was available or readily available was higher in 1989 (55 percent) than in 1980 (30 percent). It began to decline after 1989, probably because the fraction of high school seniors using cocaine had fallen sharply, but was still 46 percent in 1995. For marijuana, the figure has remained between 80 and 90 percent without any discernible trend since 1975.[30]

These findings on price and availability make it highly implausible that enforcement was the principal cause of the decline in drug use among the general population. It is possible that large numbers of arrests, seizures of great quantities of drugs (highly publicized in the 1980s though hardly mentioned during the 1990s), and dramatically rising imprisonment rates have had an important symbolic effect. This is on its face unlikely and difficult to test. The explanation for declining drug use among high school students may well be found less in policy than in attitudinal changes related to fashion and risk behaviors.

DEMAND SIDE PROGRAMS

The standard liberal critique of current policies is that they neglect the demand side programs – treatment and prevention. Prevention in particular has a strong appeal to the American sense of dealing with fundamentals; if one can reach potential users before they start, then all the adverse consequences of drug use and coercive control can be vitiated. The failure of prevention programs to capture a larger share of the drug budget is an interesting phenomenon, partly explained by the tight link in the public mind between the drug problem and crime and partly by the weaknesses of existing prevention programs (Haaga & Reuter, 1995). Treatment has done better budgetarily, perhaps because it can indeed show substantial success.

Oddly enough, given their small share of the total drug budget, we can say a great deal more about the effects of treatment and pre-

---

30. Caulkins (1999) showed that availability is negatively related to price and positively related to prevalence.

vention, which account for no more than 25 percent of this nation's public expenditures on drug control, than about the consequences of enforcement. Even more oddly, that is a consequence of the nation's dedication to punishment. Any other program has to justify itself against the suspicion that it is kind to criminals (treatment) or too diffuse (prevention). Since punishment is what drug users and sellers deserve, there is little need (in the eyes of politicians and perhaps the public) for these programs to demonstrate their effectiveness. Research funding for systematic studies of prevention and treatment may be ten times that for enforcement. Thus, we provide more precise statements about the two demand side programs.

Our purpose here is not to provide a comprehensive survey of these programs but to suggest briefly how they fit into current policies and to outline what is known about their effectiveness. These are important foundations for the legalization debate.

Treatment

Until the late 1960s, treatment for drug dependence was provided almost exclusively in two federal facilities (Fort Worth and Lexington) which had as much penal as therapeutic character. This reflected the continued legacy of the legal battles around interpretation of the Harrison Act, which ushered in national drug prohibition in 1914; court interpretations of allowable medical practice had discouraged physicians from taking on these patients (Musto, 1987).

With the introduction of methadone in the 1970s, ironically because of Richard Nixon's enthusiasm for finding a way of fulfilling his promise to use federal authority to reduce crime (Epstein, 1978), specialized programs aimed at those dependent on illicit drugs became widely available. In 1995, approximately 850,000 persons were admitted for drug treatment[31] each year from programs that receive at least some public funds; this probably represents the vast majority of the total number receiving any kind of treatment. Cocaine (300,000), heroin (150,000), and marijuana (120,000) account for the bulk of treatment episodes, classified according to primary drug of abuse. Estimates of the need for treatment suggest that about one-quarter

31. There were 590,000 people classified as receiving treatment for a primary drug problem; another 270,000 people who had a primary alcohol problem but a secondary drug problem also received treatment (SAMHSA, 1997b).

of those in need actually receive treatment in any one year (e.g., Gerstein, Foote, & Ghadialy, 1997), but those basic estimates, which are built on the houshold survey, are of questionable value since the NHSDA finds most of those in need of treatment to be users of marijuana only. The share of those dependent on cocaine and/or heroin who are in need of treatment may be substantially larger.

The public treatment system is poorly funded, provides inadequate services to its clients, and has a high drop-out rate; nonetheless, it can justify itself strongly in terms of cost-benefit ratios. Compared to the private treatment system, it must deal with more severely addicted patients who have a much poorer prognosis. Most are unemployed, poorly educated, and without stable family, three of the predictors of failure in treatment (McLellan & Weisner, 1996). Compared to the private system, publicly funded programs pay lower wages to their staff, who have less training. The staff-client ratio is higher and the number of contact hours is fewer. Yet credible, systematic studies have found benefit-cost ratios for public drug treatment programs that range from $3 to $7 for each dollar of treatment funding (e.g., Gerstein et al., 1994). Rydell and Everingham (1994) estimated that the United States could reduce cocaine consumption by 1 percent by investing $34 million in additional treatment funds, considerably cheaper than achieving the same outcome with domestic drug law enforcement ($246 million), interdiction ($366 million), or source country controls ($783 million). A later study using a similar model (Caulkins et al., 1997), estimated that $1 million spent on treatment could reduce U.S. cocaine consumption by 104 kilograms, much more than if the same money were spent on trying to lock up more dealers (26 kilograms) or providing longer sentences for convicted dealers (13 kilograms). Notably, these estimates are based on a fairly pessimistic estimate of treatment effectiveness. In their analyses, treatment's cost-effectiveness stems partly from the temporary suppression of consumption during treatment but mostly from post-treatment reductions even though they assumed on the basis of prior studies that only 13 percent of those who enter treatment remain drug-free for 15 years.[32]

---

32. A National Academy of Sciences committee (Manski, Pepper, & Thomas, 1999) argued that, given the limitations of existing data, the Rydell and Everingham conclusions are speculative; alternative modeling assumptions can support conclusions either more or less favorable to treatment. RAND has disputed aspects of this argument (RAND Drug Policy Research Center, 2000). (MacCoun was on the NAS committee.)

A major social benefit from treatment comes from reductions in crime generated by lowered drug use. The classic study of methadone programs (Ball & Ross, 1991) showed in-treatment reductions in crime of 70 percent or more. Employment rates and wage rates for clients, during or after treatment, do not show much increase, pointing to the limits of treatment for the drug-dependent population with which these programs now deal. Most of those who enter treatment will relapse into regular drug use within a few months of entry, and they will have difficulty meeting the behavioral requirements for long-term employment. It is now generally accepted by the treatment community that repeated cycles of treatment and relapse are often necessary before clients make lasting behavioral changes. Many treatment experts believe that the coercive impact of the criminal justice system plays a key role in motivating addicts to seek and complete treatment (Anglin & Hser, 1990). The recent growth of "drug courts" in Miami, Oakland, and other American cities is intended to enhance this justice system function; drug courts are formally or informally organized court procedures designed to divert nonviolent drug offenders to treatment and rehabilitation services (General Accounting Office, 1997).

Prevention

Initiation into illicit drug use, as opposed to dependence, is primarily a youth phenomenon. Eighty percent of users start before the age of 18. More than half of those who use illicit drugs are in their late teens or their twenties, and drug use peaks at an earlier age than that for alcohol, tobacco, or psychoactive prescription drugs (Kandel, 1993). Over the past 15 years, the U.S. federal government has considerably increased funding for programs to prevent adolescent involvement in licit and illicit drugs; in 1995 the figure was about $2 billion. Most of this money is spent by schools, though there is a continuing programmatic interest in other kinds of institutions, such as churches and recreational facilities, which may be more effective at reaching the highest risk groups.

Early drug prevention programs of the 1970s were largely premised on a rational choice model: if students understand the risks of drug use, they will be more likely to resist initiation. It soon became apparent that there are several problems with this approach. First, perceptions of drug risks are only one factor that influences adolescent drug use; equally or more important are peer influences and pressures (Ellickson, 1995). Second, these drug prevention programs provided "risk information" that greatly exaggerated some risks for some drugs (e.g., the addictiveness and neurological consequences of marijuana use); when students' growing samples of observations failed to concur with these messages, the programs were quickly discredited.

Contemporary programs continue to provide risk education, but many place much greater emphasis on training students to resist social pressures to use drugs (Ellickson, 1995). Ironically, at a time when many youth were ridiculing Nancy Reagan's "Just Say No" campaign, prevention experts were demonstrating that teaching youth how to say no was indeed an effective prevention strategy, at least relative to previous approaches. But the most popular American drug prevention curriculum is Project DARE (Drug Abuse Resistance Education), created by the Los Angeles Police Department in the early 1980s. The DARE program was designed as a largely atheoretical hodge-podge, mixing drug risk education, self-esteem promotion, decision-making skills, and alternatives to drug use; its most distinct feature is that the lessons are given by professional police officers. Repeated evaluations of DARE have shown no effect on drug use (Gottfredson, 1997).

In a much-cited analysis of 143 evaluation studies, Tobler (e.g., 1992) estimated that few of the evaluated programs achieved much reduction in drug use in the targeted populations. Programs were notably more effective in influencing drug knowledge and much less effective at influencing attitudes. Unfortunately, even the more successful programs rarely have effects that persist for more than a few years (e.g., Ellickson, Bell, & McGuigan, 1993). This is hardly surprising since it is unrealistic to expect a small sample of classroom experiences to have demonstrable effects on nonclassroom behavior years later. Investing in later booster sessions appears necessary to obtain sustained effects (Botvin et al., 1995).

Tobler found that programs specifically targeting tobacco were most influential; programs focusing on alcohol or both licit and illicit drugs had considerably weaker effects. The success of tobacco programs might reflect in part the sheer weight of credible evidence for the dangers of tobacco, especially relative to fairly modest rewards. Moreover, most adolescents have probably met adults who have struggled to quit smoking. On the other hand, alcohol prevention programs face a considerable challenge because alcohol is used so widely (and frequently safely) in our society.

More is known about drug prevention's effectiveness than its cost-effectiveness. In theory, prevention efforts could be made more efficient and effective by targeting efforts at those youth at greatest risk. In practice, risk and resilience factors have been identified, but it isn't clear how to single out high-risk students for an intervention without stigmatizing them (possibly undermining any positive effects). Prevention programs are almost exclusively focused on the goal of reducing prevalence. In keeping with this focus, prevention program evaluations (like many treatment evaluations) are preoccupied with establishing program effects on *whether* adolescents use, giving short shrift to the measurement of *amounts* and *styles* of drug use or the harmful consequences of that use. But the fact is that most adolescent drug users pass through a limited period of experimentation without experiencing any lasting effects or acute harms (e.g., Kandel, 1993; Shedler & Block, 1990). This raises the question of whether prevention programs shorten the drug-using careers of experimenters or motivate those experimenters to use drugs more cautiously than they might in the absence of exposure to prevention messages. If so, prevention evaluations, by relying so heavily on prevalence indicators, might be underestimating the beneficial effects of the interventions.

The most ambitious and comprehensive cost-effectiveness study of prevention was conducted by Caulkins et al. (1999). The study found that it would be possible to implement a state-of-the-art prevention program for all U.S. school children for only $550 million but that this would reduce cocaine consumption by only between 2 and 11 percent. Prevention is cheap but, perhaps because it is difficult to target, can make only a modest contribution to controlling America's drug problems.

Finally, we note that there is little research on how prevention works when implemented in schools as opposed to model programs run by researchers. Drug prevention is not central to the concept of schooling as practiced in the past, and there is evidence of considerable administrative resistance to incorporating it in the core curriculum. Moreover, it involves sensitive social messages of the kind that schools do not deliver well in those communities that most need them, namely inner-city poverty communities (Gottfredson, 1997). Whether more funding for school-based prevention would in fact have much effect on drug use is an open question.

There is essentially no research on prevention programs outside of schools. It is plausible that other institutions have more prospect of reaching the highest risk children; that plausibility remains to be tested.

CONCLUSION

Current American drug policy has massive flaws and still leaves the nation with a massive problem that affects the poor most acutely. Retaining prohibition does not require maintenance of all current policy choices. A case can be made that the United States needs to develop substantially stronger prevention and treatment programs. That seems a reasonable goal, though not one which could be achieved within a small number of years, given just how primitive is the cumulated knowledge about what works in prevention and the attitudinal barriers to providing good quality treatment. Moreover, even with better and more demand side programs, it is likely that we will be left with very substantial drug-related problems. It would be very optimistic to claim that the nation's drug problem could be reduced by 50 percent over the next five years through improved treatment and prevention.

The weaknesses of the current regime are severe enough that it is not absurd to claim that a truly radical alternative, which moved the criminal sanction to the margins of policy, could do better. We now turn to the arguments and evidence for that position.

PART II: THE ARGUMENTS

3   The Debate

For years, the topic of drug legalization was the nearly exclusive province of a handful of prominent but controversial figures; psychedelics enthusiasts like Timothy Leary, physician Andrew Weil, or novelist Aldous Huxley; libertarians like William F. Buckley, economist Milton Friedman, and psychiatrist Thomas Szasz; or Rastafarian reggae stars like Bob Marley and Peter Tosh – the latter perhaps best known for his political anthem "Legalize It." But during the past decade, the issue has gradually entered the mainstream of policy discourse. The list of prominent advocates for major drug law reform includes advice columnist Ann Landers, former Reagan Secretary of State George Schultz (though only briefly vocal on the issue), Wall Street wizard George Soros, former television talk show host Hugh Downs, Baltimore Mayor Kurt Schmoke, former San Jose police chief Joseph McNamara, neuroscientist Michael Gazzaniga, a growing list of state and federal judges, and the editorial boards of the *Wall Street Journal, Rolling Stone, The Economist, National Review*, and *New Scientist.*

The debate over prohibition of psychoactive substances is hardly anything new in the United States. The topic itself is as old as the nation (Musto, 1987) – only the substances have changed. Although the "Noble Experiment" of alcohol prohibition between 1919 and 1932 comes most readily to mind, the legal status of many other psychoactive substances has been questioned. Indeed, the first half of the twentieth century saw much change in the legal status of psychoactive drugs. In 1900, numerous states prohibited both alcohol and cigarettes but allowed cocaine and heroin; by 1933, there was a complete reversal. Over at least the past thirty years, the question of whether to relax the prohibition of the use of certain drugs – especially heroin, cocaine, and marijuana – has become a recurrent theme in the debate over drug policy.[1]

We divide advocates into three distinct groups. *Prohibitionists* defend the status quo of strict legal sanctions against all the currently illicit drugs. *Decriminalizers* would maintain the legal ban on the sale of those drugs but advocate a reduction in criminal sanctions for possession of small amounts. *Legalizers* would make the sale and use of some currently illicit drugs legal, although most advocate government regulation.

U.S. political leadership has been outspokenly in the prohibitionist camp. It is now a ritual of presidential campaigns to include calls for increasing toughness against drug sellers and no remission in sanctions against drug users. No major figure from either party has suggested significant legal change. Some liberals have expressed their distaste for the excesses of the "War on Drugs," but they have been unwilling to suggest changes in law. For example, Democratic Congressman Barney Frank, a leading spokesman for liberal positions on social policy, has criticized the current policies (Pincus, 1994) but has taken no greater initiative than to sponsor legislation that would allow research on the medicinal uses of marijuana.

Most striking though is the extent to which leading political figures speak out repeatedly against any form of legalization. Notwithstanding the broad and unvarying popular opposition to any formal legal change, almost every prominent politician has spoken more than once about the dangers of legalization. It is hard to identify another social policy issue on which a view held by such a small minority, unrepresented in the major legislatures, has attracted repeated vehement denunciations from every level of the political system.

1. In the early 1990s, the debate resurged with a virtual explosion of articles and essays (e.g., Farr, 1990; Goldstein and Kalant, 1990; Jacobs, 1990; Nadelmann, 1989; Wilson, 1990). In addition, special symposia on the debate appeared in the February 1989 issue of *American Behavioral Scientist*, the Fall 1990 issue of the *Journal of Drug Issues*, the Spring 1990 issue of the *Hofstra Law Review*, two 1991 issues of the *Milbank Quarterly* (Vol. 69, No. 3 & 4), and the Summer 1992 issue of *Daedalus*. Recent essays by leading legalization advocates appear in the 12 February 1996 issue of *National Review*. Various books have reprinted popular and academic essays by prominent advocates on both sides of the debate (e.g., Boaz, 1990; Evans & Berent, 1992; Fish, 1998; Schaler, 1998; Thompson, 1998).

Firm resistance to even a discussion of legalization has been bipartisan. When Congressman Charles Rangel, long-time chair of the House Select Committee on Narcotics Abuse and Control and generally a liberal Democrat, held the first hearings on drug legalization in 1988 (Associated Press, 1988), the proponents were held up to ridicule and given little time to speak. Representative Dick Solomon has sponsored – thus far without success – the Anti-Drug Legalization Act, which states that "no department or agency of the United States Government shall conduct or finance, in whole or in part, any study or research involving the legalization of drugs." Joycelyn Elders, President Clinton's first Surgeon General, was immediately and intensely criticized for even suggesting that the topic might be worth studying (Labaton, 1993).

Each year the Office of National Drug Control Policy (ONDCP) issues a *National Drug Control Strategy* (NDCS). Almost invariably this admittedly repetitive document contains a denunciation of legalization. For example in 1996, the President's two page trasmittal letter said, "And we will continue to oppose resolutely calls for the legalization of illicit drugs." The main body of the Strategy included among its objectives (ONDCP, 1996, p. 14):

> *A Reaffirmation of Anti-Legalization Sentiments.* ONDCP helped to reaffirm the sentiments of millions of Americans who oppose the legalization of drugs. In May 1995, ONDCP, in coordination with other Federal agencies, co-sponsored the 1995 "American Cities Against Drugs" conference in Atlanta, Georgia. Officials representing dozens of American cities, large and small, signed a declaration of resolute opposition to the legalization of illicit drugs.

Only the most cursory effort is made to rebut the substance of the legalizers' arguments. Senator Orrin Hatch, chair of the Judiciary Committee, in a routine hearing on the 1996 *NDCS*, rhetorically implored the Director of ONDCP to fight the legalizers vigorously. The Director, of course, dutifully said that he would and indeed regularly makes statements on the matter (e.g., McCaffrey, 1998). In August 1999, he issued a new report entitled *The Destructive Impact of Drugs on the United States: How the Legalization of Drugs would Jeopardize the Health and Safety of the American People and Our Nation.*

Other federal agencies also contribute to the antilegalization effort. For example, DEA put out a White Paper (DEA, 1994) intended to arm those who publicly debate the legalizers.

The debate has been given prominence by the media. For example, in 1988 the nationally prominent television program *The Koppel Report* (produced by Ted Koppel) produced a 1½ hour town meeting on the topic (American Broadcasting Corporation, 1988); in 1998 Koppel's *Nightline* devoted a show to a debate on the topic (American Broadcasting Corporation, 1998).

ELITE OPINION

To better understand the various positions and their implications, we examine both the content and the form of the legalization debate. We identify the key arguments that distinguish prohibitionists, decriminalizers, and legalizers. Some arguments involve empirical questions resolvable by systematic research, but some involve irreconcilable philosophical differences. We also assess the rhetorical styles that distinguish reformers from defenders of the current drug laws. At the very least, a better understanding of the content and intellectual tenor of the debate will highlight some of the principal issues in the dispute. It might also provide an indication of the likelihood of resolving differences and finding drug policies acceptable to more than one camp.

A major forum for the debate has been the editorial pages of American newspapers. In these pages, one finds all sides of the debate and a variety of rhetorical styles. The writers include academics, public officials, and intellectuals. To describe the form and content of the debate, we analyzed several samples of "op-ed" essays addressing the topic. The first, oriented toward the recent history of the debate, examined op-ed pieces in the *New York Times* from 1970 to 1990 (MacCoun et al., 1993); in collaboration with Beau Kilmer, we recently updated this analysis through early 1997.[2] The second,

2. These *New York Times* essays were identified from the *Information Bank Abstracts,* which is compiled by the New York Times Company. It relies on the *New York Times* as its primary source and covers the period from January 1969 to the present. Identified essays were obtained and incorporated in the sample if clearly expressing opinion rather than a news story presenting factual journalistic reporting, and if the central focus of the essay was drug decriminalization and/or legalization. Our original study (MacCoun et al., 1993) covered the period 1970–90. Our 1997 update, conducted by Beau Kilmer, covered the period from 1988 to the first half of 1997.

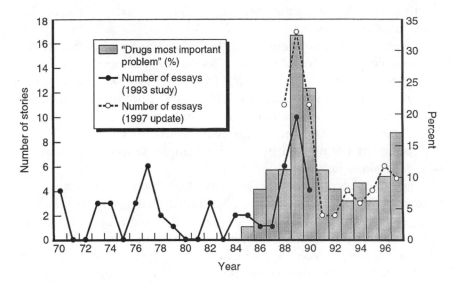

Figure 3.1 Drug law essays in the *New York Times*, January 1970 through June 1997 (Note that the final data point covers six months only.)

described in detail elsewhere (MacCoun et al., 1993), examined 133 essays published in 28 different American newspapers between July 1, 1989, and June 30, 1990 – the peak period for interest in the topic since 1970.

Figure 3.1 shows the number of op-ed essays on the topic of drug legalization or decriminalization that were published in the *New York Times* – generally considered the nation's "newspaper of record" – each year from January 1, 1970, to June 30, 1997.[3] There is a cluster of essays in the mid to late 1970s, a brief period of quiescence, and an explosion of interest in the years 1988–90 – over twice the number of essays of the earlier 1976–8 peak. Since that time, the topic has received continued attention, albeit at less feverish levels. The upturn in interest in 1996 and early 1997 is partly attributable to the debate

---

3. To calibrate the update with the earlier study, we included a three-year overlap (1988–90). As seen in Figure 3.1, our later search identified relevant articles at a higher rate – due to a more inclusive search query and improvements in the *Information Bank Abstracts* coverage. Thus, our 1970–90 yearly counts are underestimates, though the update coding qualitatively replicates the peaking in 1989.

surrounding the successful medical marijuana citizen initiatives in California and Arizona.

Superimposed onto Figure 3.1 is the percentage of American citizens naming "drugs (or) drug abuse" as the "most important problem facing the country" in Gallup polls from 1985 to 1997 (*Sourcebook of Criminal Justice Statistics 1996*, Table 2.1). The notion that elite and public concern are associated is hardly surprising, but the degree to which they move in tandem on this issue is quite striking, though elite reformers are not necessarily "opinion leaders" shaping the views of the general public.

The emergence in the late 1980s of drug law reform as a mainstream policy debate was by no means limited to the *New York Times*. During the same period, the *Washington Post* ran a lively series of essays and letters, including Baltimore Mayor Kurt Schmoke's call for decriminalization (May 15, 1988), Milton Friedman's "open letter to [drug czar] Bill Bennett" (September 7, 1989), Bennett's reply to Friedman (September 19, 1989), Friedman's rebuttal (September 29, 1989), and Bennett's "Mopping Up After the Legalizers: What the 'Intellectual' Chorus Fails to Tell You" (December 15, 1989); these letters are all reported in Evans and Berent (1992). The prestigious journal *Science* published Ethan Nadelmann's (1989) critique of drug prohibition and a less sanguine view of legalization by two neuroscientists (Goldstein & Kalant, 1990). *Commentary* published James Q. Wilson's (1990) eloquent and forceful defense of drug prohibition.

Shifts in advocacy and emphasis

The distribution of positions varied over the twenty-year period. Table 3.1 shows three qualitative shifts in advocacy since 1970. Half the 1970s essays – 61 percent of those taking a position – advocated decriminalization. (We prefer the term *depenalization*, but *decriminalization* is the term these essays used.) In the 1980s and 1990s, specifically prodecriminalization (as opposed to legalization) essays became rare, while prohibitionist essays quadrupled. Although the net effect was a prohibitionist shift, reformers were more likely to favor legalization over the more limited decriminalization. Thus, the debate became more polarized in the 1980s, shifting from decriminalization to a debate between prohibiters and legalizers. The next

Table 3.1. *Position advocated by decade*

Position advocated	1970s (%)	1980s (%)	1990s[a] (%)
Prohibition	18	59	32
Reformed prohibition	—[b]	—[b]	38
Decriminalization	50	4	3
Legalization	14	21	19
Allow medical marijuana	—[b]	—[b]	3
No position taken	18	17	5
Number of essays	(22)	(29)	(37)

[a] Through first half of 1997.
[b] Category not included in 1970–90 coding scheme.

Table 3.2. *Percent of essays mentioning each drug, by decade*

Drug	1970s (%)	1980s (%)	1990s[a] (%)
Cannabis	100	52	40
Cocaine	9	72	60
Heroin	18	59	32
LSD	9	0	3
Alcohol	9	34	24
Tobacco	5	17	19

[a] Through first half of 1997.

significant shift was the growth of a reformist, "mend it – don't end it" wing of the prohibitionist camp. These authors reluctantly endorsed prohibition but called for kinder, gentler ways of implementing it (e.g., a significant shift in emphasis toward treatment and prevention).

There was a notable shift in the drugs under focus in the debate, as seen in Table 3.2.[4] Most striking is the omnipresence of marijuana in the 1970s editorials. This is hardly surprising; the 1970s saw a rapid

4. An alternative explanation is that the publication policies of the *New York Times* editorial staff changed over time.

growth in marijuana use among American youth. During the 1970s, twelve states decriminalized marijuana: Oregon in 1973; Alaska, Colorado, and Ohio in 1975; California, Maine, and Minnesota in 1976; Mississippi, New York, North Carolina, and South Dakota in 1977; and Nebraska in 1978.[5]

In the 1980s essays, marijuana's prominence faded; no additional state decriminalized marijuana during that decade. Instead, there was a growing preoccupation with cocaine – presumably reflecting the rapid growth in the size of the underground market for that drug, especially following the emergence of crack in many cities around 1985. In the pre-crack 1970s, cocaine was perceived to be much less serious than heroin. But in the 1980s, through a combination of myth and hard reality, cocaine came to be perceived as the leading drug menace in the country (Reinarman & Levine, 1989).

Prohibitionists, decriminalizers, and legalizers emphasized different drugs. Cocaine was more likely to be mentioned by prohibitionists than by the legalizers or decriminalizers; cannabis was much more likely to be discussed by reform advocates than by prohibitionists. In part, this reflected the drug-specific nature of some proposals [e.g., calls for reform of marijuana (but not hard drug) laws]. But more generally, marijuana – widely used with relatively modest risks – seems to pose rhetorical difficulties for advocates of across-the-board prohibition. Cocaine – with its strong links to violence and loss of self control – may pose similar rhetorical problems for legalizers.

Shifts in the content of the debate

Arguments made for or against a change in drug laws are shown in Table 3.3. Although the small subsample sizes preclude strong inferences, it appears that the types of arguments changed over time, at least among drug law reformers. In the 1970s, the major argument made in favor of liberalizing drug laws was that the current laws were too harsh. In the 1980s and 1990s, the proreform faction emphasized the benefits liberalized drug laws would have on crime and the criminal justice system: reducing illicit drug markets, drug-related crimes (e.g., crimes committed to raise money to purchase drugs), and, to a

---

5. South Dakota and Alaska subsequently repealed their decriminalization laws, but the Alaska Supreme Court has muddied matters; see Chapter 14.

Table 3.3. *Arguments for each position by decade*

Arguments for drug legalization and/or decriminalization[a]	1970s (%)	1980s (%)	1990s (%)
Would decrease drug-related crime	0	57	66
Would eliminate illicit drug markets	0	43	22
Should regulate like prescription drugs	0	14	33
Should make available for medical uses	0	14	22
Current laws are too harsh	36	0	11
Current laws infringe on rights	21	14	11
Should emphasize treatment/education	14	29	22
Criminal justice system is overburdened	21	29	33
Current laws are hypocritical	—[c]	—[c]	22
Alcohol prohibition was a failure	—[c]	—[c]	44
Arguments against drug legalization and/or decriminalization[b]			
Would increase number of users, addicts	25	41	38
Would increase safety hazards	0	12	8
Would increase drug-related illness	25	65	15
Would increase drug-related crime	0	18	15
Implies endorsement, sends wrong message	50	6	12
Would disrupt families	0	18	27
Disproportionately harms poor/minorities	0	18	8
Drug use is immoral	0	6	4

[a] Legalizers and decriminalizers only.
[b] Prohibiters only (includes prohibition reformers in 1990s sample).
[c] Item not coded in 1970–90 sample.

lesser extent, the burden of drug cases on the system. Trends in the content of prohibitionist arguments are more difficult to discern. Prohibiters generally emphasized the fear that liberalized drug laws would lead to more use and/or addiction, with deleterious effects on families. Interestingly, neither side framed the debate in primarily moral terms; essayists on both sides tended to couch their arguments in terms of the purported objective consequences of drug policy choices.

In summary, over two and a half decades, the focus of elite debate shifted from marijuana decriminalization (1970s) to the legalization of multiple psychoactive drugs, especially cocaine (1980s to the present). Along with this change of focus was a major change in the arguments offered for relaxing prohibitionist laws, from a focus on the civil rights of users to an emphasis on the increase in overall criminality concomitant with forcing drugs into the criminal world. The prohibitionists, as defenders of the status quo, changed less than the legalizers and decriminalizers, but increasingly emphasized the negative consequences of drug use.

Many critics of the drug war (e.g., Lusane, 1991; Tonry, 1995) have suggested that the increasing punitiveness of American drug policy in the 1980s was a response to a shift in the demographics of the pro-totypical drug user, from white college kids smoking pot to young urban African-American men smoking crack. We have little doubt that this account has validity, but note that it is difficult to separate racial patterns of drug use from the dramatic growth of street-level drug markets in inner-city neighborhoods, and the violence they produced (see Saner et al., 1995). Marijuana is typically not associated with the criminal underworld, while heroin always has been and cocaine became so in the 1980s. The most visible counterculture members of the 1960s and 1970s were but a tiny fraction of all pot smokers. During that period, the typical user was well within the moral boundaries of mainstream society, and hence someone with a large political constituency. Indeed, cocaine, before it became associated with the poor and the criminal world, was similarly regarded. The change in class and crime associated with drugs are as plausibly related to the shift in attitudes as is race.

PUBLIC OPINION

Elite attention toward legalization seems to rise and fall with public concerns about drugs as a social problem. One might therefore assume that the ebb and flow of elite interest in drug legalization might produce, or at least be correlated with, dramatic swings in public sentiment toward legalization. An examination of public opinion trends over the past two decades suggests that nothing of the sort has taken place. The public opinion trends in Figure 3.2 show no indication of the sudden explosion of elite interest in the topic during 1989 and 1990 nor any subsequent indication that the elite debate had even taken place. There has been remarkably little variation in the opinions of American adults; for twenty years,

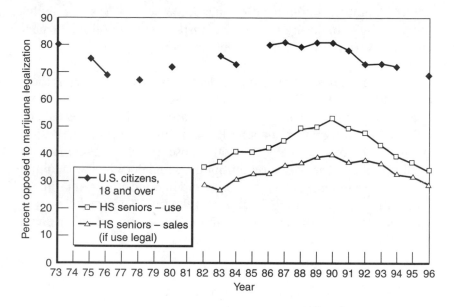

Figure 3.2 Opposition to marijuana legalization, 1973–96

between 70 and 80 percent oppose marijuana legalization, the focus of most of the polls.

The views of American adolescents are less clear. Gallup data on thirteen to seventeen year olds (not shown in the figure) shows a level of opposition comparable to that of adults in the National Opinion Research Center (NORC) data. But data from the University of Michigan's *Monitoring the Future*, an annual survey of American high school seniors, show greater support for marijuana legalization than the Gallup data would suggest. Whereas the Gallup item asks, "Do you think the use of marijuana should be made legal, or not?," MTF asks students to consider the choice between three options: "using marijuana should be entirely legal," "it should be a minor violation like a parking ticket, but not a crime," or "it should be a crime." A second question asks, "If it were legal for people to use marijuana, should it also be legal to sell marijuana?" Given these response options, outright opposition to legal change is more muted (Figure 3.2). In the senior class of 1996, for example, 31 percent would favor legalization of use, and 21 percent would make it a minor violation. If use were legal, 47 percent would make sales legal for adults; 11 percent would legalize sales for anyone. This suggests that some of those opposing legalization in the Gallup poll might have endorsed variations on complete legalization if given more response options.

Adolescent opinions also appear less stable over time than those of adults. Both the Gallup series and the MTF series describe a general increase in opposition to legalization during the 1980s. This might reflect the growth in young Republicanism during that period. Another obvious correlate of both those trends is the dramatic decline in adolescent drug use during the same decade. For example, trends in recent marijuana prevalence and in opposition to marijuana legalization show a strong inverse correlation, moving so closely in lockstep that it is difficult to attribute cause and effect in either direction.[6]

WHY HAVE LEGALIZERS HAD SO LITTLE IMPACT?

A verdict on the success of the legalization movement would be grossly premature. Such matters are difficult to quantify, but there are numerous indications that the movement continues to gather steam. One is the growing list of prominent figures willing to be associated with the cause. With the exception of Robert Dupont (and some ambiguous public backpedaling by George Schultz), few elites who have publicly endorsed legalization have later denounced it. As a result, in each passing year, the list grows longer, undoubtedly making it easier for other celebrity figures to "come out of the closet," so to speak. Second, prohibitionist organizations, both public (the Drug Enforcement Administration) and private (the Partnership for a Drug Free America), increasingly feel the need to write antilegalization position papers, surely a sign of growing nervousness about the issue. And third, financier George Soros has recently invested about $15 million into the drug reform lobbying effort, through his Lindesmith Center (Ethan Nadelmann is the Director) and support for the Drug Policy Foundation and other reform organizations.

---

6. The correlation does not change appreciably when either prevalence or opinions are lagged by one year.

Nevertheless, thus far there is little indication that the legalization movement is gaining popular support and considerable evidence that it is falling largely on deaf ears. Chapter 15 will explore reasons why public views could conceivably change, possibly very rapidly. But at present, it is safe to say that Americans are quite unpersuaded by the legalization position. Why?

One possibility is that the public is simply wrong; legalization is in fact the most defensible position, and the public is ignorant of that fact. We will spend the better part of a book making the case that matters aren't that simple. And of course, the fact that many elites support a position does not mean it is correct; history is replete with egregious examples of expert error.

A second possibility, alluded to at the beginning of the chapter, is that the problem lies with the position's advocates rather than the position itself. The public may continue to associate the topic with countercultural and libertarian figures well outside the political mainstream. But this account is becoming increasingly implausible. The most vocal and publicly visible advocate of drug law reform in the past decade has been Ethan Nadelmann, a former professor of public policy at Princeton's Woodrow Wilson School, and a serious, articulate, and well-informed spokesman. Because of their prominent positions and their experience managing drug problems, advocates like Baltimore Mayor Kurt Schmoke, New York District Judge Robert Sweet, and former San Jose police chief Joseph McNamara bring considerable credibility to the movement.

A third possibility, one we find plausible, is that a compelling set of arguments for legalization is necessarily very complex, making it difficult to communicate and difficult to accept. In part, the problem is one of comprehension; many people may not fully understand the position. But in part, the problem is that legalization – and major drug reform proposals more generally – requires tradeoffs among competing values, tradeoffs that many citizens may find unpalatable if not completely unacceptable. If drugs are evil, how can it possibly be right to allow them to be sold in legal commerce? Those who argue that legalization would reduce other evils (crime, AIDS, etc.) must overcome some very basic resistance.

To better understand the rhetorical style of argumentation in the legalization debate, we analyzed the integrative complexity of the editorials in our National Sample. *Integrative complexity* (e.g.,

Tetlock, 1983, 1989, 1993) is a concept that has been employed to study political rhetoric; among its numerous applications are speeches in the U.S. Congress, the United Nations General Assembly, and public pronouncements of U.S. and Soviet leaders. Integrative complexity involves two factors. *Differentiation* refers to the acknowledgment of different ways of looking at a problem. People who do not differentiate see the world in terms of black and white, whereas differentiators acknowledge not only shades of gray but also that things may be black on one dimension but white on another. *Integration* refers to the ability to deal with the differentiation in a constructive way, perceiving or postulating relationships (e.g., trade-offs) among the multiple differentiated dimensions. Tetlock argues that integrative complexity does not imply a value judgment about the intelligence of the source or the validity of the arguments. For example, arguments for the abolition of slavery were low in complexity but today few would question their moral validity.

Tetlock and his colleagues developed a method of coding integrative complexity on a seven-point scale (viz., 1 = low differentiation; 3 = moderate differentiation but low integration; 5 = moderate-to-high differentiation but only moderate integration; 7 = a fully differentiated and integrated argument). Figure 3.3 presents the percentage of each advocacy group at each level of integrative complexity.

The prohibitionists (mean = 2.7) showed significantly less complex rhetoric than the legalizers (mean = 4.0) and decriminalizers (mean = 3.7). Fifty-eight percent of prohibitionist essays were at levels 1 or 2, the undifferentiated "black vs. white" end of the continuum. On the other hand, most legalizers and, to a lesser extent, decriminalizers scored in the highly differentiated and moderately integrated range. Note again Tetlock's point that higher levels of complexity do not imply either higher intelligence or a more valid set of arguments. But we think the higher complexity scores of the reformers might shed light on the intractability of the debate and the difficulty reformers have had attracting public support.

Why is prohibitionist rhetoric less complex than that of the reform advocates? Three explanations come to mind. The first is the rigidity-of-the-right hypothesis that has waxed and waned in the past 50 years of social psychology (Tetlock, 1989, 1993). This hypothesis is rooted in research on the "authoritarian" personality type, work that was motivated by post-War attempts to explain the rise of Fascism. The

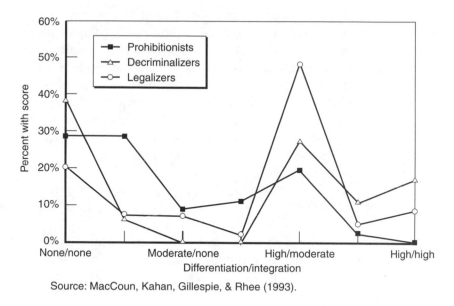

Source: MacCoun, Kahan, Gillespie, & Rhee (1993).

Figure 3.3 Integrative complexity scores by position advocated

authoritarian personality type is a cluster of traits, including political conservatism, a rigid dichotomizing cognitive style, and a punitive attitude toward deviance from conventional mainstream values and traditions. But it is notable that many prominent legalizers are conservatives – though of a libertarian rather than religious stripe (e.g., William F. Buckley and Milton Friedman).

A second explanation is that legalizers, arguing against the status quo, require more complex arguments because their task of persuasion is more difficult. Tetlock (1989, 1993) argued to the contrary; the political opposition, on the attack, can be less complex as it hammers on a weak point in the status quo. But Tetlock's recent work (Tetlock, Peterson, & Lerner, 1996) suggested that political rhetoric should be low in complexity when one's audience rewards demagoguery, but high in complexity when one's audience is skeptical. Arguably, legalizers have little to gain from demagogic posturing – except perhaps when preaching to the choir at drug reform conferences – and a strong motivation to overcome opposition and stereotyping through a careful appeal to logic and evidence.

A third explanation, not mutually exclusive, is that the philosophical bases for legalization are inherently more complex than those for prohibition. Many legalizers emphasize the complex and often unintended consequences of cocaine and heroin prohibition – in particular, the apparent role of drug prohibition in promoting income-generating crime, overburdening the criminal justice system, and diverting resources away from treatment and prevention. Superficially, legalization seems paradoxical – how can permitting a socially problematic behavior lessen the problem to society?

CONCLUSION

Though the specifics have changed, the basic debate about the proper legal status of drugs has been a fixture of American elite discourse for many decades. Interest in the topic seems to track public concerns about drugs, but elite arguments for legal change have been ignored or rejected by most citizens. Our analysis suggests that reformers' arguments are complex and multidimensional, not easily reduced to effective bumper stickers or advertisements. Chapters 4 through 6 examine the complexity of the philosophical and behavioral arguments for legalization in greater detail.

4   Philosophical Underpinnings

Many of the arguments in the legalization debate involve empirical matters – either evaluative descriptions of the status quo or predictions about the likely consequences of a change in policy. But purely moral arguments also play a prominent role. Many prohibitionists assert that drugs should be banned because drug use per se is immoral. On the other side, many legalizers and decriminalizers argue that U.S. drug laws are hypocritical, or too draconian, or that they infringe on an individual's right to take drugs. Chapter 3 showed that nonempirical arguments were outnumbered by empirical assertions (not necessarily accurate) in American newspaper essays, but quantity says nothing about the force or conviction with which the arguments were believed or felt. Nor does quantity reveal the origins of the authors' views; empirical claims may serve as a means of bolstering an essentially values-based conviction. Additionally, it may be that the kinds of people who write op-ed essays (especially those that get published) are more enamored of, or at least more fluent in, empirical argumentation. Scrolling through the messages on any of the growing number of pro- and antidrug discussion groups on the Internet, one can find a much greater reliance on nonempirical, morals-based arguments.

The debate cannot be neatly parsed by distinguishing facts and values; philosophers and scientists have long rejected a strict fact-value dichotomy as untenable (see Cole, 1992). Values affect the selection, measurement, interpretation, and evaluation of research findings (MacCoun, 1998b). Moreover, the very belief that one might use facts to help adjudicate moral issues is itself a moral position (e.g., it is a central tenet of utilitarianism). Thus, before tackling the empirical claims, we briefly survey the underlying philosophical issues. Philosophical positions are not always explicit in the policy debate, but they nevertheless shape the politics of drug policy formation. Moreover people's moral views (e.g., their respect for drug laws) influence the effectiveness of drug policies.

CONSEQUENTIALIST VS. DEONTOLOGICAL ARGUMENTS

The *utilitarian* tradition, originating in the works of Jeremy Bentham and John Stuart Mill, enjoins us to evaluate acts and rules by their consequences – specifically, by their net contribution to human utility. The term *utilitarian* carries considerable intellectual baggage and has sinister overtones for many. Most readers will have encountered thought experiments showing how chilling conclusions can follow from seemingly innocent utilitarian premises. (A surgeon has five patients facing death; each needs a different organ for transplant, but none have been donated. In walks an unwitting, healthy young flower deliveryman. . . .) Over a century of debate, the tradition has yielded many variants, each sprouting up as needed in response to utilitarianism's many critics. Utilitarian theories vary with respect to the proper objects under scrutiny (e.g., individual acts vs. rules for acting), the interpretations of utility (e.g., happiness, welfare, or the more content-free operational definitions of modern economics), and units of analysis (momentary experiences vs. individual actors vs. aggregate societies; see Parfit, 1984). We will sidestep these philosophical potholes by offering in place of utilitarianism a more general notion, *consequentialism* – the claim that it is appropriate to evaluate certain acts or rules by evaluating their empirical (i.e., observable) consequences.

Most closely associated with Immanuel Kant, *deontological* positions assert that certain moral obligations hold irrespective of their empirical consequences. Most of the injunctions of the world's leading religious traditions (e.g., thou shalt not kill) are deontological in nature, although as Blaise Pascal pointed out, the choice between salvation and damnation certainly offers consequentialist food for thought. Inherent sinfulness is frequently the argument against toleration of homosexuality and prostitution but less frequently against drug use, perhaps because though psychoactive plant use predates Biblical times by millennia, the New Testament is silent on the topic. (Drunkenness is condemned, but moderate alcohol consumption of course figures prominently in the story.) A particularly eloquent deontological statement against drug use comes from James Q. Wilson (1990, 1993):

> [I]f we believe – as I do – that dependency on certain mind-altering drugs *is* a moral issue and that their illegality rests in part on their immorality, then legalizing them undercuts, if it does not eliminate altogether, the moral message. That message is at the root of the distinction between nicotine and cocaine. Both are highly addictive; both have harmful physical effects. But we treat the two drugs differently, not simply because nicotine is so widely used as to be beyond the reach of effective prohibition, but because its use does not destroy the user's essential humanity. Tobacco shortens one's life, *cocaine debases it*. Nicotine alters one's habits, *cocaine alters one's soul*. The heavy use of crack, unlike the heavy use of tobacco, corrodes those natural sentiments of sympathy and duty that constitute our human nature and make possible our social life (Wilson, 1990, p. 26; italics added).

Deontological arguments are at least as popular on the legalization side of the debate, most prominently among libertarians (e.g., Richards, 1982; Szasz, 1974, 1987). Thomas Szasz endorses two variants of the libertarian position on drugs in the following quote:

> I believe that we also have a right to eat, drink, or inject a substance – any substance – not because we are sick and want it to cure us, nor because a government-supported medical authority claims that it will be good for us, but simply because we want to take it and because the government – as our servant rather than our master – does not have the right to meddle in our private dietary and drug affairs (Szasz, 1987, p. 349).

The affirmative argument is that we have a right to use drugs. One can readily assert a *natural* right to drug use, but it is more challenging to identify a comparable *positive* right to drug use, a right protected by the U.S. Constitution or statutory law.[1] A class of narrow exceptions involves the religious use of psychedelics by organized religious groups. The negative argument is that government has no right or standing to prohibit the ingestion of drugs (or other acts involving one's own body), so long as no one else is being harmed in the process. This latter point deserves emphasis. Few if any

---

1. Sweet and Harris (1998) provided a detailed examination of a possible unenumerated legal right to drug use under the Ninth Amendment.

libertarians believe that the law must tolerate acts by drug users that cause serious and direct harm to others (see the discussion that follows); they simply assert that such acts already fall under the purview of acceptable nondrug criminal laws.

Individuals (other than philosophers) don't fit neatly into consequentialist or deontological categories. These terms refer to types of arguments, not necessarily types of people, and most of us hold a mix of both types of views. Policy analysis tends toward consequentialist positions, but most people – analysts and nonanalysts alike – hold many categorical deontological beliefs. It is useful to think in terms of the *psychological weights* that people place on different arguments. We give arguments zero weight if they appear completely irrelevant, but also if they appear morally repugnant (Elster, 1992; Fiske & Tetlock, 1997). At the other extreme, arguments can be decisive and "trump" or preempt all others; in such cases, the individual's views are frozen and largely impervious to counterargument or evidence. But research on the psychology of attitudes suggests that, in practice, these trump arguments are rare.[2] We now examine the philosophical sources for many of the considerations that need to be weighed.

THE LIBERAL TRADITION

John Stuart Mill

John Stuart Mill's *On Liberty* (1859/1947) is the starting point for contemporary debates on the legislation of morals. It is the cornerstone for the liberal tradition in moral and political philosophy, not to be confused with the term *liberal* as used in contemporary U.S. debates. Early in the essay, Mill articulates what has come to be known as the *harm principle*; it is worth quoting at length:

> [T]he sole end for which mankind are warranted, individually or collectively, in interfering with the liberty of action of any of their number, is self-protection. That the only purpose for which power can be rightfully exercised

2. Unidimensional responses to multidimensional problems are not uncommon – we'll see that offenders sometimes choose crime that way – but the explanation often involves limited motivation or cognitive capacity rather than the press of moral convictions. A psychological implication is that overall assessments will be unstable, as weights are recomputed due to situational fluctuations in the relative salience of the various dimensions.

over any member of a civilized community, against his will, is to prevent harm to others. His own good, either physical or moral, is not a sufficient warrant. He cannot rightfully be compelled to do or forbear because it will be better for him to do so, because it will make him happier, because, in the opinion of others, to do so would be wise or even right. These are good reasons for remonstrating with him, or reasoning with him, or persuading him, or entreating him, but not for compelling him, or visiting him with any evil in case he would do otherwise. . . . The only part of the conduct of anyone, for which he is amenable to society, is that which concerns others. In the part which merely concerns himself, his independence is, of right, absolute. Over himself, over his own body and mind, the individual is sovereign (pp. 144–5).

Mill justified the harm principle on utilitarian grounds, stating, "Mankind are greater gainers by suffering each other to live as seems good to themselves, than by compelling each to live as seems good to the rest" (p. 148).[3] But as Skolnick (1992, p. 138) noted, "the enduring influence of *On Liberty* and its harm principle is derived less from some exquisite utilitarian summation than from Mill's intuitions about the despotic potential of government."

Joel Feinberg

Joel Feinberg's (1984, 1985, 1986, 1988) four-volume analysis of "the moral limits of the criminal law" is arguably the leading contemporary exposition of the Mill tradition. Feinberg offered what he believed was a more defensible statement of the harm principle:

It is always a good reason in support of penal legislation that it would be effective in preventing (eliminating, reducing) harm to persons other than the actor (the one prohibited from acting) *and* there is no other means that is equally effective at no greater cost to other values (1988, p. xix).

To this, Feinberg added an *offense principle*:

It is always a good reason in support of a proposed criminal prohibition that it is necessary to prevent serious offense to persons other than the actor and would be an effective means to that end if enacted (1988, p. xix).

For Feinberg, "the harm and offense principles, duly clarified and qualified, between them exhaust the class of good reasons for

3. Mill did not assert, as is sometimes assumed, a *natural right* to freedom from interference: "I forego any advantage which could be derived to my argument from the idea of abstract right, as a thing independent of utility" (p. 145). Nevertheless, others have derived Mill's principle from nonconsequentialist appeals to liberty or autonomy as intrinsic rights or goods (see George, 1993).

criminal prohibitions" (p. xix); together, they characterize "the liberal position." (Omitting the offense principle produces the "extreme liberal position.") Much of his four-volume work is directed toward articulating the necessary clarifications and qualifications. Two are especially important. Feinberg's harm principle applies only to *wrongful harms*, which involve "setbacks to another's interests" that violate another's rights and not to *nonwrongful harms* (setbacks that do not violate the other's rights) or *nonharmful wrongs* (violations of another's rights that do not set back another's interests). Similarly, Feinberg's offense principle only applies to *wrongful offenses*, meaning offenses "caused by wrongful (right-violating) conduct of others," but not the larger class of "disliked mental states" not caused by right-violating conduct.

Drug laws

Feinberg's offense principle is central to debates about pornography but seems largely irrelevant to the drug law debate. Conceivably certain acts committed in a state of intoxication might meet Feinberg's offense principle, but those are readily dealt with by various nondrug criminal laws (e.g., public nuisance and public decency laws). The harm principle, on the other hand, plays a crucial role in the drug legalization debate. Because the major theoretical alternatives to the liberal tradition are generally much less restrictive about the legislation of morality, one might argue a fortiori that if drug prohibition can be justified under the harm principle, it is even more acceptable under alternative moral schemes (see Moore, 1991, p. 532).

   Thus, a key question for the justification of drug laws is whether drug use causes wrongful harms to others. For decades, the term *victimless crime* was used to characterize drug use, gambling, and prostitution. But in recent years, this term has been fading from use, and to the modern ear, it already sounds quaintly naïve, or even mildly offensive. This is more of an expansion in consciousness than in conscience, reflecting not puritanism but rather an increased awareness of what economists call the "externalities" of human affairs – the many ways in which our private conduct can impose costs on others. The recent focus on the health harms of passive smoking is a prominent instance. We will later catalogue over fifty distinct classes of harms associated with drugs, most primarily borne by nonusers.

That claim in itself might appear to meet the Mill/Feinberg harm criterion decisively, and indeed we think it almost certainly does. But there are several complications. First, Husak (1992), in a particularly sophisticated defense of a right to use drugs, argued that most of the harms drug use poses to others are not "wrongful" or "criminal" harms subject to the Mill/Feinberg criterion, because they do not violate others' moral rights. Husak was most persuasive in arguing that any increase in drug use under legalization would not in itself violate anyone's rights; we surely have no right that others not use drugs. Husak is less convincing in his challenge to "a moral right that the drug user be an attentive parent, a good neighbor, a proficient student, a reliable employee" (p. 166). As stated, this seems compelling, but Husak's way of framing the issue set up a straw man. The roles of parent, neighbor, student, and employee are too heterogeneous to form a meaningful set; the risks and responsibilities that accompany parenthood are entirely different from (and more compelling than) those that accompany the roles of student or employee. And even though most readers will share Husak's rejection of government-mandated productivity, that isn't what prohibiters are demanding – criminalizing reckless or irresponsible role conduct is surely very different from mandating exemplary conduct. At any rate, the question isn't whether all or even most forms of disutility caused by drug use violate moral rights – some of them do; the question is whether they are sufficient to justify drug prohibition.

Second, not every incident of drug use harms others; in fact, the vast majority do not. Indeed, though this is difficult to quantify with existing data, it is likely that many if not most drug users *never* do wrongful harm to others as a result of their using careers – bearing in mind that the majority of these careers are limited in duration and intensity. Rather, each incident of drug use is accompanied by a *risk* that others will be harmed; some users, substances, settings, and modalities of use are riskier than others, but in no case is the risk zero. Drug use is not distinct in this regard; many prohibited acts are associated with harm only probabilistically – running red lights, driving under the influence, and so on. Of course, this is true to some degree of most licit human activities. Unfortunately, there is no obvious threshold probability of harm to others beyond which activities should be legally prohibited. For example, alcohol consumption poses greater risks to nonusers (through violence, accidents, and neonatal effects) than marijuana does, yet the former is legal and the latter is not, a puzzle we take up later in the book.

Finally, for a Millian policy analysis, establishing that drugs harm nonusers does not settle the question. Prohibiting drugs is costly, in direct expenditures, in foregone benefits, and in the opportunity costs of diverting resources and attention from other government activities. A policy that costs society more than the harms it mitigates is difficult to justify from a consequentialist perspective. A final complication is that drug prohibition may itself be the *cause* of many of these harms to others (see Chapter 6); consider, for example, the violence associated with illicit drug markets. This raises two questions regarding Feinberg's statement of the harm principle. First, is drug prohibition "effective in preventing (eliminating, reducing) harm to persons other than the actor" (1988, p. xix)? If prohibition is itself a source of harm to others, then one must ask whether its *net* effect is to reduce such harms. Second, is there "no other means that is equally effective at no greater cost to other values"? These questions will preoccupy us for the remainder of the book.

ALTERNATIVES TO LIBERALISM

Legal paternalism

Table 4.1 compares the Mill position to other major alternatives. Perhaps the major contemporary alternative is *legal paternalism*, which Feinberg defines as the belief that "[I]t is always a good reason in support of a prohibition that it is necessary to prevent harm (physical, psychological, or economic) to the actor himself" (1988, p. xix).[4] That drug use is potentially harmful to the user is beyond dispute; the risks include addiction (e.g., the suffering caused by withdrawal and craving), drug overdose, disease, drug-related accidents, criminal victimization, economic hardships, and social isolation. Note that these risks are considerably greater for some drugs (cocaine, PCP) than for others (marijuana, psilocybin) (Gable, 1993; Goldstein, 1994;

---

4. A related but distinct notion is *legal perfectionism*, the belief that laws can and should play a role in positively shaping citizens for their individual benefit. Though liberal theorists (e.g., Rawls, 1971) are generally "antiperfectionist" in this sense, and leading perfectionists are nonliberals (George, 1993), there are some notable perfectionist liberals (e.g., Raz, 1986).

Table 4.1. *Major philosophical positions on prohibition*

	Relevant criteria for prohibition?	
	Net reduction in harm to others	Net reduction in harm to users
Legal moralism	Not relevant	Not relevant
Strict libertarianism	Not relevant	Not relevant
Millian liberalism	Necessary	Not relevant
Soft paternalism	Sufficient, but not necessary	Sufficient if legal minor or judgmentally impaired
Hard paternalism	Sufficient, but not necessary	Sufficient

Julien, 1995). But a coherent paternalism must surely weight the extent to which prohibition and its enforcement creates, enables, or augments these harms. As with harms to others, the key policy questions are whether prohibition produces a *net* reduction in harms to users themselves, and whether alternative policy regimes would more effectively reduce harms to users. In Chapter 6, we attribute primary causation for each of some fifty different harms to either drug use or drug laws and their enforcement. Many of these harms are primarily borne by users, and prohibition bears the primary (but not sole) responsibility for most of these harms. Nevertheless, many of the risks drugs pose to the user are psychopharmacological effects of drug use itself – exposure to external risks produced by diminished mental capacity and psychomotor coordination during intoxication and the more direct risks of addiction and other physical and psychological harms.

Mill himself recognized a paternalistic exception to the harm principle for children and the mentally disabled:

> It is perhaps necessary to say that this doctrine is meant to apply only to human beings in the maturity of their faculties. . . . Those who are still in a state to require being taken care of by others, must be protected against their own actions as well as against external injury (1859/1947, p. 145).

This position is sometimes known as *soft paternalism*; Feinberg (1986) questioned whether it is truly an exception to the harm principle. Moore (1991) argues that Mill's paternalistic exception "offers substantial room for justifying the use of state authority to regulate drug use." Mill's notion of mature faculties can be read as requiring at least some *minimal* capacity for rational choice. This minimal requirement is clearly met for adults who contemplate drug use for the first time, except perhaps those with severe retardation or mental illness. But the threshold won't be met if judgment is impaired by either intoxication or the "weaknesses of will" caused by addiction (Kleiman, 1992a). There is a growing recognition, as well as laboratory evidence, that under the right conditions, most of us can get trapped in choices that we ourselves, if viewing the situation with no new information but a different perspective, would judge to be against our best interests (see Loewenstein & Elster, 1992; Loewenstein, 1996).[5] The argument from addiction applies with varying force across psychoactive substances; it is more compelling for drugs that produce withdrawal symptoms, obsessive craving, and/or compulsive behavior (like heroin and cocaine) than for drugs with minimal addictive potential (like psilocybin).

A vexing complication for consequentialists (e.g., Millian liberals and legal paternalists) is that a change in drug laws might have different effects at the micro level (average harm to the individual user) and the macro level (aggregate harm across drug users), a point taken up at length in the final section of the book. Imagine, for example, that a change in drug laws reduces average harm per user (e.g., through the regulation of production, purity, and labeling) but increases total aggregate harm to users (e.g., due to substantial increases in the quantity of use and/or the number of users).[6] A "macro" consequentialist should accept whichever regime minimizes *total* harm (to others, to users, or both, depending on one's views on paternalism). On the other hand, a "micro" consequentialist might accept a regime that minimizes *average* harm (to others, to users, or both), even if some alternative regime better reduces total harm (e.g., by successfully restricting total use). For the micro consequentialist,

5. An alternative perspective is Gary Becker's argument that addiction can be characterized as rational behavior given appropriate external conditions (e.g., Becker & Murphy, 1988). Becker's model is an intellectual *tour de force* of unknown relevance to the phenomenon of real-world addiction.
6. Note that average and total drug harm can diverge for reasons similar to the cases where average and total utility diverge. For the latter case, philosophers usually cite examples where the population size in question changes. In a related vein, average and total drug harm can diverge when the "population" of drug incidents changes – either because each user uses more or because there are more users than before. If use remained constant, average and total harm would always move in the same direction. (See Chapter 15.)

total harm is irrelevant as long as individual acts of drug use are made safe enough. This micro consequentialist view might seem implausible, but note that this is in fact how many activities are implicitly treated – sports, driving, and so on. Regulation generally aims at the average safety per incident of these activities (and perhaps, the worst possible harm per incident) rather than the number of incidents or the level of total participation. Increases in participation may increase total harm enough to trigger stricter regulation, but that regulation usually targets harm levels, not participation levels. (And it may be the increased salience of the harms that gets attention rather than some threshold level of their absolute magnitude).

Legal moralism

Criminalized vices are often labeled *mala prohibita* (wrong because they are illegal), as distinct from crimes that are *mala in se* (evil in themselves). Crimes in the latter category, such as homicide, rape, and armed robbery, are generally considered evil because the offenders intentionally cause wrongful harm to others. Drug use is clearly qualitatively different from such offenses. Yet many defenders of prohibition discuss drug use in terms that suggest they find it intrinsically immoral. The label *legal moralism* characterizes the belief that "it can be morally legitimate to prohibit conduct on the ground that it is inherently immoral, even though it causes neither harm nor offense to the actor or to others" (Feinberg, 1988, pp. xix–xx).

In practice, it is difficult to distinguish legal moralism from other justifications for drug prohibition. Skolnick (1992) and Husak (1992) argued that prominent drug prohibitionists view drug use in deontological terms, as *malum in se* or morally repugnant in and of itself. The earlier quote from James Q. Wilson (". . . cocaine alters one's soul . . .") seems to support this thesis. But as noted at the outset, deontology is a characteristic of arguments, not people. A closer examination suggests that prominent prohibitionists ultimately define the immorality of drug use in consequentialist terms. Authors like James Q. Wilson and William Bennett described drug use as immoral, but they made their case with references to harms to self and others. For example, in the same essay, Wilson (1990) established the consequentialist basis for his moral repugnance:

The notion that abusing drugs such as cocaine is "a victimless crime" is not only absurd but dangerous. Even ignoring the fetal drug syndrome, crack-dependent people are, like heroin addicts, individuals who regularly victimize their children by neglect, their spouses by improvidence, their employers by lethargy, and their coworkers by carelessness.

Similarly, in his introduction to the first *National Drug Control Strategy*, William Bennett (1989) indeed argued that "drug use degrades human character." But in the next sentence, he offered a clearly consequentialist rationale: "Drug users make inattentive parents, bad neighbors, poor students, and unreliable employees – quite apart from their common involvement in criminal activity."

Still, even though prohibitionists cite consequentialist arguments – the coin of the realm in contemporary U.S. policy debates – it does seem plausible that legal moralist sentiments run deep in American opposition to drug law reform. Legal moralism is difficult to defend from a Western (classical) liberal perspective, but it is consistent with what cognitive anthropologists (Haidt, Koller, & Dias, 1993; Shweder et al., 1997) have identified as an *ethics of community* (codes that dictate one's social roles and duties) and an *ethics of divinity* (codes that dictate physical purity). Some will endorse a legal moralist position on drugs because the escapist aspect conflicts with their ethic of community; others, because the chemical aspect conflicts with their ethic of divinity. But these reactions are likely to be vague, intuitive, and difficult to articulate.

Perhaps the following thought experiment provides a relevant test. Imagine a newly invented synthetic psychedelic, "Rhapsodol." Rhapsodol provides an intense (but not unduly frightening) altered state, full of intellectually and aesthetically intriguing mental imagery, and a profound sense of love for all living creatures. These sensations last for approximately 30 minutes and then vanish completely, producing absolutely no detectable changes in one's life outlook or mental or physical functioning. They can only be experienced by sitting or lying in a completely stationary position; any abrupt physical movements end the psychedelic state and return one to a normal state. Moreover, because of neurochemical processes of adaptation, the effects can be experienced only once a day. Would you consider Rhapsodol use immoral? Should it be legally prohibited? We suspect that even in the absence of any obvious harms to self or others, some Americans would still answer these questions in the affirmative.

Effects of laws on cohesion and legitimacy

In 1957, in a document now famous as the *Wolfendon Report*, a committee led by Sir John Wolfendon recommended that the British Parliament decriminalize homosexual activity between consenting adults (see George, 1993). Lord Patrick Devlin's critique of that report, later published in an expanded form as *The Enforcement of Morals* (1959/1965), articulated a fifth theoretical position on the legislation of morality. Devlin asserted that legislators are obliged to prohibit legally any act that is viewed as morally repugnant by its citizenry, if for no other reason than the necessity to preserve the society's cohesion and prevent its dissolution. Notwithstanding a superficial resemblance to other views already discussed, Devlin's position was distinct. It is not paternalistic; Devlin was not arguing that the prohibition is necessary for the good of the potential actors (see Dworkin, 1978). Nor is it simply a form of legal moralism; indeed, Devlin did not require that society's moral views must be justifiable by reasons; he simply required that these views be widely shared and deeply held (Dworkin, 1978; George, 1993). Finally, Devlin's argument should not be confused with the notion that it is adaptive for society to *define* certain acts as immoral in order to influence behavior (e.g., Chapter 5; see Wilson, 1993). Instead, Devlin's position is a novel form of consequentialist argument in which morals legislation is justified not in terms of the consequences of the *act* (harms or offenses) but rather in terms of the consequences of the moral content of the law – specifically, its role in preserving society.

Devlin's argument should not be confused with the view that drug use per se, if sufficiently widespread, would reduce social cohesion. The campus unrest of the Vietnam War era (when marijuana use first became widespread) comes to mind, but drugs are at most a partial explanation for that phenomenon. Moreover, national drug use peaked not in 1969 (the era of the Yippies and the Black Panthers) but in the late 1970s (the disco era). For some communities, the drug problem peaked a full decade later with the violence of the crack era. But note that Devlin's argument involves the prevalence of moral views, not immoral acts. Indeed, if the prevalence of antidrug attitudes and of drug use are inversely related, Devlin's model would be most applicable when drug use is rare. Devlin's argument makes no predictions about the cohesiveness of societies where most members are tolerant of drug use.[7]

Devlin's position has numerous flaws and has received some withering criticism (e.g., Dworkin, 1978; George, 1993; Hart, 1963). Ronald Dworkin (1978) offered one line of attack: "What is shocking and wrong is not [Devlin's] idea that the community's morality counts, but his idea of what counts as the community's morality" (p. 255). Dworkin complained that Devlin would allow moral opinions based on prejudice, ignorance, or irrationality to determine the content of the law, noting that "the belief that prejudices, personal aversions and rationalizations do not justify restricting another's freedom itself occupies a critical and fundamental position in our popular morality" (p. 254).

In evaluating Devlin, it is important to distinguish two issues: the validity of his theory as a description of how laws get formed and the validity of his assumptions about the stability of society. The influence of emotions and prejudice on the formation of laws and policies is documented in the sizeable literature on "moral panics," which draws on the history of American drug control for illustrations (Morgan, 1981; Musto, 1987). But Devlin's normative argument is based on a different assumption, that a society's stability depends on the congruence of its moral views and its criminal laws. As Hart (1963) pointed out, Devlin simply asserted without evidence what is in fact an open empirical question. Hart noted that Devlin's argument is tautologically true if "society" is narrowly defined as a specific set of moral principles, but he suggested that such a definition would be absurd; the history of human civilization shows no such rigid stasis. Devlin offered no evidence that societies are destroyed (or even weakened) when they legally tolerate behaviors their citizens find morally repulsive. Devlin's position is difficult to assess empirically because it is frustratingly vague. For example, what frac-

7. Ethnobotanical researchers argue that psychoactive plant rituals actually help to *promote* cohesion in some small indigenous communities, including the Huichol Indians in Mexico, the Tucano Indians in Colombia, and the Native American Church in the United States (Schultes & Hoffman, 1992). Participants in the MDMA rave scene in various American cities make similar claims; "... almost all respondents mentioned enhanced closeness and communication with other people or their environment as a major benefit of the MDMA experience" (Beck & Rosenbaum, 1994, p. 68). In both cases, it is difficult to separate the effects of the drugs from the effects of the rituals and settings in which they are being used. "Bowling alone," when the bowl is at the end of a pipe, seems unlikely to build a sense of community.

tion of the citizenry must share an antipathy to the behavior? A plurality? A simple majority? A two-thirds majority? Are opinions to be weighted by the strength with which they are held? And how should a society's cohesion be defined? What constitutes a breakdown in cohesion?[8]

Robinson and Darley (1997) recently offered what might be characterized as a neo-Devlinian hypothesis, specifically, that a congruence between lay intuitions about legal liability and those embodied in the Model Penal Code enhances both legitimacy and compliance. Their research identified numerous gaps between the Code and lay views, but these discrepancies involved differential reactions to legal elements of a crime (e.g., attempts vs. actual commissions) rather than the criminalization or noncriminalization of acts like drug use. Though they did not directly test their hypotheses about the consequences of these gaps, many recent studies have documented the correlation between perceived legitimacy of the law and legal compliance (e.g., Tyler, 1990).[9] Though very little is known about these linkages, this line of research does take seriously the possibility that the match between the content of those laws and public sentiments might have important behavioral consequences.

The *direction of the discrepancy* is likely to be both normatively and behaviorally important. A "sin of commission" would occur if the law criminalized acts citizens failed to recognize as immoral; a "sin of omission" would occur if the law failed to criminalize acts the citizenry found immoral. Devlin is concerned with sins of omission; implicit in Robinson and Darley's discussion is a concern with sins of commission. Normatively, our rights-based constitutional democracy poses more constraints against the elimination of sins of omission, though in recent years, shifts toward greater leniency have posed greater political risks. Almost by definition, sins of commission attract attention under a prohibition; it is impossible to observe whether legalization would produce sins of omission of comparable or greater magnitude. Many Americans are angry at smokers and problem

8. For a critical analysis of the cohesion concept in the context of heterosexual antipathy toward homosexuals in the military, see MacCoun (1996).
9. Tyler's study was not designed to test Devlin's theory, and his analyses are only indirectly relevant. He measured legitimacy in part as a willingness to obey laws even when one disagrees with them. This willingness is indeed correlated with actual compliance. A more direct test of Devlin would examine compliance as a function of the gap between one's own moral views and one's perception of the content of the law.

drinkers, but does this translate into reduced legal compliance or social stability? Absent more direct evidence, Devlin's position is a much weaker foundation for drug prohibition than the harm-based rationales discussed earlier.

The benefits of drug use

Largely absent from this discussion has been any analysis of the benefits of drug use and their role in the moral assessment of drug prohibition. Indeed, the notion that the currently illicit drugs have benefits is almost completely ignored in the policy analytic literature on drug control (Gable, 1997). Arguing from the so-called *revealed preference* principle, many economists argue that the fact that individuals choose to use such drugs establishes de facto that they have benefit (see Becker & Murphy, 1988). Many will reflexively reject this notion. One sophisticated argument for rejecting it is Mark Kleiman's (1992a) observation that many of these drugs instigate neurological and psychological processes that motivate compulsive use, even among those who freely acknowledge they would prefer to stop using. As Kleiman would no doubt agree, this argument has more force for highly addictive drugs like nicotine, cocaine, and heroin than for cannabis or the psychedelics.

Rather than inferring the benefits of a drug by its consumption, one might explicitly identify properties of the drug experience and argue for their benefits empirically or philosophically. Interestingly, the least addictive illicit drugs – cannabis and the psychedelics – have generated the largest endorsement literature. The psychedelics in particular have been defended (subject to various caveats about safe modalities of use) by respected ethnobotanists and pharmacologists (e.g., Schultes & Hoffman, 1992), religious scholars (see Forte, 1997), literary figures (see Strausbaugh & Blaise, 1991), and psychiatrists (e.g., Bravo & Grob, 1996; Strassman, 1995). Indeed, the latter authors are conducting federally approved controlled trials to examine the safety of methylene-dioxy-methamphetamine (MDMA) and other psychedelics with a hope of eventually testing their psychotherapeutic potential. Many such claims may eventually fail the tests of science or cultural experience – witness Freud's notorious endorsement of cocaine – but others may well be substantiated in time.

In the end, it is no more important for consequentialists to agree on the benefits of drug use than it is to agree on the relative importance of its harms, or the harms of prohibition. Just as readers will differ in the weight they place on the freedom to use drugs, or the immorality of drug taking, it is likely that they will differ in their willingness to place positive value on the drug-taking experience.

IMPLICATIONS

This chapter has attempted to articulate the major theoretical positions on the legislation of morality. We would probably characterize ourselves as soft paternalists, but we have no intention of imposing our moral views. Instead, the examination of these moral models is intended to identify underlying points of contention in the policy debate and places where empirical research and analysis might have leverage in shifting people's views. Only two positions – legal moralism and extreme libertarianism – are purely deontological and hence impervious to research evidence or policy analysis. Nothing in the remainder of this book is likely to change the views of such readers, although we hope that we can help them anticipate the likely empirical consequences of their preferred policies so that they can ponder possible policies of mitigation. But the remaining positions – liberalism, hard and soft paternalism, and Devlin's hypothesis – each require relevant evidence and analysis regarding harms to users, harms to nonusers, and/or the effects of laws on social stability.

Many legal liberals and paternalists will argue that the harms of drug use are already sufficiently apparent to justify drug prohibition decisively. But note that liberalism does not *require* prohibition in the presence of harms to others, nor does paternalism *require* prohibition given harms to self; rather, they *permit* prohibition in those circumstances. In our view, the critical questions involve the *relative* harms to self and others under prohibition versus alternative legal regimes.

5   How Does Prohibition Affect Drug Use?[1]

A key point of contention in the drug law debate is whether legalization would open a floodgate – a dramatic escalation in drug use – or merely loosen a spigot. Most legalization opponents assert that use would increase substantially. Moreover, some are willing to quantify this, although clearly most have aimed high for rhetorical purposes, and none provide more than the most superficial account of the basis of their estimate. Even Herbert Kleber, the most serious scholar among those providing estimates, simply asserted that "if cocaine were legally available, as alcohol and nicotine are now, the number of cocaine abusers would probably rise to a point somewhere between the number of users of the other two agents, perhaps 20 to 25 million." Table 5.1 compares recent prevalence estimates with various predictions of prevalence in a postlegalization regime. Most are nothing short of apocalyptic; they range from Morton Kondracke's lower bound 40 percent growth for marijuana and light cocaine use to several predictions of tenfold growth in heroin and cocaine addiction.

Legalization advocates are more circumspect about the prevalence issue; in Chapter 3's content analysis, drug use rates were discussed by 60 percent of prohibition advocates but only 5 percent of legalizers. Few legalizers contend that ending prohibition would actually

1. This chapter updates an earlier *Psychological Bulletin* article by MacCoun (1993). That article provides a more extensive discussion of the psychology of deterrence and a more complete bibliography of relevant research.

Table 5.1. *Current drug prevalence and predictions about postlegalization prevalence*

Drug	Recent prevalence	Predicted prevalence after legalization
All illicit use	13 million monthly users in 1996 (6.1% of population aged 12 and older)[a]	26–39 million (Kondracke, 1988) 40–50 million "heavy users" (Bennett, 1995)
Marijuana	10.1 million current (past month) users in 1996 (4.7% of population aged 12 and older)[a]	50–60 million (DuPont, cited in Kondracke, 1988) 4–6 million extra users (Kondracke, 1988)
Cocaine	Estimates range from 600,000 to 3,600,000 weekly users circa 1996.[a]	". . . [a]ddicts will number somewhere between 8.5 million (if regular usage doubles and 70 percent become addicted) and 42 million" (Kondracke, 1988) 10–32 million "compulsive users" (Homer, cited in CASA, 1995) 20–25 million; compulsive users might be 9 times higher than at present (Kleber, 1994) 50–60 million (DuPont, cited in Kondracke, 1988) 60–70 million (Branch, 1988, citing unnamed experts) 60–100 million (Pollin, cited in Goode, 1997)
Heroin	Lower bound estimate of 216,000 current (past month) users in 1996[a] Expert estimates range from 500,000 to 1 million regular heroin users	10 million (DuPont, cited in Kondracke, 1988) 10 million (Branch, 1988, citing unnamed experts)

[a] National Household Survey on Drug Abuse (annual); see *http://www.health.org/pubs/nhsda/96hhs/*; Rhodes et al. (1997).

reduce drug use.[2] Most who address the issue argue that any increase would be minimal. For example, in his 1989 *Science* article,

2. An exception is David Boaz (1990). Observing that illicit use was currently climbing while licit use (alcohol and tobacco) had been declining, he predicted that a short-run increase in newly licit use would be followed by a long-run decline. This is dubious logic and a selective use of history.

Nadelmann argued that "there are . . . strong reasons to believe that none of the currently illicit substances would become as popular as alcohol or tobacco even if they were legalized" (p. 945). Dennis (1990, p. 128) is unusual among legalizers in offering a point prediction; he expected an "immediate and permanent 25 percent increase in the number of addicts and the costs associated with them" – but still anticipates a net social savings of about $25 billion due to ending the costs of the drug war. Unlike most authors, he is explicit about the calculations underlying his estimate; unfortunately they are based on some sweeping assumptions about things that are simply not known.

This chapter reviews and evaluates what is known about the impact of drug prohibitions and their enforcement on levels of drug use in modern America. We compare three policy regimes. The baseline case is contemporary American prohibition – in particular, the aggressive enforcement-oriented approach championed by William Bennett in the Bush Administration, and largely sustained by the Clinton Administration. Against that baseline, we examine theoretical predictions regarding the effects of two generic alternatives; as is traditional in the debate, neither alternative is articulated in any detail. For the purposes of this chapter, *depenalization* (often confusingly called decriminalization) refers to a substantial reduction of penalties for possession of modest quantities of prohibited psychotropic drugs (e.g., civil monetary fines). In this regime, the sale and manufacture of these drugs remains illegal and that prohibition is aggressively prosecuted at current levels. The term *legalization* refers to a new regime in which currently prohibited psychotropic drugs are regulated using the contemporary American alcohol model (e.g., cocaine, marijuana, and heroin available in retail stores for those over 21 years of age). Intermediate medical and regulatory models are considered in Chapters 13 through 15.

This chapter makes two points. It is plausible that drug penalties could be substantially reduced without significantly increasing use but also that legalization might lead to sizeable increases in use. The two positions are not contradictory, nor are we trying to occupy a cautious "middle ground" position. Greatly curtailed user sanctions might have *qualitatively different* effects than changes in the legal status of drug manufacture and sales.

To many, it may seem obvious that legalization would increase drug use. But an earlier article (MacCoun, 1993) argued that this might not be the case. Like this chapter, that essay identified seven distinct mechanisms by which drug prohibitions affect drug use and reviewed the extant theoretical and empirical literature on each mechanism. Most of these mechanisms discourage drug use, but a few appear to actually encourage it; they are among the many unintended consequences of drug prohibition. The 1993 article argued that ignorance regarding the magnitude of each these effects – particularly at the licit-illicit threshold – precluded any confident predictions about whether legalization would influence use, much less the size of any increase.

But since 1993, several lines of new evidence (described in this chapter) reinforce the common intuition. Notwithstanding some perverse effects, the *net* effect of legalization would almost certainly be a nontrivial increase in the prevalence of drug use. Granted, that statement hardly clarifies the debate. For starters, there is no credible basis for deciding whether that "nontrivial" increase is 10 percent or 1,000 percent, though it likely falls somewhere in that broad range.

Recent analyses have gone beyond these qualitative assertions, attempting to provide point predictions about the magnitude of growth (Grossman, Chaloupka, & Brown, 1998; Homer, 1993b; Saffer & Chaloupka, 1995). For example, Saffer and Chaloupka projected that the number of occasional heroin users would grow 54 percent, with a 100 percent increase in total consumption. For occasional cocaine use, the relevant estimates were 33 percent and 50 percent, respectively. These efforts are to be applauded for improving the scientific basis of the legalization debate. Still, the projections are unconvincing; they are too heavily based on a narrow economic conceptualization of drug use, and on parameter estimates within an existing legal regime. This chapter identifies reasons to expect that legalization would produce qualitative changes in behavior not captured by an extrapolation from drug use in a world of prohibition.

For nonconsequentialists who view drug use as intrinsically bad, a prediction of increased use provides a sufficient case against legalization. But for consequentialists, matters are not so simple; much depends on what fraction of the new users will become regular heavy users, as opposed to occasional recreational users. Most illicit drug-using careers are limited to a brief period of casual experimentation without harmful consequences (see Johnston, O'Malley, & Bachman,

1989; Shedler & Block, 1990). A notable minority of users are seriously harmed by their use, or cause harm to others, but, as Chapter 6 explains in some detail, some harms resulting from any individual's frequent use may go down. Thus, the key consequentialist policy question, though not the only one, is whether, notwithstanding increases in use, there would be a net increase or decrease in drug-related harms.

THE ECONOMICS OF DRUG DEMAND

The dominant paradigm for projecting the effects of legalization is the rational choice perspective of modern economics, which emphasizes three mechanisms of influence – drug availability, drug prices, and the deterrent effects of punishment (Miron & Zweibel, 1995; Thornton, 1991; Warner, 1991). Interestingly, prohibiters draw upon the economics of consumption to argue that prohibition is helpful, whereas legalizers draw upon the economics of supply to argue that prohibition is harmful (see Chapter 3). The rational choice perspective has received considerable criticism for its narrow and often demonstrably invalid assumptions (see Hogarth & Reder, 1986; Mansbridge, 1990), but it is a productive starting point for analyzing drug law effects.

Basic microeconomic principles suggest that toughly enforced prohibitions will raise prices above their level in an untaxed legal market. If the demand for drugs is sensitive to price, price increases should also discourage drug use. The price elasticity of demand – the percentage change in demand for a 1 percent increase in price – is difficult to estimate for illicit drugs. For the licit substances, estimates cluster around −0.4 for cigarettes and −0.7 for alcoholic beverages (Manning et al., 1991); in contrast, elasticity is around −1.5 for automobiles and −3.5 for movies. Generalizing from the licit psychoactives, some analyses have assumed low sensitivity to price among illicit drug users, at least for highly addictive drugs like heroin. For example, Moore (1991) and Becker, Grossman, and Murphy (1992) cited evidence for a price elasticity of demand for heroin at around −0.2 to −0.3; by way of contrast, they cited estimates in the −1.0 to −1.5 range for marijuana, a drug with much lower dependency potential. In their cost-effectiveness analysis of strategies for reducing cocaine consumption, Rydell and Everingham (1994) assumed an elasticity of –0.5 for cocaine.

But several new studies suggest much greater price sensitivity, with elasticities for cocaine ranging from –0.7 to –2.0 (Caulkins, 1995; Grossman, Chaloupka, & Brown, 1995; Saffer & Chaloupka, 1995). Van Ours (1995) estimated demand elasticity near –1.0 for opium in the Dutch East Indies prior to World War II. A possible explanation for the high elasticity among heavy users is that they spend most of their earnings on the drug and may respond to the increased difficulty of maintaining desired consumption levels (i.e., avoiding withdrawal) by seeking treatment.

Irrespective of price, evidence is mixed as to whether the mere availability of intoxicants influences their consumption levels. Analyses of national survey data suggest that variations in perceived availability of marijuana and cocaine are correlated with high school drug use (Caulkins, 1999), but multivariate analyses suggest availability played little or no causal role (Bachman et al., 1988; Bachman, Johnston, & O'Malley, 1990). For alcohol, several studies have documented effects of minimum drinking ages on the alcohol consumption of 18- to 21-year-olds (Bonnie, 1986), but this intervention confounds availability with deterrence effects and other causal factors discussed later. On the other hand, the recent privatization of bottled wine and spirits distribution in Iowa appears not to have resulted in significant consumption increases, despite a massive increase in availability (Fitzgerald & Mulford, 1992). One recent study of geographic fluctuations in alcohol consumption suggested that *perceived* availability matters more than actual availability (Abbey, Scott, & Smith, 1993). Subsequent chapters will draw on evidence from gambling, tobacco, alcohol, and the Dutch cannabis coffeeshops to argue that commercial promotion may matter as much or more than the mere availability of a substance (or vice) per se.

Logically, there must be threshold levels of low availability and high price beyond which drug use becomes impossible for the consumer, but those levels are difficult to achieve through drug law enforcement. Beyond the mere fact of illegality, enforcement activities are surprisingly limited in their ability to influence the availability and price of illicit drugs (DiNardo, 1993; Reuter, Crawford, & Cave, 1988). For example, a massive increase in the severity of punishment for cocaine selling has failed to increase the price of that drug (Caulkins & Reuter, 1998). But most studies have only examined variations in levels of enforcement, rather than compare enforcement to its absence. Even though the availability and price of drugs are only modestly affected by variations in the current levels of enforcement or interdiction, they would likely be more dramatically affected by the complete elimination of enforcement brought about by legalization or by substantial reductions in the penalties for use.

DETERRENCE: THE FEAR OF LEGAL SANCTIONS

Deterrence theory is rational choice theory as applied to the decision to commit crimes. It originates in the political philosophy of Jeremy Bentham (1789/1948) and Cesare Beccaria (1764/1963), who assumed that human nature was essentially hedonistic, so that crime will be motivated by potential gains but deterred by the prospect of certain, swift, and severe punishment. Irrespective of its role in providing retribution or incapacitation, incarceration should discourage other would-be offenders from engaging in criminal acts (general deterrence) and discourage the offender from recidivating upon release (specific deterrence).

Modern deterrence theory (e.g., Blumstein, Cohen, & Nagin, 1978; Zimring & Hawkins, 1973) is an application of the rational choice paradigm, rooted in Bentham's utilitarianism, that is so influential in contemporary economics. Rational choice theories assume that actors rationally select those actions that will maximize their expected utility. Deterrence theories thus postulate that an actor will engage in a criminal act whenever its expected utility exceeds that of the most profitable alternative. The expected utility of the crime is positively related to the gains from successful completion of the crime multiplied by the subjective probability of obtaining those gains and negatively related to the costs of legal sanctioning if the actor gets caught, multiplied by the subjective probability of legal sanctioning. The latter two components are generally referred to as the *severity* and *certainty* of legal sanctions and serve as the primary focus of most deterrence research. A third component, *celerity* (the speed with which the sanction is applied), has received less attention.

Deterrence theory's implication for the drug policy debate is clear; ceteris paribus, if depenalization or legalization were to reduce the severity of, or even eliminate, legal sanctions, the result should be an increase in the expected utility of using drugs and, hence, an increase in the prevalence of drug use.

Effects of penalties and their enforcement on crime rates

Many of the strongest tests of deterrence theory have examined the effects of legal interventions against drunk driving, a crime arguably of greater relevance to the drug policy debate than the violent or property crimes more frequently studied. Like the illicit drugs, alcohol is a psychoactive substance commonly ingested to achieve a state of intoxication that, as a by-product, can produce serious externalities for other people. Ross and his colleagues (Ross, 1992) have challenged what he calls "the Scandinavian myth" that Norway and Sweden have dramatically reduced drunk driving using per se laws in which driving with a blood alcohol level exceeding a certain threshold – generally 0.08 percent to 0.10 percent – constitutes an offense, regardless of the conduct or demeanor of the driver. These laws are intended to increase the certainty of legal sanctions. Evaluations of per se laws consistently find that they achieve an immediate deterrent effect, often measured by a reduction in road fatalities, but that the effect is generally short-lived, and the problem returns to baseline levels within a year (Ross & LaFree, 1986).

Other jurisdictions have attempted to deter drunk driving by increasing sanction severity. Ross and LaFree (1986) report failures of such interventions in Finland, Australia, and Chicago. West et al. (1989) documented an immediate reduction in traffic fatalities in the wake of Arizona's extremely punitive 1982 policy against first-time drunk driving offenders, but the fatality rate gradually returned to baseline levels within two years.

Ironically, severity-based policies appear to undermine the certainty of punishment. The ceteris paribus logic of deterrence theory is subverted by the dynamics of the criminal justice system, whose actors have considerable discretion to respond in ways that undermine the intent of formal policies. This tendency has been established very clearly for policies that increase sentence severity. First, defendants are more aggressive in fighting the charges. Following New

York's 1973 adoption of a strict drug sentencing law, the percentage of defendants demanding trial increased from 6 percent to 15 percent (Association of The Bar of The City of New York, 1977). Similar responses have followed various state and local efforts to increase drunk driving penalties (West et al., 1989; Zamichow, 1990) and in the aftermath of California's 1994 "Three Strikes" law (Legislative Analyst's Office, 1995).

Second, various actors in the criminal justice system tacitly conspire to avoid imposing the harsher penalties (Tsebelis, 1990). "Mandatory" penalties are weakened by prosecutors during plea bargaining and by judges during sentencing (Ross, 1976; Ross & Foley, 1987). And as penalties become more severe, judges and jurors are more likely to acquit defendants (Kerr, 1978); this leniency has been observed following changes in drug sentencing and drunk driving laws (Goode, 1989; Ross, 1976) and implementation of California's Three Strikes law (Legislative Analyst's Office, 1995). Because the certainty component appears to have a greater deterrent impact than the severity component, these policies may actually reduce the general deterrent effects of the law.

Perceptual deterrence research

Ross (1982) speculates that the effects of drunk driving crackdowns and other deterrence-based interventions may be short-lived – fading out soon after they lose the temporary salience provided by media coverage. This underscores the point that deterrence theory is a *perceptual theory*, a theory of how the individual actor's own perceptions of risks and rewards motivate decisions (Waldo & Chiricos, 1972). Policy makers can only influence perceived sanctions indirectly, by controlling actual sanctions and perhaps by using publicity to enhance or exaggerate those perceptions. Information about laws and enforcement policies is diffused through the mass media, interpersonal channels, and personal experience (Geerken & Gove, 1975). Because laws and enforcement policies may not be implemented as written or intended, the public may receive mixed threat signals. An example might be the disjuncture between federal "zero tolerance" rhetoric and state and local tolerance of marijuana possession.

When social diffusion distorts or weakens legal threat messages, efforts to achieve general deterrence are probably more like pushing a string than cracking a whip – modest gains require a lot of effort. The relationship between actual sanctions and behavior is only as strong as the intermediate link – the subjective perception of risk.[3] When the association between legal sanctioning and crime rates is observed to be weak or unreliable at the aggregate level, the weakness might lie in the enforcement-perception link, the perception-behavior link, or both. This association raises two questions for researchers. First, how accurately do citizens perceive legal sanctions? Second, do the *perceived* sanctioning risks – the risks of arrest and punishment – deter criminal conduct?

How accurate are legal risk perceptions? Most of the information Americans receive about the criminal justice system comes from fictional depictions in the movies and on television, and given the "just deserts" schema so prevalent in Hollywood plot logic, it has long been known that the general public tends to exaggerate the risks of arrest and punishment for many crimes (e.g., California Assembly Committee on Criminal Procedure, 1968; Erickson & Gibbs, 1978). This is can be explained by the *availability heuristic* – the tendency for people to exaggerate the likelihood of events that are vivid and salient and come readily to mind (Tversky & Kahneman, 1974). Because of this tendency, highly visible enforcement campaigns can enhance and even exaggerate perceived sanctioning risks. For example, during a period in which the actual arrest rate for drunk driving was higher in Fairfax County, Virginia, than in Montgomery County, Maryland, residents of both counties nevertheless estimated a higher rate for Montgomery County, apparently because of that county's regular use of roadside sobriety testing checkpoints (Williams & Lund, 1984).

Indeed, deterrence theory suggests that the general public's exaggerated belief in the law's omniscience may help to preserve the social order. Although even researchers have difficulty estimating the actual likelihood of arrest or imprisonment for any given criminal act, the true sanctioning risks for many crimes are quite low, particularly crimes involving drug and alcohol

3. A dynamic model of deterrence by Sah (1991) implies that the influence of changes in sanctioning severity can take years, or even generations, to be observed. Evidence cited later in this section, however, suggests that highly salient enforcement can have immediate, if short-lived, effects.

use.[4] For example, the probability of arrest for drunk driving has been estimated at somewhere between 1 in 200 to 1 in 7,500 (Turrisi & Jaccard, 1991). Chapter 2 argued that the risk per transaction for either drug users or drug dealers is probably less than 1 in 3,000. On the other hand, the *cumulative* legal risks associated with using or selling drugs are much steeper. For users, we estimated that the average annual risk of arrest is about 3 percent for marijuana users and 6 percent for cocaine users. Note that many of those arrested for possession are actually drug dealers. In Washington, DC, in 1988, for street-level drug dealers (selling about twenty-five times a week), we estimated a 1 in 5 likelihood of incarceration in a year of dealing, with an arrest risk perhaps twice as high.

Some empirical studies have shown that the more experienced an offender, the lower his assessment of the risk of arrest (e.g., Horney & Marshall, 1992; Paternoster, 1987). It is not clear whether offenders are simply more optimistic about avoiding sanctions, or whether they are better at estimating sanctioning risks. Possibly they believe that they have learned to reduce their risks. Studies of drug dealers (Ekland-Olsen, Lieb, & Zurcher, 1984) and shoplifters (Weaver & Carroll, 1985) found that experienced offenders develop strategies for reducing sanctioning risks.

Perceptual tests of deterrence theory. Do perceived legal risks deter criminal behavior? One source of evidence is studies that simply ask people whether they view the law as a deterring influence on their own conduct. For example, surveys of male college students find that about 35 percent report some likelihood that they would commit rape if they could be assured of not being caught and punished (Malamuth, 1981). In a 1988 national survey of high school seniors (Johnston, O'Malley, & Bachman, 1989, p. 144), 69 percent said they would not smoke marijuana if it were to become legally available, 7 percent said they would try it, 13 percent said they would use it about as often as they do now, 4 percent said they would use it more, and 2 percent said they would use it less. Taken at face value, these findings might suggest that the law is a necessary deterrent for rape but

---

4. Research on boundary effects of vague risk information (Casey & Scholz, 1991) suggested that enhanced enforcement clarity might actually reduce compliance when enforcement risks are this low.

relatively inconsequential for preventing drug use. But responses to such questions are vulnerable to social desirability bias, and people are surprisingly inaccurate in understanding the causes of their own actions (see Nisbett & Ross, 1980).

A better strategy is to see whether there is a correlation between people's perceptions of legal risk and their self-reported criminal activity (see Paternoster, 1987; Williams & Hawkins, 1986). For present purposes, the most relevant data come from studies of the deterrence of marijuana use.[5] Paternoster's (1987) review suggested that the average correlation between perceived *certainty* of punishment and marijuana use is about –0.21 after controlling for experiential effects. For perceived *severity*, the average correlation is –0.17, and Paternoster argues that even this small effect is inflated because many studies measure severity in ways that include both formal sanctions and informal nonlegal sanctions. As a result, he concluded that "perceived severity plays virtually no role in explaining deviant/criminal conduct" (p. 191), a conclusion that accords with the results of aggregate-level studies cited earlier.

Why does severity matter so little? Theoretically, severity should matter less if punishment is improbable. But it is unlikely that even our most aggressive enforcement efforts have – or even could – raise the certainty of punishment to high levels.[6]

The empirical record suggests that deterrence theory is at best a partial explanation of drug use decisions. As noted earlier, its effects are quite modest in size, generally accounting for 5 to 10 percent of the variance in marijuana use reported in perceptual deterrence surveys. This does not imply that legal sanctions have no policy significance for achieving general deterrence; at the national level, an influence of such small magnitude can have an impact on a large number of lives (see Rosenthal, 1990). But it is clear that most of the variance in marijuana use remains to be explained by other factors.

In considering the implications of the deterrence literature for the drug law debate, it is important to bear in mind that these studies

5. See MacCoun (1993) and Paternoster (1987) for a listing of relevant studies.
6. Formally, severity and certainty are predicted to combine multiplicatively rather than additively (Grasmick & Bryjak, 1980). Of those studies testing the certainty × severity interaction, some have found it and others have not (see MacCoun, 1993). But additive effects tend to be more robust than multiplicative effects in regression models (Dawes, 1988).

examine the effects of variations in the certainty and severity with which criminal sanctions are meted out or the effects of variations in individuals' perceptions of certainty and severity (Cook, 1980; Nichols & Ross, 1988). What they don't do is compare criminalization regimes to depenalization or legalization regimes – the focus of this book. This has both methodological and substantive implications.

Statistically, this results in a "restriction of range" in the deterrence variables – a "floor effect" that will underestimate any absolute effects on behavior that they might have in principle (Nunnally, 1978). For this reason alone, absolute deterrent effects are likely to be larger than relative deterrent effects. Psychologically, a given increment in sanctioning risks (e.g., a 10 percent increase) would likely have the greatest impact at the transition from a zero to nonzero probability. Category boundary effects are predicted by prospect theory (Kahneman & Tversky, 1984), which contends that people give more weight to the difference between zero probability and a very small probability (e.g., 0.00 vs. 0.01) than to a comparably large increment between any two nonzero probability values (e.g., 0.50 vs. 0.51). In addition, the mere fact that an act is illicit may influence behavior independently of the actual magnitude of the threat of punishment. This *symbolic threshold hypothesis* is discussed in more detail later.

Limited rationality and deterrence

Expected legal risks do have an influence on decisions, but their effects are considerably more muted than generally assumed. Part of the problem is that people just do not seem to combine information in the manner suggested by rational choice theories (see Dawes, 1988; Kahneman & Tversky, 1984). For example, Carroll (1978) found that when evaluating hypothetical crime opportunities, few adult and juvenile offenders focused on more than one of the four key deterrence factors: probability of success, amount of gain, probability of capture, and size of penalty.

And the factors that do matter are more likely to involve carrots than sticks. Studies comparing the relative influence of the rewards and risks of crime suggest that criminal gains are more influential than penalties, and the probability of success is more influential than the probability of capture (Carroll, 1978; Piliavin et al., 1986). Unfortunately, none of these studies examined drug use. But the expected rewards of drug use are quite familiar. People seek drugs for stimulation, entertainment, escape, personal or spiritual exploration, or, in the case of addiction, the cessation of withdrawal symptoms (Siegel, 1989; Weil, 1972). Of course, these effects don't appeal to everyone. In public opinion surveys, nonusers are much more likely to mention "not interested" than "fear of legal reprisals" as the primary reason why they don't use marijuana (Maloff, 1981).

One reason gains generally loom larger than risks is that the gains tend to be immediate, whereas legal sanctions are not only uncertain but also in the remote future. Criminal offenders are particularly prone to impulsiveness and an inability to delay gratification (Gottfredson & Hirschi, 1990; Wilson & Herrnstein, 1985). This suggests that the swiftness of punishment – or *celerity* as it is called by deterrence theorists – should play an important role in the deterrence process. Little is known about the effects of celerity, though existing tests provide mixed support (Howe & Brandau, 1988). In an attempt to deter drunk driving, some communities have enhanced punishment celerity by using administrative rather than criminal sanctions such as confiscating drivers' licenses when they fail or refuse to take blood-alcohol level tests (Nichols & Ross, 1988). There are limits to the ability of the criminal justice system to mete out punishment for drug offenses rapidly enough to counteract impulsivity effects without greatly curtailing civil liberties (Gendreau & Goddard, 1991; but see Kennedy, Piehl, & Braga, 1996).

This is not to say that potential drug users are mostly impervious to the risks of their actions. Perceived *health* risks may be more influential than legal risks. Schelling (1992) documented the singular role that health information has played in bringing about a dramatic decline in cigarette consumption in the United States, a trend that occurred well in advance of any serious mobilization of the force of law. Bachman et al. (1988, 1990) presented evidence that a rise in health-related concerns played a major role in the decline in drug use among high school seniors during the 1980s.

When people do reason about risks and rewards, it is clear that they do not always do so in accordance with the dictates of expected utility theory. But the rational choice paradigm is also unrealistic in its assumption that actions are necessarily reasoned at all. Like

many behaviors, repeated drug use comes under the control of uncon-
scious physiological and cognitive influences (Ronis, Yates, & Kirscht,
1989). Indeed, it is surprisingly difficult to draw a hard and fast line
between physiological and psychological processes of addiction
(Baker, 1988; Marlatt et al., 1988). A continuum of mechanisms
can influence behavior in the absence of explicit reasoning, ranging
from higher-level cognitive processes to very low-level neurological
mechanisms.

A mechanism at the higher end of the continuum is the *self-concept*
(Oyserman & Markus, 1990). Many people may never bother to
ponder the risks and rewards of drug use because they simply conclude that drug use doesn't match their self-definition: "I'm not that
kind of person." At a lower level are automatic cognitive "scripts"
(e.g., for operating a car or playing a piano piece), well-rehearsed procedures that eventually run more or less autonomously with little
conscious attention or instigation (Uleman & Bargh, 1990). Lower
still are conditioned responses, which are known to play a major role
in the development of drug dependence (see Baker, 1988; Marlatt et
al., 1988). For example, users often learn to experience craving for a
drug in the presence of environmental cues that have been frequently
paired with the drug in the past. Of course, this craving mechanism
is not unique to psychoactive drugs, as dieters, ex-smokers, and
Pavlov's dogs have all discovered.

As drug use (or any behavior) becomes habitual, it becomes
increasingly "mindless," and any new information about the behavior that the individual subsequently encounters may have relatively
little influence on behavior (Ronis et al., 1989). This suggests that
legal sanctions should have the most influence on a person's initial
decision to use drugs and then steadily diminish as use becomes more
frequent. Thus, Paternoster (1989) observed a reliable certainty-of-
punishment effect on adolescent marijuana use in an initial set of
interviews but no such effect in later interviews when they were more
experienced.

INFORMAL SELF AND SOCIAL CONTROLS

Social scientists have long recognized that informal personal and
social norms and sanctions play a major role in the regulation of

conduct (e.g., Cialdini, Kallgren, & Reno, 1991). Although our primary concern is with the effects of formal legal controls on drug use, a brief consideration of informal personal and social norms is relevant because of the possibility that informal norms may influence the effectiveness of formal laws.

Morality and legitimacy

As a framework for thinking about legal compliance, deterrence theory lends itself to an overly cynical view of human nature, suggesting that laws are effective only if backed by strict punitive enforcement. This ignores the crucial moral force of law (Tyler, 1990). Although violations of personal moral standards may be "costly" to the individual, moral judgments are both conceptually and empirically distinct from instrumental judgments about risk and reward (see Grasmick & Bursik, 1990; Klepper & Nagin, 1989). Three different categories of noninstrumental personal judgments affect compliance decisions – the perceived morality of the act, the perceived morality of the law, and the perceived legitimacy of the law.

Some theorists have suggested that the perceived *morality of the act* may moderate deterrence effects of legal sanctions. Specifically, sanction threats are hypothesized to be irrelevant to individuals who have either internalized the legal norm or judged the behavior to be morally repugnant (e.g., Gibbs, 1975; Zimring & Hawkins, 1973). Evidence for this proposition is mixed (Grasmick & Green, 1981; Grasmick & Bursik, 1990; Paternoster, 1989). It may be that deterrence effects aren't moderated by the perceived morality of the *act*, but rather the perceived morality of the *law*. Research on moral reasoning and legal socialization (e.g., Cohn & White, 1990; Kelman & Hamilton, 1989) suggests that people differ in their reasons for choosing to comply with laws. Following Kohlberg's theory of moral development, Tapp and Kohlberg (1971) categorized responses to questions such as "Why do you follow rules?" in terms of a progressive scale of three different levels of legal development. It is interesting to speculate about how individuals at each level might be affected by legal sanctions against drug use.

Individuals at the *preconventional level* have a "rule-obeying" perspective; they comply with laws to avoid punishment by authorities. These individuals would seem to be most susceptible to the deterrent effects of drug laws. In fact, the image of the citizen offered by deterrence theory is strikingly similar to this category. Thus, the relationship between the perceived certainty and severity of punishment should be strongest for this group, and its members should be deterred only to the extent that they think that detection and punishment of users is likely.

Individuals at the *conventional level* have a "rule-maintaining" perspective; they exhibit an approval-seeking conformity, or emphasize the importance of maintaining the social order. For this group in particular, the mere fact that an act is illicit might have an impact on behavior independent of the actual magnitude of the threat of punishment. As mentioned earlier, this *symbolic threshold effect* is one reason why legalization should have more dramatic consequences than depenalization, which leaves the drug's legal status intact.[7] If this is the case, this group might be quite susceptible to a change in legal status, even if its members currently believe that sanctioning risks are quite low.

Finally, individuals at the *post-conventional level* have a "rule-making" perspective; they evaluate laws in terms of abstract philosophical principles. Relative to the other two groups, these individuals should be influenced relatively less by sanctioning risks and legal status and more by their own beliefs about the morality and appropriateness of drug use (Meier & Johnson, 1977). These individuals are unlikely to be completely impervious to sanctioning risks, but if such risks are already perceived to be low, then drug legalization might have relatively little effect on their decision to use drugs. If they are already using drugs, they would continue to use them; if they don't currently use drugs, they would be less likely than the other groups to start.

A third consideration is the perceived *legitimacy* of the law (Tyler & Lind, 1992), the evaluation of the source of the laws and the process of their implementation. Tyler and Lind argue that the perceived fairness and legitimacy of authorities and laws are important noninstrumental determinants of legal compliance. Thus, Tyler's (1990) study found that perceptions of the legitimacy of laws and the fairness of their enforcement significantly influenced the general public's subse-

---

7. Note that the symbolic threshold effect is not a deterrence effect; the distinction between the two corresponds closely to French and Raven's (1959) distinction between legitimate power and coercive power.

quent compliance with laws. Although Tyler and Lind have not specifically examined drug use, their analysis has an important implication for drug policy. As already seen, many feel that drug laws constitute an invasion of privacy, that sentences for drug offenses are too harsh, that minorities are singled out for enforcement, and that the licit status of alcohol and tobacco makes the current regime hypocritical. Tyler and Lind's work suggests that such perceptions might well undermine the effectiveness of drug laws.

"Forbidden fruit" effects

There is a popular intuition that the illicit status of marijuana and other drugs might even heighten their attractiveness for young people – a *forbidden fruit effect*. In a sense, this is the opposite of a symbolic threshold effect, although the psychological mechanisms probably differ. Some policy analysts (Moore, 1991; Wilson, 1990) have expressed skepticism regarding the forbidden fruit argument. Nevertheless, there are several psychological mechanisms that might produce such an effect.

First, *reactance theory* (see Brehm & Brehm, 1981) predicts that restrictions on freedom of choice enhance the attractiveness of an object or activity. Second, the principle of scarcity (Cialdini, 1985; Lynn, 1992) suggests that artificial scarcity can enhance the desirability of a commodity, because of the learned association between scarcity and quality.[8] Third, forbidden fruit effects might reflect a disposition for risk seeking (Lopes, 1987) or sensation seeking (Zuckerman, 1994) – a heightened attraction to the thrill and mystery of psychoactive drugs and a diminished fear of the legal risks that accompany them.

The drug research literature has no systematic research on the forbidden fruit hypothesis. Nevertheless, there is rigorous empirical support for similar effects from experiments in other domains of social policy. For example, two-year-olds are significantly more interested in playing with toys when they are placed behind a barrier that restricts their access (Brehm & Weintraub, 1977). People become

---

8. This might help to account for the lack of consistent availability effects discussed earlier. Whereas the opportunity perspective suggests that availability should promote use, this principle suggests that under some conditions, *scarcity* might promote use. Perhaps these are offsetting effects.

significantly more interested in information when it is being censored by authorities (e.g., Worchel & Arnold, 1973; Zellinger et al., 1975). Experiments conducted as part of the recent National Television Violence Study indicate that "parental advisory," "PG-13," and "R" labels make TV programs and movies significantly more attractive to 10- to 14-year-old boys (Cantor, Harrison, & Krcmar, 1995). And there is a documented "Romeo and Juliet" effect (Driscoll, Davis, & Lipetz, 1972), in which young couples experience heightened feelings of romance as parental interference in their relationship increases. Drug prohibition may actually motivate some drug use through a forbidden fruit mechanism, but the magnitude of such effects is unknown.[9]

Informal social controls

Social norms. Considerable social-psychological research demonstrates that the effects of informal social norms on behavior are measurable, reliable, and often quite powerful (see Ross & Nisbett, 1991). Informal social norms can either promote or discourage drug use, depending on their source (see Elliott, Huizinga, & Ageton, 1985). Cialdini and his colleagues (1991) demonstrated the value of distinguishing two types of norms. *Injunctive norms* are one's perceptions of how other people believe one should behave. In the case of drug use, the content of injunctive norms involves the appropriateness of obedience to drug laws versus the acceptability of drug use and/or intoxication. Of course, different sources – peers, parents, siblings, coworkers, neighbors, the mass media, authority figures, one's church – convey different injunctive norms. The power of injunctive norms varies directly with one's bonding to the source (Hirschi, 1969) and motivation to comply (Ajzen & Fishbein, 1981). The forbidden fruit effect shows that a source may be influential, but in a contrary

---

9. The nature of these reactance and scarcity mechanisms may impose boundary conditions on the phenomenon. Reactance effects should be stronger following the active removal of an existing freedom than when one is exposed to an object or experience that has always been prohibited (Brehm & Brehm, 1981). And restrictions on freedom may be tolerated when an acceptable rationale is provided (Tyler, 1990). Most importantly, although a forbidden fruit effect may occur when other factors are held constant, in natural settings, other factors may covary with drug prohibition in ways that weaken the effect – "forbidden fruits" are often less available, more expensive, less healthy, and more stigmatized than many unprohibited products and activities.

direction – I may decide to do something because you *don't* think I should do it.

Descriptive norms are one's perceptions of how others actually behave – not what they say or believe, but what they *do*. Descriptive norms provide contextual cues as to appropriate or acceptable situational conduct (Cialdini et al., 1991), and they provide a powerful means for vicarious learning (Bandura, 1986). Studies show that if people learn that others have broken a law, they are more likely to break that law (Cialdini et al., 1991; Mullen, Cooper, & Driskell, 1990; Stalans, Kinsey, & Smith, 1991).

Informal sanctions. Norms are passive sources of information, but they can be expressed by active social sanctioning (e.g., overt expressions of disapproval, ridicule, resentment, or rejection). Thus, informal norms have an instrumental dimension. When deciding whether or not to engage in deviant behavior, potential offenders may consider not only the legal risks but also the shame, embarrassment, or harm to their reputation that they might suffer if observed engaging in deviant behavior (see Braithwaite, 1989; Grasmick & Bursik, 1990).[10]

The *labeling theory* tradition in psychology and sociology (see Braithwaite, 1989) suggests that the stigmatization associated with criminal sanctioning can produce harmful effects. Labeling theory predicts that legal sanctions, rather than deterring criminal behavior, can actually *enhance* the likelihood of future offending. In essence, the argument is that the stigma associated with criminal sanctioning alienates the individual from conventional society, promoting contact with deviant referent groups and enhancing the likelihood of future deviance befitting the label – a self-fulfilling prophecy. Braithwaite's (1989) theory of "reintegrative shaming" is the most sophisticated contemporary statement of labeling theory; he predicted that deleterious effects of labeling can be avoided if social disapproval is temporary, occurs in a context of interdependence and communitarianism, and is followed by gestures of forgiveness and reacceptance. Under such conditions, social shaming is predicted to increase subsequent compliance. Absent such conditions, shaming is "disintegra-

10. Job-related sanctioning mechanisms, like mandatory drug testing, fall in a gray area between formal and informal controls. An important question is whether they would remain in place or be lifted following drug legalization.

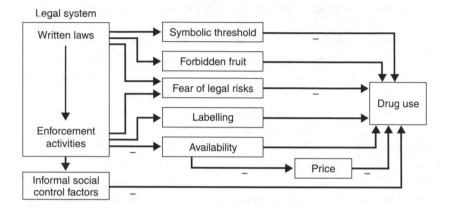

Figure 5.1 Potential pathways of legal influence over drug use (Relationships are positive unless otherwise indicated.)

tive" and can foster the stigmatization effects predicted by labeling theory (see Orcutt, 1973, for a similar distinction between "inclusive" and "exclusive" reactions to deviance). Unfortunately, the conditions for reintegrative shaming are frequently absent for many drug law offenders in contemporary American society, a point taken up in Chapter 15.

SUMMARY OF MECHANISMS

Figure 5.1 provides a summary framework involving seven distinct causal pathways between drug laws and drug use. The rational choice paradigm suggests three pathways: the perceived fear of legal sanctioning, the availability of drugs, and the price of drugs. Social-psychological research suggests four additional pathways: the symbolic threshold effect, the forbidden fruit effect, stigmatization effects, and the mediating effects of informal social control factors. The last pathway represents the potential effect of drug laws on the net antidrug thrust of the descriptive and injunctive norms, informal sanctions, and drug-related information in the social environment. Of course, these informal social control factors directly influence drug use, regardless of whether they actually mediate the influence of formal social controls.

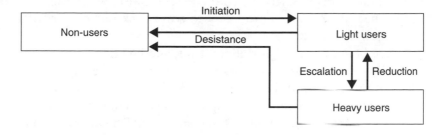

Figure 5.2 Flows between nonuse, light use, and heavy use

Assume for simplicity that variations in consumption frequency and quantity can be characterized by a simple dichotomy between light and heavy users (Everingham & Rydell, 1994). Then "use" can be decomposed into several qualitatively distinct phenomena: *initiation* into drug use, *escalation* from light use into heavy use, *reduction* from heavy use into light use, and *desistance* from either level of use, as seen in the flow model in Figure 5.2 (adapted from a similar figure in Everingham & Rydell, 1994). *Prevalence* levels are determined by initiation and desistance rates, whereas *consumption* levels are primarily determined by escalation and reduction rates.

It is not clear which of these flow rates are most sensitive to formal sanction threats. In general, heavy users are at considerably greater risk than light users because of more frequent purchases. On the other hand, the risk perception literature cited earlier suggests that nonusers might overestimate their true sanction risks, whereas experienced users may fail to appreciate the cumulative nature of their risk, developing an exaggerated sense of their own invulnerability. Heavily dependent users may simply fail to consider legal risks.

Availability and price mechanisms should have greater influence on consumption levels than on prevalence levels. First, availability and price will matter little to those who have categorically rejected drug use; hence, only a fraction of nonusers will show any sensitivity to these economic factors. This is especially likely during periods when a drug is most heavily stigmatized (e.g., cocaine in the late 1980s vs. the early 1970s). At the other extreme, highly dependent users are most likely to have established ready (and perhaps multiple) sources of availability, and in theory, to be "price inelastic" in their demand for their drug (though the little relevant evidence cited earlier fails to substantiate this prediction). To the extent that they are sensitive to price, heavy users are more likely to scale back on consumption than to quit altogether.

The symbolic threshold, forbidden fruit, and labeling mechanisms jointly should have a greater influence on prevalence levels than on consumption levels. Each of these mechanisms will be more sensitive to the boundary between legal compliance and noncompliance than to any variations in the extent of noncompliance. The effects should be greatest on initiation rates. Those most sensitive to the symbolic moral threshold are least likely to cross that Rubicon in the first place; for others, that is where forbidden fruits should have the greatest allure. Though labeling might be a matter of degree, one must generally become a drug user to be labeled as such; once labeled, various disintegrative social forces can conspire to encourage movement farther past the boundary, rather than back across it (Braithwaite, 1989).

IMPLICATIONS FOR POLICY

Effects of depenalization on drug use

The cumulative effect of drug laws on drug use across all seven mechanisms is not known. Figure 5.1 suggests five pathways by which the current regime *discourages* drug use (the symbolic threshold effect, fear of legal risks, availability and price effects, and the reinforcement of informal social controls), and two by which it can inadvertently *encourage* drug use (forbidden fruit and labeling effects). Prohibitionist drug laws would actually increase use if the latter effects predominated, but this seems implausible. Though forbidden fruit and labeling effects are quite real (and need to be taken seriously by policy makers), the bulk of the evidence suggests that the dominant mechanisms are price, availability, deterrence, and the symbolic threshold. (Social norms are at least as important an influence on drug use, but the effect of legalization on these norms is uncertain.) Hence, the net effect of drug laws is probably to reduce drug use substantially below the levels in a full legalization regime.

Nevertheless, existing data are inadequate to estimate the strength of each effect. Some of the mechanisms – symbolic threshold effects,

Table 5.2. *Effects of legal change on drug use*

Drug law mechanism[a]	Impact of depenalization		Impact of legalization	
	On mechanism	On use	On mechanism	On use
Availability (−)	Little or no change	Little or no change	Less availability	Increases
Price (−)	Little change	Little or no change	Lower price	Increases
Fear of formal sanctions (−)	Less fear	Increases	Less fear	Increases
Symbolic threshold (−)	No change	No change	Weaker effect	Increases
Forbidden fruit (+)	Little or no change (use is still banned)	Little or no change	Eliminates (adults) or weakens (youth)	Decreases
Stigmatization/ labeling (+)	Weaker effect	Decreases	Eliminates (adults) or weakens (youth)	Decreases
Bolstering of informal norms (?)	Unclear	Unclear	Unclear	Unclear

[a] (+) denotes that mechanism encourages use; (−) denotes that mechanism discourages use.

forbidden fruit effects, stigmatization effects – would be extremely difficult to operationalize in a fashion permitting reliable estimates of their magnitude in nationally representative samples (or even small, local convenience samples). More importantly, effect sizes estimated within a criminalization regime will probably fail to capture the full impact of a shift to legalization.

Table 5.2 presents our qualitative predictions for the effect of depenalizing or legalizing a drug on each of these mechanisms. Depenalization reduces the penalties for using a drug – and in practice leads to reduced enforcement efforts against users (Single, 1989) – but leaves its legal status intact. Depenalization should reduce deterrence effects and labeling effects, although it may not eliminate them. Recall that the deterrent effects of drunk driving crackdowns tend to be temporary. Thus, the effects of depenalizing a drug may be similarly short-lived, but in the opposite direction: an immediate reduction in perceived risk followed by a gradual return to baseline. When depenalization first takes place, the publicity may heighten the salience of the reduced risks, but with the passage of time, fewer individuals who know that the drug is illegal will know the specific penalties for possession and use.

Many of the seven mechanisms should be little affected. The drug's continued illegality will still motivate some people to avoid it – the symbolic threshold effect – and others to seek it out – the forbidden fruit effect. Because depenalization leaves sanctions against drug sales intact, it should have a negligible effect on a drug's manufacture and distribution. Enforcement against retail transactions would become more difficult, but unless the reduction in deterrence increased demand substantially, any effect on drug availability and price is likely to be quite modest. Most importantly, because the legal prohibition remains intact, informal control factors should remain largely unaffected.

Research on the effects of marijuana depenalization illustrates the plausibility of these conjectures. Marijuana has been depenalized in twelve U.S. states,[11] in some regions of Australia, and (as discussed in Chapters 10 and 11) in the Netherlands, Italy, and Spain. Italy and Spain have also depenalized possession of heroin and cocaine; the Netherlands and Australia have not.

Several lines of evidence – on the deterrent effects of marijuana laws, and on decriminalization experiences in the United States, the Netherlands, and Australia – suggest that eliminating (or significantly reducing) criminal penalties for first-time possession of small quantities of marijuana has either no effect or a very small effect on the prevalence of marijuana use.

There are several statistical analyses of survey data on marijuana use in depenalization and nondepenalization states. Survey analyses in depenalizing states have found either no change in marijuana use or an increase that was slight and temporary. Depenalization was not associated with any detectable changes in adolescent attitudes toward marijuana. Most cross-state comparisons have found no difference in adolescent marijuana use in depenalization vs. nondepenalization states.[12] Only two studies offer possible contradictions to this con-

---

11. These states include Oregon in 1973; Colorado, Alaska, and Ohio in 1975; California, Maine, and Minnesota in 1976; South Dakota, Mississippi, New York, and North Carolina in 1977; and Nebraska in 1978. South Dakota repealed its new law almost immediately. Alaska repealed its law almost twenty years later, but court rulings have created an ambiguous status; see Chapter 14.

12. See DiNardo & Lemieux (1992), Johnston, O'Malley, & Bachman (1981), Maloff (1981), National Governor's Conference (1977), Single (1989), and Thies & Register (1993).

clusion.[13] Model (1993) reports a small increase in mentions of marijuana in emergency room records in depenalization states. This seems less likely to reflect an increase in the number of users than an increase in consumption by *existing* users – Model argued that this is in part a substitution away from hard drugs – or perhaps an increased willingness to acknowledge marijuana use. An unpublished analysis (Saffer & Chaloupka, 1995) estimated somewhat higher levels of use in depenalization states. This study differs in several respects from previous analyses (a different survey instrument, a different time period, inclusion of adults in the sample, and different statistical techniques), any one of which might account for the discrepancy with the published literature.

Depenalization involved changes in marijuana laws and their enforcement that were fairly subtle; arrest rates for marijuana possession are the same in those U.S. states that decriminalized and those that did not, though in the decriminalization states the penalties are presumably less severe. In at least one state, California, the policy change was significant. According to Aldrich and Mikuriya (1988), California felony marijuana arrests fluctuated between 73,000 and 100,000 in the four years preceding the Moscone Act of 1976, which depenalized marijuana. In 1976–85, the first decade of depenalization, felony marijuana arrests dropped to the 17,000 to 24,000 range – a quarter or less of the previous steep rates. On the other hand, misdemeanor arrests rose from around 3,500 a year before depenalization to an average of 39,000 in 1976–85. Although the reduction was real, it might have been psychologically subtle. Arrest is a rare phenomenon, news stories and anecdotes might have failed to distinguish felony vs. misdemeanor charges, and people have difficulty estimating low-probability events. When MacCoun asks his undergraduate students at Berkeley whether they favor California removing penalties for the possession of small amounts of marijuana, about two-thirds say yes, and the rest are opposed. Almost none know that it occurred twenty-five years ago.

But the conclusion that cannabis depenalization in the United States had little or no effect is bolstered by evidence from a similar policy change in the Netherlands (from 1976 to the mid-1980s) and

13. A possible third is Segal's (1990) comparison of drug use in Alaska and other states. As explained in more detail in Chapter 14, Segal correctly asserted that for methodological reasons the study does not inform the depenalization issue.

two regions of Australia. Studies of depenalization in South Australia (P. Christie, 1991; Donnelly, Hall, & Christie, 1995) and in the Australian Capital Territory (McGeorge and Aitken, 1997) reported no changes in marijuana use associated with this legal change, and no differences in marijuana use between these regions and nondecriminalization regions of Australia. Chapter 11 assesses the Dutch experience in detail, arguing that depenalization – as distinct from the later de facto legalization of cannabis – had no detectable effect on levels of use.

Effects of legalization on drug use

The right-hand side of Table 5.2 depicts the situation after *legalizing* a drug, and shows graphically how depenalization and legalization differ in their behavioral implications. Legalization changes both the legal status and its enforcement. It opens the possibility of radical changes in a drug's distribution. This possibility is often viewed as a major benefit of legalization (Nadelmann, 1989) because it would dramatically reduce criminal drug markets and their attendant corruption and violence. The effects of legalization on a drug's availability and price would depend on the nature of the postlegalization market and the manner in which it is regulated (Jacobs, 1990; Warner, 1991).

Although the sheer prevalence of drug selling in some neighborhoods suggests the difficulty of deterring street-level dealers, the current drug laws deter legitimate firms – for example, the tobacco and alcohol industries – from selling illicit drugs. Moore (1990) estimated that heroin, marijuana, and cocaine are sold illicitly at seventy, fifteen, and eight times their licit prices, respectively. While prices might be propped up using "sin taxes," if rates are set too high, the black market might well resume – witness Canada's recent failed experiment with steep tobacco taxes (Gunby, 1994). And unless strict regulations are adopted, a legalization regime might well lead to the kind of aggressive marketing of psychoactive drugs used now for tobacco and alcohol (see Chapter 8). In that sense, drug legalization might indeed open the floodgates.

Legalization should also significantly reduce deterrence, symbolic threshold, forbidden fruit, and labeling effects, at least for adults, although legal controls for minors might well remain in place, as in the case of cigarettes and alcohol today. Since the latter two effects are thought to encourage use under prohibition, their elimination might help to reduce the magnitude of any increase in use.

A key question is: How would legalization affect informal self-controls and social controls regarding drug use? The existing social science research indicates that these informal factors play a major role in regulating psychoactive drug use (Elliott et al., 1985; Paternoster, 1989). Even in the absence of formal legal controls, informal social-control and self-control factors might prevent most people from serious drug involvement. If so, legalization might open some spigots, but it wouldn't open any floodgates – people who don't use under prohibition would also abstain under a legal regime.

Thus, much would depend on the effect of a change in the law on informal controls. The relationship between law and informal controls is complex and still poorly understood (Black, 1976; Ellickson, 1987; Heckathorn, 1990). Many laws are a *product* of social norms. For example, a popular social movement appears to be driving anti-tobacco legislation today (Schelling, 1992), and a particularly aggressive grass roots movement was responsible for the adoption of alcohol prohibition earlier this century. It is also likely that the law plays a reciprocal role in shaping and reinforcing informal norms and beliefs so that legalization might weaken existing social norms against drug use. Critics often argue that it would "send the wrong message," implying a tacit endorsement of drug use. This doesn't appear to have happened after marijuana depenalization (Johnston, O'Malley, & Bachman, 1981; Single, 1989), but legalization might send a stronger message, particularly for individuals at the conventional level of moral reasoning. Also, some of the informal sanctions that Williams and Hawkins (1986, 1989) have identified as deterrence factors – the embarrassment and threat to relationships and opportunities that can result from being arrested – would no longer be operative in a legalization regime.

Black (1976, p. 107) offered a different hypothesis about the relationship between law and norms: "Law varies inversely with other social control." Black did not stipulate the direction of causality, but his discussion emphasized how the erosion of informal controls tended to result in the emergence of new formal controls. Does the erosion of *formal* controls similarly result in the emergence of stronger informal controls? Ross (1976) suggested that the same homeostatic dynamics that undermine attempts to strengthen legal control, discussed earlier, might also lead actors to compensate for *reductions* in legal control, by more vigorously enforcing related laws and norms that remain intact. Wilde (1982) proposed a *risk homeostasis* hypothesis, suggesting that people will compensate for overprotective policies by behaving more recklessly and for underprotective policies by behaving more cautiously. If Ross and Wilde are correct, legalization might actually strengthen informal self-controls and social controls. Of course, this argument is quite speculative and requires a great deal more research attention. But it suggests that the erosion of informal controls cannot be taken as a given. Chapter 15 will consider this important question in more detail.

The effects of drug laws on drug use are considerably more uncertain and complex than is generally acknowledged by advocates on either side of the drug policy debate. The current state of knowledge, based on research examining minor variations in enforcement *within* a drug prohibition regime, does not provide a basis for projecting the consequences of stepping outside that regime altogether. There are too many unknowns to predict the effects of drug legalization with any specificity, and advocates on either side who suggest otherwise should be greeted with healthy skepticism. Chapters 7 through 12 will attempt to step outside of prohibition, looking at experiences with alternative regimes in other places and times and with other vices.

6   How Does Prohibition Affect Drug Harms?

The damage that drugs do to society is a function not only of the number of users but inter alia of the quantity they consume, the amount they spend, and the mode and circumstances of sales and consumption. For example, it is the income generated by drug sales rather than the quantity consumed that determines many of the problems associated with drug markets. Indeed, higher consumption at lower prices may reduce dealer earnings and related violence. Similarly, the fact that heroin is usually injected (partly a function of its extraordinarily high price) rather than snorted or smoked is the major factor linking heroin use and HIV; large numbers of heroin smokers might produce less harm than smaller numbers of injectors. All these harms are influenced by policy as implemented, particularly enforcement. This chapter examines that connection.

We begin by identifying the major harms associated with drugs under current policy. Not all harms are included. In particular, we do not consider the loss of liberty or of the possible benefits of drug use that loom large for some legalization advocates. It is not that we think those matters unimportant, as Chapters 4 and 13 make clear, but they are very much a matter of dispute and not susceptible to measurement.

The number of harms listed here (almost fifty) is daunting, but the elaboration is not mere pedantry. The harms are highly variegated and that variety is part of the policy problem, since it prevents effective aggregation and thus straightforward comparison of different regimes. For many reasons, there are not even approximate

101

numbers on most of the harms under the current regime, let alone for any hypothetical regime that is substantially different. Again that uncertainty, like the variety of harms, is itself an important aspect of the legalization debate; it biases the decision against the unpredictable change. The final complication is that the gains and losses under different regimes are likely to be unevenly distributed across different population groups. These implications are taken up in Chapter 13.

The first part of this chapter is a general theoretical discussion of these aspects of assessing legalization, decriminalization, prohibition, and their variants. That is followed by an examination of enforcement's unintended and potentially harmful effects, which are so prominent and have been at the heart of the pragmatic case against prohibition. Massive black markets accompanied by corruption, disorder, violence, and the wrecking of inner-city communities are perhaps the central harms associated with current U.S. drug policies, though their divisiveness and intrusiveness also merit discussion.

A TAXONOMY OF DRUG-RELATED HARMS[1]

No drug policy is without adverse consequence. Making choices involves comparing those adverse consequences, best translated into costs so that systematic comparison can be made.

Assessment of costs under a given regime usually requires at least three distinct steps: identifying all the relevant dimensions of consequences, estimating their magnitudes, and then assessing the costs of those consequences. All present major problems here.

First in the absence of an established academic framework for drug policy analysis, participants in drug policy debates are quite selective in highlighting the particular dimensions of harm that serve their rhetorical purposes. For example, as described in Chapter 3, legalization advocates emphasize drug prohibition's affront to civil liberties and the incentives it creates for black market crime and violence; pro-

---

1. This section draws largely on an article written jointly with Thomas Schelling; see MacCoun et al. (1996).

hibiters emphasize the risks of addiction and its pernicious effects on families, neighborhoods, and the workplace. Clearly, one has to take all these into account, and developing a full list is itself a difficult undertaking.

Second, little is known about the magnitude of the relevant consequences. For example, it is extraordinarily difficult to estimate the number of premature deaths caused by cocaine use under the current regime, much less a hypothetical alternative. Data are available from the Drug Abuse Warning Network for twenty-five or so major cities (SAMHSA, Annual) and from Vital Statistics nationally, but it is impossible to do much better than say that the number is between 4,000 (the DAWN figure) and 10,000,[2] using a very narrow definition that excludes deaths due to many effects of chronic use (e.g., stroke, heart attack) or indirect effects (homicide) (National Institute on Drug Abuse, 1991; National Center for Health Statistics, 1991). Compared to the mortality estimates for alcohol and cigarettes, with their exquisitely sophisticated epidemiological databases (see, for example, Manning et al., 1991), the figures for illicit drugs are embarrassingly primitive.

Third, even less is known about how to translate such consequences into costs. Only occasionally will a consequence be, in its raw or original form, an express monetary value. "Fines collected," "drug enforcement budget," and "costs of treatment" are already in monetary terms; many consequences – infringement on personal liberty, the fear of apprehension, and the sense of public disorder – will not be. Generally, attaching monetary values to these consequences, to make them commensurate with each other, is at least as difficult and uncertain as estimating the raw consequences in the first place. Even though there is a growing literature on "the costs of drug abuse,"[3] it is of limited value because it examines just a fraction of the relevant cost factors, generally those most readily quantified. For example, fear of crime, as opposed to defensive expenditures, is not included (e.g., Harwood et al., 1998).

2. DAWN collects data from approximately 140 Medical Examiners officers that account for 70 percent of all autopsies performed in the United States (SAMHSA, 1997). Given the concentration of cocaine use in metropolitan areas, it is likely that they account for an even higher share of drug abuse-related autopsies. The 10,000 figure is a crude judgment about the share of cocaine-related deaths that might be due to acute effects.
3. See, for example, Collins & Lapsley (1992), Harwood et al. (1998), Rice, Kelman, & Miller (1991), and Votey & Phillips (1976).

The current situation might reasonably be taken as providing the baseline for comparison. However it is extremely difficult to find a parsimonious quantitative characterization of what constitutes current policies, let alone of their consequences. For example, estimates of total (as opposed to federal only) expenditure on drug enforcement are available for only 1990 and 1991 (Office of National Drug Control Policy, 1993), and even those are questionable (Reuter, 1994). Just determining the number of persons incarcerated for drug offenses strains existing data systems nationally; for example, many persons are incarcerated for violation of a parole or probation condition that they remain abstinent from illicit drugs, but existing data systems keep track only of the original crime of conviction. Reuter (1991) explored the problems of determining whether the punitiveness of drug enforcement had increased or decreased during the 1980s; he found the result very sensitive to whether the denominator was an estimate of the number of users or of transactions.

The question then is how much harms are changed by differences in regimes. For example, under almost any imaginable regime there will be drug-related deaths. What must be determined is whether there would be more or fewer, and whose deaths they would be (users, sellers, innocent parties), under specified alternative regimes, since we might place higher value on those (e.g., bystanders caught in drug dealers' cross fire) who are innocent victims of others' decisions to violate the law.

Given the enormous difficulties of assessing the characteristics of the status quo, the challenge of anticipating the relative costs of alternative regimes is a daunting one. For example, in considering a change in drug laws or enforcement, an important consequence is certain to be something like "number of dependent users." Whether this number goes up, goes down, or is substantially unchanged is an important consequence, as are the number of deaths due to overdose, number of illegal transactions occurring, quantity of drug consumed, and number of annual person-years in prison, among others. Yet most of these consequences remain unexamined. For example, existing studies of state marijuana decriminalization have looked only at short-term changes in prevalence and not at lengths of drug-using careers or intensity (see Single, 1989). Furthermore, as argued in Chapter 5, there is no systematic basis for assessing the impact of decriminalizing the use of cocaine on the number of users, or, even if that number were agreed upon, the consequences that would result.

The dimensions of drug-related harm

Of the three assessment tasks – identifying the relevant dimensions, estimating the magnitude of consequences, and assessing the resultant costs – this chapter tackles only the first. The other two present major empirical challenges, requiring new data and modeling; however, we offer some provisional estimates of certain major items, just as anchor points.

To encourage a more systematic comparison of drug control regimes, Table 6.1 provides a multidimensional assessment matrix. Its first dimension, namely the regime under consideration, has already been described. Though for simplicity we refer to "the policy dimension," this actually refers to a series of subdimensions: the who, what, where, and when of restriction; the certainty, severity, and nature of sanctions; and so on.

The second dimension is the array of alternative drugs under consideration. It seems advisable to treat each drug separately. The consequences of tightening or loosening the heroin laws in the United States, for example, are so different from the likely consequences of comparable changes in the regime governing marijuana – in terms of the numbers and kinds of people involved, the health effects, the burdens on the enforcement system, the associated crime or violence, the transmission of disease – that no assessment of an alternative regime for heroin could be directly translated into an assessment for marijuana (or alcohol or frequently abused prescription drugs). Similarly, psychedelic drugs like LSD, MDMA, and psilocybin differ sufficiently from cocaine and heroin that it makes little sense to simply lump them together as "hard drugs." However, note the considerable complication presented by the fact that the effects of a specific regime for one drug may depend on the regime applied to other drugs that are potential substitutes or complements; one of the harms of a tough cocaine regime may be increased use of heroin.

In addition to these two dimensions, at least three others need to be included in our evaluation matrix; all three relate to drug-related costs (damages, harms, losses). These appear in Table 6.1; we omit the policy and drug dimensions to simplify the presentation, so that what

Table 6.1. *Taxonomy of drug-related harms*

Category	Harm	Who bears the harm/risk						Primary source of harm
		Users	Dealers	Intimates	Employers	Neighborhood	Society	
Health	Public health care costs (drug treatment, other)	x			x		x	Use
	Private health care costs (drug treatment, other)	x			x			Use
	Suffering due to physical illness (acute, chronic)	x		x				Use
	Suffering due to mental illness (acute, chronic)	x		x				Use
	Addiction	x		x				Use
	Effects of maternal use on infants	x		x			x	Use
	HIV/other disease transmission	x		x			x	Use, illegal status
	Prevention of quality control	x						Illegal status
	Inhibition of voluntary pursuit of treatment			x				Enforcement
	Restriction on medicinal uses of drug	x					x	Illegal status
Social and economic functioning	Reduced performance, school	x		x	x		x	Use
	Reduced performance, workplace	x		x	x		x	Use
	Poor parenting, child abuse	x		x		x	x	Use
	Influence on others' using	x		x		x	x	Use
	Harm to self-esteem associated with use	x						Use, illegal status
	Harm to reputation associated with use	x						Use, illegal status
	Harm to employability associated with use	x			x			Use, illegal status
	Accruing criminal experience	x		x			x	Illegal status
	Acquaintance with criminal networks	x	x	x		x	x	Illegal status
	Elevated dollar price of substance	x	x				x	Enforcement
	Infringement on personal liberty	x	x		x	x	x	Enforcement
	Prevention/restriction of benefits of use	x					x	Illegal status

Category	Item	1	2	3	4	5	6	7	Source
Safety and public order	Accident victimization (work, road, etc.)					x	x		Use
	Property/acquisitive crime victimization	x			x	x	x		Use, enforcement
	Violence, psychopharmacological		x		x	x			Use
	Violence, economic compulsive		x			x			Enforcement
	Violence, systemic (associated with markets)		x	x	x	x			Enforcement, status
	Fear, restricted mobility			x					Use, enforcement
	Sense of public disorder and disarray				x		x		Use, enforcement
	Reduced property values near markets				x		x		Enforcement
	Observably widespread violation of law							x	Illegal status
Criminal justice	Increased police costs							x	Enforcement
	Increased court costs							x	Enforcement
	Increased incarceration costs							x	Enforcement
	Preempting of scarce jail/prison space							x	Enforcement
	Court congestion and delay							x	Enforcement
	Police invasion of personal privacy	x		x		x			Enforcement
	Corruption of legal authorities							x	Enforcement
	Demoralization of legal authorities							x	Enforcement
	Violation of the law	x		x				x	Illegal status
	Devaluation of arrest as moral sanction							x	Enforcement
	Interference in source countries							x	Enforcement
	Strained international relations							x	Enforcement
	Fines	x		x	x				Enforcement
	Time and income lost (in court, in prison)	x		x	x	x			Enforcement
	Legal expenses	x		x	x				Enforcement
	Stigma of criminal record, prison record	x		x	x			x	Enforcement
	Fear of apprehension	x		x	x				Enforcement

appears in Table 6.1 is just one of a series of conceivable matrices; specifically, the status quo for heroin and cocaine. The matrix might appear very different for an alternative regime and/or type of substance (e.g., the medical prescription of heroin for maintenance purposes).

One dimension specifies *the nature of the harm or cost*. Table 6.1 lists nearly fifty such harms; the list could undoubtedly be expanded and refined, but it provides a reasonable first approximation of the full range of costs associated with drugs in an industrial society. For convenience they are clustered into the categories of health, social and economic functioning, safety and public order, and criminal justice. It is important to identify the full range of these harms/costs because they are not all positively related to the extent of drug use or to any other single metric; a policy that increases drug use may reduce other harms and vice versa.

Some of these consequences are much more important than others. For example, direct criminal justice costs in the current regime are in the order of tens of billions of dollars; how many billions depends on how much one believes that crime is elevated by drug use in the current regime. Similarly, a number of studies (CASA, 1994; Phibbs, Bateman, & Schwartz, 1991) found that illicit drugs contribute substantially to health care costs. Others may be quite minor. For example, harm to reputation associated with use of illicit drugs may be minimal now because those who use frequently either conceal that or associate with other frequent users so that they suffer no loss that they care about. But the list must include some that are minor currently if it is possible that they would become substantial in another regime.

Another dimension specifies: *who bears the cost*. Costs can be borne by users of the drug, users' intimates (family, lovers, friends), dealers, taxpayers, innocent bystanders, neighborhoods, society in general; for example, funding the increased criminal justice system costs is borne by taxpayers, whereas intimates, friends, and users are primarily affected by addiction itself. A careful identification of all possible bearers of cost or damage need not imply that costs are even commensurable across bearers; if anything, attention to this dimension discourages attempts to treat all costs interchangeably, precisely because it stresses their heterogeneity. It also encourages one to think explicitly about the allocation of harms across different groups under different policies (see Moore, 1976). The interests of groups may be in conflict; for example, measures that increase the extent of cocaine use but reduce the aggregate violence and disorder surrounding distribution of the drug (perhaps by allowing open retail sale and purchase in one location) may benefit neighborhoods but increase the damage suffered by intimates.

The final dimension specifies *the primary source of the harm or cost.* There is an ample supply of published hypotheses on this issue (e.g., Kleiman, 1992a; Moore, 1991; Nadelmann, 1989); our own hypotheses appear in the final column of Table 6.1. Four potential categories of causes are trafficking in the drug, use of the drug, illegality of the drug per se, and enforcement of drug laws. Only the latter three are used, and exclusion of the first – trafficking – requires explanation. The harms and damages due to trafficking in a prohibitionist regime are mainly of two kinds. One is obviously that trafficking is the medium through which use is supplied; if use can be blamed on traffickers, then "harms due to use" can be traced back into "harms due to trafficking." But since the harms due to use are typically identified with users and their associates – ruined lives or careers, ill health, and the like – nothing is gained and something is lost if the accounting framework suppresses users and identifies the harms and losses with trafficking.

The other kind of cost (harm, damage) due to trafficking is mostly associated with enforcement of the laws. It includes direct costs – specifically budgeted drug law enforcement. It also includes indirect costs – the crowding of courts and prisons; the drug-market violence and neighborhood deterioration associated with illegal black markets and criminal competition; the loss of lives and careers of young people drawn into criminal activity, perhaps arrested and incarcerated and often permanently removed from the legitimate labor force; and all the attendant social demoralization and loss of confidence in law and order. To associate these harms with enforcement of the law is not to "blame" law enforcement for the evils of criminal drug-market activity but to recognize that among the costs of prohibition are the side effects of what is necessarily imperfect and incomplete enforcement of the law. These are just as real and as "enforcement related" as are police deaths and the budgetary costs of law enforcement. Of course, enforcement can only generate these costs when there are consumers attempting to purchase and use drugs, but we attribute these costs to enforcement if there is reason to believe that the costs would not be incurred in the absence of prohibition.

However, some of traffic-related violence is not attributable to enforcement but to illegality per se. Young males in an illegal commerce, with valuable goods to sell and without access to courts to resolve disputes, are likely to use violence to resolve disputes, whether about territory, payment, or the quality of goods, even if enforcement is minimal.

The illicit status of the drug per se also generates a variety of other costs and damages. When a person purchases and consumes an illicit drug, there is a cost to society and, arguably, to that individual, simply due to the fact that the transaction and the consumption are illegal and the person has, in buying and consuming the item, committed a crime. Just as unenforced or unenforceable speed laws may produce law breaking and disrespect for traffic laws, incompletely enforced or unenforceable drug laws make the ensuing drug purchases criminal acts, and the person an unapprehended "criminal." These social and individual harms might be assimilated to the costs of law enforcement – as "costs" associated with imperfect and incomplete enforcement. But they would be accrued even in the absence of enforcement. Because these harms are a matter of the legal status of the drug, it is useful to keep them as a separate category.

Subtler costs arising from illegality include the reduced availability for medical research and use of a substance with potential medicinal benefits that is deemed, as a matter of legal policy, unacceptable for any use. A controversial example is the use of marijuana for appetite enhancement for AIDS patients and nausea relief for cancer patients undergoing chemotherapy. The reason for prohibiting or severely restricting research on this use is presumably not that the use for AIDS treatment is itself contrary to policy but that allowing that use is somehow incompatible with marijuana laws and their enforcement (Hecht, 1991). The initial governmental reaction to the passage of Proposition 215 in California certainly confirmed that suspicion (Chapter 15).

When in doubt as to whether a cost (e.g., lack of sterile needles) requires enforcement above and beyond legal status, the cost is attributed to legal status per se; this assumes that mere legal status has an important symbolic role with or without the instrumental impact of enforcement.

Some costs are probably determined jointly by both drug use and enforcement *or* illicit status. In such cases, drug prohibition arguably adds to the costs that would already be incurred in the absence of prohibition. Uncertainty about the purity of, and diluents in, heroin, arising from enforcement and illegality per se, contribute to the number of overdoses by heroin users; but given poor self-control on the part of the heroin-addicted, it is likely that some of these deaths would occur even if the drug were legally available. None have been reported in the Swiss heroin maintenance experiment discussed in Chapter 12, but that is an extremely tightly controlled environment in which injection takes place under professional supervision. Similarly, prohibition contributes to the stigmatization of drug users, but drug users might well be stigmatized in the absence of prohibition, as increasingly is true of cigarette smokers in the United States (Schelling, 1992). Through its effect on prices, law enforcement inadvertently promotes acquisitive crime and its attendant violence – what Goldstein (1985) calls "economic compulsive" violence aimed at generating cash for drugs. But for some substances and dosage levels, intoxication per se can promote impulsiveness and criminality (see Bushman, 1993; Fagan, 1990). In these cases, we list both causes to indicate our ignorance as to the *primary* source of the cost.

A simplistic reading of Table 6.1 might imply that drug prohibition is in total a greater source of harm to society than drug use per se (which is cited only half as frequently). Indeed, many have argued this position (e.g., Nadelmann, 1989). But, as we noted earlier, one's position on this question will depend on how one weighs alternative harms and how the harms compare across regimes. Four facts suggest that evaluating and comparing total harm is largely a task of judgment rather than arithmetic. Three were noted earlier – we currently lack relevant empirical evidence for many of the harms that are at least quantitative in principle, many of the quantifiable harms aren't readily translated into monetary terms, and many of the harms are intangible and inherently subjective; our relative aversion to them is a matter of personal (dis)taste. A fourth is that it is easier to perceive the presence of harms than their absence; we may blame a regime for the harms that it allows or creates but fail to credit it for the harms it reduces or prevents (Kleiman, 1992a). As argued in Chapter 5, drug use is less than it would be absent prohibition, but that reduction cannot be estimated yet. On the other hand, measuring the number of actual overdoses or criminal earnings (at least approximately) is possible. The remainder of this chapter attempts to describe and assess more carefully some of the major harms of the current U.S. regime, giving special attention to the extent that those harms might be affected by enforcement.

THE IMPLEMENTATION OF PROHIBITION AND SPECIFIC HARMS

The economics of black markets

Prohibition of certain drugs generates black markets, which are the source of many harms only slightly related to the goods or services involved. They provide illegal incomes to many, including some who otherwise would be much less involved in crime. Some participants earn enormous incomes (almost as much as American CEOs or athletes!), which creates socially damaging role models in some inner-city communities and political destabilization in some producer nations. Rayful Edmond, Jr., the principal cocaine distributor in Washington, DC, in the late 1980s, was earning tens of millions of dollars before he was convicted in 1989; he was only 24 years old when his career ended (Walsh, 1989). The major Colombian traffickers may have acquired fortunes in the hundreds of millions of dollars (Lee & Clawson, 1996). Further, these incomes provide the basis for much corruption of law enforcement, particularly police.

Central to American concerns with current drug policies, and constituting a large share of the costs attributed to our current policies, are the violence and disorder that surround some drug markets. Enforcement shapes black markets and associated harms, as well as their form and distribution in society.

Ubiquity of drug selling in inner-city communities

One harm of current American prohibition policies that is unquestionably concentrated in inner-city communities and has serious long-term consequences for those communities is the extraordinary prevalence of drug selling. That selling not only produces massive incarceration rates for young minority males, particularly African-

Americans but also affects the viability of those communities in both economic and social terms.

Data on Washington, DC, provide perhaps the clearest evidence on the prevalence of drug selling. We examined who was charged with drug selling in the District of Columbia, 1985–91, a city with a population of about 575,000 in this period (Saner et al., 1995). Using police records, we calculated that at least 23,156 different DC residents were charged with selling in that 7-year period; 85 percent were male and 60 percent aged 18 to 29. Most striking, 98 percent were African-American. Even in a city that was 65 percent African-American in 1990, that figure stands out; for other criminal offenses the percentage African-American ranged from 85 percent (nondrug misdemeanor) to 95 percent (drug possession).

This is consistent with the cruder national indicators presented in Chapter 2. For example, in 1994 African-Americans (12 percent of the general population) constituted two-thirds of admissions to state prison for drug offenses, compared to slightly less than one-half for all nondrug offenses.

What the more specific DC data permit, though, is estimation of the probability of a charge for drug selling among a particular high-risk demographic groups. Given that the charged population is overwhelmingly African-American, young, and male, the calculations were done for successive birth cohorts of African-American males resident in DC. After adjusting census data for known undercounts, it was estimated that 30 percent of black males born in 1967 and resident in the District of Columbia were charged with drug selling between 1985 and 1991 (i.e., ages 18 to 24). For each of the previous five birth cohorts, going back to 1962, the comparable rate ranged from 26 to 30 percent.

Thus in the late 1980s, drug selling was attracting a substantial fraction of all young African-American males resident in the nation's capital city. Moreover, notwithstanding its reputation as a troubled city, Washington was a city with a poverty rate close to the average for large cities (21 percent compared to 19 percent for large cities as a group in 1990), and employment rates and wages for African-American residents that were high for large cities in the United States.

Two general caveats need to be made about these findings. First, the figures reported for DC refer only to those charged with drug offenses as adults; some drug sellers may evade law enforcement over a long period of time and others may desist following careers as juvenile dealers. Second, in 1986, 279 juveniles were charged in DC with drug selling. To that extent, the preceding figures underestimate the prevalence of drug selling by males under 24 in this population. Both effects are probably small. Selling drugs on the street over a period of years is a risky business, and few are likely to avoid an occasional arrest. Drug selling at a young age is likely nowadays to lead to frequent use of the drug sold and thus to dependence; that makes exit difficult. On the other hand, to the extent that some charged are not guilty, then these figures are overestimates; while allowing for errors in justice, again this is probably a modest source of error.

Second, the dominance of African-Americans among the population charged with drug selling clearly overstates their share of the total drug-selling population either in Washington or the United States. Those who sell expensive drugs in exposed settings are at much higher risk of being caught than those who sell in private settings. Marijuana selling is mostly done without such exposure (frequently to friends in school or college dorms) and though the total number of marijuana sellers is much larger than the number of cocaine or heroin sellers, marijuana-selling arrests annually average only about 70,000, compared to about 220,000 for these other drugs. African-Americans may be disproportionately represented among those who sell in outdoor markets, in part because they are such a large share of the urban poverty population (41 percent of those living in poverty in center cities in 1990 were African-American[4]). Finally, Caulkins and McCaffrey (1993) found, in an analysis of the National Household Survey on Drug Abuse, that though only 19 percent of self-avowed dealers are African-American, they accounted for 64 percent of self-reported arrests. Although this survey omits a large fraction of frequent drug users[5] who are the most active sellers, it does suggest that African-Americans who sell drugs have a higher arrest risk than their white counterparts.

The harms that flow from this high prevalence of drug selling in the inner city are varied and deep. Drug dealing itself generates drug

4. More refined analyses of 1980 Census data that focus on the most extreme poverty households show even more concentration. For example, Rickets and Sawhill (1988) estimated that in those tracts that they classified as "underclass," 59 percent of that population was African-American.
5. Frequent users are hard to interview when in households, and many of them are currently incarcerated or homeless.

dependence (Altschuler & Brounstein, 1991), it lessens attachment to the work ethic and conventional social ties. It encourages violence for self-protection both at the individual and community level. The development of the crack market in the mid-1980s has been credibly blamed for the upsurge in youth violence generally, providing the lethal weaponry that has been increasingly used for settlement of minor disputes (Blumstein, 1993).

For those who get caught, there is not only the time in prison, which can hardly be called rehabilitating in these days of over-crowded prisons and reduced prison training programs, but also the loss of time to develop as members of the community, family, or work-force. Studies of the effect of a criminal conviction on employability produce ambiguous results; Grogger (1992) finds that much of the black/white youth wage differential can be accounted for by differences in arrest rates. Bushway, Nagin, and Taylor (1995) find that there may actually be a short-term wage increase resulting from arrest; this could be the consequence of shifting the arrestees onto a career path that gives them higher immediate wages but sharply reduced prospects for future growth, since firms will invest less in their training. Marriage prospects presumably decline for those involved in the drug trade, since its long-term risks are at least as conspicuous as its short-term rewards for prospective brides (the business being predominantly male). The sharp decline in marriage rates among inner-city black females with children has many sources (Wilson, 1996). However, the dramatic increase in incarceration rates among African-American males of the birth cohorts 1960–75 that has been fueled by the drug trades undoubtedly has worsened matters, though it must be noted that marriage rates for college-educated African-American males have also been declining.

At the community level, drug dealing has decreased the availability of positive adult male role models. Young women may not want to marry dealers but younger boys may seek to emulate them, in part because of the shortage of financially successful males in legitimate pursuits in those communities and in part because of a lack of belief in their own long-run prospects. Crime rates are exacerbated by the ease of access to drugs and in attracting more drug-dependent users who are either potential victims or offenders, depending on their immediate economic circumstance.

Those who sell drugs are not innocent victims of prohibition. They choose to deal; many similarly situated persons do not. Yet absent prohibition, the opportunity for drug selling would not exist for these groups; it would at most become a marginal activity like after-hours sales of liquor or clandestine distribution to underage buyers. Thus, the damage that arises from the creation of these opportunities must be taken as among the harms to ascribe to our current policies.

How much are they driven by the enforcement, its intensity, or strategies of enforcement, as opposed to prohibition itself? One mechanism connecting enforcement and the extent of drug selling is the creation of new selling opportunities through incarceration. A major distinction between drug selling (indeed the distribution of illegal goods and services generally) and other crimes is that the demand for the service remains and users are willing to compensate new sellers for entering the business. In our DC study for 1985–7 (Reuter, MacCoun, & Murphy, 1990) we estimated that a dealer selling regularly (at least two days per week) had about a 2 in 9 chance of being imprisoned in the course of a year; this figure does not take into account time incarcerated before the charge is disposed of, so it somewhat underestimates the extent of churning in the market resulting from the jailing of offenders. The data do not permit estimation of the replacement of incarcerated dealers by new recruits, but it is plausibly substantial. If so, unless there is a substantial deterrence effect, incarcerating dealers might simply expand the pool of people who become dealers.

Imprisoning dealers may still raise prices and thus reduce drug consumption, though, as already noted, the evidence that imprisonment risk raises price is weak. But whether there are other enforcement strategies exist that can keep prices high or restrict access without incarcerating so many is an important question. There is a general discomfort with what is sometimes characterized as "trail 'em, nail 'em, jail 'em" strategies, which inter alia may encourage the survival of more violent organizations that use intimidation and the threat of killings to prevent employees from informing. Community policing, with its emphasis on a more sensible use of police resources and breaking up markets rather than arresting offenders, offers a general framework for accomplishing this (Kennedy, 1993), but it has not so far made a major impact on drug enforcement in U.S. cities, at least in terms of reducing drug-selling arrests.

Corruption

American drug prohibition has been associated with some of the most significant criminal corruption of modern times in other countries. As this book was being written in 1998 and 1999, the nation was assailed daily with stories of drug-related corruption in Mexico, implicating the head of the Mexican equivalent of the Drug Enforcement Administration (Golden, 1997), many senior officials in the supposedly reformed elite drug unit, and possibly a number of even more senior officials in the previous Salinas administration (Golden, 1998). In 1995 it was Colombia's turn to catch the international eye; former president Ernesto Samper was credibly accused of financing his 1994 election campaign with $6 million from the principal Cali drug exporters. It is hard to think of any bolder act by a criminal group than the Medellin cartel's 1989 assassination of the leading Colombian presidential candidate, Carlos Luis Galan. Peru's corruption has not been as integral to the political system, but it has been pervasive and, in the late 1980s, contributed to the undermining of legitimate authority and the rise of the Sendero Luminoso as a threat to the state.

The corruption generated in producer and transshipment countries is horrific, but it has to be seen in the context of political and enforcement systems that show little capacity to deal with a wide array of threats to integrity. For example, the privatization of Mexico's state-owned enterprises in the Salinas administration was accompanied by extraordinarily large bribes to senior officials (Celarier, 1997). Drug prohibition certainly exacerbates this problem, but it is not the origin of it.

The U.S. Congress, enraged by evidence of Mexican government officials' complicity in the torture/murder of DEA agent Enrique Camarena in 1985, imposed a requirement that the President certify annually that the governments of other countries from which U.S. consumers purchase drugs are cooperating with the U.S. in trying to suppress that export. This has become a major source of friction between the United States and its Latin American neighbors. In particular, Mexicans object to the world's largest consumer of illicit drugs labeling the producer countries as the problem (*The Economist*, 1997). Note that this tension is one adverse consequence of current U.S. prohibitionist policies. It is certainly not inherent in prohibition itself. Western European nations, though much afflicted by illicit drugs, have adopted less aggressive policies toward the producer countries; see, for example, Joyce's (1998) discussion of the more nuanced policy of the British government toward the cocaine source countries.

Perhaps *real politique* would claim this as one of the unhappy obligations of the world's last remaining super power, but it appears mostly as a consequence of domestic politics, which encourages cheap posturing about the irresponsibility of source governments.

Strikingly, the nature and extent of corruption in the United States itself has been far less significant. Though the most recent police scandals in New York, associated with the Knapp Commission in the early 1970s and the Mollen Commission in the early 1990s, have been drug related, they have been much narrower than earlier scandals centered on other illegal markets. They have involved fewer officers and reached less high up into command structure. For example, the 1950s scandal around gambling, in particular a Brooklyn bookmaker named Harry Gross, showed highly systemic corruption, as had prostitution and vice scandals uncovered by the Lexow Committee in the 1890s (Kornblum, 1976). These earlier scandals involved very senior police officials and connected with the core political machine of the city. The most recent major gambling corruption case, involving the Philadelphia Police Department in the 1980s, also went high in the department, leading to the conviction of the second-ranking official (Gruson, 1986).

The older corruption was far more systemic and involved whole precincts, largely because that was the only protection of value for a retailer whose business operated in a conspicuous fashion on a continuing basis (Reuter, 1984a). This was true in cities other than New York. For example, Beigel and Beigel (1977) described similar systemic corruption around gambling enforcement in Chicago in the early 1970s. Though a number of rings of corrupt police have been found in many cities (e.g., the L.A. County Sheriff's office in the late 1980s and the Miami Police Department homicide squad in the early 1980s; Rosenblatt, 1981) they have not penetrated the senior ranks. The drug-related corruption of recent years has generally involved small groups or individuals working opportunistically, robbing dealers or offering protection for a particular deal.

Corruption in the principal federal drug enforcement agencies has so far been slight. A total of sixteen DEA agents have been charged with corruption over a 10-year period; for an agency with 3,600 investigators this is something less than a wholesale integrity problem (Jones, 1997). Moreover, there has been a dearth of allegations against senior officials. It is always difficult to be confident that the bulk of corruption has been uncovered. However, given the density of informants and the overlapping jurisdictions of many agencies, it seems unlikely that serious drug-related corruption can be hidden for long periods. Drug traffickers facing long sentences in federal court have strong incentives for providing information on any agents whom they have paid; indeed providing information useful to law enforcement is the only basis for mitigation of penalties under federal sentencing guidelines.[6] The fact that a major trafficker has to be concerned about a plethora of local, state, and federal agencies also reduces the value of protection afforded by any one agency.

A more subtle kind of institutional corruption of enforcement agencies has received attention in the last decade. Federal and state laws allow law enforcement agencies to earn money for seizures and forfeitures related to drug enforcement. The sums generated have been large; the federal government had earned $4 billion by the end of fiscal year 1994 from these actions; one-third of this had been distributed to state and local law enforcement agencies (U.S. Department of Justice, 1995). Mast, Benson, and Rasmussen (1997) show that police departments were responsive to the rewards provided through these forfeitures; departments in states returning a higher fraction of seizures to their police budget increased their rate of drug arrests.

Some state and local agencies[7] have been credibly accused of targeting enforcement not on the most serious offenders but on the most lucrative prospects. For example, in a notorious 1992 incident, Los Angeles County sheriff's deputies killed a wealthy recluse when they raided his property in search of marijuana plants. The owner of the

---

6. Jonathan Caulkins points out that this is an instance in which intense sustained enforcement may be corruption reducing, even though it is not explicitly aimed at that corruption.
7. Federal agencies must turn over these moneys to the general treasury. However, they benefit from the laws because federal laws allow generous payments (up to one-half) to state and local agencies involved in a federal seizure, thus giving these agencies a strong incentive to bring the cases into federal jurisdiction.

property had no criminal record and no marijuana plants were discovered; yet the deputies stormed into his house in the early morning and shot him when he emerged from his bedroom with a gun, apparently drawn in self-defense against night intruders. It appeared that the sheriff's office was hoping to earn large sums from confiscation of the property; the Narcotics Bureau earned almost 13 percent of its funding through such confiscations (Fessier, 1993). The head of a state law enforcement agency told one of us that he was expected to raise about one-third of his budget from seizures and forfeitures and was concerned about the effect on targeting decisions.

Yet another consequence of drug enforcement may also be labeled corruption. Drug enforcement is a particularly degrading and dangerous type of police activity. It requires undercover work, which erodes trust within a police agency. Informants are central to the business and, even when run honestly, create morale problems. Drug enforcement encourages police brutality because drug dependence in modern America so debases the lives of many addicts, making them careless of their health and negligent in their dealings with others (Simon & Burns, 1997). Police become less concerned with the rights of those they arrest because so many drug users arouse feelings of disgust. That induces more tension between the community and police, even though there is undoubtedly strong community support in inner cities for ridding the neighborhood of the visible sores of open-air markets. The sheer volume and repetitiveness of drug cases affects prosecutors as well; they become more inured to police manipulation of the court process in providing routine perjury about the circumstances of an arrest or seizure.

Any corruption is a cause for concern, and these institutional failures are very serious. But certainly when compared to Prohibition, the corruption generated by drug prohibitions in this country seems quite modest. Allegations of political (rather than police) corruption around protection of the drug trade have been negligible; there has been nothing like the corruption of Chicago city politics that deprived alcohol Prohibition so rapidly of its moral legitimacy. The effects on the police are more serious but still seem to pose something less than a crisis. It is the impact of U.S. policies overseas that has generated the most distinctive corruption problems. Perhaps, as was true for Prohibition in the United States, it is the low integrity prior to the creation of the large black market that produces such massive corruption, which then further complicates the task of generating honest administration.

Violence and other crime

Many illegal markets show low levels of violence or disorder. As discussed in Chapter 7, prostitution though frequently unsightly and sometimes a nuisance, does not generate much by way of additional violence. Bookmaking, notwithstanding the drama of the film *The Sting*, was also a generally peaceful affair; bookies were more likely to die in bed than on the battlefield of competition. Even for some drugs, the markets generate little violence; marijuana in general does not spark much injury as the result of competitive or transactional disputes.[8]

However, some drug markets are clearly very violent; many participants are at risk of being killed or seriously wounded by others in the same business, either as buyers or sellers, and there are unintended shootings of innocent by-standers. Though the FBI figures suggest that only about 5 percent of homicides in recent years are drug related, studies of a few cities suggest that this substantially underestimates the contribution of the drug trade.[9] Blumstein (1993) showed that the beginning of the crack epidemic in a city was associated with a sharp increase in homicide rates.

Paul Goldstein, in three widely cited articles (Goldstein, 1985; Goldstein, Brownstein, & Ryan, 1992; Goldstein et al., 1989), explored both conceptually and empirically the connections between violence (principally homicide) and drugs. Conceptually he provides a three-part classification: psychopharmacological (violence due to the effect of the drug itself), economic compulsive (violence for the purpose of generating money for expensive drugs), and systemic (violence to protect turf, contracts, or reputation). This is a very rough classification scheme,[10] but it does make useful distinctions. In par-

---

8. In the District of Columbia in the late 1990s, it was reported that some street gangs were in violent disputes over the marijuana market (Pierre, 1996).
9. The explanation for the underestimation may lie in the technique used by the FBI in its Supplemental Homicide Reports, which allows for only one cause of the homicide; thus, a dispute about a drug deal may be classified either as a fight or as drug related. The former may be easier to determine.
10. For example, Goldstein does not distinguish among two forms of psychoactive-related violence – aggression and victimization. Those visibly intoxicated are easy marks.

ticular it isolates one source of violence that is driven primarily by drug use itself.[11]

In his study of homicides in New York City, Goldstein and his colleagues found that drugs and alcohol were an important cause for a large share of all incidents in 1984 and 1988. For 1988, near the height of the crack epidemic, they classified 53 percent of homicides as being drug-related or alcohol-related; there was also a substantial percentage whose drug-relatedness could not be determined. Of those that were drug-related, 14 percent were psychopharmacological (68 percent alcohol, 16 percent crack), 4 percent were economic-compulsive, and 74 percent were systemic (61 percent crack, 27 percent powder cocaine). By contrast in 1984, before crack, only 42 percent of homicides were drug- or alcohol-related, 59 percent were psychopharmacological (79 percent alcohol), 3 percent were economic-compulsive, and 21 percent were systemic. The difference between the findings of the two years is a useful reminder that these numbers are not eternal verities but come out of a complex process of market dynamics. A second measure of the significance of drug market-related violence is the probability of a market participant being killed or injured as a consequence of participation. Our own research on drug selling in Washington, DC, examined drug-related violence. The Metropolitan Police Department estimated that between 50 and 80 percent of homicides in 1988 were drug-related, though it did not break down the figure by specific drug or cause. We estimated that 24,000 persons were drug sellers on at least a regular (though mostly part-time) basis and that the risk of being killed in the course of the year was about 1 in 70; the risk of being seriously injured (requiring a hospital admission) was about 1 in 14. By any standards, these were extremely high rates; the homicide rate was probably thirty times that found among young adult African-American males in American cities in the late 1980s.[12]

---

11. It is probably not prevalence but the extent of frequent use that is most significant, since a small share of all users account for the vast majority of all drug consumption; Everingham and Rydell (1994) estimated that 22 percent of cocaine users in 1992 accounted for 70 percent of the quantity consumed. Moreover, frequent users are most likely to be made aggressive by their cocaine use or are most visibly unable to defend themselves.

12. The FBI reported rates of homicide victimization per hundred thousand African-American males, steadily rising from 48 to 61 between 1985 and 1989 (FBI, annual). This includes both those involved in the drug trade and those not involved. If 30

Why are these drug markets, particularly that for crack, so violent? The acute effects of the drug itself may not be directly responsible for much of it; that at least is the implication of the more recent Goldstein study. Certainly it is not difficult to identify other potentially important factors.

1. *The youth of participants.* Rates for violent crime peak early, at about ages eighteen to twenty-two. The young are particularly likely to lack foresight and thus engage in violence to settle disputes. The crack market was the first mass drug market in which most of the sellers were very young.
2. The *value of the drugs themselves.* The cocaine that fills a plastic sandwich bag is worth thousands of dollars. The return to sudden, situational violence was unusually high.
3. *The intensity of law enforcement.*[13] Transactions are carried out under considerable uncertainty as a consequence of this intensity. Disagreements are particularly likely where written records are lacking, participants speak in code, and there is always doubt about whether one of the participants is an informant. Intensified enforcement increases all three of these risk factors.
4. *The indirect consequence of drug use.* Users are more violent and aggressive, and this encourages dealers to prefer selling out of doors. It also promotes unreliable behavior among user/dealers and thus more retaliation by their suppliers.

Probably the combination of these factors, rather than any one of them, accounts for the extraordinary violence associated with crack markets in the late 1980s. That violence seems to have fallen substantially in the late 1990s, perhaps reflecting the aging of participants in crack markets (Golub & Johnson, 1997), though violence itself, as well as enforcement, may also have selected out the most violent participants.

Rasmussen, Benson, and their associates examined whether more intensive drug enforcement increases violent crime; much of this work is summarized in Rasmussen and Benson (1994). The mecha-

percent were involved in that trade, then drug dealers would need to have a rate 30 times that of the remainder.
13. Miron (1998) analyzed homicide rates since 1900 and found that the intensity of prohibition enforcement (including that against alcohol 1920–32) accounts for much of the variation. The use of a questionable proxy for enforcement intensity (expenditures by specialized federal enforcement agencies) raises serious questions about this finding.

nisms involved are quite varied. For example, enforcement might lead to more violence in competition. Benson et al. (1992) found that the violent crime rate in a community was increased by more drug arrests in a neighboring community. This they argued is a displacement effect, as dealers move from the targeted community to the neighboring one and struggle over the establishment of territories. Another mechanism works through the limited capacity of the correctional system; increased prison space for drug offenders reduces the penalties for other crimes, including violent crimes, and thus induces higher victimization. Benson and Rasmussen (1991) showed that, even assuming that prison is effective only through incapacitation and not deterrence, the observed rise in the resources devoted to drug enforcement in Florida in the 1980s might have increased other crime by 10 percent.

This work supports the finding of a much earlier study by Silverman and Spruill (1977) that higher heroin prices increase property crime. The assumption here is that (1) tougher enforcement raises prices, (2) demand for heroin is inelastic, and (3) the larger expenditures for heroin are generated by more property crime. These are all reasonable but assailable assumptions. In particular, the new literature on the demand for drugs suggests that it is far more price responsive than previously thought (Caulkins & Reuter, 1998), though perhaps only in the long run.

Aggressive enforcement may have other adverse consequences. It is oft claimed (e.g., Thornton, 1991; Rasmussen & Benson, 1994) that tougher enforcement leads to higher potency drugs. After all, higher potency reduces the bulk of the illegal transaction and thus lowers enforcement risk, a principal source of costs. However, the available evidence is quite mixed. On the one hand, it is true that Prohibition generated a shift to the stronger spirits, away from beer. On the other hand, during the period when cocaine was legal, it was sold in high-potency forms (Chapter 9). Also heroin, seen as the drug subject to the toughest enforcement for many years, was sold in very low purity in retail markets until the early 1990s. Indeed, it is routinely asserted that higher enforcement will lead to lower purity, as well as higher per pure milligram prices; curiously, there is no theoretical account of why that should be the case. Thus, the effects of enforcement on potency are ambiguous.

Health consequences

Under current U.S. policies it appears that the health costs (mortality, morbidity, and the costs of treating drug use and its sequelae) of drug use under prohibition are substantially smaller than those arising from crime (mostly criminal justice and the losses borne by those incarcerated). Rice et al. (1991) estimated that over two-thirds of the total costs associated with illegal drugs ($58 billion in 1988) are crime or crime-control related. The more recent figures from Harwood et al. (1998) suggested a slightly lower 60 percent (of $98 billion) for 1992.[14] This is a consequence of the relatively small user base for illicit drugs, certainly when compared to alcohol or cigarettes.

Nevertheless, the health consequences are substantial and not necessarily well reflected in these "cost of illness" studies, which are limited by the lack of good long-term studies of mortality and morbidity associated with drug use. The association between injecting drug use and infectious diseases, most notably HIV, is one of the few links that has been well studied, as summarized in Chapter 2.

Some of the morbidity and mortality associated with the use of cocaine, heroin, and other illicit drugs is a consequence of drug use itself. Cocaine dependence induces careless behavior, particularly with respect to sex; under any regime, cocaine might be expected to be associated with high rates of venereal disease. Phencyclidine induces aggression that is likely to be associated with injury. Intoxication, whatever its source, will increase the incidence of automobile injuries.

However, much of the current damage is unquestionably the consequence of prohibition. Most heroin overdoses are the result of uncertainty about potency, which could be avoided in a legalized and regulated market. The sharing of needles, which is central to the spread of HIV, is motivated in some areas primarily by the need to conceal needles, which are so strongly indicative of use of the illicit drugs. Indeed, making needles legally accessible in pharmacies, as

---

14. Given the roughness of these estimates, 60 percent may not be significantly different from two-thirds, but it is possible that there has been a decline as the result of the aging of the drug-dependent population between 1985 and 1992.

they are in nine U.S. states and most Western European countries, turns out to have only a modest effect on the prevalence of needle sharing. Arguably, in the context of prohibition, the incentives for clandestine use of heroin lead to needle sharing.

Aggressive syringe-exchange programs, which aim at more than simply improving legal access, can reduce the risk substantially. Stimson (1996) argues that Britain has avoided an epidemic of HIV among injecting drug users through these efforts. The cost resulting from prohibition then is not excess HIV-related mortality and morbidity but the cost (including intrusiveness) of that needle exchange program. Absent prohibition, heroin might well be legally sold with syringes, hence vitiating the need for a campaign. The politics of the continued opposition to federal funding of needle exchange are discussed in Chapter 15.

Intense enforcement of prohibition provides incentives for use of more potent forms of drugs.[15] Heroin is injected in most countries because that is the most efficient mode of consuming a fabulously expensive substance; recent shifts to snorting and smoking heroin in the United States are probably related to the sharp decline in price of the drug. Diluents, which are occasionally toxic, are added by dealers for the same reason. If more potent marijuana is a source of greater health risks, which is widely believed but for which there is no specific evidence, then that can be marked down to enforcement rather than prohibition per se.

Perhaps the most general way in which prohibition worsens the health consequences of drug use is by making prices so high that little money or attention can be spared for anything unrelated to the drug itself. Heroin addicts in modern America are in extremely poor health. They have weak attachment to a treatment system whose own manifest frailties are themselves partly a function of prohibition precisely because the clinics deal with such a criminally active and economically marginal population that it is hard to get sustained support for providing good quality services. Those dependent on cocaine are little better off, but the drug itself, precisely because it is positively reinforcing, must take more of the blame.

15. Legal markets for cocaine and heroin might generate a range of potencies. Alcohol is sold as beer (8 percent alcohol), wine (14 percent), and distilled spirits (40 percent); cigarettes include a range of nicotine levels. For cocaine and heroin, low potency would facilitate physical handling of the drug.

CONCLUSIONS

There is no doubt that current policies generate enormous gross harms, though that is of itself not enough to condemn them. It is impossible to divide the damage associated with illegal drugs currently between prohibition per se and U.S. implementation of it. The task is inherently difficult, and little research has targeted it.

Note that the harms described and analyzed here are highly specific to this period. The harms of prohibition in the United States in 1960, when there was very slight prevalence of marijuana use or cocaine or heroin dependency, were very much lower than they are now. The comparative merits of different regimes change over time, perhaps representing changes in social conditions and attitudes generally, even further complicating the problem of projecting the consequences of major changes in the legal regime.

Nonetheless, it is reasonable to conclude that tough enforcement is responsible for much of the observed damage. The extraordinary prices of cocaine and heroin, the massive involvement of young minority males in center cities, foreign corruption, and the violence of the drug trades are all plausibly much increased by the nation's decision to be highly punitive toward these drugs. Prohibition might be implemented differently with much less of this specific collateral damage.

PART III: THE EVIDENCE

7 Other Vices: Prostitution and Gambling

The legalization debate gives almost no attention to two vices, prostitution and gambling. Yet both share important attributes with illegal drugs; they bring pleasure to large numbers, pose a moral issue for many people despite attracting a substantial share of the total population (males only in the case of prostitution), and create massive illegal markets when they are prohibited. Gambling, but not prostitution, becomes habit forming[1] and causes harm to a modest or large fraction in the long-run. Legal control of these vices, in particular whether they should be prohibited, has been a matter of debate for over a century.

Both vices raise issues for regulation and prohibition similar to those encountered in the drug legalization debate. For example, how great are the harms of the activity or substance itself? How does one weigh the moral consequences of widespread flouting of the law against the increased prominence of the disapproved behavior accompanying legalization? Is there a mode of regulation that approximately achieves the control level of prohibition without creating the illegal market? They also raise common political issues: how are choices about prohibition and regulation framed politically?

Something can also be learned from the differences in the fates of the regimes for these two activities. Illegal gambling and prostitution were both central problems for city governments until the 1960s

---

1. That is not to say that an obsessive interest in prostitutes is unknown. However, there is no claim that this is a common phenomenon or that it accounts for a substantial share of all visits to prostitutes.

because they were so closely connected with organized crime and urban corruption. Gambling has mostly been legalized through a series of state actions since 1970, with the development first of state lotteries (now available in thirty-seven states) and then of casinos (thirty states, including those with tribal casinos). Prostitution, in contrast, remains prohibited in all states except for the rural counties of Nevada, where it is subject to rigorous state regulation. Outside of San Francisco, notoriously the most liberal city on matters of sex regulation, there is hardly even a whisper of the old debate about legalizing the activity.[2] The chapter briefly discusses why this has been so.

GAMBLING

Gambling as behavior

The impulse to gamble has a universality comparable to the desire for occasional intoxication. About 68 percent of the adult population in 1998 reported having participated in some form of recreational gambling in the past year (NORC, 1999); in that same year, about 64 percent consumed alcohol (SAMHSA, National Household Survey on Drug Abuse, 1998). Gambling is distinctive in being an element of both recreation and commerce, though gambling in the context of commerce is frequently seen as constructive and wealth enhancing while recreational wagering, as for example in the state lottery, is merely redistributive. To be a "gambler" is often seen as admirable; it means a capacity to rise above the hum drum and risk loss in order to achieve more.

Most recreational gamblers wager small sums in any one session or over the course of a year. While wagering, they do not make important decisions – the kind that have profound effects on their welfare and that of others – that they later regret. Their conduct may be impulsive and may even lack prudence, but it falls well short of the dramatic loss of control we take as a distinctive feature of addiction and intoxication.

2. The Board of Supervisors of San Francisco created a Task Force on Prostitution, which considered various legal options and "recommended that the City departments stop enforcing and prosecuting prostitution crimes" (San Francisco Task Force on Prostitution, 1996).

Some fraction of bettors do however suffer a loss of control. Gambling becomes for them, as heroin injecting becomes for the heroin-dependent, the dominant activity in their lives, and they are no longer capable of consistently regarding the welfare of others or indeed their own. They will engage in behaviors, such as theft, that they would otherwise regard as abhorrent. Though there is no evidence of any physiological withdrawal symptoms associated with compulsive gambling, there is some research showing neurological changes associated with gambling behavior in some individuals (see, for example, Koepp et al., 1998, cited in Chapter 4 of Committee on Social and Economic Impact of Pathological Gambling, 1999).

Pathological gambling is a clinical condition, listed in the American Psychiatric Association Diagnostic and Statistical Manual, fourth edition (APA, 1994):

> The essential features . . . are a continuous or periodic loss of control over gambling, a progression, in gambling frequency and amounts wagered, in the preoccupation with gambling and in obtaining moneys with which to gamble and a continuation of gambling involvement despite adverse consequences.

There is also a broader category of problem gambling, defined by one author simply as "the losing of an excessive amount of money" (Rosencrance, 1989). This condition may be seen as the counterpart to drug abuse, while pathological gambling is more comparable to drug dependence.

The prevalence of pathological and problem gambling behaviors in the U.S. population is a matter of intense speculation and little systematic research. Using an earlier era's definition and terminology, the first of two national surveys of the behavior found 0.8 percent of U.S. adults in 1975 were "probable compulsive gamblers" and another 2.4 percent were "potential compulsive gamblers" (Kallick et al., 1979); note that this prevalence would translate into about 1.6 million compulsive gamblers in 1996. A second national survey in 1998 found, using a more rigorous measure, that about 0.8 percent of the household population had lifetime experience of pathological gambling and using a broader measure (covering both pathological and problem gambling) that the figure rose to about 2 percent (NORC, 1999; p. 25).

Most research has been done only at the state level and has generated somewhat higher figures for a fuzzier measure of "probable *lifetime* pathological gambling." The instruments used to develop these estimates do not inspire great confidence, and the figures should perhaps be regarded as upper bound estimates. A new meta-analysis of over 120 surveys of problem and pathological gambling, which took account of differences in quality and the measures used, concluded that the prevalence in the adult population was about 1.3 percent in the mid-1990s and that it had not increased in the last decade, notwithstanding the increased availability of legal gambling outlets (Shaffer, Hall, & Bilt, 1997).

Data on lottery expenditures suggests that the distribution of gambling expenditures like that for other dependency-creating behaviors, is highly skewed, with a small fraction of all players accounting for a large share of total expenditure. Clotfelter et al. (1999) estimated that the most active 5 percent of players account for 54 percent of total lottery spending; each of these players buys at least $3,870 in lottery services each year. The top 20 percent (spending at least $1,619) account for 82 percent of the total.

The severity of pathological gambling – just how much harm it causes to the pathological gambler and society – is also a matter mostly of speculation. In the political battles surrounding the establishment of casinos in various states, wild figures are often thrown around. Small-scale samples, drawn from the already tiny population seeking treatment or the not much larger Gamblers Anonymous (GA) membership,[3] are extrapolated to the general population of those with gambling problems. For example, Goodman (1995, p. 61) cites Volberg as stating that "the cost to the public of the average pathological gambler in 1981 was approximately $13,600," a figure which turned out to come from study of the small number of gamblers whose problems were so serious that they went to the Johns Hopkins University gambling treatment clinic.

The claim that "forty percent of all white collar crime is generated by problem gambling" is a universal among casino opponents (see e.g., Goodman, 1995), who cite a study by the American Insurance Institute. It turns out that no such organization has ever existed, and it appears that no one who cites the study has actually seen any document (Kelly, 1995). However, there is no question that the tens of

3. An official of the national Council on Compulsive Gambling recently estimated active GA membership at any one time as only about 12,000 persons (personal communication).

thousands who regularly participate in Gamblers Anonymous have suffered and caused serious problems because of their obsession with gambling. Family breakdown, child abuse, embezzlement, and severe depression are just some of the problems reported; for some gamblers the problem seems to be a chronic, lifetime, relapsing condition.

History of control

Attitudes toward gambling have been extraordinarily variable since the eighteenth century. As many authorities note (e.g., Ezell, 1960), lotteries provided a major source of public and private funds in the colonial and early federal eras. The Virginia Company sponsored a lottery in 1612 to offset the costs of colonization. Colleges such as Columbia, Harvard, Princeton, and Yale relied heavily on lotteries in their early days, as did colonial governments seeking funding for major projects. By 1831 eight states sponsored 420 lotteries yielding $66 million, over five times the budget of the federal government.

Bookmaking on horse races was also a major activity. In the late nineteenth century, seats on the New York Stock Exchange and its bookmakers' equivalent sold for the same amount, about $7,000. Casinos, though never legal, were numerous in major cities; for example, New Orleans was reputed to have 500 gambling houses, with other Southern cities such as Mobile and Vicksburg also being well known for their gambling attractions (Asbury, 1938).

Some religious groups were fervently opposed to all forms of wagering, though the Bible is silent on the matter (Bell, 1976). There was also recognition both in literature and regulation that some people could not control their gambling. It was however generally viewed as a healthy recreational activity in the colonial and early federal eras. Nineteenth-century churches, of all denominations other than the Quakers, were active promoters of lotteries for their own activities; the nobility of the purposes was taken to justify the means. For example, Pennsylvania granted ninety-eight lottery licenses to churches before ending all lotteries in 1833 (Ezell, 1960, p. 140).

A wave of nineteenth-century scandals in the operation of state lotteries, along with a concern about crime generated by lottery expenditures and exploitation of the poor, led to prohibition and tough enforcement against all gambling activities (Ezell, 1960). The scandals included the rigging of winning numbers and payments to officials for licenses. The most notorious and longest lasting operation was the Louisiana Lottery, which bribed officials in many states and used its money to influence elections (Fact Research, Inc., 1976). By 1894, after a complicated battle involving ingenious maneuvers around Congressional efforts to deny lotteries use of the mails, lotteries were effectively prohibited throughout the nation.

Horse racing, with associated betting, was restricted to just three states (Kentucky, Maryland, and New York). One reason that horse wagering survived in a few states was the development of the pari-mutuel system, a very early form of automated accounting, which removed the need for the disreputable profession of bookmaking and allowed the state to operate risk-free pools, from which it drew healthy revenues to assuage its conscience.

Beliefs about what gambling did to players, as well as problems of ensuring honest operation, were critical to the prohibition. Tales of gamblers losing everything, so that their families had to march off to the poorhouse, were a standard part of the litany of gambling-related evils that sustained the strict prohibitionist regime from 1900 to 1960. There were also "true confessions" conveying the same message: a young businessman told of deserting friends, giving up work, and losing his health as a result of involvement in lotteries (Ezell, 1960, p. 183).

The prohibition was also sustained by the very problems that it generated. The fact that organized crime, mostly the Mafia after 1920, was believed to be the dominant supplier and heavily dependent on illegal gambling was an argument for vigorous enforcement of laws against gambling. *A Two Dollar Bet Means Murder* (the title of a popular book by Cook, 1961) conveyed the notion that there was no such thing as an innocent bet; each wager fueled the coffers of America's most dangerous criminals, a notion that is also part of current discussions about marijuana. Even into the 1980s the FBI claimed that illegal gambling was organized crime's most important source of income (President's Commission on Organized Crime, 1986).

Gambling was probably the most important source of police corruption for many decades following Repeal. The Kefauver Committee, in the investigation that launched the American fear of the Mafia as a national menace, identified gambling-related corruption as the most prominent element of Mafia activities around the country (Moore, 1974). As already mentioned, gambling was central in most of the major police corruption scandals that erupted approximately every twenty years between 1890 and 1970 in New York City (and more episodically in Chicago and Philadelphia).

Illegal numbers and horse bookmaking generated systemic corruption that posed a peculiarly serious threat to the integrity of big-city police departments (Reuter, 1984a). For example, each numbers outlet served numerous customers each day, typically before 11 A.M. Operators had difficulty concealing the location of their sales outlets; a patrol officer would soon notice the large numbers of customers who came into a store for just a minute and left without any visible purchases. Only if the entire precinct force was corrupted could these operations continue undisturbed.

While big-city police devoted significant resources to gambling enforcement, their efforts were essentially ritualistic. For example, in the late 1960s the New York Police Department (NYPD) made 11,500 gambling arrests annually, of which almost 5,000 were for felony offenses (Reuter & Rubinstein, 1982, p. 122).[4] About 700 officers, in a department of 25,000, were devoted exclusively to gambling enforcement; in addition, the detective division was expected to make many gambling arrests as well.

However, the high arrest activity covered the lack of real commitment to tough enforcement, which was reflected in the indifference of prosecutors and judges in New York:

> [G]ambling cases were handled as low level routine prosecutions, to be disposed of as expeditiously as possible. For some time during the 1950s and 1960s there existed in New York a unique institution called "Gambler's Court." All but a few gambling cases were disposed of here by a court which could impose only minor fines and very short (less than 90 days) jail sentences. The cases were handled by the most junior prosecutors. It was in fact one of the traditional first assignments for new Assistant District Attorneys. A prosecutor might dispose of 10 cases each day in this court where perjured testimony by police officers was an accepted part of the routine (Reuter & Rubinstein, 1982, p. 133).

Another study found that only one out of fifty felony gambling convictions in New York City courts resulted in a prison sentence

4. This compares with 70,000 drug arrests in the city in 1991, of which 43,000 were for felonies.

(Lasswell & McKenna, 1972). Indeed, notwithstanding fulmination about the evils of illegal gambling and organized crime in New York, where Tom Dewey and Frank Hogan made national reputations as the most prominent rackets prosecutors from 1930 to 1970, the state only created felony gambling statutes in 1963. Until then no person could receive more than a 12-month jail sentence for any gambling offense.

Comparable enforcement data are not available for other cities in that era, but some national figures point to the lack of stringency in enforcement. Arrests were quite numerous for a while, reaching 115,000 in 1962 for approximately half of the nation for which data were available (approximately 61 arrests per 100,000 population over the age of 18 in the jurisdictions covered) but fell rapidly. By 1975 only 50,000 arrests were recorded, and in 1994 the figure had fallen still more to 14,500. No national prosecution figures are available.[5]

Federal enforcement showed the same pattern, with few arrests generating significant prison terms. To raise funds for the Korean War, Congress imposed a 10 percent excise tax on all wagers and a $50 occupational tax on anyone employed in taking bets. Illegal book-makers were expected to pay taxes on their gross wagers, and the reputation of the FBI was sufficiently intimidating that some bookies are thought to have ceased operation for a while. However, even though the tax was set at a punitive level and well-publicized raids were made by the Internal Revenue Service, it failed to curtail either notorious casino towns (e.g., Covington, Kentucky, and Hot Springs, Arkansas) or the continued operation of bookmakers in major cities through-out the nation (Carlisle, 1976). Even after the Supreme Court ruled that IRS filings under the Tax Act could not be used for criminal investigation and prosecution, thus removing an important legal defense (namely a claim that filing taxes violated the Fifth Amendment right against self-incrimination), payments under the Gaming Tax Act were negligible (Duncan, 1976).

In the 1960s the McClellan Committee[6] held hearings, with star witness Joe Valachi providing dramatic testimony on the power and

---

5. Indicative of how minor the penalties are for gambling, we were unable to find any data on gambling offenders in state prisons.
6. The name universally given to the Permanent Subcommittee of Investigation of the Senate Government Operations Committee chaired by Senator John McClellan (D, Arkansas) from 1956 to 1976.

ruthlessness of the Mafia; again the hearings showed the centrality of gambling and related corruption. These hearings, together with the report of the President's Crime Commission of 1967, led to passage of the Organized Crime Control Act of 1970. Predicated on the continuing corruption of local law enforcement by organized crime in its gambling activities, this Act enormously increased federal criminal jurisdiction and for the first time gave the Department of Justice the authority to make wiretaps (Reuter, 1983). The vast majority of those wiretaps in the first four years targeted gambling activities – 72 percent out of 957. But federal courts proved indifferent; senior Mafiosi convicted of running bookmaking or lottery operations received short or suspended sentences. By 1978 gambling accounted for only 7 percent of federal wiretaps, though still 42 percent of all wiretaps nationally (Reuter & Rubinstein, 1982, p. 140). The federal organized crime task forces, set up along with the Organized Crime Control Act as elite units independent of the more political U.S. Attorneys' offices, after focusing on gambling cases in their first five years, moved on to other matters, before disappearing entirely in 1989.

In summary, gambling enforcement in the late twentieth century became a largely symbolic activity. It generated headlines, mostly about corruption, but there was discernibly little faith that it accomplished much by way of crime control. Moreover, the underlying assumption, that the activity itself needed to be criminalized, simply dissipated as a wealthier society sought more modes of exercising its freedom.

The current regime

The major forms of gambling are now readily available in legal forms, with the important exception of wagering on sports events. State lotteries, with a growing array of products including all those offered by the old illegal numbers game, are available in 37 states. Casinos, restricted to Nevada until 1978, are becoming increasingly accessible, partly through the unexpected backdoor of the Indian Gaming Regulatory Act. Off-track betting is now spreading throughout the country, allowing bettors to wager on horse races nationally, exactly the service offered by the classic bookmaker depicted in the film *The Sting*. Sports wagering is unavailable except in Nevada casinos.

Legal wagering has grown dramatically in dollar volume; gross revenues (after paying off winners) rose from $10 billion in 1982 to $40 billion in 1994.[7] Much of that was the result of additional forms of gambling becoming newly legal in various states. Casinos were the largest single generator of gambling revenues ($15 billion), and there is a consensus that this sector will grow rapidly. Lotteries generated almost as much and also have been growing rapidly; pari-mutuel wagering, mostly on horse racing, provides a rapidly declining share of the total.

The first wave of new state lotteries in the period 1967–76 was driven largely by fiscal concerns (Clotfelter & Cook, 1989). Certainly the basis for selling these lotteries to the populace in the required referendum was that the lottery would provide a large source of government revenues that did not constitute taxes because they were voluntarily paid. Competition with illegal operators was very much a secondary argument, though it certainly was mentioned. New Hampshire, the first state to create a lottery in the modern era, was hardly a state in which illegal operators constituted a major threat to the state. As a low-tax state, New Hampshire eagerly embraced the lottery because most of the revenues would come from out-of-state visitors. A second wave of lotteries in the early 1980s was also intended to help states struggling with a weak economy and cutbacks in federal grants.

The states have aggressively promoted their own lotteries, offering a growing range of products, ranging from the relatively passive classic lottery, in which the buyer does not even pick the number of his ticket and gets the result of his bet days later, to the game of keno, which gives very rapid feedback and incentives for continued betting. For example, Maryland runs keno games every five minutes, the bettor can wager between $1 and $20 and win prizes up to $100,000. As a result of this creation and promotion of new products, lottery revenue now constitutes the third largest source of revenues for the states, providing a total of $10 billion, about 3 percent of total state revenues in 1994.

Many observers have expressed uneasiness over the states' direct involvement in this activity. The states are not just passively providing a service desired by its citizens, which would otherwise be provided

7. Data on gambling volume is taken from Ernst and Young, *Compilation of Gaming Data.*

illicitly. They are directly stimulating demand to generate revenues from the high tax rate on lottery play. However, the justification for that high tax is the belief that gambling is an activity of questionable worth (Galston & Wasserman, 1996); these are hard to reconcile when the state creates new players.

State lottery promotions have been highly stimulative. A New York state lottery ad proclaimed, "We won't stop until everyone's a millionaire." California does not lag in this respect: "Everybody gets lucky sooner or later, so don't take any chances." Some states are starting to impose restrictions on their own ad agencies. For example, the Massachusetts legislature cut the state lottery's budget from $12 million to $400,000, and Minnesota has directed the lottery not to run ads that stress the lottery as a means for solving personal financial problems. There have been references to politicians' "qualms about brazen promise of easy money" (Sterngold, 1996).

The decision to have the state operate the lottery directly, rather than franchise private operators, reflects beliefs about the corruptibility of private operation and the ability of the state to maximize revenues by direct operation. This may be naïve (government operations tend not to be entrepreneurially efficient, and corruption can be internal as well as in the contracting process), but the shadow of the Louisiana Lottery is still present. State operation makes the promotional activities even more troubling.

The current casino wave, which started with the passage of the federal Indian Gaming Regulation Act in 1988 and Iowa's authorization of riverboat gambling in 1989, is also driven by economic forces, this time in the form of economic development (Goodman, 1995). For example, in Maryland the casino industry argued that the state could create an industry with 20,000 new jobs, possibly generating a total employment gain of 60,000; the added taxes on wagering itself were fairly incidental in that analysis (Joint Executive-Legislative Task Force, 1995). The opposition takes two forms: one is principally moral (casinos generate crime and human misery), whereas the other is economic (casino jobs come at the cost of other local employment).

States have not operated the casinos but have always franchised private operators, subject to moderately heavy taxes (ranging from 6 to 20 percent of gross revenues) and to quite stringent regulation, particularly aimed at the fiscal probity of the firm and employees. In

Nevada, organized crime played a major role in the creation of the industry; when it was a pariah activity, as it was nationally until the late 1960s, only pariahs could invest without loss of reputation (Skolnick, 1978). In the last two decades, there has been little credible evidence of continued organized crime involvement as major hotel and entertainment corporations have built large casino operations. Even in New Jersey, with its rich history of organized crime activity, there have been few accusations, and none proven, of major casino corruption, beyond that routine to state-regulated industries. That record is particularly remarkable given the location of the industry in Atlantic City, many of whose modern mayors have been either convicted of bribery or have left office under a legal cloud.

States have not attempted to restrict casino advertising and promotion systematically, though federal law does prevent the casinos from advertising their gambling, as opposed to recreational activities, in non-casino states. This promotion contrasts vividly with casinos in Europe, which are frequently not permitted to place any promotional sign on their building; a typical French casino is a bland building with a discreet sign saying "Casino." British regulations do not allow the distribution of liquor to patrons at gaming tables or the extension of credit by the casino operator; however, both are regarded as critical to the successful operation of American casinos. Such restrictions are probably not even legally permissible in the United States in the context of the Supreme Court's broad interpretation of freedom of speech and increasingly stringent requirement that the state show a compelling interest in its regulation of economic behavior.

A few states (e.g., Texas and Virginia) have introduced race tracks as a new wagering outlet but the principal means by which horse betting has become accessible to more people has been through the spread of off-track betting parlors, which allow bettors in any location to place wagers on tracks in many states. Off-track betting has been viewed for the last decade purely in terms of the interests of the racing industry. Do the gains from having more bettors off site outweigh the loss of track attendance? Illegal bookmakers have become essentially irrelevant, since bookmakers are now principally dependent on sport wagering.

The continued prohibition of sports wagering is obviously an interesting counterpoint to the changes that have occurred elsewhere. It is no longer sustained by puritanical attitudes toward gambling generally but rather by narrower concerns about the threat it would pose to the integrity of games that are close to holy rites in contemporary American life. Congress, usually loath to intervene in matters concerning gambling, did pass a law that essentially prevented states from allowing betting on sports events if they had not done so by a specified date. Only Nevada and Oregon[8] at present are permitted to license such gambling.

Assessing the current regime

What have been the consequences of legalizing the major forms of wagering? Given the dearth of research, most of the following assertions are merely plausible conjectures, but they are probably uncontroversial. The volume of gambling (combining both legal and illegal) has increased, perhaps very substantially. State governments have been able to avoid politically painful increases in more visible taxes and charges. Systemic police corruption has diminished substantially. More speculatively, the prevalence (if not average severity) of problem gambling has increased, and the moral authority of the state has been eroded by its promotion of lottery gambling.

No study has estimated the impact of the introduction of lotteries, casinos, or off-track betting on the fraction of the population that engages in gambling or the amount that is spent, simply because there are no state-level studies of pre-lottery/casino betting levels. The 1975 national survey (Kallick et al., 1979) found higher rates in those few states that had established lotteries then, but this is a thin reed, given that the early lottery states were also the states in which the illegal numbers game had been most prominent, such as Illinois, Massachusetts, and New York. More recent studies (e.g., Volberg, 1994) attempted to estimate whether legalized gambling has increased the extent of problem gambling and reported high figures (e.g., for Iowa, Volberg estimated that lifetime problem gambling rose from 1.7 percent in 1989 to 5.4 percent in 1995, following the introduction of riverboat casinos and the expansion of other gambling opportunities). However, the methodological weaknesses of these

---

8. The Oregon exception arose from the fact that its state lottery used the results of a large number of sports events for the purpose of generating a winning number.

studies make them suspect.[9] The 1998 national study found no signficant effect of casino availability on the prevalence of pathological and problem gambling, but its small sample size constituted a weak test.

Nonetheless, it seems very likely, given the massive expansion of the last ten years in recorded legal gambling expenditures, that indeed legalization has greatly increased betting by the U.S. population. One indicator, albeit a weak one, is that 400 new chapters of Gamblers Anonymous enrollments were formed between 1990 and 1995 (Reno, 1996). Interestingly, a form of betting commonly reported by those with serious gambling problems is the one that is still not generally legal, namely sports wagering.[10] That may be the consequence of removing the stigma attached to gambling in general that follows from allowing state lotteries, casinos, and the like. Certainly the casinos believe that their own respectability has been enhanced by state promotion of lotteries.

A standard critique of state lotteries is that they impose sharply regressive taxes on the poor. The state keeps approximately 35 percent of total wagers, after paying out 55 percent in winnings and 10 percent for expenses (including promotion); that amounts to a 35 percent tax on the initial payment, higher than any other sales tax except that on cigarettes.[11] Clotfelter et al. (1999) find that households with less than $10,000 in annual income spend as many dollars as those with incomes up to $50,000, after which the figure drops substantially. Households with less than $10,000 in income on average wager $520 per annum. Though the expected return is about 55% of wagers, the payments are so skewed that most households lose almost the entire amount. Thus lottery expenditures for poor households may average about 5 percent. For households with incomes between $50,000 and

9. Lester (1994) reported a modest correlation between the number of gambling outlets in a state and the number of chapters per capita of Gambling Anonymous. Since chapters of Gamblers Anonymous vary in size and state outlets are a weak measure of the accessibility of legal gambling, this is not a particularly persuasive finding.
10. About one-third of those who in 1995 called a national hotline to assist problem gamblers reported that they were involved with sports gambling. Casino gambling was the most frequently mentioned form (60 percent of callers) (Council on Compulsive Gambling, 1996).
11. It can be argued that the tax rate is actually 350 percent since the price of a lottery ticket (in terms of expected loss) would otherwise be only 10 cents, compared to the actual 45 cents.

$100,000 the comparable figure is less than 0.5%.[12] Ten percent of those spending more than $1,619 per annum (the top 20 percent of players) were from households with incomes less than $10,000, but adults in such households constituted only 5% of the adult population.

Such regressive taxation may be bad public policy, but in assessing the current regime a central issue is how the burden compares with that under a prohibition, when operators, like the government now, retained approximately 45 percent of winnings (Reuter, 1983). That portion went to payment of bribes to police and for compensating commission agents for taking various kinds of risks, from honest enforcement and from competitors. Even in our current antigovern-ment era, it is presumably less harmful to enrich government than criminal organizations. Moreover, though there is little relevant data, play in the illegal numbers game probably was even more concen-trated among lower income groups, the more affluent being more sensitive about legal stigma.

Conclusion

The legalization of gambling has indeed brought great gains, even if one does not include the pleasures that many derive from the ability to indulge in fantasies of sudden wealth. Moneys that previously went to criminals and corruption have been diverted to public coffers. But two consequences are less attractive and highly relevant to the debate about drug legalization.

First, state governments have become greedy boosters of a be-havior that clearly causes problems. Stimulating the demand for lotteries, particularly for games like keno that allow rapid repeat play, poses a real danger of triggering obsessive gambling. The sharp regressivity of lottery taxes (concealed as operating profit to the state) makes this only more questionable. Though states generally seem to have maintained strict and effective control over casino oper-ations, the power of the industry in New Jersey has started to erode some of those controls. Occasional scandals have occurred in Louisiana (Sack, 1995), a state with a rich history of such corruption problems. Regulation of horse racing has been another source of

12. These calculations assume that the average income for households with less than $10,000 is $7,500 and that small prizes account for about 10 percent of total payments.

state-level corruption because of the highly discretionary character of the regulatory regime, though scandals have been rare since the conviction of Maryland Governor Marvin Mandel in the late 1970s (later overturned on a technicality).

Second, operators of bookmaking establishments have probably benefited from this expansion, and this has been treated as a matter of indifference. Recent testimony from a major figure in the Chicago bookmaking business includes a claim that each expansion of legal gambling had helped his operations (Jahoda, 1995). Gambling is legitimized and the stigma of betting with bookmakers rather than legal operations seems to be declining.

There is little harking back to the earlier era. That is not to say that we are, as a society, better off with the current regime. But there is an air of historic inevitability to this regime; gambling is obviously a harmless indulgence for most of us and the intrusion of the state into private lives represented by the prior prohibition seems pointless and unwarranted. What is less obvious are the costs generated, the reverse of our drug policies in which the costs are more conspicuous than the gains. The moral debasement of state government is a phenomenon that only a few academics and preachers bemoan; in an era whose Calvin Klein advertisements border on child pornography, state lottery advertisements scarcely stand out. The regressivity of taxes and the expansion of problem gambling, perhaps with more white collar crime, are not matters that attract attention. The social costs of the current regime are quite concentrated but among a group that is not likely to be able to create politically potent organizations.

PROSTITUTION

Drug taking and sexual activities with prostitutes have more striking differences than similarities. Dependency and loss of control, the frightening characteristics of drug taking, are not central to society's concern with prostitution, surely to be found more in the exploitation of women, the erosion of trust in spousal relations, the transmission of disease, and the debasement of sexual relations. Prostitution is included here primarily because it offers the best instance of a very large illegal market subject to minimal enforcement, one of the alternatives to current drug policy within the prohibitionist framework. How well does this approach control the harms associated with prostitution? Secondarily, it is worth examining why there has been so little movement with respect to its legalization, as has been the case for drugs other than alcohol and cigarettes; this stasis is particularly surprising in light of the well-documented existence of reasonably compelling European models of legalization.

Characterizing the prostitution problem

The discussion is limited to female prostitutes serving male clients, probably still the principal form, though there is more awareness now of male prostitution than was the case twenty years ago. Prostitution involving juveniles is discussed only occasionally as it presents quite a distinct social problem.

The harms of prostitution include the exploitation of women, their clients, and their employers; perhaps the spread of sexually transmitted diseases (STDs);[13] criminal victimization of customers by prostitutes and vice versa; the corruption of police; unsightly solicitation of customers; the debasement of sexual relations; and the generation of criminal incomes. Some are inherent in the act of commercial sex; many could at least be ameliorated by legalization and regulation.

Data on the extent of prostitution is slight. Decker (1979, p. 94) estimated, on the slender basis of a survey in a single city, that in 1976 there were about 340 million acts of prostitution nationally. This number is perhaps one-third to one-quarter the number of purchases of cocaine annually.[14] Simon and Witte (1982) estimated 80,000 to 500,000 Full-Time Equivalents (FTEs) in the industry, a fanciful measure that they resorted to because there were no data on the extent to which women worked full-time as opposed to part-time.

13. Recent research consistently finds that prostitutes account for a small share of STDs. For example, in the tests conducted on prostitutes in Colorado Springs, CO, from 1987 to 1991, only 4.4 percent were found to be HIV positive (and most of these women shot-up as well); in 1991, 4.7 percent had *N. gonorrhoeae* and 7.4 percent had *C. trachomatis* (Woodhouse et al., 1992). Big cities with higher rates of female crack use may show higher rates for prostitution-related STDs.
14. It is estimated that 300 tons of cocaine are consumed annually. If purchases are made in 200 pure milligram units, 1.5 billion purchases are generated. However, a substantial fraction of the purchases are made in larger units.

Vorenberg and Vorenberg (1977) claimed that about 500,000 women worked as prostitutes at least occasionally in the course of a year. There are hints that quite significant numbers of women engage in prostitution part-time for a few years and otherwise lead lives that would be deemed "respectable." For example, the National Task Force on Prostitution, an advocacy group, asserts that "over 1 million people in the U.S. have worked as prostitutes" (Prostitution Education Network, 1998).

History and regulation

The regulation and abolition of prostitution were major issues for social reformers in America at the turn of this century. In the years preceding the Progressive Era (1900–30), most local governments did not single out prostitutes as a distinct class of deviants; that process occurred later (Hobson, 1987). As with drinkers, gamblers, and poverty-stricken individuals, city officials wanted simply "to keep [the prostitution] trade beyond the view of respectable folk" (Hobson, 1987, p. 26).

Interestingly, the religious reformers that sprang up in the early- and mid-1800s viewed prostitution as more than an immoral activity. Hobson (1987) suggested that they viewed it as an economic problem because it gave sons a reason to squander the fortunes of their fathers or defraud their employers and creditors. Most locales before the Progressive Era maintained the prohibition on prostitution, but this was not a uniform policy. San Francisco, then as now a leader in liberal vice policy, created zones of tolerance for prostitutes and attempted to integrate the prostitutes into civil society.

Prostitution is, for both social and economic reasons, principally an urban phenomenon; social control is tighter in rural and village settings, and a single prostitute is likely to require a substantial number of clients for adequate support. Thus, the massive growth of cities in the last half of the nineteenth and early twentieth centuries led to an apparent growth in the activity. Greater visibility drove city governments to take action in the early 1900s; in some large cities, this took the form of the creation of vice commissions. The Chicago Vice Commission stated in its 1911 report that "Continual and persistent repression of prostitution the immediate method; absolute annihilation the ultimate ideal." The commission also found that this was the general approach of the "morals" laws of other states as well (Hall, 1979). The legalization of prostitution was not even an option for most Americans in the Progressive Era.

The lack of discussion about prostitution policy options (other than criminalization) can be attributed to an early study by The New York Committee of Fifteen. This committee, created by the Chamber of Commerce to study prostitution, was the first expression of concern over the activity in the Progressive Era (Connelly, 1980). The committee's 1902 study, *The Social Evil: With Special Reference to Conditions Existing in New York City*, evaluated other prostitution policies, primarily those of the European states. Connelly (1980) reported that "the committee admitted that regulation and medical inspection was the preferred European policy but argued that it had not worked" (p. 13). It recommended continued enforcement of the existing criminal laws, only with harsher and better advertised punishments.

The increased publicity led to additional laws to discourage prostitution: tenement house laws, judicial reforms, public health ordinances, and revisions of the national immigration statutes in 1903, 1907, and 1910. These changes had little effect, and Connelly (1980, p. 25) quoted a New York attorney as saying that New York's prostitution laws were "ill considered, scattered, inconsistent, and chaotic."

Nonetheless, by the end of the Progressive Era, government officials and reformers were claiming victory in the "war on brothels." Consistently arguing that their efforts were responsible, reformers forgot about the "other contemporary and cultural changes – the advent of the automobile, the increased availability of telephone service, shifting neighborhood patterns, the proliferation of apartment buildings, and, most important, changing moral standards" – that decreased demand for centrally located brothels (Connelly, 1980, p. 26). Citizens in the 1920s were elated that most brothels were no longer visible and perhaps did not care if prostitution was occurring somewhere else. This was the beginning of America's de facto tolerance for the activity.

Red light districts were an accepted part of American cities until the First World War when the association of brothels with venereal disease, a major hazard to the armed services, led to a general effort to close them down (Milman, 1980). They were replaced by areas of highly concentrated street prostitution and probably some smaller brothels. Interestingly, brothels, subject to a great deal of official control, remained a visible part of the environs around major military establishments in U.S. cities, such as Norfolk, Virginia. Military police worked with local authorities to ensure that the women were subject to regular health checks to reduce the risk of sexually transmitted diseases.

Organized crime involvement in prostitution was a major issue in the first half of this century. The connection with organized crime arose from the police corruption that was endemic in that period, around all illegal markets. For example, Lucky Luciano, a leading figure in the New York Mafia from 1930 to 1950, was successfully prosecuted for operation of a brothel by Thomas Dewey, when Dewey was a crusading District Attorney for Manhattan. In recent decades though, there has been little concern with this; brothel operators retain their evil reputation but seem not to be involved in any other substantial criminal activities. The generally successful campaign against the Mafia in the last two decades has included little allegation of involvement in prostitution.

Prostitution among juveniles is often the source of public concern, fueled by publication of sensational estimates; for example, Katyal (1993, p. 794) cited Congressional hearings for the source of the statement that "[o]f an estimated 1.5 million children who flee their homes each year or are homeless, fifty percent engage in prostitution." These figures, baseless claims by problem-mongers, are particularly important because they identify a part of the prostitution problem that is not amenable to reform; no one proposes that prostitution be legal for women under the age of 18.

Nevada legalized brothels in 1971 on a local option basis in all counties with populations of less than 200,000, thus excluding the only two large cities (Las Vegas and Reno). Possibly this was an effort to ensure that the less-developed counties had their own tourist base. The brothels are subject to local regulation, which includes tight restrictions on advertising and regular health checks. In some counties, there are also restrictions on the mobility of the women; for example, "[t]he town of Winnemucca does not allow prostitutes to have friends within the town, including pimps, boyfriends or husbands" (Vorenberg & Vorenberg, 1977, p. 30).

The law in most states has a clear hierarchy of acts: promotion or pimping (primarily a male activity) draws the heaviest statutory penalties; prostitution itself is criminalized, though typically only as a misdemeanor; the purchase of services by the customer is frequently not itself explicitly a criminal offense, though liberal interpretation of the "promotion" section can lead to inclusion of purchase of services.

Arrests for prostitution remain numerous; Pearl (1987) examined sixteen of the nation's largest cities and estimated that prostitution arrests equaled the number of arrests for violent offenses. Nationally the numbers showed rapid increase from 1963 (26,000) to 1980 (85,000) before plateauing in the late 1980s; recent figures have been around 100,000 annually (FBI, annual). It is peculiarly a big city enforcement activity; the arrest rate per capita for the fifty-four largest cities was reported to be twenty-three times that for cities with population between 25,000 and 50,000 (Flanigan & Maguire, 1984, Table 4.2).

Few of these arrests generate incarceration; Pearl (1987) reported that 11 percent of prostitution convictions produced sentences of incarceration (compared to approximately 70 percent for felony drug offenses). The average time in jail was estimated in the mid-1980s to be about 54 days; taking account of these figures, the expected jail time per prostitution arrest was between 1 and 2 days. Pearl (1987, p. 785) also reports that in San Francisco the public defender estimated that prostitution accounted for 10 to 20 percent of his caseload. Christopher Archer, a Washington, DC, police officer working on the prostitution squad, reported that when he checked the recent court experiences of five well-known prostitutes, he found that none received anything more severe than a suspended sentence, even though they had between five and sixteen prior convictions (Archer, 1995).

Control of prostitution causes considerable difficulty to the police in many U.S. cities. Often arrests can only be made under circumstances that put the police in awkward positions; for example, in New York the prostitute must make an explicit offer to perform a sexual act before an arrest can be made. If the prostitute requires the customer to undress first before any such discussion takes place, as is apparently the usual requirement in massage parlors, the officer is exposed (in multiple senses) to an embarrassing situation. Efforts to pursue customers by having female officers pose as prostitutes are also not well regarded and can create physical hazards for the officer.

The "pussy squad" as the specialized prostitution units are universally and vulgarly known, are among the least well regarded of specialized assignments.

Pearl (1987) cited a number of studies of the criminal justice system which found courts to regard prostitution as a very minor offense; for example, she cited a New York judge as saying, "Most judges do not feel [the prostitute's] crime merits jail – not when they are constantly faced with more serious crimes like robbery and murder" (p. 788, fn 113). The low seriousness assigned to prostitution in the criminal justice system is consistent with popular views. A Justice Department survey of crime seriousness in 1985 (Bureau of Justice Statistics, 1985) listed 204 different offenses; prostitution was ranked 174th in seriousness, immediately followed by "a store owner knowingly puts 'large' eggs into containers marked 'extra large.'" Wolfgang et al. (1985), in their survey of perceived seriousness of offenses, reported a score of 1.4 for "a person smokes marijuana," 1.6 for "a person is a customer in a house of prostitution," and 2.1 for "a woman engages in prostitution." In contrast the score is 4.5 for "a person cheats on his federal income tax return."[15]

The primary goal of enforcement against prostitutes seems to be control of harms to others, in particular the visibility of street solicitation.[16] Efforts at reform without new legislation (e.g., the creation of the Combat Zone in Boston, an area in which the police explicitly tolerated various sex-related businesses) are aimed at controlling the location of visible soliciting. Call girls (i.e., prostitutes who solicit business by phone either through a network of contacts, such as bartenders, or through advertisements in adult magazines) are apparently at very slight risk of arrest, though Weitzer (1997) reported that some police departments maintain units that specialize in controlling such activities. The much greater attention to street prostitutes can be given numerous interpretations, some more benign than others. It may be taken to represent class bias on the part of the police (since

15. Curiously, similar studies by Rossi et al. (1974) and Howe and Brandau (1988) didn't even include seeing a prostitute among the crimes they studied.
16. In Britain the famous Wolfenden Committee Report provides a good articulation of this, though it appears not to have had any particular impact on U.S. policing policies. The report asserted that the law should only be concerned with "the manner in which the activities of prostitutes and those associated with them offend against public order and decency, expose the ordinary citizen to what is offensive and injurious, or involve the exploitation of others."

call girl clients are likely to be more affluent than those of streetwalkers). Alternatively, it can be interpreted as an appropriate focus on the segment of the trade that causes most community concern.[17] Massage parlors are sometimes targets for enforcement, in part because they may generate a great deal of undesirable traffic in their neighborhoods. Whether there is racial bias, intended or not, in enforcement is not a topic that seems to have generated discussion; that bias may come either in the choice of whom to arrest or in the choice of neighborhoods in which to allow the markets to settle.

Reform models

Models of effective prostitution reform are available in Europe and have been prominently discussed in the United States ever since Flexner (1914) published the first major public health study of prostitution early in this century. The regulation of prostitution in West Germany is distinctive in a number of ways:

- Prostitution may not be banned in cities with more than 20,000 population.
- Pimping and procuring are illegal.
- Prostitution is not allowed in schools, churches, cemeteries, or houses where people are under eighteen years of age.
- Prostitutes must be eighteen years of age and must be citizens of West Germany
- Boys between fourteen and eighteen may purchase services only with parental permission.
- Each of the states is responsible for public health control, including venereal disease (VD) checks.
- Income from prostitution is subject to income tax, but prostitutes are not eligible for unemployment compensation, social security benefits, or national health insurance.

Yondorf (1979) found that in large part the West German system worked as designed and that there was little public concern about prostitution.

---

17. Weitzer (1997) reported a Canadian survey that found that "while only 11 percent of the population found street prostitution acceptable, a higher number accepted brothels (38 percent), escort and call girl services (43 percent), and prostitution on private premises (45 percent)" (p. 15).

Many European cities, notably Amsterdam, Copenhagen, and Hamburg are well known for the open availability of legal prostitution, as described in a generally admiring scholarly literature (e.g., Vorenberg & Vorenberg, 1977; Rio, 1991). The women are less likely to be victimized, soliciting is less troubling, police are relieved of a burdensome and awkward responsibility, and sexually transmitted diseases are better controlled. No one claims that these models are perfect, but few identify any disadvantages (other than the basic morality of not prohibiting the activity) compared to the current U.S. system of discretionary enforcement of criminal prohibitions. But there are no studies of prevalence to test whether legal availability increases the extent of prostitution among women or the use of prostitutes by men.

Anglo-Saxon countries other than the United States, with similar traditions of highly prohibitive regimes, have recently reformed their prostitution laws. For example, the Australian state of Victoria in 1986 repealed criminal laws against prostitution by adult women and gave local governments control over the location of brothels; operators and managers of brothels were to be licensed (Neave, 1988). Canada also removed the criminal sanction against prostitution in 1985, though it also strengthened a series of related criminal prohibitions against communications related to prostitution or living off income from others' prostitution (Freeman, 1989–90).

Attitudes and politics

The shame attached to patronizing a prostitute is about equivalent to that associated with the use of marijuana, if the seriousness ratings mentioned earlier are the correct measure. But use of a prostitute is, outside of group settings such as the military or college fraternities, taken as evidence of failure as a man or poor taste, at least in this nation and this era. This was not true in Western Europe in the nineteenth century, though perhaps a distinction between a paid mistress and a shared prostitute, even if a beautiful and well-paid one, was important. Proust, in *Swann's Way*, presents Odette as just such an ambiguous figure who moved, with some shadows over her, in fashionable circles in Paris in the late nineteenth century.

Prostitution is now simply an accepted part of the urban fabric of the United States. A concern about transmission of HIV via prostitutes to the general heterosexual population has subsided. Many liberals believe that the continued criminalization of prostitution serves to exploit women and to create unnecessary criminal incomes, but the issue is not sufficiently weighty for it to be high on the agenda of any major reform organization. COYOTE (Cast Off Your Old Tired Ethics), an organization of prostitutes pressing for reform, has faded from its 1970s prominence.

Surveys show mixed support for prostitution reform. Weitzer (1991) reported results from a number of local or state surveys, generally showing declining support. For example, the Field survey, a leading California poll, asked whether "[I]t is a good idea or bad idea to legalize prostitution to provide more tax revenues and help control the disease and crime that now result from uncontrolled prostitution." In 1971, 50 percent thought it a good idea and 42 percent, a bad idea; in 1984, the figures were 41 percent and 54 percent, respectively (p. 30). The only national data come from a Gallup poll in 1991 which included the question: "Some people feel that in order to help reduce the spread of AIDS, prostitution should be made legal and regulated by the government. Do you agree or disagree?" Forty percent agreed and 55 percent disagreed (Gallup Organization, 1991, p. 73). A search of op-ed columns in the 1990s yielded only two essays ("A foolish proposal," 1996; Archer, 1995).

One argument is that prostitution must be on the decline as premarital sexual activity, including cohabitation, becomes much more widely accepted. "[F]ewer than 6 percent of American women born before 1911 reported that, before they were nineteen, they engaged in premarital sexual activity. . . . For the 1959–61 birth cohort, by contrast, in the [National Survey of Family Growth] 1982, more than 62 percent of women reported premarital sexual intercourse before age nineteen" (Laumann et al., 1994, p. 324). The figure was still rising in 1991 (Laumann et al., 1994).

Relatively few U.S. males report that they are sexually active outside of marriage (Laumann et al., 1994). With men able to have sexual relations with women of their own class, the demand for prostitution should be much reduced. More directly, Geis (1971; cited in Simon & Witte, 1982) reported a decline over twenty years in the percentage of males whose first sexual experience was with a prostitute, from 23 percent to 7 percent. A recent survey on U.S. sexual practices found only 3 percent of males reporting that their first sexual experience involved payment; for women, the figure was only 0.1 percent; for males aged 55 to 59, the figure was about 7 percent, compared to only 1.5 percent for those aged 18 to 24 (Laumann et al., 1994, pp. 330–1).

That line of argument perhaps misinterprets the role of prostitution in male sexual lives. Some men may relish the lack of commitment, as well as the ability to indulge fantasies and peculiar sexual practices. The clustering of young males in various communities in isolation from females (e.g., military camps, new immigrant communities) also suggests that the demand for prostitution will continue to flourish. Enough women lack good labor force opportunities, or are drug-dependent, that there may well be a substantial supply. Feminists have suggested that the current criminal laws against prostitution are also an essential part of the legal system, which ensures male control over women's sexuality (McKinnon, 1982).

Weitzer (1991) offered two factors to account for the lack of feminist support for prostitutes' rights. The first is simply the contamination resulting from association with deviants; moreover prostitutes are popularly seen less as victims than opportunists, though this view seems to be changing over time. The second is the division in the movement about the appropriate view of prostitution: "A libertarian faction sees it as a valid occupational alternative, which decriminalization would make safer: abolitionists consider it inherently sexist and degrading" (p. 35).

An assessment

In striking contrast to illicit drugs, the prevalence of prostitution is a minimal concern. The number of prostitutes, either nationally or locally, is unmeasured in any systematic way. Use of prostitutes by males is not measured at all and plays no role in the public discussion. The focus is exclusively on a few specific harms and on morality.

Street markets for drugs and for prostitution have some similarities. Both generate undesirable concentrations of people who are likely to be disrespectful of others and who produce unease among nonparticipants. Drug buyers and sellers are likely to include many who are menacing and perhaps intoxicated. The customers of prostitutes are frequently intoxicated and perhaps menacing as a consequence; prostitutes themselves are only ambiguously menacing.

Policing can, in most communities, confine the visibility of prostitution to acceptable levels. It does so at some cost in terms of debasing the police in public esteem, as well as conspicuously diverting resources from other police functions that have more public support. But neither these issues nor the evident continued existence of prostitution have been enough to generate more than modest and episodic calls for legal reform, notwithstanding some fairly effective working models of alternatives. Though there is little systematic evidence on the matter, it appears that the prevalence of prostitution, no matter how measured, is declining or at least not expanding.

Neave (1988, p. 205) suggests that policing and law can make a substantial difference to the way in which the prostitution industry operates:

> [T]here is ample historical evidence demonstrating that changes in prostitution laws determine whether those working as prostitutes seek their clients on the street, in brothels or through escort agencies. . . . [E]nforcement policies reflect social concerns about the visibility, rather than the existence of prostitution but often increase the vulnerability of women working in the business. Women working in brothels can usually get help if a client becomes violent, but women who work for escort agencies visit their client's hotel rooms or homes, where they may risk injury or even death.

The source of active resistance to reform in the United States is hard to identify, precisely because the debate has been so muted. We are inclined to attribute it to the same factors that create such suspicions about harm reduction in drug policy in the United States. Reform, if it means permitting legal operation, condones immoral behavior; regulation indeed involves government complicity. The degrading of government is itself an argument against removing criminal prohibitions, even if reform would reduce the harms from prostitution.

It may also reflect that the act itself has a different moral status from the others considered in this chapter. Purchase of a lottery ticket or a visit to a casino involves no loss of repute to the individual; it is not clear that revelation of betting on sports events with a bookmaker would be very damaging to one's reputation. Even elected officials can openly engage in such activities without risk. It is only excessive involvement that creates problems; the stigma attached to excess also holds true for alcohol. Nevertheless, to be known to patronize a prostitute brings a variety of social stigmas into play: sexual inadequacy, untrustworthiness (if the customer is married), and exploitation of women. That would not be changed if the activity were legal, since it is the act itself rather than the legal status that is the source of the stigma.

Why has the United States been able to sustain a moderate and public health-oriented regime of policing within the prohibition context? Morris and Hawkins (1970) argue that there can be no regulation when there is prohibition; enforcement cannot be refined to the subtle requirements of regulation but must be a blunter instrument. Prostitution seems to offer a counterexample. Perhaps it is the relative lack of concern about the adverse consequences of the act itself to either the individual customer or the community that allows the police a more regulatory function. Prostitution is now seen only as an immoral activity, no longer one constituting a threat to the community; that perception alone may not be enough of a basis to sustain tough and intrusive policing.

8   Other Substances: Alcohol and Cigarettes

Any sustained debate about legalizing drugs eventually includes reference to alcohol, a habit-forming psychoactive substance that causes enormous damage as a result of its behavioral and physiological effects. The failure of Prohibition (a constitutional amendment, no less), as illustrated by the passage of Repeal just 13 years later, is the standard cite in the argument for legalizing the currently illegal substances. The first half of this chapter examines Prohibition and the regimes that have evolved since Repeal.

The debate gives little attention to tobacco, the habit-forming psychoactive substance responsible for the greatest number of deaths, beyond occasional reference to the recent declines in cigarette use through regulation and education without prohibition. Yet a great deal of insight about legal regimes for addictive substances can be obtained from examination of experiences with cigarette regulation and use since the 1964 Surgeon General's Report first made the dangers of smoking a matter of common knowledge.

This chapter makes three substantive points. First, the parallel between Prohibition and current drug policy is compelling, but the lessons are quite obscure, primarily because of differences in the history surrounding use of the two substances. Second, U.S. policy toward alcohol and cigarettes has performed poorly in terms of protecting public health; these substances are now the leading causes of preventable death. Third, the reasons for the failures are not idiosyncratic to those substances but are rooted in characteristics of the American legal and political systems. These matters have to be taken seriously for projecting what legalization regimes are feasible.

ALCOHOL

The experience of the Prohibition era remains deeply etched in the American memory, even 60 years after Repeal. Except among a few revisionist cognoscenti (e.g., Burnham, 1968–9), it is almost universally seen as a great social disaster, and, notwithstanding the many harms attributable to alcohol consumption, there has been no consideration of returning to a prohibition regime. Moore and Gerstein (1981), observed: "It is widely believed that Prohibition was a failure and that it demonstrates once and for all the futility of attempts to legislate morality" (p. 62), though they themselves do not endorse that position. The truth is, of course, more complicated than the folklore. Prohibition may have reduced alcohol-related disease, notably liver cirrhosis, quite sharply and had a moderate effect on drinking. It might still be judged a failure, but the lessons learned about other prohibitions (and other eras) are quite uncertain. This section first examines the sources and nature of Prohibition's failure, assesses its relevance to prohibitions more generally, and then analyzes the operation of the current alcohol control system.

Prohibition

National Prohibition was the culmination of a long series of temperance measures taken at the state level and inspired by a paternalistic concern about the consequences of working class drinking (Aaron & Musto, 1981). It came after a period of modest decline in alcohol consumption.[1] The temperance movement believed that individual rights had to be sacrificed for the common good. A prominent

---

1. The time series on alcohol consumption from 1880 to 1915 shows substantial year-to-year variations, which suggest poor measurement, but no clear trend. The 1915 figure is slightly lower than the average for 1900–10, but we see no basis for others' conclusions that drinking was clearly on the decline before the restrictions put in place because of World War I. It is, however, true that widespread antialcohol sentiment preceded Prohibition – surely a prerequisite for its adoption – and that sentiment rather than Prohibition might deserve credit for any subsequent declines in consumption.

spokesman, later a Repeal advocate, asserted in an influential pre-Prohibition book: "You may exercise your personal liberty only in so far as you do not place additional burdens upon your neighbor, or upon the state" (Stelzle, 1918, p. 84). The saloon, seen as the center of disorder and vice in working class communities, was an important target for prohibitionists, an instance where the exercise of personal liberty would indeed create additional burdens for others by its mere existence.

In retrospect, the optimism about Prohibition's effectiveness as a declarative statement and the lack of concern about enforcement seem breathtakingly naïve given the nation's experiences with other illegal markets, such as those for prostitution and bookmaking, particularly in big cities. Aaron and Musto (1981) summarized the belief of the contemporary Temperance movement: "Once the destruction of the 170,000 saloons had been achieved and the systematic spread of addiction stopped, it was believed that the appetite for drink would wither away without the artificial stimulation of an organized traffic" (p. 159).

Prohibition did not include criminal penalties for the possession (as opposed to purchase) of alcohol, though apparently some courts treated possession as effective evidence of intent to distribute. It was in fact close to what is called decriminalization in the contemporary drug debate. Even home brewing or wine making was legal, provided none of the product was sold. Partly to ensure political support for the movement, agents were also restricted from intruding into private residences to detect drinkers. Indeed, many historians believe that the passage in 1929 of the Jones Act, which massively increased the severity of penalties for first-time offenders (5 years imprisonment and $10,000 fines), provided a major boost to the Repeal movement (see, for example, Clark, 1976).

Nor could agents effectively track diversion of licitly produced alcohol, theoretically intended for use in industrial activities in a denatured form (i.e., after addition of chemicals that made it unfit for human consumption). Unsurprisingly, industrial demand for alcohol increased sharply with the arrival of Prohibition. Initially, physicians were also allowed to prescribe alcohol to patients; that loophole was rapidly closed with a 1921 law that limited prescriptions to one pint every 10 days, hardly enough to slake the thirst of even a moderate drinker.

Enforcement was corrupted from the beginning. Urban corruption, an endemic problem of the early part of this century, seemed to reach its peak during Prohibition; certainly it was never more visible. The federal presence in Prohibition did not help. Kobler (1973) cited a 1921 grand jury report from New York stating that "almost without exception the [Prohibition Bureau] agents are not men of the type of intelligence and character qualified to be charged with this difficult duty and federal law" (p. 247). This no doubt reflected the early decision, pushed by advocates of Prohibition, to exempt the Prohibition Bureau from civil service regulation and ensure that agents would be enthusiastic advocates of enforcement. As a result, appointments to the Bureau became primary patronage. It was estimated that one out of twelve Prohibition Bureau agents was dismissed for misconduct before the Bureau was folded into the Justice Department in 1928.

Moreover, enforcement was never very intense. The states mostly refused to devote any significant effort to the matter; only 18 appropriated money for a prohibition unit, and three appropriated less than $1,000, a derisory amount even then. New York made 7,000 arrests in 1921 and 1922, but this produced only 20 convictions; in 1923 the state-level prohibition was repealed. Appropriations for the federal Prohibition Bureau, which accounted for most enforcement activities, rose from $6.3 million in 1921 to $13.4 million in 1930 (U.S. Department of Treasury, 1930, p. 2: cited in Miron & Zwiebel, 1995, p. 186); if one-third of the adult population drank on an occasional basis, a modest estimate, this amounted to less than $0.30 per drinker. It is true that federal arrests were quite numerous, never less than 42,000 after the first year and reaching 98,000 in Fiscal Year 1933; conviction rates were usually over 80 percent. Yet prior to the passage of the Jones Act, the average prison term was only 35 days, accompanied by a $100 fine. Even after that act, the prison time average never rose above 6 months (Meier, 1994, pp. 142–7). What was striking about Al Capone's 1931 eleven-year sentence for tax evasion (of which he served seven years) was precisely that long prison terms were so rare for the leading bootleggers. They were public figures, much discussed in the press, leading open lives, in sharp contrast to the shadowy existence forced on major drug dealers in the United States in our own era. Those few that did serve long terms were generally convicted not of bootlegging but of violent crimes.

Prohibition also generated horror stories about overly aggressive enforcement and entrapment. Prohibition Bureau agents were indicted for twenty-three civilian deaths by local grand juries (*Chicago Tribune*, November 11, 1928: cited in Meier, 1994, p. 145)[2]; the federal government had all charges moved to federal courts and dismissed there. Credible claims of entrapment were also common, and the courts expanded law enforcement rights, such as double jeopardy (allowing prosecution under both state and federal law) and warrantless searches (Solomon, 1985). The dominance of federal law enforcement, a novel aspect of Prohibition, was also a source of unease.

Though organized crime existed in American cities well before Prohibition, the creation of a national market in bootlegged liquor increased its influence, visibility, violence, and wealth. Prohibition also forged connections among gangs in the various cities that had not existed before; much alcohol was imported, and the importers served many cities. This provided the basis for the growth of the national Mafia as an organization.

Homicide rates rose sharply during the 1920s, and this has frequently been attributed to Prohibition (e.g., Friedman, 1991). Contemporary scholars certainly thought that the two were connected (e.g., Landesco, 1929/1968; see also Sinclair, 1964). Spectacular incidents like the St. Valentine's Massacre of seven bootleggers in Chicago provided vivid evidence, though some scholars have been dismissive of a claim that smells of journalistic exaggeration. There are some anomalies. Homicide rates certainly do decline sharply in 1933, suggesting that it was indeed Repeal rather than the Depression (beginning in 1930) that drove them down, but the decline continues for some years after 1933, which is inconsistent with a one-time event, like Repeal, unless competition and conflict among criminal suppliers networks took several years to dissipate. It is unlikely that the elimination of the bootlegging market explains all the decline, but it was an important influence.

Recent research (Miron & Zwiebel, 1991) affirmed findings of the classic study of Warburton (1932) that reductions in alcohol consumption were moderate during Prohibition (one-third to

2. Meier cites Woodiwiss (1988); our efforts to find the same information in the *Chicago Tribune* have so far been unsuccessful, but that may be nothing more than an error in the cited date.

one-half), notwithstanding roughly a tripling of the retail price of alcohol.[3] Perhaps the major surprise is the size of the price increase, given the low stringency of enforcement; perhaps the high incomes of bootleggers represented primarily compensation for the risks imposed by other participants in the trade, to adapt a framework that Reuter and Kleiman (1986) developed for illegal drug markets. The implied price elasticity of demand for alcohol is very slight indeed, suspiciously so since the largest reductions seem to have been among heavy drinkers; rates for cirrhosis of the liver fell by 50 percent early in Prohibition and recovered promptly after Repeal in 1933. "[T]here can be little doubt that during the few years of Prohibition in Canada, Finland and the USA, all indicators of alcohol consumption and alcohol problems reached the lowest level achieved in any period for which there are relevant data." (Edwards et al., 1994, p. 131).

The price rise may have had most impact on working class drinkers, who were in fact the principal target of the more pragmatic Prohibition advocates. There appears also to have been a substantial shift from beer and wines to distilled liquors; this probably was driven by the fact that beer and wine were bulkier per unit alcohol content, and bulk was the principal source of risk and costs for both bootleggers and speakeasies.

Repeal

Reductions in alcohol-related problems (not well estimated or known at the time) did not seem worth the vast criminal problems created by Prohibition. The Temperance movement had been primarily a moral movement, with public health concerns as a convenient tool;

---

3. A new, unpublished paper by Jeffrey Miron (1997) reports very different results. Miron found that alcohol consumption, along with a measure of the age composition of the population, explained liver cirrhosis rates for the period 1910–93, omitting Prohibition. When he applied the same equation to the cirrhosis figures for 1920–33, he found that the implied reduction in consumption from Prohibition was negligible; indeed, under some specifications, consumption actually was increased by Prohibition. He suggested that the most likely explanation for this is that prices did not rise much during Prohibition but offers only the briefest interpretation of why the standard data (see Thornton, 1991) should not be taken at face value. The conventional account in fact has serious anomalies. Though Miron presented the most sophisticated statistical analysis, his account had its own anomalies. For example, Miron claimed that most of the tripling to quintupling of prices in Irving Fisher's price series resulted from a failure to adjust for inflation; yet inflation was low at the time. For the moment, we stick with the older account.

the obvious moral failure of Prohibition was particularly troubling. Moreover the rate of violations seemed to be increasing as the years wore on; the rising number of convictions for violations of the Volstead Act were not a source of comfort, given the initial faith that the demand for alcohol would decline with the disappearance of the saloon. The increased intrusions by the federal government into private life also disturbed many of the business leaders prominent in the Repeal movement. The very elite Association Against the Prohibition Amendment (AAPA), chaired by Pierre DuPont, was a major force and represented just such concerns. John D. Rockefeller Jr., whose 1932 conversion to the Repeal movement after being a prominent supporter of Prohibition was a major event, saw the problem as growing disrespect for the law, bred by an unreasonably broad restriction on personal behavior.

Prohibition, apparently permanent in the late 1920s even as the prestigious Wickersham Commission provided a sophisticated critique of its operations (National Commission, 1931), collapsed rapidly, almost without resistance, by 1933. The onset of the Depression, which of course generated a crisis of government finance, led to strong economic arguments for reviving a major fiscal base for state and federal governments. Alcohol taxes had accounted for 32 percent of federal revenues in 1913 (Meier, 1994, p. 140); it was credibly estimated that repeal could provide $1 billion to the federal government, whose 1932 revenues totaled only $2.25 billion. Franklin Roosevelt ran on a strong Repeal platform in 1932, though not previously an outspoken foe of Prohibition. Three-quarters of the states had ratified Repeal within eight months of its passage by Congress, even though Congress, concerned with the possibility that rural-dominated state legislatures would block passage, required state referenda be held (Kyvig, 1979). The vote was 15 million for repeal and only 4 million for maintenance of Prohibition.

It is worth contemplating just how extraordinary an accomplishment Repeal represented. Certainly even many of the most fervent Prohibition critics believed prior to 1930 that there was no prospect of meeting the onerous requirements of a constitutional amendment. Thirteen states could block Repeal and the thirteen smallest states, predominantly rural and Protestant, had a population of only 5 million, about 5 percent of the national total. "In light of the widespread view that the Eighteenth Amendment could never be rescinded, opponents of national prohibition in the early 1920s diverted their attention toward the more modest and seemingly more attainable goal of rendering the law less obnoxious in practice" (Kyvig, 1979, p. 54). Efforts, for example, were made to raise the allowable alcohol content from 0.5 percent (specified by Congress but not in the Eighteenth Amendment itself) to allow low-alcohol (2.75 percent) beer.

The speed with which Repeal swept the nation is of great interest because it suggests the possibility that current drug prohibitions might also be frailer than they look, a matter taken up in Chapter 15. However, it is worth noting that there were clear signs of the erosion of popular support for Prohibition by the late 1920s. In 1926, five state referenda approved pro-Repeal measures; by 1930, a national poll found only 40 percent favoring continuation of the existing universal prohibition (with one-third choosing exemption for wine and beer). The Wickersham Commission reported that during its work period, 1929–1930, "adverse public opinion in some states and lukewarm public opinion with strong hostile elements in other states [presented] a serious obstacle to the observance and enforcement of the national prohibition laws" (National Commission, 1931, p. 49). Moreover the temperance organization principally responsible for the passage of Prohibition, the Anti-Saloon League, had fallen apart following its legislative triumph (Kerr, 1985); the resistance to Repeal lacked organization and strong commitment.

Assessment

One plausible view is that alcohol Prohibition failed because it was never seriously attempted. The loopholes in the basic law, the lack of political willingness to close them once it became clear that the law was not self-enforcing, along with a failure to commit resources for enforcement or to respond effectively to the corruption that was generated, all point to what has been characterized as a symbolic crusade (Gusfield, 1963) rather than a public policy reform effort.

Could Prohibition have been made more effective? That it was not enforced seriously does not mean that more aggressive and honest enforcement would have done much beyond somewhat increase the price of beer and push greater numbers to home brew and wine production. It might have galvanized the population against the Volstead

Act earlier, just as the Jones Act helped reignite the Repeal movement. Moreover, more aggressive enforcement by state and local agencies, which surely would have had to bear the principal responsibility if Prohibition were to succeed in that pre-New Deal era, might have generated even more corruption, given their general integrity problems. Zimring and Hawkins (1992) also suggested that the task of interdicting smuggled liquor at the coast and borders was well beyond the capability of the federal government at that time.

The parallels between Prohibition and contemporary drug prohibitions are obvious and strong. The vast illegal markets and the dramatic violence are the most striking. Drug dealers may not have the cachet of Dutch Schultz or Frank Costello, but their enormous financial success is seen also as corroding values in the inner city. Both then and now, there was concern about the growth of federal government criminal justice activities and the increasing intrusiveness of law enforcement generally, as well as the corruption of law enforcement agents faced with remarkably lucrative opportunities. Finally, there is the widespread sense in both instances that the policy is an expensive and morally repellent failure.

Yet it is worth noting also the major differences. Some problems were worse in Prohibition. The corruption associated with drug enforcement in the last decade has been nonsystemic and confined to policing, reflecting changes in political structure (the shift to federal powers) and the increased professionalization of the criminal justice system (Reuter, 1984a). Even allegations against prosecutors are quite rare, and no significant politician has been implicated. This lack of corruption, of course, contrasts sharply with Prohibition, when the Chicago mayoral election was largely manipulated by Capone from his base in neighboring Cicero, and senior managers of police departments in most major cities were in the pay of bootleggers.

On the other hand, Prohibition brought no equivalent to AIDS. Toxic alcohol was occasionally a source of great damage, as in the "Jamaica Ginger" disaster (Morgan, 1982) when 50,000 people suffered paralysis as the result of drinking contaminated alcohol, a devastation far worse than any acute effect caused by strong or contaminated heroin in modern times. But the public health concerns, though present, were less acute than those surrounding contemporary drug use.

The political dynamics were different, too. The level of support for Prohibition was clearly very strong when it was first enacted. The state-level prohibitions that preceded national prohibition were largely enacted through popular vote at referenda rather than by legislative action. Even in 1928, Herbert Hoover won election easily on a strict Prohibitionist platform. However, the experience of Prohibition itself gradually eroded support.

In part, this was because alcohol was not regarded by most of the population as evil in itself. There was too much respectable and indeed honored imbibing throughout Western society for that to be the case. Edith Wharton's characters may be prone to imprudence after wine, but their drinking is not a subject of condemnation, and Shakespeare offers many instances of wine as a balm to the troubled soul.[4] The Prohibition was intended to reduce harms; drunkenness was indeed a major social problem, and perhaps many moderate drinkers were willing to give up their own pleasures to rescue others from their lack of control. But this "reluctant intolerance" (to adapt Kleiman's "grudging tolerance") is not the kind of attitude that encourages stringent punishment of low-level retailers, let alone drinkers. It is also an attitude that might respond to experience.

This contrasts sharply with current attitudes toward the use of cocaine and heroin, which are generally regarded as dangerous and addictive. It is easy to portray any seller of those drugs as a merchant of evil, profiting from the probable misfortunes of others. Marijuana comes closest to 1919 alcohol in terms of public perceptions of harms. It is generally accepted that most who use marijuana suffer and cause little damage as a consequence but that perhaps it causes enough damage that society as a whole needs to be restrained. Only about one-quarter of high school seniors are persuaded that occasional marijuana use is hazardous (Johnston, O'Malley, & Bachman, 1997). It is perhaps unsurprising then that marijuana enforcement has been less consistently stringent. As discussed in Chapter 2, many are arrested for minor marijuana offenses (mostly possession) but probably face very minor penalties as a consequence.

---

4. For example: "Let me play the fool: With mirth and laughter let old wrinkles come, And let my liver rather heat with wine Than my heat cool with mortifying groans" (Gratiano in *The Merchant of Venice*, Act I, Scene 1) or "Come, come, good wine is a good familiar creature if it be well used: exclaim no more against it" (Iago, in *Othello* Act 2, Scene 3).

Apart from the success in raising prices of cocaine, heroin, and marijuana to unimaginable levels, perhaps the principal difference between Prohibition and current drug prohibitions is experiential. The citizenry of 1932 did not have to imagine society with alcohol legally available; they could *remember* it. Whether systematically or not, they could make a comparison between conditions under Prohibition and those that had prevailed before U.S. entry into World War I, when it had been possible to openly purchase drinks. In 1933, they were voting for restoration of what they had previously rejected but which now, after a decade of Prohibition, looked preferable. Arguably, Herbert Hoover's famous phrase about "the noble experiment" was correct; they had tried the experiment and interpreted it as a failure. Though, as we shall see in Chapter 9, the nation has historical experience with legal availability of cocaine, heroin, and other opiates, but it is so distant that no social memory remains. Thus, the argument about legalization of drugs involves exchange of impressions about what would happen, depriving it of the clear focus of the Repeal debate.

Current policy

Though Prohibition and Repeal are a part of the legalization debate, it is useful also to analyze post-Repeal experience with alcohol. This history illustrates the difficulties of creating a sensible regulatory regime for a powerful industry distributing a substance that is highly attractive and addictive for a significant part of the population.

Alcohol is a major public health problem in modern American society. Alcohol consumption accounts for about 100,000 excess deaths annually in the early 1990s (Institute for Health Policy Research of Brandeis University, 1993). For some population groups, it has even more devastating effects. Native Americans are particularly susceptible to alcohol, their rate of alcohol-related deaths is five times that of the population as a whole (U.S. Department of Health and Human Services, 1993). Epidemiological studies in the mid-1980s estimated that in a single year about 7 percent of the population was either alcohol dependent or abusing alcohol (Robins & Regier, 1991). The beneficial effects of moderate drinking have received considerable attention in recent years. There is mounting evidence that one to two drinks per day reduces mortality rates, primarily due to lower cardiovascular disease (e.g., Anderson, 1995). However, there is no claim that these benefits come close to compensating for other alcohol-related costs with present consumption patterns.[5]

Alcohol is also implicated in a majority of homicides and a large share of violent crimes.[6] Alcohol-related offenses, such as driving under the influence (DUI) and drunkenness and related disorderly conduct account for several million arrests each year out of a total of about 12 million arrests for all offenses (FBI, annual). It was estimated that in 1992 alcohol abuse and dependence cost U.S. society $150 billion (Harwood et al., 1998), mostly related to increased morbidity and mortality.

This evidence that alcohol problems are widespread and extremely costly has been insufficient to create any serious interest in the restoration of Prohibition or indeed to create a stringent regulatory apparatus, beyond an increase in the minimum drinking age from 18 to 21 in the late 1970s. For example, alcohol is subject to quite modest taxes. The average tax burden per drink is only 35 cents[7]; revenues from alcohol taxes totaled about $17.5 billion in 1994 (DISCUS, 1996). The Clinton administration's efforts to impose higher federal taxes on alcohol as part of its effort to finance the health care reform package failed in the face of industry resistance. See Krauss (1993).

Moreover, the real value of the tax per unit consumption has declined for most of the postwar period. In 1990 Kenkel (1996) estimated that the average tax rate on alcohol was just over 20 percent, compared to 60 percent in 1950. Yet it is clear that higher alcohol taxes reduce drinking significantly and that the reductions are particularly large for those who drink most heavily (see e.g., Coate & Grossman, 1988). An economic analysis using fairly conservative assumptions about the economic costs of alcohol consumption borne by others found that the 1988 tax levels were only half of what they should have been to cover the external costs of drinking (Manning et al., 1991).

---

5. Eric Single et al. (1996) suggested that alcohol consumption does actually reduce the number of deaths annually but not the number of years of life lost, since alcohol-related deaths occur at a relatively young age.
6. "Alcohol is a key factor in up to 68 percent of manslaughters, 62 percent of assaults, 54 percent of murders/attempted murders, 48 percent of robberies, and 44 percent of burglaries" (U.S. Department of Health and Human Services, 1987).
7. This estimate is adapted from Manning et al.'s (1991) estimate of 23 cents per ounce of alcohol, assuming there are 1.5 ounces of alcohol in the typical shot of distilled spirits.

Restrictions on access and promotion have been mild as well. In some states and counties, there is a government monopoly on the retail sales of alcohol, intended in part to reduce availability, but this covers only 28 percent of the population (DISCUS, 1997) and does not prevent aggressive promotion by brewers and distillers. One study of alcohol control agencies concluded that, for the period 1950–75, "economic considerations overruled preventive concerns" (Mäkelä et al., 1981, p. 84). Efforts to restrict promotion have been subject to effective legal challenge. For example, in 1996 the Supreme Court struck down a Rhode Island statute prohibiting billboard advertising by liquor stores as a violation of the First Amendment.[8] There are voluntary prohibitions on television advertising of distilled liquor, but wine and beer restrictions are quite limited; the actual consumption of alcohol cannot be shown. The alcohol industry spends $1 billion on media advertising annually and perhaps as much again in other promotional activities.[9] The industry is a potent force politically; for example, Seagrams, one of the industry leaders, was rated as number two among soft money donors for the 1995–6 election cycle.[10]

The light regulation found currently is a striking contrast to the systems that were created after Repeal. Fifteen states initially established state monopolies; only nine states allowed retail sale of alcohol without food. In some states patrons could only be served at tables; standing at a bar was believed to encourage overindulgence. Sunday sales were forbidden. The erosion of these restrictions probably owes as much to a declining acceptance of government regulation of personal behavior as to any lobbying activity by the liquor industry's various sectors, but the latter certainly has been aggressive. Unsurprisingly, there have been only modest declines in drinking and related problems. Per capita alcohol consumption has fallen somewhat from 2.04 gallons of pure alcohol per capita in 1975 to 1.68

8. *Liquor Mart Inc. v Rhode Island*, May 13, 1996.
9. "According to LNA Multimedia Report Service (1995), the alcoholic beverage industry spent more than $1 billion in 1994 for traditional media advertising (i.e., broadcast and cable television, radio, magazines, billboards, and newspapers). In addition, *The Economist* ("Smoking 'em out," 1990) estimated that the industry annually spends a roughly equal amount on other forms of promotion, such as store displays, consumer novelties, and sponsorship of cultural and sports events" (Saffer, 1996).
10. Common Cause (1998) estimated that the alcohol beverage industry distributed $8.6 million in PAC and soft money contributions in the 1995–6 election cycle.

gallons in 1995, but it is still well above the levels prior to Pro-hibition.[11] The number of driving fatalities related to intoxication has fallen more sharply,[12] reflecting the efforts of organizations such as Mothers Against Drunk Driving to increase the strictness of enforcement and punishments and to encourage programs such the designated driver and driver education (Ross, 1992). But heavy drink-ing among high school seniors and college students continues at a high level; the percent of seniors reporting consumption of five drinks at a session at least once in the previous week fell from 41.2 in 1980 to 27.5 in 1993 and has risen since then to 30.2 in 1996 (Johnston, O'Malley, & Bachman, 1998). School-based prevention programs have been handicapped by society's ambivalence about alcohol consumption itself. Not only is alcohol heavily advertised, but most children live in households in which adults drink at least occasionally and a "responsible use" message is far more difficult to convey than abstinence (Ellickson, 1998).

The significance of this for the drug legalization debate is taken up in the concluding section of the chapter, since the experience in regulating tobacco is very consistent with that of regulating alcohol in late twentieth-century America.

CIGARETTES

Tobacco use has been prohibited, indeed subject to draconian crim-inal penalties, in other countries and other eras.[13] Even in the United States, fourteen states prohibited tobacco at some stage between 1895 and 1921 (Troyer & Markle, 1983). These prohibitions were based on a concern about smoking by children (allegedly stunting their development) and women (a "cosmopolitan" habit and threat to traditional American values of femininity). The prohibitions and

11. Per capita consumption of distilled spirits fell from 0.79 gallons in 1975 to 0.49 gallons (38 percent) in 1995 (DISCUS, 1996).
12. Between 1985 and 1993 the percentage of automobile fatalities involving a participant with more than 0.10 blood alcohol content fell from 41.2 percent to 35.0 percent. Total fatalities declined over that same time period from 39,195 (18.4 per 100,000 popula-tion) to 35,747 (15.6 per 100,000 population) (National Highway Transportation Safety Administration, annual). The implied decline in fatalities involving high alcohol impair-ment was thus from 7.6 to 5.5 per 100,000 population, a relative decline of 27 percent.
13. An extreme example is the Chinese law of 1638, which provided for decapitation for using or distributing tobacco (Borio, 1998).

associated antismoking movement fell apart after World War I, at least in part because cigarette smoking was associated with soldiers and patriotism (Gusfield, 1993).

There is no longer any consideration of such prohibition in the United States. Even in the mid-1990s, with the antitobacco public health advocates in full cry and the tobacco industry very much on the defensive politically and legally, outright prohibition was never proposed as an alternative. The shadow of Prohibition, as well as a general repulsion against criminalizing the behavior of tens of millions of people who bear the primary costs of their own bad habits, militate against this. For example, Beierer and Rigotti (1992) asserted that "the failure of alcohol prohibition suggests that a ban on tobacco sales would be similarly difficult to enforce" (p. 526). Most analysts dismiss the possibility in even fewer words (e.g., Warner, Slade, & Sweanor, 1997).

Nonetheless, the regulation of tobacco can provide useful insights for the legalization debate. Here is an instance of a substance for which it is agreed that there is no safe dose and whose addictiveness to most users is no longer a matter of scientific disagreement[14] which accounts for a large share of all deaths. There is evidence that it harms others, through exposure to second-hand smoke (Environmental Protection Agency, 1993). Many children receive strong messages in schools about the dangers of smoking and certainly are exposed to numerous billboards and Public Service Announcements denouncing the dangers of smoking. Increasing restrictions have been placed on where and when cigarettes may be consumed, particularly in workplaces and public entertainment facilities (Schelling, 1992). The sale to minors has been prohibited for years, and more efforts are being made to enforce these prohibitions. Very senior officials with high credibility, such as former Surgeon General C. Everett Koop, have inveighed against the behavior.

Nonetheless, the fraction of adolescents who begin smoking has scarcely declined since 1980 (Johnston, Bachman, & O'Malley, 1998) and 25 percent of adults continue to consume cigarettes daily.[15] Monitoring the Future, the annual survey of high school students, reported

14. Addiction experts Jack Henningfield and Neal Benowitz (in Hilts, 1994) each rated it as higher in dependency potential than heroin, cocaine, alcohol, caffeine, or marijuana.
15. The American Heart Association (1998) reported that 25.9 million men and 23.5 million women were current smokers in the United States.

sharp declines in the late 1970s for high school seniors. Daily cigarette use fell from about 29 percent in 1976 to 21.3 percent in 1980. Since then, though there have been substantial year-to-year fluctuations, the trend has been essentially flat, with the 1996 figure at 22.2 percent. Delaying initiation past sixteen might produce major reductions in the prevalence of adult smoking rates, though the probability of going on to regular consumption is less age-related than for other substances. The 1990s have also not seen a continuation of the 1980s gains in cessation by adult smokers.

Much of the explanation for the stasis seems to lie in the difficulty of effectively regulating the tobacco industry itself. It has maintained considerable political power, through skillful engagement in financing political campaigns and creation of broad alliances with other groups. This has ensured the industry's continued ability to promote the drug aggressively so that the antismoking message provided by schools and other institutions are frequently drowned out by the plethora of prosmoking messages delivered by the industry itself. Notwithstanding legal restrictions, minors continue to have ready access to cigarettes. Taxes remain nonpunitive. The stock market predicts continued profitability for these already very wealthy companies, though some of that also represents the continued growth of foreign markets in which American cigarettes retain a particular cachet.

Cigarette consumption and its problems

Perhaps no health behavior has been as well studied as cigarette smoking. The list of diseases associated with cigarette smoke continues to grow; whereas lung cancer was the principal focus initially, smoking is now also implicated in 21 percent of deaths involving chronic heart disease. It also contributes to most involving pulmonary disease. The Surgeon General issues regular reports on smoking and health; these have been a principal means for conveying to the general population that smoking accounts for 400,000 excess deaths annually (CDC, 1993). Indeed, the 1964 Surgeon General's report (U.S. Public Health Service, 1964) was an absolute landmark in changing public attitudes toward smoking.

The drop-off in smoking rates has been much sharper since 1970 for the college-educated than for those who have not completed high school; in the 1996 National Household Survey on Drug Abuse only 18 percent of the former smoked, compared with 34 percent of those without high school education. This has reinforced dramatic changes in attitudes toward smokers and smoking. "By the 1990s, the smoker was not only a foolish victim of his or her habit but also an obnoxious and uncivil source of danger, pollution and illness to others" (Gusfield, 1993, p. 63). There are now substantial population pockets (e.g., college faculty) in which smoking is a highly deviant behavior (e.g., one colleague reported embarrassment when another faculty member paid an unexpected visit to his house and found him smoking a cigar on the verandah).

The declines in smoking rates among adult men in the United States are typical of the Western world. Some nations have seen more rapid declines; for example, the Netherlands rate was about 80 percent in the mid-1960s and had fallen to 33 percent in 1994. Others have seen slower declines; for example, Norway's rate was 60 percent in the mid-1960s and was still above 35 percent in 1994. No Western nation had a rate lower than 23 percent in 1994, though many have adopted much more restrictive policies.[16]

Policy

The principal levers for reducing smoking are education, taxation, restrictions on access and promotion, restrictions on places of use, and treatment and regulation of labeling and contents. Education and use restrictions have been enormously expanded, whereas the others (apart from treatment) have been largely thwarted by the tobacco industry. In the late 1990s, one might add lawsuits as an independent lever for raising price (through large payments to the states) and restricting promotion.

The youth market is crucial because the vast majority of adult daily smokers become daily users by age 20 (89 percent); indeed, a majority begin at or before age 16 (62 percent). Antismoking messages are nonetheless not yet a standard part of elementary and secondary education today because health education is not part of the core curriculum of schools (Lynch & Bonnie, 1994). Many model programs have been shown to be moderately effective in reducing initiation

16. Prevalence rates are from the World Health Organization (1996).

rates among adolescents at least in the short run. For example, one meta-analysis of forty-seven studies of school-based programs found that programs emphasizing social influence lowered smoking rates by 4.5 percent compared to control group rates (Rundall & Bruvold, 1988; cited in Lynch & Bonnie, 1994). Newer experimental programs show even larger effects for at least some subsamples.[17] For example, in a 3-month posttest, Gilbert Botvin's Life Skills Training project reported declines of 56 percent (relative) among African-American urban youth who smoked in the past month (Botvin et al., 1989). There are few long-term evaluations, and these have found that the effects tend to decay substantially after two years, though booster sessions in high school may be able to counter that.[18] In Botvin et al.'s six-year follow-up study on a prevention program with multiple booster sessions, they found that "monthly and weekly cigarette smoking were 15 to 27 percent lower and heavy cigarette smoking was 25 percent lower in intervention subjects. Effects of this magnitude could prevent 60,000 to 100,000 tobacco-related deaths each year" (Botvin et al., 1995, p. 111). Such potential gains follow arithmetically from the figures Botvin presents, but there is little likelihood of achieving such strong results in a mass program.

Programs that involve community institutions to reinforce the school have shown stronger effects that may be more enduring. A component of the Minnesota Heart Health Program, in which an experimental community received more adult smoking-cessation programs, risk-factor screening efforts, and consideration of anti-smoking ordinances, showed a 40 percent reduction in student smoking rates over a 6-year period (Perry et al., 1992). These model programs have been implemented in only a few communities to date; most schools and communities still use much less refined approaches, though not much is known about what programs are in fact adopted.

17. For example, Botvin reported results for schools that implemented his program with "high fidelity" and ascribed all the difference to his programs. Jonathan Caulkins, personal communication, suggested the possibility that the differences may relate to the schools themselves.
18. For example, a social influence program developed in Waterloo, Canada, reported substantial differences at the end of eighth grade, for an intervention that began in sixth grade. But a six-year follow-up found that "[s]ignificant program effects that had been observed earlier . . . had faded into statistical significance by the latter [sic] high school years" (Gerstein & Green, 1993, p. 91).

Taxation of cigarettes in the United States remains moderate by both historical U.S. and contemporary international standards. In late 1993, the average tax per pack of twenty cigarettes (including both federal and state taxes) was 56 cents; this tax rate compared to $3.48 in Denmark (the highest), $2.85 in the United Kingdom, and $2.04 in Germany (cited in Lynch & Bonnie, 1994, p. 184). Taking account of its relative wealth, the U.S. tax rate was remarkably low. Moreover, the inflation-adjusted value of the taxes had fallen in the United States over the prior 40 years; the 1993 figure was only 56 percent of the 1955 tax rate. The inflation-adjusted price of cigarettes rose over the same period but only because the cigarette companies raised their wholesale prices (Tobacco Institute, 1994). Only with the large settlements in 1998 and 1999 between the tobacco companies and the states has the effective tax rate begun to increase markedly.

Tax rates matter because the demand for smoking, particularly initiation rates, is sensitive to prices. Many studies have found that a rise of 10 percent in cigarette prices will reduce demand by about 5 percent (e.g., Lewitt, 1989). For adolescents, most of whom are not yet addicted to nicotine, the estimated price responsiveness is much greater, perhaps 15 percent for a 10 percent increase (Lewitt, 1989). The erosion of tax levels thus has a demonstrably negative effect on health.

Labeling, aimed at ensuring that smokers are constantly reminded of the health risks, has been a major battleground in the past, the size and specificity of the messages being the principal points of contention. From a fuzzy "Warning: Cigarettes may be hazardous to your health," the FTC has moved to a rotating set of four much more declarative messages such as "Smoking causes lung cancer, heart disease, emphysema, and may complicate pregnancy."

Restrictions on where cigarettes can be smoked have become substantially more stringent over the last decade (Lynch & Bonnie, 1994). Many workplaces now have bans on smoking; this is truer of large employers, particularly government, than of small businesses. The Department of Defense, for example, prohibits smoking in any of its facilities worldwide, affecting approximately 3 million employees. Many restaurants, shopping malls, and sports stadiums have restricted smoking.

Cessation programs for smokers are, like those for other addictive behaviors, effective enough to justify their costs but usually involve multiple episodes before success and still do not offer a great deal of promise for cutting smoking rates substantially. Schauffler (1993, p. 200) reported a variety of 1-year quit rates for participants in self-help programs, ranging from 11 to 27 percent. For those who used smoking-cessation clinics, the rates ranged from 20 to 40 percent (MMWR, 1992). Given that relapse rates for substance abuse treatment programs generally rise substantially after twelve months (Anglin & Hser, 1990), these are hardly encouraging results. Indeed, only about 10 percent of smoking quitters used any formal assistance.

Health insurance companies have resisted covering cessation programs, in large part because the reductions in health costs come so much later that the insured will have moved to a different carrier. Moreover, there is a large direct financial incentive for the smoker herself; a group cessation program, costing on average $120, will repay a 1 pack a day smoker within 2 months, if successful. More than half of former smokers report at least three attempts to quit before succeeding (Schelling, 1992, p. 431); few of these attempts involve formal cessation programs.

A vast panoply of criminal laws surround cigarettes (e.g., prohibitions on the sale of cigarettes to minors). These get little attention from the usual authorities for enforcing criminal laws, namely the police. Zimring suggests that this is a consequence of the extent of allowed use: "It is impossible to prohibit what you regulate" (1993, p. 105). This itself is a sensible corollary to Morris and Hawkins' proposition, "It is impossible to regulate what is prohibited" (1977, p. 21), mentioned in the discussion of policing of prostitution. Creating specialized agencies for which this is the central activity, like inspector generals in various federal agencies, is an alternative, but it is fraught with its own problems of corruption and quality such as attracting good-quality personnel for such limited functions.

The federal government has attempted to have the states enforce regulations against sales to underage customers. However, published reports of the frequency of noncompliance detected when agencies do undercover tests suggest that the 500,000 outlets for cigarettes still do not take these obligations seriously. For example, Lynch and Bonnie (1994) cited a Surgeon General's report that reviewed thirteen studies of over-the-counter sales (i.e., not including vending machines); it found that "the weighted average of the percentage of minors able to purchase tobacco was 67%" (p. 202). Neither enforcement nor the penalties are tough enough; almost none involve criminal sanctions, and police agencies give this kind of enforcement low priority (Lynch & Bonnie, 1994, pp. 220–1).[19]

Smoking promotion and politics

American society has thus been active in trying to reduce smoking in many aspects of life, with institutional lethargy as an important barrier. But in accomplishing the goal of smoking reduction, it has had to confront an aggressive opponent.

The tobacco industry has been a power in politics at every level of government. In the 1995–96 national campaign cycle, it contributed $9.9 million, making it the leading industry for such contributions (Common Cause, 1997). It has formed coalitions with other interest groups to defeat particular initiatives. For example, "To defeat proposed legislation restricting cigarette print media advertising, the tobacco industry established the Freedom to Advertise Coalition, which included the American Association of Advertising Agencies, the Outdoor Advertising Association of America, and the Association of National Advertisers. The industry's position was also supported by magazine and newspaper publishers and by the influential American Civil Liberties Union, which announced its strong opposition to cigarette advertising restrictions on First Amendment grounds" (Kagan & Vogel, 1993, p. 37). The result was that none of the restrictive legislation even reached the floor for debate. To defeat large increases in federal tobacco taxation, the industry allied itself with groups fighting against tax increases generally.[20] It has also used donations to nonprofit groups very successfully to broaden its political base.

19. One senior federal official told the following story. An undercover purchase had just gone successfully; the clerk in the store had refused to sell to an underage, undercover purchaser. The adult police officer was writing up the incident report when he heard a tapping at the passenger-side window, where the adolescent was sitting. Another clerk had seen the incident and didn't want the kid to feel bad, so he had brought out a pack of cigarettes for him to buy!
20. It can find allies for fighting its other enemies as well. "Major business groups including the U.S. Chamber of Commerce said yesterday that they are intensifying their efforts to derail a Senate tobacco bill in part because they fear it will help their mortal enemies: trial lawyers. The Chamber began airing a new TV commercial blasting the proposed 'tobacco tax' and 'millionaire trial lawyers' who, the ad says, 'will pocket billions' from lawsuit settlements mandated in the tobacco measure" (Torry, 1998).

It has succeeded until now in maintaining statutory prohibitions on regulatory activities by federal agencies, particularly the Food and Drug Administration. Equally important, though peculiarly unpublicized, is the continuing federal prohibition on states or municipalities regulating tobacco advertising and promotion activities that occur entirely within the borders of the state or municipality.

The power of the industry, even after wide publicity for documents that showed it long concealed evidence of the hazards of smoking (Glantz et al., 1995), was demonstrated most vividly in 1998. The industry had negotiated multibillion dollar payments to a number of states which had filed suits claiming reimbursement for Medicaid payments for treatment of smoking-related illnesses. The release of documents had caused it concern that juries might start to find for individual plaintiffs, perhaps even award ruinous punitive damages.

The industry negotiated a settlement with a coalition of state Attorneys General and private plaintiffs' attorneys in 1997. That settlement would have required the industry to pay out $368 billion over 25 years and to accept restrictions on promotion and product regulation by the FDA. In return, it would have received a limit on annual payments to plaintiffs. Since this agreement required federal legislation, Congress drafted its own bill, which imposed heavier penalties and strictures on the cigarette manufacturers, including substantial excise taxes. Late in this process the industry decided that it would contest the legislation. This posed a serious threat since numerous legal obstacles could be raised that would, at a minimum, delay implementation of the bill for a few years. Though the Senate Commerce Committee nonetheless voted out the bill in its tough form, it failed to attract enough votes on the Senate floor. Most observers believe that this was a consequence of the industry's $40 million ad campaign, depicting the bill (with its large tax increases) as a greedy effort on the part of politicians to fund unnecessary programs.[21] In late 1998

---

21. See *Washington Post* stories of June 17, 1998 (Torry & Dewar, 1998) and August 8, 1998 (Eilperin & Torry, 1998). "[W]hen Republican pollsters asked voters whether supporters of the tobacco bill are mainly seeking to cut teen smoking or to get additional tax revenue, 69 percent said they were seeking tax revenue. . . . The theme of huge, new taxes to expand government has echoed for weeks in the industry's commercials. Its latest offering shows a Christmas tree in front of the Capitol, as a voice tells listeners, 'It's the season of giving in Washington, but remember it's your taxes they're giving away'" (Torry & Dewar, 1998).

the states reached a settlement requiring payment by the companies of $250 billion over 25 years. The Supreme Court ruled in April, 2000, that the FDA lacked jurisdiction to regulate cigarettes (*FDA v. Brown and Williamson*, 2000).

The industry has been as aggressive in state as in federal politics. For example, the long-time Speaker of the Californian State Assembly, Willie Brown, protected tobacco interests in a state known for its liberal activism in regulation. "Other than a minor tax increase in 1967, it was not until 1988 that any state-level legislation relating to tobacco use or taxation was passed in California, and even that occurred only by popular vote on a ballot initiative. The legislative leadership in California had consistently turned back every other piece of proposed anti-tobacco legislation" (Bal and Lloyd, 1994, p. 2068). Even after passage of Proposition 99 (which imposed a new 25 cent tax per pack and gave substantial revenues for antitobacco advertising and education), the industry was able to postpone its implementation for nine months.

At the local level, the industry has been less successful in fighting the activists. Literally hundreds of municipalities have enacted restrictions on where smoking can take place. Kagan and Vogel (1993) argue that this is because activism flourishes at the grass roots and the cigarette industry cannot mount campaigns on so many local fronts. However, municipal governments have limited powers so that these victories have limited consequences. For example, higher local cigarette taxes are likely to be thwarted by the intercity purchases.

The tobacco industry is among the major advertisers in the United States. Much of the policy action has shifted to the promotional activities of the tobacco companies. They were estimated to spend $4.6 billion in 1991 for advertising and promotion, with the latter now accounting for the vast majority of the total. Long banned from television, the cigarette companies now devote much of their effort to such activities as billboards (for which they are the single most important purchaser), display ads at point of sale, sponsorship of sporting events and public entertainment, and distribution of promotional gifts (tee-shirts, caps, etc.). These activities help create the sense that tobacco smoking is a normal and acceptable behavior, very much countering the effects of school-based prevention programs. Studies of other nations that have implemented much more sweeping bans on advertising, such as Canada, which prohibits cigarettes from print media or even promotion of sporting events, have found a substantial impact on smoking rates (Toxic Substances Board, 1989).

Smoking messages are ubiquitous in the United States and many other countries and convey a variety of implicit messages. A 1986 British survey reported that 44 percent of citizens assumed that the government would not permit cigarette advertising if the product were seriously dangerous (cited in CDC, 1990). Cigarette firms have been particularly skillful at creating images attractive to potential youth smokers; the Joe Camel ads, purportedly designed to discourage youth from smoking, notoriously have accomplished the opposite, being the best known images among adolescents and making smoking an attractive "cool" behavior (DiFranza, Richards, & Paulman, 1991).

Low-tar and -nicotine cigarettes have been an important instrument for maintaining the credibility of prosmoking messages. It is now well established that smokers adjust their behavior so that low-tar cigarettes pose no less a risk to health than do regular cigarettes (Kozlowski & Pilletteri, 1996). Ads that stress the ability of the smoker to make a positive decision on his or her own behalf have added to the attractiveness of smoking, particularly for the young.

Smoking and the future

As others (e.g., Schelling, 1992) have noted, one can be impressed either by the fact that over half of all daily smokers in the United States have managed to give up what is clearly an extremely addictive substance or by the fact that nearly one-quarter of adolescents, despite a multitude of messages about the dangers of smoking, are daily smokers by the time they leave school. Clearly there are strong forces at work both to make smoking more difficult and to promote the use of cigarettes and tobacco.

The long-term prognosis is surely in favor of the antitobacco advocates. Their substantive case is strong, and the growing stigmatization of smokers and smoking may have a tipping effect (i.e., when smokers constitute a small share of a group, they may find themselves subject to such ostracization and with so few allies that their numbers fall sharply in a short period of time). That is at least a partial account of the dramatic declines in smoking among the highly educated and suggests that it may also occur for other groups in society.

Yet for our purposes, it is the negative aspect of the story that seems most telling; a (modern) generation after the 1964 Surgeon General's Report first made the negative health consequences of smoking popular knowledge the nation is still engaged in a battle to make daily smoking a rare behavior. Even the growing stigmatization both of the behavior and of smokers has had only moderate impact. The sluggish response of schools with respect even to developing smoke-free policies for their staff,[22] though there is evidence that this has a significant impact on student smoking, is indicative of the barriers to mobilizing institutions to combat consistently a health threat that is integrated into everyday behavior.

A combination of First Amendment rights, strongly protected by the courts over many decades, and the highly fragmented nature of American politics have complicated the task of reining in the cigarette industry. The release of various papers (see, for example, Glantz et al., 1995) showing that the industry suppressed research results on the dangers of tobacco and that it may have tampered with the nicotine content of cigarettes may weaken the defense in liability cases, but that will merely punish past actions of the current manufacturers, not much impede the ability of companies generally to continue to market and promote cigarettes.

Tobacco prohibition, outlandish as it may appear now, is not without its attractions. A large black market might be tolerable if it reduced premature deaths by even, say, one-quarter (i.e., by 100,000). There is growing evidence that quitting is possible and some evidence that increasing the difficulty of smoking conveniently, as with workplace programs, has an impact on smoking rates (Bierer & Rigotti, 1992). The growing stigmatization of the product and the behavior provides a credible political basis for such actions. Whether it is technologically feasible to implement an effective ban and what kinds of adaptations smokers might make to thwart it are matters that need serious and detailed consideration. But that prohibition is given no consideration in the current debate is again a tribute to the power of popular interpretations of the experience of Prohibition.

22. A Pittsburgh school garnered national attention when it posted a sign in one of the student bathrooms announcing that it was "Nonsmoking"; the implication was that the others did allow smoking.

CONCLUSION

Alcohol, cigarettes, and gambling are all sold in markets that are subject to quite modest regulation. Efforts to increase the stringency of that regulation have been met by well financed, politically skillful, and legally resourceful campaigns that have kept public health concerns at the margins of public policy.

This should be no surprise. Regulating the conduct of business has always been particularly difficult in the United States. The great struggles over workplace safety and environmental protection in the 1960s and 1970s are merely recent illustrations of a continuing problem that is a natural consequence of both American ideology and the structure of political finance. Advertising has been particularly difficult to regulate because of First Amendment protections that have been given broad interpretation by the courts. Yet promotion is almost the central issue with respect to these vices, which depend so much on manipulation of attitudes to ensure that potential buyers view them as respectable purchases.

In projecting the consequences of legalizing drugs like cocaine or heroin, the experience with the alcohol, gambling, and tobacco industries suggests the difficulty of maintaining regulation that is guided by the public interest, particularly public health. Critical in these cases has been the growth of large corporations or state enterprises, capable of effective strategic decisions. Perhaps it is possible to design a legalization regime with a dispersed industry of atomized firms. There are economic forces, mostly associated with economies of scale in national marketing, that generate concentration in these markets, but perhaps statutes could prohibit any corporation from attaining more than a fixed share (say 5 percent) of the national market, though there is no precedent for such a restriction.

For gambling, the nation has been through a complete cycle, from almost universal legal availability to almost complete prohibition back to near universal legalization. The changes seem to be driven by shifts in attitudes toward prudence generally and towards individual rights and in beliefs about the vulnerability of individuals to pathological gambling. The evils caused by prohibition have not been central to the modern shift. Rather these evils have served as a prop for economic interests, including state governments, seeking to expand their markets. What was once treated as a vice is now treated as just another product; considerations of gambling-related harms get no attention in the regulation of the activity.

Prostitution in some ways reinforces this lesson. For whatever reason, the nation has accepted a harm reduction approach to control of this activity. The harms of prostitution are certainly influenced by prohibition; both customers and prostitutes are at higher risk of infection and criminal victimization when the activity is prohibited rather than regulated. But compared to a highly promoted legal industry might bring, the harms may not look so terrible.

Our goal here is not to design optimal policies for these other vices but to suggest how little data and analysis support the current policy choices and the obstacles to maintaining stringent regulation of those that are legal.

9 U.S. Experience with Legal Cocaine and Heroin

(with Joseph Spillane)

The United States is not without experience of legally available cocaine and heroin. From the early 1880s until about 1905, there were no criminal prohibitions against either the sale or use of these drugs, as indeed there were no regulations governing the use and distribution of any psychoactive substances, except for alcohol. By 1905, various state laws were passed prohibiting the sale or distribution of opiates and cocaine and in 1915 the Harrison Act closed down legal retailing nationwide. Ironically, between about 1890 and 1920, it was possible in many states to purchase heroin or cocaine legally, though the sale of alcoholic beverages and cigarettes was prohibited.

History does not repeat itself; at best it crudely paraphrases. Late twentieth-century America – affluent, suburban, postindustrial, with its emphasis on individual rights and self-expression – is so different from the nation of a century ago that only the most naïve would expect legal opiates and cocaine to produce the same patterns of use, abuse, and related problems. Yet the experiences of that time are a frequent reference in the contemporary legalization debate, usually in the form of "we tried legal availability and it failed," the antithesis of the more ubiquitous "we tried Prohibition and it failed." Even the proponents of legalization seem uneasy about the historical experience with legal cocaine and opiates, though they emphasize the slight relationship between drug use and crime prior to prohibition (e.g., Miller, 1991). Our interpretation of that period is that what existed came to be seen as "ugly" and that with the same great naïveté that led to alcohol Prohibition, the problems of abuse were to be legislated out of existence. Naïve or not, the effort did result in sharp reductions in the use of opiates and cocaine for two generations, until the explosion of heroin use in the late 1960s.

U.S. experiences with legal opiates have been well described and analyzed, first in David Musto's classic *The American Disease* (1971/1987) and more recently in David Courtwright's *Dark Paradise* (1982). We give more attention here to the less well-studied experience of legal cocaine, drawing primarily on Joseph Spillane's (2000) *Cocaine: From Modern Marvel to Modern Menace in the United States, 1884–1920*, which was funded by the Sloan Foundation as part of the research reported in this book. The experience with opiates is more briefly described later in this chapter. The final section presents our analysis of the relevance of these experiences to the current legalization debate.

COCAINE

The story of legal cocaine can be readily summarized. Discovered in 1884, the drug quickly found its way into the pharmacopoeia as a major addition to the weak arsenal available to doctors. Indeed, in the 1880s it constituted something of an elixir and was freely prescribed for a wide range of ailments. The next two decades saw a steady rejection of the drug, first by doctors, then by pharmacists, and finally (and most reluctantly) by the pharmaceutical manufacturers themselves. The change in attitude reflected many factors: evidence of the addictive potential of the drug, the destructive effect of the drug on those who did become dependent and their occasionally violent behavior, and finally the low socioeconomic status of those who continued to use it after the dangers became known.

States began passing criminal prohibitions on its sale (never on its manufacture) and it was included in the Harrison Act, the 1914 federal legislation that has formed the basis of the prohibition regime ever since. This followed over a decade of efforts at regulating the promotion by patent medicine manufacturers of cocaine-based cures and then the dispensing of increasingly potent forms of the drug. These efforts failed to prevent the moderate growth of a recreational market for the drug, though consumption always remained at levels well below those witnessed in our own times.

In contrast to opiates, the decade following the Harrison Act saw little evidence that cocaine users needed treatment for their problems or that there was a significant cocaine market, notwithstanding the continued production of cocaine in the United States and its use as an anesthetic.

The medical phase

Initial enthusiasm. The discovery of the physiological properties of cocaine was seen as a major breakthrough for modern medicine. In 1884, Carl Koller in Vienna demonstrated that it could be used as a topical anesthetic in operations on the eye, providing doctors with an anesthetic that permitted the patient to stay awake during the operation without feeling pain, did not induce nausea, and was apparently without risk to the health of the patient.

Further research, much done in the United States, found that cocaine had broad applications as a topical anesthetic for a variety of other operations (e.g., on the throat and nose). Sensitive areas could be explored in nonsurgical procedures (e.g., physicians examining patients with painful throat conditions were able do so painlessly by employing a cocaine solution sprayed in the throat).

In 1891 Roberts Bartholow (1900), a leading advocate of the new physiological research wrote "No remedy in modern times – probably in any age of the world – has become so famous in so short a time as cocaine, and no remedy has so been subjected to the tests of physiological experiment and clinical observation." Even those who had been skeptical about the effect of coca, which had been tested in the previous decade and generally found wanting as a therapeutic, were impressed. E. R. Squibb (1884), a coca skeptic, wrote, "It is exceedingly rare that a novelty in the materia medica is so easily and so quickly tried, and still more rare that one is found that is so very definite and so very important in its results, and the future utility of which is so quickly and so easily established." Its discovery in Germany and Vienna, then centers of medical research, gave the drug an attractive air of modernity in an era that was beginning to look skeptically on traditional and untested remedies. This, of course, was prior to the creation of the FDA or any other regulatory authority overseeing the safety and efficacy of new drugs; no formal tests were required before a drug was allowed in the marketplace.

Cocaine's uses quickly spread beyond surgery. It could be used as a diuretic, for treatment of nausea and vomiting, and, more controversially, as a tonic for neurasthenia, the standard term for a variety of nervous disorders. Cocaine's stimulant qualities were highly regarded. A Portland, Maine, physician reported that he took cocaine for sleeplessness and "felt wide awake in a moment and was able to read understandingly a very abstruse book" (Woodman, 1885, p. 287).

Opiate addiction, usually brought on by careless prescribing habits, was also an important target for cocaine treatment. Cocaine seemed initially to offer a means for assisting withdrawal, apparently the most significant obstacle to curing addiction. The most common treatment plan involved gradually reducing an addict's dose of opium or morphine and substituting frequent (and sometimes increasing) doses of cocaine. The gradual reduction treatment was spread over varying lengths of time, usually about a week. At this point, most physicians attempted to have their patients discontinue cocaine. Other physicians encouraged its continued availability, suggesting its use whenever the patient felt the desire for opiates.

Finally, cocaine's most common application, and ultimately its most destructive, was in the treatment of respiratory problems. Dr. Franke Bosworth, an early pioneer of its application in this respect, claimed in 1884 that "there is no longer any excuse for anyone suffering from a cold in the head" (1884). Numerous cocaine-based medicines were developed to soothe coughs and related respiratory diseases. While as an anesthetic the drug was administered only once or a few times to a patient, it was used much more frequently by those taking it as a cure for catarrh or hay fever, or for treatment of melancholia; the manufacturer might recommend that it be taken multiple times a day for a period of a week. Many of the preparations used coca rather than cocaine, often dissolved in wine. But cocaine was also frequently injected, the hypodermic having only become readily available in the 1870s. Moreover, as the price of cocaine fell [from $1 per grain (70 milligrams) in 1884 to about 2 cents per grain in 1887], sniffing powdered cocaine became affordable, and many doctors began to prescribe that mode.

Doubts. The medical profession soon became aware of some problems from regular use of cocaine, though initially this was described as cocaine "poisoning." Cases resulting in death were rare, but there were some strong adverse reactions, particularly when the drug was used as an anesthetic since that involved large doses, often administered by hypodermic. Patients might vomit, become nauseous, lose consciousness, and so on. The behavior was particularly troubling because it seemed so unpredictable; some patients reacted adversely to very modest doses, others had no problem with very large quantities.

Behavioral problems also manifested themselves fairly quickly. For example, one doctor reported a case in which a patient "became maniacal, and under the delusion that he been attacked by a robber, sprang from his seat, seized the doctor by the throat and began to beat him" (Mattison, 1886–7, pp. 572–3). Others had patients who began to hallucinate, speak disconnectedly, or suffered paranoid delusions.

The addictiveness of cocaine was a matter of controversy for some time. A former Surgeon General, William Hammond (1886), said that "[a]s to the cocaine habit, he regarded it as similar to the tea or coffee habit and unlike the opium habit. He did not believe there was a single instance of a well pronounced cocaine habit, the patient being unable to stop it at any time if he chose to do so."

But opinion gradually changed. Three factors contributed to the view that cocaine use was extraordinarily risky: the ease and rapidity with which cocaine abuse developed in some users; the severe physical and mental effects of cocaine abuse, unlike anything encountered in opiate abuse; and the tenacity of cocaine abuse, despite the fact that it did not lead to a physical addiction. Whereas opiate addicts often lived with their addictions for years without seriously impairing their ability to work, most case histories of cocaine abuse mentioned startling physical deterioration.

The initial medical reaction was that the problems were largely the result of their own overprescription, and thus that they could bring the problem under control. The early addicts were mostly male professionals; doctors themselves were particularly likely to show up, in part because of the frequency of self-experimentation, as well as easy access. This helped explain the relatively benign response to the problem; it was socially unthreatening. Doctors drastically reduced their prescription volume. Though a small number of doctors sold prescriptions later on, allowing addicts to obtain the drug more easily (and perhaps more cheaply), the medical profession soon came to have a modest role in the provision of the drug. Despite the promotional efforts of manufacturers such as Parke-Davis, the medical market for cocaine began to decline sharply by the end of the 1890s. This was due in part to the development of alternatives that had few of the undesirable side effects of cocaine, as well as to the changing attitudes of physicians. For example, procaine (novocaine) entered the market as an alternative anesthetic.

Patent medicine and the promotion of cocaine

The medical profession lost control of the provision of cocaine by the end of the 1890s. The market continued to grow, largely through the efforts of manufacturers, who publicized selective medical opinion to promote the drug and created their own popular market by ignoring the guidelines of standard medical practice. This market expansion was helped by the development of alternative medical approaches such as homeopathy and eclecticism as well as by a host of fringe practitioners and quacks. Many consumers avoided medical advice altogether and opted to make their own decisions about medicines.

The pharmaceutical industry of the late nineteenth century was divided into two groups of firms. The "ethical" manufacturers supposedly aimed at meeting the medical need and marketed primarily to physicians. The patent manufacturers bypassed the physician and marketed directly to the buyer.

Cocaine was among the most important products of the European and American pharmaceutical/chemical industry, and the supply of the drug far exceeded the limited requirements of medical practice. Moreover, whereas the medical market was dominated by low-potency coca products, the new market was flooded by more powerful forms. Efforts of an anticocaine coalition of doctors and reformers to define standards of appropriate use were undercut by manufacturer promotion of cocaine products primarily aimed at nonmedical and recreational use. There was no regulation of the manufacturers prior to the Harrison Act.

Since cocaine could be purchased without a prescription, influencing the attitudes of retail druggists was important for establishing confidence in the product. The ethical industry initially differed little from the patent manufacturers in this respect, though it did try to shape physician attitudes as well as those of druggists. Parke-Davis, the most prominent of the ethical firms in the cocaine industry, published a whole stable of magazines aimed at influencing physicians and pharmacists; these magazines selectively reprinted reports from medical journals favorable to the use of cocaine. Indeed, it carried this further in its publication of what was ostensibly a reference book *The Pharmacology of the New Materia Medica* in 1892; this contained 240 pages on coca and cocaine, of which only three contained negative reports, even though much had already been learned about the dangers of cocaine.

Favorable reports were also reprinted many years after they had been superseded by other findings. Of particular concern to cocaine manufacturers were published accounts in medical journals of patients experiencing toxic reactions. Selling the safety of cocaine was central to the appeal to a medical audience. Fortunately, medical theorizing provided the manufacturers with a credible explanation – that these reactions were, in fact, due not to cocaine but to impurities and by-products in the cocaine they had used. Parke-Davis and the other large firms thus emphasized the purity of their product.

Cocaine was one of the first major drug discoveries to benefit from the ability of drug makers to communicate directly with consumers about its uses. All cocaine manufacturers advertised and promoted their product extensively, including some of the earliest celebrity endorsements. For example, Sigmund Freud was persuaded to endorse the quality and purity of Parke-Davis cocaine. More notoriously, patent manufacturers, such as the Mariani Company, enlisted popes and presidents to extol the virtues of their products.

Mariani produced the most common of the early patent medicine forms, coca-based wines; by the early 1890s, a New York wholesale dealer listed nineteen varieties of coca-laced wines in his catalogue. The wines were soon succeeded by coca based soft drinks, Coca-Cola being the most prominent. John Pemberton, Coca-Cola's creator, was an Atlanta pharmacist who also did some manufacturing for a limited market. Among Pemberton's products was a coca wine, which he called Peruvian Wine Cola. When the city of Atlanta adopted prohibition in 1886, Pemberton was forced to develop a nonalcoholic alternative to Peruvian Wine Coca. The syrup that resulted from his experiment he called Coca-Cola. From the beginning, this product was intended to serve a medical market, albeit through a delicious fountain drink. In its early advertising, Coca-Cola not only openly acknowledged its coca content but also ardently invoked accepted medical knowledge of coca to make its sales pitch. Though its later ads made fewer therapeutic claims than the early ones, even in 1907 it was coyly advertising the benefits of the small amount of coca it contained.

These wines and colas contained very little cocaine. For example, some of the soft drinks had barely 1 milligram per fluid ounce; a 12-ounce drink then gave the consumer less than one-twentieth of what would be in a line of cocaine. Even Vin Mariani is estimated to have had only 6–8 milligrams per fluid ounce. Though these were habit-forming substances, they did not induce in their consumers the fearsome decline in health and the exacerbation of aggressive behavior experienced by iatrogenically addicted cocaine users.

However, a second class of patent medicines that developed in the second half of the 1890s presented much more serious problems to their buyers. By 1900, catarrh cures were unquestionably the leading form of cocaine product. These typically contained 3 to 5 percent cocaine, so that 2 ounces of Agnew's Catarrhal Powder had more than 1 gram of cocaine: "This quantity was supposed to be harmless, but every druggist knows how the sale of these 'catarrh cures' grew enormously on the strength of its cocaine content" (Towns, 1917). The catarrh cures were the source of most of the cocaine abuse involving patent medicines. Many of them involved inhalers, thus allowing for the sniffing of cocaine.

These products required substantial doses to achieve their intended curative effect. Moreover, increasing doses were usually necessary to provide the same amount of relief. The manufacturers further contributed by encouraging repeated and excessive use. A circular for Ryno's Hay Fever and Catarrh Remedy, which contained nothing but cocaine, advised for its use in "hay fever, rose col, influenza or whenever the nose is 'stuffed up', red and sore" the remedy should be employed "two to ten times per day, or oftener if really necessary." For "chronic catarrh," Ryno noted that the remedy should be employed two or three times a day but that "this disease is often very intractable, sometimes requiring several months to cure." Compounding the problem was that many of the catarrh cures did not reveal that cocaine was one of the ingredients.

Recreational use

Significant recreational use unrelated to medically related abuse had become noticeable by 1895. The medical profession believed that the drug could still prove valuable, provided doctors kept much closer control of dosing. However, with pharmaceutical manufacturers and patent medicine makers steadily increasing production (and ignoring the cautions of physicians), cocaine started to gain popularity among new groups of consumers in the mid-1890s. Total production by the early 1900s was five times as high as it had been in 1890 when the drug was still being widely prescribed by physicians. One of the early recreational uses reported was as a stimulant among stevedores on the waterfront in New Orleans. According to the *Medical News*:

> The cocaine habit began among the negro roustabouts of New Orleans, who found that the drug enabled them to perform more easily the extraordinarily severe work of loading and unloading steamboats at which, perhaps for seventy hours at a stretch, they have to work, without sleep or rest, in rain, in cold and in heat. The pay is high, $150 a month, but the work is impossible without a stimulant. Whisky, while protecting the negro against the rain and cold, did not given him the endurance against fatigue that was needed, Cocaine proved to be the very stimulant needed. Under its influence the strength and vigor of the laborer is temporarily increased, and he becomes impervious to the extremes of heat and cold (Spillane, 2000, p. 92).

Clearly this was completely detached from any pretended therapeutic use. This behavior appeared to have spread throughout the South. *Medical News*, in the same article, reported that "On many of the Yazoo plantations this year the negroes refused to work unless they could be assured that there was some place in the neighborhood where they could get cocaine, and one big planter is reported to keep the drug in stock among the plantation suppliers and to issue regular rations of cocaine just as he was accustomed in the past to issue rations of whisky." Though there is little evidence that cocaine was more prevalent among Southern blacks than whites, there had been a concerted effort to control blacks' access to alcohol, making the unrestricted cocaine more attractive, accessible, and cheap.

Some industrial employers in the Northeast also found it useful to provide cocaine so as to ease problems related to various conditions (e.g., dust irritation, which could be ameliorated by a menthol and cocaine spray). The drug became popular too in Western mining communities, though "the white crystals quickly acquired a reputation for inciting violence and insanity" (Whiteside, 1978).

One might treat the use of cocaine in strenuous or difficult work situations as self-medication. But there grew up yet another market that was unquestionably recreational and came to bear the brunt of contemporary condemnation. Those involved in dealing with juvenile delinquency at the turn of the century reported that cocaine was a serious problem; cocaine was more attractive than morphine to young males. For example, a description of cocaine use in Newark stated that

> "the cocaine habit is steadily growing in Newark among the boys who pool in the upstairs pool and billiard rooms and that the usual way of taking the powder is by snuffing it up the nostrils from a quill. . . . [T]he assertion is made that scores of young men have recently lost ambition and employment by the use of the drug in this manner and that several deaths have recently been caused by the habit" ("Boys who use cocaine," 1904).

Surveys of those who were addicted around 1914 (the year of the Harrison Act) found that even though most opiate addicts had acquired the habit under medical supervision, cocaine addiction was almost exclusively acquired through association with other users. It was also begun at an earlier age, frequently 16 to 18. The anecdotes suggested that dependence led to acquisitive crime, partly because it was expensive to acquire cocaine in the form of these catarrh medicines but also because it engendered violence among its habitués.[1]

Legal but unrespectable

What had once been a principal drug in materia medica had been relegated to a very specialized role by 1900. Pharmacists, like physicians, seeking to improve their professional standing in the community, sought to restrict the dispensing of cocaine-based cures. Thus, even before the Harrison Act of 1914, cocaine was no longer readily obtained from mainstream pharmacists, who insisted that purchasers present legitimate prescriptions. In the face of continued recreational

---

1. Indeed, the drug's reputation for engendering violence may well have led users to take it to steel themselves for occasions when violence was appropriate, just as alcohol is frequently imbibed as a preparation for difficult encounters.

demand for the drug, not yet criminalized, a fringe distribution system developed, centered on pharmacists who basically offered no other product. Associated with these pharmacists, the object of much ire to the professional organizations, were networks of peddlers who distributed the drug to the users.

This market had some similarities to the late twentieth-century illegal market. First, the price was much higher than that charged for prescription cocaine. Musto (1990) estimated that, in terms of hourly earnings, cocaine cost as much in New York in 1912 as it did in the late 1980s, though the price (25 cents for 85 milligrams) strikes us now as absurdly low. Second, the drug was frequently much diluted; though the diluents were apparently not toxic, they did generate adverse reactions in some patients. In his account of the drug culture of San Francisco, Fred Williams (1920) claimed that "[n]ine out of ten dope users have sores all over their bodies – due to the sugar of milk with which the drug is adulterated." Third, the markets tended to be located in socially marginal areas, often vice districts where other kinds of illicit enterprises were already concentrated. Finally, the customers were predominantly from lower socioeconomic groups. Writing of New Orleans' famous red-light district, Storyville, Hair (1976) observed that "by 1900 cocaine had become by far the most common hard drug taken by poorer blacks and the prostitutes, black and white, who worked in or around Storyville" (pp. 76–7). A 1903 American Pharmaceutical Association report (cited in Spillane, 2000, p. 98) concluded that "the use of cocaine seems to be rapidly supplanting in part the use of morphine among men and women of the underworld."

Not that cocaine and opiates were always substitutes. An 1899 survey of 1,000 drug patients all of whom had applied for treatment at the Keeley Institute in Dwight, Illinois, suggested that the institution was already treating many poly-drug users. According to the report, 166 used combinations of opiates and cocaine and only 18 used cocaine alone.

As Courtwright has shown for opiates, it was the change in the character of users rather than increases in the amount consumed that definitively changed public attitudes toward the drug. Now it was clearly a vice, not simply a powerful medicine whose misuse under medical supervision could lead unfortunate victims to a career of addiction.

Prevalence and problems

There are no meaningful estimates of the extent of cocaine use in 1900. Some contemporary reports made claims about the number of cocaine addicts in a particular town but provided no supporting evidence. For example, in Dallas, a city of 40,000 in 1894, a correspondent to a pharmacists' journal asserted that there were 500 to 600 people (1.2 to 1.5 percent) with a "cocaine habit," while in 1910 a New Orleans grand jury estimated that about 5 percent of the city's population used cocaine.

Nor is it easy to develop estimates of how much cocaine was being consumed at the time; only imports of the leaf were subject to duty, and this provided incentives for importing refined and semirefined cocaine, for which there were no tax-based records. The available industry data, along with tariff records for leaf, suggest that total consumption never totaled more than the equivalent of 8 tons of pure cocaine. This should be compared to about 300 tons now estimated to be consumed in a nation with almost three times as many citizens.

The prevalence of frequent cocaine use must have been sharply lower than it is now. The fact that the drug was cheaper in 1905 (even after adjusting for differences in earning power) meant that those who were cocaine dependent probably consumed on average substantially more than their 1990s counterparts. If they consumed just 100 grams a year, about the current figure, and all 8 tons were consumed by addicts, then there would have been 80,000 cocaine-dependent persons in the United States around 1905, the peak consumption year. That should be compared with the approximately 1.5 million nonincarcerated cocaine addicts estimated for 1990. The prevalence rate for cocaine dependence was probably only one-fifth and perhaps as little as one-tenth of the current figure.

The involvement of cocaine in the criminality of the time seems to have been limited. Hamilton Wright, a major figure in the negotiation of the early international conventions on drug control, was informed that 5 percent of New York City prisoners were cocaine users. Observers also believed that most of the crimes of cocaine users were minor misdemeanors. Then as now, there was a debate about the nature of the relationship between cocaine use and crime. The Bronx District Attorney believed that the connection was almost exclusively through the need to commit crimes to support what had become an expensive habit. He could cite only one case in which the drug itself seemed to lead to violence. On the other hand, a prominent textbook of the time saw the drug as changing behavior and attitudes toward violence. Reviewing a case of a boy who regularly used cocaine and had numerous contacts with the criminal justice system, the author observed, "If we saw the case . . . a few years later we should probably find him a most dangerous fellow, carrying weapons and willing to do anything desperate" (Healy, 1915, p. 278). There is a striking lack of reference to violence around the selling of the drug.

Responses

The very rapid onset and marked deterioration in physical and mental states of the cocaine addict suggested the need for treatment. However, the public response was limited by the perception that cocaine addiction, unlike opiate dependence, was principally a vice rather than a medical problem.

In 1906, the Pure Food and Drug Act was passed, creating the framework for regulation of drugs and medical products. Cocaine was only one of many targets of the reformers but it certainly received attention as one of the patent medicine ingredients most regularly abused. Samuel Hopkin Adams, the most prominent of the muckraking journalists on this issue, was particularly scathing about Vin Mariani. The regulators and their supporters were uninclined to make distinctions on the basis of the quantity of cocaine in a medicine; they were as aggressive about low-potency coca wines as the high-potency catarrh mixtures. This was consistent with the letter of the law because the Pure Food and Drug Act authorized the regulators only to judge whether a product was misbranded or adulterated; the quantity of cocaine made little difference.

Less attention however was paid to the large quantities of pure cocaine being manufactured and distributed by the ethical chemical and pharmaceutical firms. As odd as it sounds in retrospect, cocaine itself, provided it was pure, was not subject to similar regulatory oversight. Thus, the consequence of regulation was to accelerate the decline in the medical use of coca and cocaine and increase the importance of pure cocaine. However, the act did require that the contents of each medicine be listed on the label; that was itself enough to bring about some decline in use of medicines whose coca content was not well-known.

Post-Harrison Act

Because the Harrison Act of 1914 was primarily aimed at the opiate problem, we leave our discussion of the circumstances and meaning of that Act to the section on opiates. After 1914, cocaine was still being imported legally in quantities that were only modestly reduced. The totals did not fall sharply until after 1920.

Nonetheless, it is striking just how rapidly cocaine disappeared as a problem drug. In 1937 the notorious Harry Anslinger, head of the Federal Bureau of Narcotics, not a public official with a strong dedication to the truth and inclined to overstatement of drug problems, stated that "Cocaine addiction has disappeared" (cited in Courtwright, Joseph, & Des Jarlais, 1989, p. 352). Consistent with that statement were seizures in the mid-1930s totaling less than 1 kilogram annually. The oral reminiscences of addicts recorded by Courtwright et al. also suggested that cocaine was not much used.

The public treatment system saw very few cocaine-dependent patients. For example, a survey of 393 drug addicts in treatment in Massachusetts in 1917 found only one who was addicted solely to cocaine. Nearly 40 percent reported multiple dependence on cocaine and opiates; very few of these were being treated in the public system, which handled most of those who were dependent solely on opiates. Though cocaine remained a reference for popular culture and is associated with the jazz scene of the first half of the twentieth-century, it was certainly a very minor drug.

THE OPIATES

Although the era of legal cocaine has received only passing attention in the legalization debate, probably reflecting the lack of good historical writing that has been available, the pre-Harrison Act era for opiates is frequently cited. There are differences both in factual claims and interpretations of the experience by the two sides.

Prohibitionists often assert that the prevalence of opiate addiction in 1900 was substantially higher than it is now. For example, Courtwright et al. (1989) estimated 300,000 opiate addicts in 1900, a figure comparable to that provided by Musto reporting on estimates made at the time, though Courtwright et al. used other sources and techniques for their estimates. Courtwright et al. asserted that there were 500,000 heroin addicts in 1990, which would represent 2 per 1,000 population, compared to 3 per 1,000 for 1900. However, the quality of these estimates is so low that the differences should be treated as nonsignificant. The half million figure for 1990 (cf. Rhodes et al., 1997) ignores those heroin addicts who have been incarcerated, which may add 100,000 to 300,000 to that estimate. Moreover, in 1990 there was a much higher prevalence of cocaine dependence, perhaps 6 to 10 per 1,000 versus less than 1 in 1,000 in 1900; it is unclear how that should be weighted in making the comparisons of the two eras.

For legalizers, it is less the numbers than the behavior of users that deserves attention.

> Throughout the 1800s no link between drug use and crime was observed. Authorities denied any link between opiates and "sexual psychoses." . . . [H]istory has answered questions that Americans of the era raised about the effect of widespread drug use on national productivity; the post-Civil War years are remembered as a time of economic and intellectual vigor (Miller, 1991, p. 87).

Though the latter statement is hardly of evidentiary value, it is true that the opiates were not considered a major problem for the labor force.

The history of opiate control prior to the Harrison Act is broadly similar to that of cocaine. Refined opiates (developed in the early nineteenth century) were a major innovation for the medical profession, providing doctors with their first powerful analgesic, particularly when the hypodermic needle was developed just before the Civil War, allowing carefully titrated doses to be delivered very rapidly. Initially unaware of the addictive potential of the drug (indeed, unaware of dependence as a general behavioral problem), there was a great deal of overprescription and a class of iatrogenic addicts was created. Middle class women were particularly affected because doctors were inclined to find the source of these patients' medical problems in nervous disorders for which a narcotic was appropriate.

Eugene O'Neill's moving portrayal of his mother's addiction in *Long Day's Journey into Night* remains the classic description of this phenomenon.

Addicts also were older and generally of middle class background in the late nineteenth century. For example, an 1885 survey of addicts in small towns in Iowa reported an average age of 46.5, while only 6 percent of an 1889 survey of 446 Massachusetts druggists reported their opiate customers as primarily lower class (Brecher, 1972, pp. 18–19). Opiate use was also not particularly prevalent among blacks at that time. The only minority strongly associated with opiates was the Chinese, who accounted for most opium smoking and whose preferred mode was subject to the first prohibitions, starting with San Francisco in 1875, an event frequently cited to illustrate the enduring use of drug prohibitions to oppress minorities.

By the 1870s American doctors were aware of the seriousness of opiate addiction and had moved to more responsible prescribing regimes. However, again the absence of any effective regulation of pharmaceutical manufacturers or pharmacists ensured that opiate-based medicines continued to be widely available for a long time. The Iowa survey conducted between 1883 and 1885 reported that the 2 million residents of the state had access to 3,000 retail outlets selling opiates; that figure did not include prescriptions filled by private physicians themselves, a common practice at that time (Brecher, 1972, p. 3).

Opiate addiction was never viewed as constituting a social problem comparable to alcoholism. In part, this was because of the behavior of most addicts when using the drugs; they became more passive rather than aggressive. The numbers were also much slighter; even the most generous estimates of opiate dependence suggest that its prevalence was an order of magnitude smaller than that for alcohol at the same time.

Politically this meant that the effort to prohibit opiates never generated the same political intensity as the fight for alcohol Prohibition. An 1881 article in the *Catholic Weekly* noted the lack of powerful organizations fighting for the prohibition of opiates. The Prohibition movement gave little attention to opiates. On the other hand, the Harrison Act generated no equivalent to the "wet" organizations that fought for repeal of the Volstead Act, and the addicts of the time were as poorly organized as those of our own era and did not generate any political pressure.

Courtwright (1982) showed that the transformation of the opiate-using population largely preceded the Harrison Act. The image of the opiate addict was altered not simply by the press and popular preju-dice but also by the changes in who used opiates and why. The number of middle class and female opiate addicts fell, largely because of changes in medical practice and growing stigmatization of opiate dependence, but the number of lower class, male, recreational users rose moderately. These changes were a necessary condition for the passage of a law, the Harrison Act, which had as its original goal the regulation of medical practice but which, because of Supreme Court interpretations of responsible medical practice, became the basis of contemporary drug prohibition.

Controls

The early opium prohibitions were clearly racist in intent. The San Francisco City Council was concerned by reports that white women and young girls were visiting opium smoking dens; it prohibited the operation of such dens, though not opium smoking itself. Eleven other states had imposed similar prohibitions by 1900. However, they were generally seen as ineffective, so Congress passed legislation in 1883 raising the tariff on opium imports from $6 to $10 and then in 1887 prohibited the importation of the low-potency opium favored by smokers. The 1887 law also contained a prohibition on opium importation by Chinese; only U.S. nationals were allowed to bring in the drug.

At least one court made note of the racist aspect of these kinds of law. An Oregon appellate court in Oregon concluded, "Smoking opium is not our vice, and therefore, it may be that this legislation proceeds more from a desire to vex and annoy the 'Heathen Chinese' in this respect than to protect the people from the evil habit" (Brown, 1993 in Bertram et al., 1996, p. 65). The prohibition was regarded by federal officials as unsuccessful. The Secretary of Treasury wrote to the Speaker of the House of Representatives in 1888 that Chinese groups were involved in extensive smuggling: "Although all possible efforts have been made by this Department to suppress the traffic, it is found practically impossible" (cited in Terry & Pellens, 1928/1970, p. 747).

The first major federal intervention into drug control was the Pure Food and Drug Act of 1906. This merely required that labeling for patent medicines be truthful and complete. It is believed that this was sufficient to reduce the sale of opiate-laced patent medicines by about one-third because many users for the first time became aware of the narcotic content of their favorite nostrum. There was, however, some concern that it also led to the addicted being able to identify more readily the stronger, and hence more attractive, forms of the drug. The reformers who had pushed for the act in the belief that it would eliminate the opiate market were disappointed and hoped to move to a ban on all opiate-based patent medicines.

However, the Harrison Act was passed primarily for reasons other than controlling domestic opiate problems. It illustrates a relationship between diplomacy and drug policy that has been an important, indeed sometimes dominant, influence, throughout the modern drug control era. This era starts with the Chinese Opium Wars of the mid-nineteenth century, sparked by the British opposition to Chinese efforts to restrict opium imports from colonial India. The passage of the Harrison Act is also useful in illustrating the multiple motivations for drug control in the United States.

The United States had acquired the Philippines in the Spanish War of 1898. Along with that conquest came responsibility for governing a nation with a large Chinese population, including many dependent on opium. The Spanish government had licensed and taxed a monopoly supplier of opium; that license lapsed with the removal of the Spanish government, and the new U.S. authorities had to find some way of dealing with the matter. Continuation of the monopoly, the first alternative considered in 1903, was met with vigorous opposition from religious leaders, outraged at the notion that the U.S. government would promote the distribution of opiates to "degenerate peoples" (in a contemporary phrase). Congress insisted on prohibition of opiate use, though it allowed a 3-year transition period for non-Philippinos (i.e., Chinese). There is no systematic reporting of how well that prohibition worked; Musto (1987) cited a 1927 study (Opium Research Committee, 1927) reporting that smoking opium was still widely available 20 years later.

American reformers who had fought for prohibition in the Philippines now sought to extend this prohibition to the rest of Asia, particularly China. For that purpose, they proposed an international conference, whose primary goal was to end the Sino-Indian opium trade. This trade had been forced on the Chinese through the most imperialist of means, resulting in two wars between China and Britain. It had also long been a source of uneasiness to British social reformers who were well aware that the Chinese government saw opium addiction as a major problem but was far too weak to stand up to the British government pressure. The Shanghai Commission, with the United States as the most active government (a role it has invariably played at major international drug control conferences), proposed a series of restrictions on opium and opium derivatives to be adopted by member nations.

The U.S. interest in solving the Chinese opium problem has many roots. There was unease about the moral basis of the exclusion act that ended Chinese immigration and thus an interest in making a positive gesture toward the welfare of the Chinese nation. Missionaries actively agitated for U.S. pressure to support a growing Chinese republican movement, which took the opium traffic, undoubtedly a major social problem in late Ching China (Spence, 1975), as an important symbol of the failures of the imperial regime. A clear commercial motive is hard to detect, though some U.S. businessmen thought that the elimination of British-Indian opium imports would create a greater demand for their goods.

The driving force for domestic legislation was the necessity of avoiding embarrassment in dealings with other nations by having the U.S. adopt legislation consistent with the Shanghai Commission. Initially, the concern was only with the opium trade. The U.S. efforts to restrict the British export of opium to China were complicated by the fact that tariffs on imported smoking opium yielded the U.S. government a tidy source of income, $1.5 million in 1909, out of total federal revenues of $604 million. This led to the passage of the 1909 Opium Act, which stirred little domestic resistance because the trade was mostly in the hands of Chinese dealers, and there was no medical use of this form of opiate.

The Harrison Act was a more complex legislative achievement, since it involved significant states' rights concerns and the interests of professional organizations (pharmacists and physicians) and commerce (pharmaceutical industry). It was again inspired by a need to meet international obligations, this time generated by the third of the international conferences, at which the United States had pushed for increasingly restrictive domestic controls on the distribution of opiates. That stance called for further legislation in the United States to meet the requirements that it had pushed on other nations.

The legislation did not initially appear to be prohibitory. Instead, it merely required that certain drugs be purchased only with a prescription, that tax be paid, and that the prescription only be provided by a doctor for the purpose of medical care. The interpretation of the act, in particular the notion that addict maintenance did not constitute medical care, occurred over an almost 10-year period and, if Congressional intent means anything, almost certainly was court written.

Whether in fact the court interpretation made any long-run difference is a fascinating question that only Courtwright has directly tackled. Physicians are not fond of addict maintenance, except perhaps when the patient has become addicted as the result of medical treatment. Although that was certainly the origin of addiction of many of the pre-1914 addicts, by the 1920s an increasing share were likely to have become addicted in the course of recreational use. They may not have found it easy to get prescriptions for what was still regarded then as a habit, even in the absence of the prohibitions contained in the Harrison Act.

CONCLUSIONS

We focus here on cocaine because it best illustrates the relevant lessons. It is clear that the U.S. cocaine problem during the legal era was very modest as compared to now. The amount consumed was slight indeed – on a per capita basis no more than one-fifth of estimated 1990s consumption. The related crime was also slight, notwithstanding the growing association with the criminal subculture of the time. Consumption was not escalating; the annual figures for imports and manufactures show some spikes but no clear upward trend. In the case of opiates, the figures show decline prior to the passage of the Harrison Act.

Why then did the United States move to total prohibition rather than regulation? In part, it may be taken to reflect relative naïveté about the consequences of prohibition. Though it is hard to see how contemporary observers could have overlooked the scale and problems of illegal gambling and prostitution, there was enough moral earnestness to the era, a lack of the well-developed cynicism of our own time, that drug prohibition was not considered likely to generate serious harms itself. The debate about these decisions contained few warnings about illegal markets and their consequences. Moreover, the prohibitionists obtained much of their objective; dependence on cocaine or opiates appears to have declined steadily and substantially after 1914 until the 1960s.

How should we judge the success of the era of legal availability? Note that the cocaine experience was not a homogeneous episode. A medically controlled substance in 1885 became primarily an adjunct to entertainment in the urban underworld by 1910. The forms in which it was used changed over time, from the less potent cordials and the like to very pure powder for snorting, partly in response to regulations that focused only on one segment of the problem. Controls were established only slowly; weak self-regulation by the medical profession became formal (though still weak) FDA regulation two decades later. Judging how well the nation fared with legal cocaine depends on the part of the period chosen. We choose to focus on how it appeared late in the period, since that was when there was a better knowledge of cocaine's pleasures and of the technology for efficiently attaining those pleasures.

The move to prohibition of cocaine was no doubt partly another manifestation of the temperance and paternalistic and class-based reform movements of the time. But it was also a response to a drug that seemed to present peculiarly severe problems to its users and that had not been effectively controlled by voluntary regulation. The continuation of the legal cocaine market after the dangers of the drug became evident can clearly be ascribed to the aggressive promotion and distribution of the manufacturers. Medical practice marginalized the drug quite rapidly, and most pharmacists were also concerned about abuse of the drug. But the manufacturers, even after the creation of the FDA and regulations aimed at limiting distribution, continued to push the product. Their power was insufficient to fight back prohibition when international obligations seemed to require that.

Cocaine played a much smaller role than opiates in the struggle over implementation of the Harrison Act, even though many believed that cocaine presented the greater problem in 1914. Physicians were interested in maintaining the opiate-dependent patients; various clinics were set up to accomplish this until the courts ruled against addiction maintenance as legitimate medical practice. However, there is no record of any effort to continue providing cocaine to those already dependent on it; either these addicts switched to other drugs or they found other ways of coping with the loss of supplies. Most accounts suggest the former. Nevertheless, total imports of leaf and refined products in 1920 were still almost two-thirds the peak levels of the first decade of the century; export to Canada and illegal reimport to the United States may have accounted for a substantial fraction of this total.

Consider now the relevance of this to the contemporary legalization debate. It is implausible that we would return, through legalization, to the situation (in terms of use or abuse) of 1900. The nation now has 2.5 to 3.5 million persons already dependent on cocaine; the figure may even be closer 4 million if one includes those who are not actively dependent because they are incarcerated. Legalizing the drug is unlikely to induce any of these users to reduce their consumption, so that we start with a base rate far higher than that ever experienced pre-Harrison Act. Nor is legalization likely to persuade them to use less harmful forms of cocaine, in particular coca products rather than refined cocaine. On the other hand, the sophistication of potential regulatory schemes is much greater; the nation is unlikely to repeat the naïve behavior of the infant FDA. Public health messages would surely be much stronger, though our review of the limited effectiveness of anticigarette messages should give pause as to what these can accomplish.

The results of legal availability were unattractive to that period. If compared to 1950, with low heroin addiction rates and minimal cocaine use, they might still look unattractive. A comparison with the 1990s complicates matters; the nation did have a smaller drug problem when cocaine and heroin were legal. Thus, the historical experience provides no unequivocal verdict; by selective use of evidence, advocates on both side can find support.

10 Learning from European Experiences

References to the drug control experiences of Britain (medical prescription of heroin) and the Netherlands (the regulated sale of marijuana by coffeeshops) have long been a commonplace of the American drug policy debate. The Zurich Platzspitz ("Needle Park") experience and the recent Swiss heroin maintenance trials have entered that debate more recently (e.g., Nadelmann, 1998). In the United States, descriptions of these policies and assessments of their effectiveness fall somewhere between casual and negligent. For example, a common claim is that the British made heroin legally available before 1967. In support of legalization, some then cite the low number of heroin addicts during most of that period; their critics then cite the large percentage increase in addicts when a few doctors began prescribing recklessly. In fact, the pre-1967 regime was not legalization, and not, in legal terms, very different from what replaced it; the growth that led to the 1967 change involved in absolute terms only a few hundred heroin users. Britain's major heroin epidemic occurred much later and – as discussed below – was not unlike that experienced in other industrialized nations (see Johnson, 1975; Pearson, 1991, 1992; Strang, 1989).[1]

Nevertheless, Western European nations have indeed adopted a wide variety of policies toward controlling illicit drugs. This variation

---

1. In absolute terms, Britain's major heroin epidemic occurred well after Americans had already begun reaching conclusions about the "British experience"; for example, in a 1976 discussion of the 1967 change in law, Votey and Phillips (1976) noted that "there is no significant illicit market for hard drugs in Britain."

makes the study of Western European experiences so interesting for those concerned with U.S. drug policy, particularly for those calling for a major retreat from the "war on drugs." The Drug Policy Foundation (1993), one of the most prominent of the reform organizations, describes European cities as providing "Laboratories of Reform." Depenalization, needle exchange, heroin maintenance, and the de facto legal availability of "soft drugs" – all staples of the reform agenda – have been tried in Western Europe; ergo an examination of how these policies have worked in Europe might tell us how they would work in the United States.

All European countries prohibit the consumption and sale of the same drugs that are prohibited in the United States (Leroy, 1992), as required by the various international conventions to which they are signatories.[2] But they have gone about implementing those prohibitions in quite varied ways. For example, Italy and Spain impose no criminal sanctions for possession of small amounts of prohibited substances, whereas Norway and Sweden aggressively seek out drug users and at least threaten incarceration or mandatory treatment. Switzerland, concerned with the spread of AIDS, has developed programs that allow heroin injectors to consume their drugs under supervision and in government-financed facilities. The Netherlands, while retaining the formal prohibition on cannabis consumption or sale, permits the sale of cannabis by coffeeshops.

Nor is the variation only in use of criminal sanction; it also shows up in treatment and prevention. For example, methadone is the principal modality of treatment for heroin addicts in Great Britain and the Netherlands (where it is liberally available), but it was not generally permitted in France[3] or Sweden.[4] until recently. Some countries that allow methadone (notably Italy) do not permit its use in the maintenance mode that is customary in Britain and the United States. Secondary prevention programs in Britain and Spain target needle users and emphasize "safe use," whereas France, Norway, and Sweden provide only abstinence messages.

---

2. These conventions include Single Convention on Narcotic Substances, 1961; Convention on Psychotropic Substances, 1971; and Convention against Illicit Trafficking in Narcotic Drugs and Psychotropic Substances, 1988. They are all UN conventions.
3. "Up until 1993 there were only three [methadone] programmes in France" (Farrell et al., 1996, p. 41).
4. Sweden allows only 450 methadone slots in four programmes; only 370 were used in 1992 (Swedish National Institute of Public Health, 1993, p. 24).

This chapter along with chapters 11 and 12 examines and interprets the drug control experiences of ten Western European nations – Denmark, France, Germany, Great Britain, Italy, the Netherlands, Norway, Spain, Sweden, and Switzerland – and compares them to experiences in the United States. It is motivated by a somewhat parochial interest, namely what can be learned about the effectiveness of alternative drug policies that might help the United States deal with its own drug problems. Chapter 11 focuses on Dutch cannabis policy since 1976, an intriguing blend of prohibition, depenalization, and commercialization. Chapter 12 focuses on the European harm reduction movement, including the Zurich Platzspitz experience, needle exchange, and heroin maintenance.

This chapter's task is to support two claims. First, the policy variation across Europe is real; it is less extreme than American caricatures would suggest, but European policies reach far more tolerant levels than seen in this country in many years. Second, the variation in the toughness of enforcement within prohibitionist regimes appears to have little systematic influence on the prevalence of drug use.

CHARACTERIZING DRUG POLICY

Is "national drug policy" a relevant construct in European nations? Is the drug problem salient enough in the ten nations we are studying that drug policies receive significant political attention? One useful piece of data comes from a survey of attitudes toward health problems, conducted in the European Community nations (including all sample countries except Norway, Sweden, and Switzerland). The question asked was: Thinking about public health in our European countries, please tell me what, in your opinion, are currently the greatest dangers or the most serious problems? (Commission of the European Communities, 1989).

Drug addiction was spontaneously identified by 42 percent of respondents, following only cancer (48 percent) and AIDS (43 percent); it was identified far more often than cardiovascular disease (24 percent) or alcoholism (15 percent). Drugs were identified as the leading public health problem in Italy (57 percent), Germany (51 percent), and Spain (45 percent), but were ranked third in France (38 percent) and the Netherlands (28 percent) and fourth in Denmark (20 percent) and the United Kingdom (27 percent). In no country was it lower than fourth on the list. Thus, the drug problem is reasonably salient in at least those nations. In Switzerland, the intense discussion about the Platzspitz and the recent heroin maintenance experiment show that drug control is a very prominent issue politically. Drug policy is not then simply an American construct artificially imposed on minor European concerns.

Drug policy crosses many domains of social policy. Criminal justice, health, and education are all major elements of what is usually described as a drug policy. A major task for this study has been finding a way of parsimoniously characterizing policy so as to allow for systematic comparison across nations.

In their cross-national examination of AIDS policy, Kirp and Bayer (1992) described national strategies as varying between the polar extremes of *contain-and-control* and *inclusion-and-cooperation*. Even though Kirp and Bayer made no claim to be able to provide a cardinal measure, they did find that nations clearly fall nearer one pole than the other. We have toyed unsuccessfully with similar categorizations – tolerant vs. intolerant, moral vs. medical model, criminal justice vs. public health orientation, and use reductionist vs. harm reductionist. On reflection, each turns out to pose a false dichotomy. Tolerance is in the eye of the beholder, and under any reasonable definition, most nations engage in both tolerant and intolerant practices. At the rhetorical level, every nation (including the Netherlands) includes a blend of the moral and the medical; at the programmatic level, policing and public health interventions coexist in every national repertoire. Finally, as seen in Chapter 12, even nations at the vanguard of the harm reduction movement are still actively involved in reducing the prevalence of drug use.

Thus, no single dimension can capture the variation in national strategies. Ideally, one would characterize nations in a multidimensional policy space. For example, Spain has foresworn the use of criminal penalties against drug users, but it has failed to pursue harm reduction strategies such as the provision of methadone maintenance or ready access to treatment. Sweden has aggressively asserted the centrality of criminal sanctions against drug users and has firmly rejected both needle exchange and the provision of methadone on essentially moral grounds; yet it just as aggressively provides high-

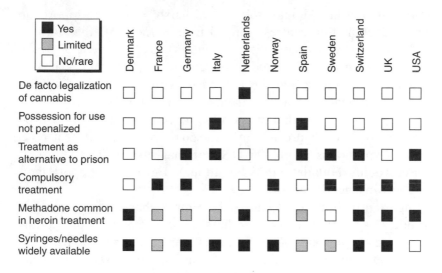

Figure 10.1 Policy indicators (circa 1990)

resource treatment and a wide range of social services to drug addicts. Figure 10.1, itself an oversimplification, illustrates some of the multidimensional complexity, comparing eleven nations on seven dimensions circa 1990. Though the figure characterizes *national* drug policies, in some nations there is a great deal of local autonomy. For example, the political structure of Germany allows a great deal of discretion to the individual states (Länder) in social policy; liberal Hamburg and conservative Munich may be almost as far apart in policy terms as Barcelona and Oslo. In the decade since 1990, most of these nations have moved further in the direction of reduced law enforcement and increased access to methadone – and even prescription heroin (in Switzerland and experimentally in the Netherlands; see Chapter 12), with serious debate about more radical legal changes in the United Kingdom, Switzerland, and Portugal.

A second indication of the multidimensionality of drug policy comes from a 1992 Eurobarometer survey of citizens in various Western European nations (Ødegard, 1995). Eight of the ten nations we are examining (all but Sweden and Switzerland) were included. Across these eight countries, there was remarkably little variation in the level of support for certain drug policies, and the patterns of support do not fit a simple "tolerant vs. harsh" schema. Support for "open rehabilitation centres" ranged from 84 percent (the Netherlands) to 93 percent (the United Kingdom). Endorsement of "treat with a drug substitute" ranged from 55 percent (Italy and Spain) to 69 percent (Denmark and the United Kingdom). Support for "distribute free needles" ranged from 40 percent (Germany) to 59 percent (Denmark), with a mean of 48 percent. Note that no European country had a figure as high as the 66 percent supporting needle exchange programs in a 1996 U.S. national survey (The Henry J. Kaiser Family Foundation, 1996), though European support may have grown since 1996.

Importantly, Europeans cannot be simply characterized as "soft on drugs" – tolerant rather than harsh. Endorsement of the option "crack down on dealers" was almost universal, ranging from 92 percent in Spain to 98 percent in Denmark. There was somewhat less consensus regarding user sanctions; the item "crack down on or isolate addicts" was endorsed by 77 percent in Great Britain but only 38 percent in Germany, 36 percent in Spain, and 29 percent in Italy.

ANALYTIC FRAMEWORK

Even with a complete and accurate database, there are daunting obstacles to a rigorous assessment of the policy-outcome link (see Cook & Campbell, 1979; King, Keohane, & Verba, 1994). It is tempting to think of drug policies and outcomes in terms of a simple causal chain:

Goals → Policies → Implementation → Prevalence of Drug Use → Prevalence of Drug Harms

In fact, the situation is almost certainly more complex, as depicted graphically in Figure 10.2. First, many exogenous factors influence both drug policy and drug outcomes: international treaties, health and welfare policies, individual rights, the authority and autonomy of physicians, and sociodemographics. Second, goals directly influence not only formal policies but also their implementation. Indeed, in some nations (most notably the Netherlands), implementation more closely reflects national goals than do formal drug laws. Third, as

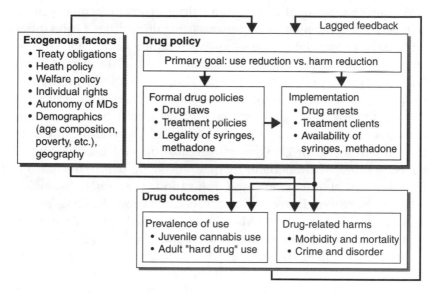

Figure 10.2 Analytic framework

discussed in Chapter 5, formal policies have symbolic influences that transcend the intensity of their implementation; they make moral statements, and thus influence the perceived fairness and legitimacy of authorities, which in turn influences compliance (Tyler, 1990). Fourth, formal policies and their implementation each have a direct influence on drug-related harms that may be largely independent of their effects on levels of drug use; Chapter 12 shows that this is the central insight of the European harm reduction movement (O'Hare et al., 1992; Heather et al., 1993). And finally, prevalence and harms have a lagged feedback effect on drug policy. For example, European drug policies have evolved considerably over the past two decades in response to a heroin epidemic (beginning in the 1970s) and an AIDS epidemic (surfacing in the 1980s). A liberal policy in a nation with a severe drug problem may be a response to perceived failure of an earlier, more repressive, policy. That the problem remains severe is not necessarily a failure of that new policy, but perhaps a reflection of the intractability of severe drug addiction in a cohort of long-time users. Preventing a worsening of that problem may be itself a significant accomplishment.

Measuring the extent of a nation's drug problem[5] requires more than estimating the number of persons using illicit drugs. Drugs differ in the damage that they cause users (e.g., cocaine's acute and chronic harms are greater than those of cannabis) and in the damage that their users cause to the rest of society. There may also be differences in the way in which the drugs are used, as summed up in Zinberg's (1984) phrase of "set and setting", which would have important consequences for the extent of harms suffered by users. Societies in which the goal of drinking is intoxication and loss of control will suffer more social damage than those in which the goal is increased social interaction and relaxation, the usual distinction between Northern European and Mediterranean drinking norms (Bucholz & Robins, 1989; Mäkelä et al., 1981). Evidence from both aboriginal and cosmopolitan populations suggests that cultural norms may regulate the use of other psychoactive drugs as well (Schultes & Hoffman, 1992; Zinberg, 1984). And a society in which the illicits are more expensive may suffer greater crime from any given level of use.

After so much hand-wringing about the hazards of cross-national drug comparisons, the reader might wonder whether they are worth pursuing. The Pompidou Group's multicity study (Hartnoll, 1994) placed the following banner atop many of its tables of cross-city drug indicators: *Warning! These data are not directly comparable.* That label is perfectly justified, and we are tempted to affix the same flag on each of the tables and figures that follow. But pragmatically, there is little point in assembling comparative data unless one is prepared to risk error and make comparisons and to make it easier for readers to do the same. Moreover there is good reason for doing so. Given the difficulties of "learning by doing" in any one nation's battle against drug problems, people inevitably look to cross-national comparisons for guidance. Our hope is to clarify what can and can't be learned from them.

5. Again note that we consider here only illicit drugs; in particular, no effort is made to examine policies toward alcohol, though alcohol is responsible for vastly more morbidity and mortality than all the illicits put together (Rice et al., 1991). A sizable comparative literature on alcohol already exists (e.g., Edwards et al., 1994; Smart, 1989). The difference in both quantity and quality between international alcohol data and international data on illicit drugs is a telling indication of the analytic drawbacks of a prohibition regime, though this should hardly be listed as a major harm of prohibition.

LAWS AND THEIR ENFORCEMENT

Though policy as implemented is quite different from the law, nonetheless the law has influence, particularly on enforcement, and important differences exist among nations. For example, German criminal law does not give police discretion (though it does allow prosecutorial discretion) when observing an offense; this contrasts with the United States and United Kingdom. On the other hand, the ability to issue cautions for simple possession of cannabis gives the British police an option unavailable in most of the United States. These legal variations often have surprising enforcement consequences. For example, when British police gained the ability to issue cautions, drug arrests did not decline; indeed, total police sanctions doubled between 1992 and 1995, suggesting that cautioning is often applied to individuals who would have otherwise been let off without formal sanctioning.[6] The recent depenalization of cannabis in South Australia (the "expiation scheme") led to an increase in the number of persons incarcerated for marijuana possession offenses because so many were jailed for failure to pay the fine (MacDonald & Atkinson, 1995).

Italy and Spain are distinct because their drug laws do not impose criminal sanctions for possession of small amounts of drugs for personal use; this covers not just "soft drugs" but all psychoactive substances. Such possession remains illegal, but the only sanctions available are administrative sanctions. These laws have been in place in Spain since 1983 (Zorilla, 1993) and have been subject to little debate. Policy discussion seems to center around the possibility of criminal penalties for use in public settings; for example, in 1989 the Mayor of Toledo imposed a 1,500 peseta fine (approximately $15) for "consumption of drugs in public thoroughfares . . . discarding or leaving behind syringes or residues that are used or usable for drug consumption" (Epoca, 1989). Italy has made many changes in criminal sanctions for possession; we examine their "natural experiment" in depenalization in some detail later.

The German constitutional court ruled in 1994 that criminal sentences could not be imposed for possession of hashish or cannabis for "occasional private use and if there is no danger to third parties." The

---

6. Data provided to us by the Home Office.

court said that it was not legalizing these drugs but recognizing that these offenses were minor and did not merit the resources of prosecution. It allowed the individual states to define "small quantities" and "occasional private use." The result has been many different interpretations of the maximum "small quantity," ranging from 35 grams in Hamburg and Baden-Wuerttemberg to 6 grams in Bavaria (Die Welt, 1994; Bild, 1995). North Rhine Westphalia has also proposed allowing for possession of small amounts (perhaps less than 0.5 grams) of heroin, though the court ruling applied only to cannabis. In March 1996, Germany also legalized the agricultural cultivation of hemp (Allgemeine, 1996), though a national poll later that year found that only one in four supported the idea of legalizing soft drugs for personal consumption (Die Welt, 1996).

The Netherlands has adopted a nonprosecution policy approximating de facto legalization for possession and sales of less than 5 grams of cannabis, recently reduced from the 30-gram limit in force from 1976 to 1995. Cannabis is widely available for retail sale in Dutch coffeeshops and in some nightclubs. Nonetheless, cannabis is formally illicit, and the production and wholesale distribution of cannabis are subject to significant enforcement activities. The Dutch regime is the only contemporary model that approximates legalization of a major recreational drug currently banned in the United States; we devote all of Chapter 11 to it.

Drug seizures

The quantity of a drug seized is a much-used indicator of the extent of drug use, in part because it is one of the few relevant figures readily generated by official administrative systems. Clearly, it is an imperfect indicator since it is a function of at least three factors: the quantity shipped (some of which may be transshipped to other nations), the care taken by smugglers and dealers to protect shipments, and the stringency of enforcement. It is very difficult to obtain any independent measures of the second and third factors, though we can offer some speculations about some of the factors that drive them. For example, smugglers will spend less to protect shipments if the replacement cost of the drug falls. Thus, seizure rates (as measured by the fraction of shipments intercepted by Customs and other interdiction agencies) are expected to rise as export prices fall. Similarly,

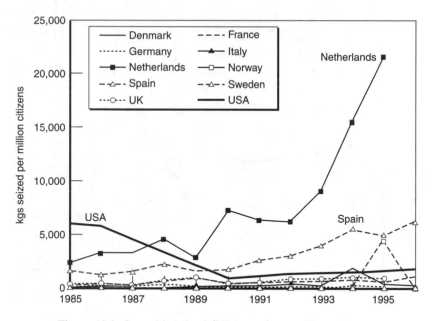

Figure 10.3 Cannabis seized (kilograms) per million citizens, 1985–96

if the drug problem is perceived to be worsening, one might expect the stringency of enforcement to rise. However, the state of knowledge about these matters does not permit estimation of a model that explains total seizures in terms of the three factors. We use seizure data as a very gross measure of shipments to a country, but (because of transshipment) not necessarily of consumption.

Figures 10.3 to 10.5 present data on seizures per million citizens for marijuana, heroin, and cocaine for ten European nations and the United States. In interpreting these figures, notice their year-to-year instability. For a country that seizes fewer than 5 tons, as most do, a single very large seizure can make a large proportionate change in a particular year. The U.S. rates are more stable since they are much larger in total.

Compared to nine other Western European nations in 1985–94, the Netherlands had a consistently higher rate (expressed in terms of drugs seized per million citizens) for all three major drugs.[7] This may

7. European seizure statistics are also analyzed in Farrell et al. (1996).

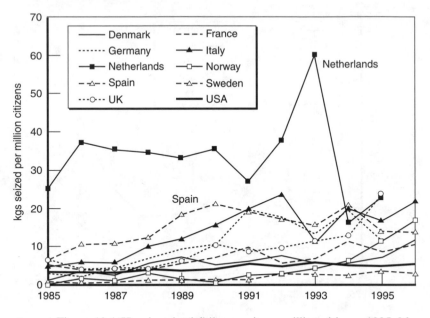

Figure 10.4 Heroin seized (kilograms) per million citizens, 1985–96

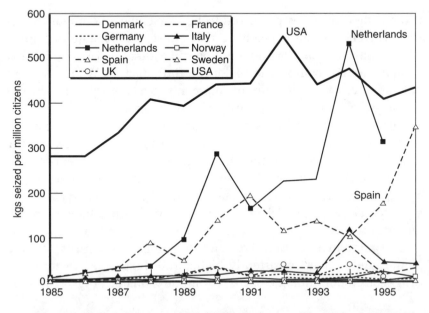

Figure 10.5 Cocaine seized (kilograms) per million citizens, 1985–96

reflect Rotterdam's importance in legitimate commerce; it is the largest port in the world, as measured by tonnage of cargo. Since drugs mostly travel in the pipeline of legal commerce and traffic, Rotterdam is a natural entrepôt for drugs, regardless of Dutch consumption levels and enforcement efforts. Seizures are dominated, in terms of weight, by interceptions at or near the borders; some part of the seizures in the Netherlands probably represents transshipment to other European nations.[8] Neighboring countries argue that the large transshipment flow is a consequence of the laxness of Dutch drug policy generally. On a priori grounds, Rotterdam's size seems more relevant since the Netherlands seeks out smugglers aggressively and punishes them heavily when caught. However, neither factor explains why the Netherlands' share of total European cannabis seizures should have risen in recent years, or why Dutch seizures of heroin and cocaine rose abruptly in 1994 and then dropped abruptly in 1995.

Spain consistently records the second highest seizure rate for all three drugs. For cocaine, that might reflect the strong ties, and substantial traffic, between Latin America and the Iberian peninsula. Though total freight movements through Spain are not particularly large, that nation does get a disproportionately large share of Latin American commerce and air traffic. The high marijuana figure represents Spain's proximity to Morocco, a principal source of hashish and marijuana to the European market. The high figure for heroin is more likely to reflect Spain's large heroin addict population than any special role in the drug trade.

Comparisons with the United States are difficult to interpret. For heroin, a number of European nations have consistently higher rates per capita than does the United States. Indeed, in 1995 the United States would have ranked only eighth among the eleven countries. Two specific factors about trafficking may explain the low heroin seizure figure. First, the United States imported substantial quantities of heroin from Mexico. This heroin had a much higher export price (i.e., replacement cost) than did Asian heroin imported into Europe so that smugglers probably took greater care to protect it, generating a low seizure rate. Similarly, the Mexican border allowed for

---

8. Transshipment routes for drug are sometimes very complicated. For example, a cocaine shipment may be intercepted in Vienna after traveling from Bogota, through Stockholm, to St. Petersburg, with an intended destination of Munich.

easier penetration than the international borders of Western Europe, so distant from the major sources. Mexico also plays an important role in the cocaine and marijuana trades destined for the United States, but for those drugs the replacement cost in the producer country is low compared to Europe, which may produce less care and higher seizure rates.

U.S. marijuana seizures are also now well below those for the Netherlands and somewhat lower than those for Spain. This may reflect both declining political interest in marijuana in the United States through 1993 and the fact that a significant share is produced within the U.S. borders and thus is less susceptible to interception.

Arrests and imprisonment

Drug law violations can be counted by both the number of individuals arrested (offenders) and the total number of violations (offenses) by these individuals. Since a single arrest corresponds to one or more drug-related charges, the number of offenses will exceed the number of offenders in any given period. Figure 10.6 presents arrest rates defined as number of individual offenders per 100,000 population. A more informative index might express the number of individuals arrested as a fraction of the number of individuals who use drugs. Unfortunately, as discussed later, national prevalence figures mostly cover heroin use only, and the arrest statistics presumably include a large number of marijuana users but are rarely broken down by drug.[9]

Figure 10.6 shows the United States to have higher and generally faster rising arrest rates. U.S. drug arrest rates are generally two to four times higher than those in Europe. Also, as described in Chapter 2, U.S. rates rose dramatically during the 1980s, while rates are relatively flat in Europe (except Switzerland). But the contrast is visually distorted somewhat by the difference in the absolute magnitudes of the rates, with the U.S. logging between 250 and 500 arrests per

---

9. Since nations operate under unique criminal codes, the definition of what is reported as an arrest may not be uniform. Generally, an arrest involves bringing formal criminal charges against an individual. However, the United Kingdom reports "persons found guilty, cautioned, or dealt with by police or other agencies," and not arrests per se (Home Office, 1992). Germany reports "investigations against the drug law," which also differs slightly from our traditional interpretation of arrest counts. These slight differences in definition are the inevitable consequence of different penal systems.

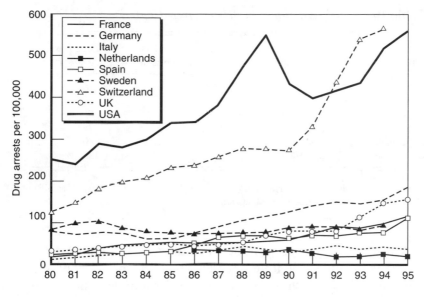

Figure 10.6 Arrest rates per 100,000 from 1980 to 1995

100,000 and most European nations under 100. In fact, drug arrest rates have grown steadily in much of Western Europe, especially Switzerland, Germany, and the United Kingdom. The exceptions are the Netherlands and Italy.

Taking out the two expected extremes in terms of total drug arrests (the United States for the high end, the Netherlands for the low end), there is still a threefold range from 45 arrests per 100,000 in Italy to 158 per 100,000 in Germany. Italy's low figure probably represents the fact that simple possession is not itself an offense subject to criminal penalties; an arrest for possession is possible only if the police are not certain whether the amount will meet the criterion "intended only for personal use." Arrests can also be classified by the type of offense involved: possession or trafficking, misdemeanor or felony, serious or not. Though directly comparable figures are not available, the vast majority of drug arrests in Italy and the Netherlands involve drug distribution, a reminder that lenient policies toward users are compatible with tough enforcement against dealers. Nevertheless, distribution arrest rates in those countries are still just a fraction of the comparable U.S. rate.

Table 10.1. *Drug offenders in prison circa 1990*

City	Population	Drug law offenders sentenced to prison	Drug prisoners per 100,000 citizens
London	6,700,000	430	6
Hamburg	1,600,000	351	22
Oslo	460,000	233	51
Rome	2,817,000	2,120	75
Copenhagen	500,000	398	80
Los Angeles	3,600,000	4,627	128

Sources: European data from Hartnoll (1994); Los Angeles data from California Bureau of Criminal Statistics in Reuter & MacCoun (1992, p. 241).

Arrest is, of course, only the beginning of the criminal justice process; of comparable if not greater interest is the severity of punishment received by those arrested in the form of detention (pretrial or otherwise) and fines and other penalties. In the United States, the increase in the stringency of drug enforcement in the 1980s has come from the rapid rise in the probability of imprisonment given arrest for a drug felony (*Sourcebook of Criminal Justice Statistics*, annual). It rose from 4 percent (23,900 state and federal inmates/581,000 drug arrests) in 1980 to 19 percent (253,800/1,350,000) in 1994, leading to a more than tenfold increase in the population of drug offenders in prison.[10] Similar data are not consistently available for any of the European study nations; only partial snapshots are available. In most of these nations, somewhere between a quarter and half of all prisoners in the early 1990s were imprisoned for drug offenses. At the national level, Denmark is at the low end, Sweden and Norway are at the high end, and the Netherlands is in the middle of that range. Table 10.1 shows the number of drug prisoners per 100,000 citizens circa 1990 for several European cities where estimates are available (derived from Hartnoll, 1994).

The purpose of drug enforcement is more than simply to raise the risks of those participating in an illegal trade. Open-air drug markets have also been a major concern in some cities but not in others.

10. This increase arises partially from a shift in the composition of arrests toward more serious offenses (distribution rather than possession) and more heavily penalized drugs (cocaine and heroin rather than marijuana).

Among those cities where the problem has been enduring and prominent are Amsterdam, Frankfurt, Madrid, and Zurich. For example, the city of Frankfurt, not generally regarded (as Amsterdam and Zurich have been for a decade) as a major center of drug use, has been concerned with a central city "drug scene" since the 1970s (Schneider, 1994). Police took action against a stable scene near the central city train station, involving about 200 to 300 users (primarily of hashish but also heroin); the result was apparently a constant movement of the scene to various areas in the inner city. In 1988, it was back at its original location, but now it involved more than 1,000 users, mostly of heroin. Deaths involving heroin, mostly around this market, totaled 148 in 1988. The police then asked for a change in policy and agreed to tolerate use (but not dealing) in a specific area, where social service agencies set up a number of facilities, providing clean needles, methadone, warm shelter, condoms, and other health services. Enforcement against nonaddicted dealers was aggressive during this period. Schneider (1994) stated that the result was increased use of all services by addicts, decreased health problems (emergency room admissions, death) and crime (robberies in the inner city, drug-related car break-ins), with outside dealers largely eliminated from the market.

Chapter 12 discusses efforts to deal with the Zurich drug scene, where a zone of tolerance had much less success. Violence around drug distribution is far less central to European drug concerns than is the case in the United States; nonetheless, the disorder and petty crime around such markets has been a significant issue for police in some cities. Why these scenes have not formed in other major cities, such as London and Rome, with substantial populations dependent on heroin, is an intriguing question for which we have not even the beginnings of an answer.

THE PREVALENCE OF DRUG USE

Meaningful cross-national comparisons of the prevalence of drug use in the general population are difficult.[11] Few nations conduct regular

11. Cross-national European comparisons have been greatly improved by the efforts of the European Union's European Monitoring Center for Drugs and Drug Addiction (EMCDDA) in Lisbon. Important early comparative efforts include Bless, Korf, and

surveys; indeed, until recently, some conducted none at all, in itself an interesting indication of differences in attitudes toward drug use.[12] Moreover, the surveys often have important differences in their population coverage, the mode of questioning,[13] and the questions asked. Coverage is a particularly vexing problem. For some adult surveys, the sampling frame is all those older than a particular age, whereas others have an upper age bound. Given that drug use was a rare behavior for those coming to adulthood prior to 1965, rates for the total population over the age of 18 are likely to be much lower than for the population between, say, ages 18 and 45.

The surveys support a few conclusions about prevalence, across nations and over time. Throughout the past two decades, marijuana was used by a moderate to high fraction of youth in most Western European nations. U.S. rates, though declining rapidly throughout the decade, were very much higher than those in Europe. Every nation in our sample, except perhaps Sweden, suffered at least a moderate heroin epidemic in the last 20 years. Italy, Spain, and Switzerland, all relative late starters, have been particularly badly affected. Cocaine has still not had a major impact on Europe, notwithstanding large and growing seizures. Amphetamines are at least as serious a problem as cocaine in most of Europe. Hard drug addiction is mostly an adult affliction; most nations have attempted to estimate their total addict population. We discuss each set of estimates in turn.

Juveniles. For cannabis, there are many more surveys of juveniles than of adults, reflecting concerns about both youthful drug initiation and the ease of surveying school-based samples relative to household populations. The school surveys are more comparable in terms of the

---

Freeman (1993), Hartnoll (1994), Reuband (1990, 1995), and Smart and Murray (1985). Earlier versions of our own cross-national comparisons appear in MacCoun et al. (1995).

12. The United States, with its emphasis on reducing the number of drug users rather than lowering the harms associated with drug use, has given much more attention to measuring general prevalence than the extent of addiction or related problems. Britain, with a policy that almost explicitly slights occasional use of drugs, has almost no prevalence data; a few questions in the Britain Crime Surveys of 1981 and 1992 (Mott, 1985; Mott & Mirrlees-Black, 1995) constituted the only nationally representative prevalence estimates in Britain until quite recently (Ramsay & Percy, 1997). It has, however, maintained a very careful addict register since at least 1950.

13. For example, Gfroerer et al. (1997) showed that classroom-based surveys, with their true anonymity, consistently generate higher self-reported rates of drug use for youth than do in-person household surveys.

ages covered; they are also less affected by differences in when drugs first became readily available in the nation.[14] Figure 10.7 shows estimates of the percentage of the "juvenile" population reporting at least one experience of using cannabis in their lifetime, within a year or so of 1990. Better data for several nations are available since the mid-1990s and will be examined in Chapter 11. But the period around 1990 is of special interest. At this point, the Reagan-Bush drug war was arguably at its peak, making the contrast between American and European policies particularly dramatic.

For two reasons, the likelihood of lifetime cannabis experience rises with age. Older adolescents are traditionally more likely to experiment with drugs, and the fact that they have lived longer means that, everything else being equal, they have had more opportunities for drug experience. The latter problem would be mitigated by past-month or past-year estimates, but such estimates are scarce in European surveys. Unfortunately, because of sample size constraints, most surveys report prevalence by age groupings, not specific ages. Thus, a 20 percent rate among 16 to 20 year olds in Denmark may not indicate higher prevalence than a 6 percent rate among 16 year olds in Sweden. With age as the horizontal axis, estimates with wide boxes in Figure 10.7 represent broad age ranges. Ranges as broad as 12 to 17 (the U.S. NHDSA) or 12 to 24 (a 1990 Hamburg survey) are almost useless for comparative purposes (though such estimates are valuable for analyzing trends and correlations). Estimates in Figure 10.7 are most comparable to the extent that they are vertically aligned.

Despite its particularly harsh antidrug climate, U.S. prevalence rates stand out. A higher percentage of U.S. youth have tried some illicit drug. Other data show that more have (a) become regular users of drugs for an extended period of time (at least some months) and (b) suffered serious harms as a result, at least as reflected in the number that are classified as dependent. Yet experience with marijuana and other drugs is by no means a rarity for younger cohorts in most nations. Chapter 11 will examine patterns of youthful cannabis use in greater detail, in a series of more focused comparisons with the Netherlands, the nation with the most tolerant cannabis policy.

14. For example, most of Western Europe experienced a sharp increase in marijuana use in the late 1960s, whereas Spain had low rates until the death of General Franco in 1975. Thus, those aged 45 in 1990 in Spain were much less exposed than their counterparts in Sweden or Germany to marijuana use during their high-risk years.

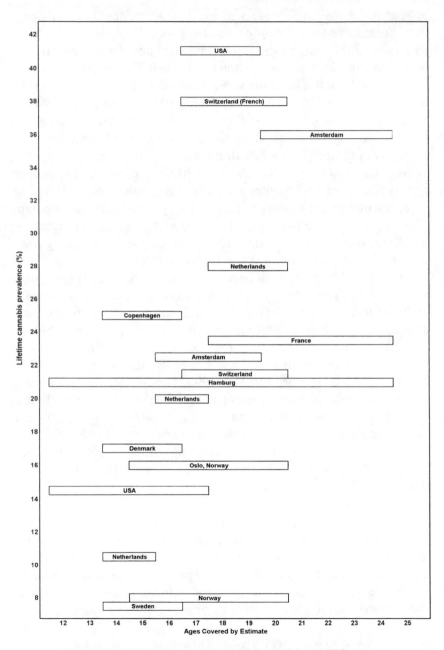

Figure 10.7 Lifetime cannabis prevalence (circa 1990)

Heroin addiction

Heroin is the major source of drug problems in Europe, as it was in the United States until the 1980s cocaine epidemic. Each of the European nations except Sweden experienced a heroin epidemic sometime in the past 20 years. Epidemics in Germany and the Netherlands began in the early 1970s; Spain's epidemic started sometime in the early 1980s. In the United States, a sharp decline in the prevalence of drug use among the general population did not lead to a decline in the extent of drug dependence and related problems (Everingham & Rydell, 1994; Reuter, Ebener, & McCaffrey, 1994). The same appears to be true of Western Europe. The resolution of this apparent paradox lies in the fact that drug dependence is a chronic, lifetime, relapsing condition for many current addicts. The drug addicts of the early 1990s mostly became dependent many years earlier. The prevalence of drug use among the general population determines the flow of new addicts so that the decline in that prevalence simply lowered or ended the growth in drug dependence. That trend is best indicated by the increasing age of the heroin dependent in Western Europe. For example, in Sweden a case-finding study in 1992 found that only 10 percent of heavy drug abusers were under 25 years old, compared to 37 percent in 1979 (Swedish Council for Information on Alcohol and Other Drugs, 1993).

Figure 10.8 gives another measure, and one with even lower quality supporting data, of differences across nations in the extent of drug use. The entries are estimates of the number of heroin addicts. Heroin is the single drug that has caused the most damage in most European nations, and it has also been a major problem in the United States. Elsewhere, Reuter (1984b) described in great detail the "mythical" status of earlier U.S. estimates of hard drug prevalence. Though these have now been refined (Rhodes et al., 1997), there is little reason to have greater faith in the estimates of European bureaucrats as compared to U.S. bureaucrats. The estimates summarized in Figure 10.8 come from authoritative sources, but those sources provide little or no documentation of the method used to generate the estimate. The usual procedure is to start with a measure of something countable but only indirectly linked to addict prevalence – number of addicts known to treatment providers, number known to the police, number of drug overdoses – and then adjust upward based on intuitions about

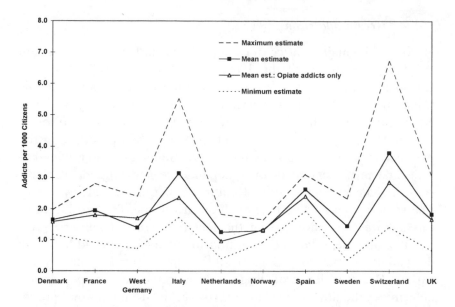

Figure 10.8 Estimated number of addicts per 1,000 citizens, early 1990s

the percentage of all addicts "captured" by that recording system. This kind of "anchoring and adjustment" strategy is an untrustworthy estimating device (see Tversky & Kahneman, 1974). But as soon as such estimates become available, they take on a life of their own and become dissociated from their sources as they get cited and re-cited without documentation. For example, Interpol publishes annual counts of known traffickers and addicts per country. For many nations in many years, the trafficker count exceeds the addict count. If these numbers had any validity, they would surely describe the ultimate buyer's market.

Figure 10.8 shows the striking variation between low-end and high-end estimates. To sort out this variance, we simply averaged together the available estimates for each country (all from the first few years of the 1990s); estimates that appeared in more than one expert or government document were therefore weighted more heavily. These mean estimates are much less variable, mostly falling in the range of 1 to 3 addicts per 1,000 citizens. We also present a second average limited to those estimates specifically referring to opiate addicts, which indicates that opiates are responsible for the lion's share of hard drug addiction in Europe.[15] Available U.S. estimates of "hard-core" users (once a week or more) suggest a higher hard drug adduction rate than any European nation – 12 per thousand for cocaine and 3 per thousand for heroin. Some heroin adducts are also heavy cocaine users, so the sum would be less than 15 adducts per thousand.

A consortium of European researchers recently conducted a sophisticated cross-national prevalence comparison of "problematic drug use" rates (defined as intravenous drug use or long duration/regular use of opiates, cocaine, and/or amphetamines) in France, Italy, Germany, the Netherlands, and Sweden (Simon et al., 1996). They derived estimates using several different methods of extrapolation from drug treatment and/or law enforcement data from the early 1990s; available data for Sweden could not support these methods. Rates of problematic drug use per 1,000 citizens ranged from 5.3 to 6.6 for France; 7.6 to 12.4 for Italy (8.7 using multivariate synthesis); 1.9 to 6.0 for Germany (3.9 using multivariate synthesis); and 2.8 to 3.4 for the Netherlands. These rates are generally higher than those in Figure 10.8; the discrepancies might reflect several factors – more recent data, more inclusive sources, and the inclusion of cocaine and amphetamine users. But the rank ordering is quite similar.

Cocaine: A "stealth" drug? American discussions of illicit drugs are dominated by cocaine (including crack), heroin, and marijuana; other drugs are either of local or ephemeral interest. That is not so true of Western Europe. Amphetamine abuse has been a long-standing problem in northern Europe. Indeed, in Sweden, amphetamine problems are as serious as those from heroin; for example, 22 percent of treatment clients mostly use amphetamines, whereas 29 percent mostly use heroin (EMCDDA, 1996).[16] That amphetamines are a stimulant drug with already established distribution systems in Europe may help explain why cocaine receives relatively little

15. For West Germany this actually produces the anomaly of an estimate of heroin addicts higher than the estimated number of persons addicted to any drug, further evidence of the noisiness of these figures.
16. Amphetamine use was actually more common than heroin use in earlier years. A 1979 "case-finding" study of drug abuse in Sweden found that more than 60 percent of the "heavy abuser" population used central stimulants, compared to only about one-quarter using heroin (Orvar Olsson, Swedish Council on Alcohol and Other Drugs, personal communication, Stockholm, 19 March 1993).

attention in the European media and, unfortunately, in European drug research. Prevalence estimates for cocaine are hard to come by. The best estimates come from Amsterdam, with a lifetime prevalence in 1994 of about 7 percent for those 12 and over; under 1 percent were recent (past month) users (Sandwijk et al., 1995). City-level studies circa 1991–2 estimated that about 2 percent of adults in Rotterdam, and just under 1 percent in Turin, were cocaine users (Bieleman et al., 1993). In contrast, the National Household Survey suggests that lifetime cocaine prevalence for Americans 12 and over was in the 10–12 percent range in the 1990–5 period. Crack, more rapidly addictive than powder cocaine, has not yet appeared in sizable quantities in Europe, though some British sources report pockets of use in poorer areas of some large cities.[17]

There are indicators that cocaine availability has risen in recent years, as South American traffickers seek new markets for expanding cocaine production. Large and rapidly rising cocaine seizures, particularly in Spain and Italy, the major southern points of entry, suggest massive increases in the trans-Atlantic cocaine traffic. In 1985, 650 kilograms were seized, but by 1990 the figure was 12 tons, almost exactly paralleling the increase in the United States between 1979 and 1984.[18] Though the figures rose sharply in 1994, they dropped almost as sharply in 1995, and the total has remained smaller than U.S. levels over the last decade.

Prices also seem to have declined, though they have remained well above U.S. levels, the opposite pattern to that for heroin. For example, in Hamburg the 1990 price for heroin was about $75 per street gram, about 40 percent pure, yielding a per pure gram price of about $190 (Hartnoll, 1994, Tables 16 and 17). This compared with a New York price per pure gram in 1990 of about $500. In contrast, cocaine sold in Hamburg for a pure gram equivalent of about $150, a little higher than the New York equivalent retail prices. But notwithstanding the price decline and evidence of increased availability of cocaine, the traditional indicators of a drug epidemic – medical emergencies, overdose cases, a growing demand for treatment – are still not showing much problematic use in Europe. Only in Spain is there some indi-

---

17. See, for example, Campbell (1993), who reported arrests of nineteen for crack offenses in London. Crack does appear in isolated reports from other countries.
18. The U.S. seizure figures continued to rise; the 1991 federal total was over 100 tonnes, and stabilized there for the rest of the 1990s.

cation; almost 40 percent of all those entering treatment (almost all for heroin abuse) around 1990 reported cocaine as a secondary drug of abuse (Cami & Barrio, 1991). One explanation may be that cocaine remains largely a middle and upper class drug, as it was in the United States in the 1970s and early 1980s (Cohen, 1989). Whatever health problems occur at this level are handled mostly through private physicians rather than public hospitals and clinics; they would then not show up in many official indicator systems, though the Spanish data cited earlier contradict that assumption.

Having said all this, the seizure figures constitute a troubling phenomenon. Unless European customs and police authorities are much better at their task than their U.S. counterparts, which is possible but implausible, the seizures suggest a sizeable market for cocaine.

Interpreting the prevalence estimates

The available data on drug prevalence in Europe are thin and vary widely in quality. Simple cross-sectional comparisons are unlikely to yield strong conclusions about the relationship between policies and prevalence. Even if the estimates were reliable and directly comparable, our analytic framework (Figure 10.2) suggests that prevalence reflects many factors other than drug policy – indeed, prevalence may sometimes determine policy. Moreover, it appears that drug prevalence and drug-related harms are only loosely coupled (see Chapter 12); nations vary in the health, longevity, and criminality of their addicts. As a result, authorities in nations with high addict problem rates (e.g., AIDS cases among injection drug users) might be able to detect and count more of their addicts.

Bearing these caveats in mind, our own view is that these prevalence data fail to reveal any pattern that resoundingly implicates drug policies. Sweden and Norway, the least tolerant European nations we have examined, have relatively low rates of drug use. But the Netherlands – typically depicted as the drug mecca of Europe – actually has similarly low levels of hard-drug use, and had very low levels of cannabis use until fairly recently (see Chapter 11). Italy and Spain (two depenalization regimes) have somewhat higher rates of addiction, as does Switzerland (an active experimenter in harm reduction interventions). But these high and low means generally fall within the minimum-to-maximum ranges of the other nations.

A stronger strategy for learning about policy effects is to combine cross-national comparisons with information on changes over time in nations that have made significant changes in their drug policies. The remainder of this chapter illustrates this strategy using Italy's on-again, off-again variations in the depenalization of drug use. Chapter 11 looks at a more dramatic policy change, the Dutch de facto legalization of cannabis sales.

ITALY'S "NATURAL EXPERIMENT" WITH DEPENALIZATION

As discussed earlier, existing U.S. analyses (e.g., Johnston, O'Malley, & Bachman, 1981) suggested little, if any, effect of cannabis depenalization on prevalence or consumption levels, a conclusion that accords well with our theoretical analysis (Chapter 5). But confidence in that inference is necessarily limited. One problem is that the policy change was fairly subtle (except, of course, from the perspective of arrested marijuana users). But a more fundamental problem is methodological. The depenalization of marijuana was not carried out in a manner that permitted strong causal inferences. There are two plausible evaluative strategies: longitudinal analyses of drug use trends in depenalizing states and cross-sectional comparisons to nondepenalizing states. (Johnston and colleagues used both approaches.) Each is a weak form of inference that is open to multiple interpretations. It helps that findings from both approaches seem to converge on a common conclusion, in this case, that depenalization had little effect on use. But the noisiness and sparseness of the data bias each analysis against detecting anything but fairly powerful policy impacts.

In the abstract, the Italian experience ought to provide a unique opportunity to learn more about the effects of depenalization. The volatility of Italian policy making may make life difficult for local officials and citizens, but it is a potential boon to policy researchers. Over the course of two decades, Italy has depenalized drugs (1975) – not just cannabis, but all the major street drugs – repenalized them (1990), and then redepenalized them (1993). This is not a true experiment (compare the Swiss heroin trials in Chapter 12), but it is a fine example of a "natural experiment" – a common but curious phrase, because there's rarely anything natural about such policy changes, except perhaps in twentieth-century Italy.

A brief history[19]

Italy's formal drug prohibition dates back to the 1923 Drug Act, which was exceedingly mild by contemporary standards. The maximum sanction for trafficking was 6 months, and the law established no criminal sentences for either possession or drug use. The language of the act hints at Italian views of drugs during the early years of the Mussolini regime, attributing their use to the "well-off" and "indolent" classes. Seven years later, the 1930 Penal Code stiffened trafficking sanctions (a 3-year maximum); use still went unpenalized, except when the user could be found "in a state of serious psychic disorder." Solivetti (1994) argued that "the rationale of the provisions was therefore that of allowing people to indulge in drug use as long as they showed the proper discretion and self-control." This is a decidedly harm-minimizing orientation toward drug control and anticipates Mark Kleiman's (1992a, 1992b) negative licensure proposal, discussed in Chapter 13.

The 1954 Drug Act (Law 1041/1954) first defined drug use as a serious criminal act, eliminating the earlier legal distinction between drug traffickers and drug users; both could now receive sentences of 3 to 8 years. Solivetti argued that the 1954 law was in response to Italy's status as a signatory to various international conventions and did not reflect any significant upswing in drug problems, which were quite modest. He also noted that the enhanced strictness of the 1954 law failed to prevent rapid growth in soft drug use in the late 1960s and the spread of heroin in Rome and other cities in the early 1970s.

By 1975, the Sicilian Mafia and other forms of organized crime were actively involved in heroin trafficking, and there were indications that opiates were supplanting soft drugs in the Italian drug scene. The policy response was a curious one. Rather than ratcheting up penalties (the typical American reaction) or lifting the trafficking prohibition (the legalizer's preferred remedy), Italy reverted to a

---

19. Our discussion borrows heavily from written essays by Enrico Tempesta (1991), Luigi Solivetti (1994), and Giancarlo Arnao (1994), as well as discussions with Tempesta, Solivetti, and criminologist Ernesto Savona.

depenalization model – depenalizing personal use. The 1975 Drugs Act (Law 685/1975) increased the maximum trafficking penalty to 18 years, though penalties for trafficking in cannabis were reduced. But the most important change was the new law's medical orientation toward substance abuse. Chronic drug use was redefined as illness rather than criminality, and personal use, and the possession of small quantities, were made nonpunishable offenses. Social, medical, and psychiatric services were established for addicts. Tempesta suggested that the 1975 law was a historic compromise between the principles of two intellectual traditions, communism and human rights, during a period of great tension between individualist and collectivist strains in Italian culture. Solivetti (1994) noted that even though the new law's medical approach to users may seem benevolent, it also introduced the option of compulsory treatment.

As shown in more detail later, a decade later Italian drug policy was in serious crisis, with a dramatic growth in drug-related deaths during the 1980s and the explosion of the AIDS epidemic among IVDUs. A 1985 Italian public opinion poll found that 77 percent viewed drugs as the nation's most serious problem; 28 percent wanted addicts to be punished "even if they had caused no harm to anybody else" (Solivetti, 1994). The government's response was to reverse the 1975 law. Effective July 1990, the 1990 Drug Act redefined users as criminal offenders, repenalizing personal use and the possession of amounts exceeding an "average daily dose" set for each drug. But even though trafficking penalties were stiffened once again, a system of graduated penalties was established for users. Initial offenses were handled administratively by the local police, who could serve warnings, suspend drivers' licenses, seize vehicles, or mandate treatment. Repeated offenses and/or failure to complete treatment could lead to incarceration for up to 3 months. In these respects, Italy's 1990 law anticipates the "drug court" model that has recently emerged in Miami, Oakland, and other American cities.

But the 1990 law was short-lived; its provisions were largely reversed by a 1993 referendum sponsored by a coalition of radical, ex-communist, and Green parties, which passed with 55 percent of the national vote.[20] The 1993 law deleted the phrase "personal use of

20. Whether this vote reflected a firm constituency for drug reform isn't clear; it may have been swept up in the enthusiasm for three unrelated political reform referenda that passed by overwhelming majorities.

psychoactive drugs is forbidden" from the 1990 Drug Act, eliminated the average daily dose, and effectively ended the repenalization of drug possession, though administrative sanctions were retained to keep Italy in compliance with the 1988 UN Convention (Italy votes against drug war, 1993).

For the time being, Italy is once again a depenalization regime for drug use.

Effects of legal change on drug problems

The 1993 reversal was largely attributed to the perceived failure of the 1990 repenalization. This raises two questions: First, what was the basis for that perception, and second, was the inference justified?

Arnao's (1994) essay suggests that the 1993 referendum had more to do with the agendas and marketing of Italian political parties – especially the Coordinamento Radicale Antiproibizionista – than with any changes in drug problems between 1990 and 1993. (This accords with our own impressions during visits to Italy in 1992 and 1993.) Indeed, statistical evidence on Italian drug trends is hard to come by; most notably, the country lacks nationally representative (indeed, even regional) drug prevalence surveys. Only a few indirect indicators are available.

Figure 10.9 shows the two longest running series, the annual number of drug deaths (1967–95) and arrests for drug offenses (1973–95) (EMCDDA, 1997; Solivetti, 1994). The figure is divided into four panels, corresponding to the 1954 penalization, the 1975 depenalization, the 1990 repenalization, and the 1993 redepenalization. The drug death figures are particularly striking, with a slow rise in the late 1970s and early 1980s, a dramatic rise in the late 1980s, an abrupt drop after the 1990 repenalization, and an apparent rise back up in 1995, just 2 years after drugs were once again depenalized. On its face, this pattern is consistent with the hypothesis that repenalization reduced drug overdoses and that redepenalization increased them – presumably indirectly via changes in drug prevalence rates. And in fact, an Italian newspaper contends that after drug deaths declined in early 1992, supporters of the 1990 law were "exultant; the results they were counting on are beginning to arrive" (*Turin La Stampa*, March 31, 1992, p. 11). An antiprohibitionist spokesman

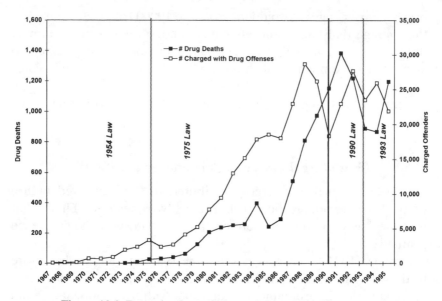

Figure 10.9 Drug deaths and charged drug offenders in Italy, 1967–95

countered (unconvincingly) that "a government that plays with statistics on the dead is acting in an indecent manner."

But even without invoking a government conspiracy, the available data are ambiguous. Drug death counts are generally a lagged indicator of drug (particularly injection drug) prevalence – a combination of overdoses and the chronic health consequences of a career of injection drug use in unsafe conditions. If this interpretation is correct, then an effect of the legal changes is hard to identify, since the number of charged offenders (mostly for trafficking offenses, under all four laws) dropped steeply 2 years *before* the 1990 law was introduced, and began its climb up again 2 years *before* the 1993 redepenalization.

Public treatment rates (Figure 10.10) offer further evidence against the hypothesis that repenalization reduced drug use and its consequences. The general trend between 1985 and 1995 was a steady increase in the number of drug treatment cases; indeed the largest increase occurred in the years immediately following the 1990 repenalization. But treatment rates are ambiguous; they can reflect increased drug use or increased enforcement, or both.

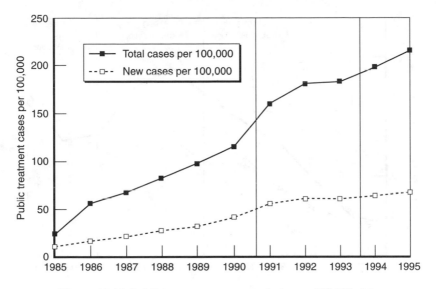

Figure 10.10 Public treatment cases in Italy per 100,000 citizens

Finally, cross-national comparisons also fail to support the notion that drug laws influenced Italian drug use and drug deaths. Figure 10.11 compares Italian, Spanish, and German drug death rates between 1985 and 1995. Spain is another depenalization regime, but maintained its policies during the 1990–3 period when Italy repenalized. Germany maintained a consistent policy of strict enforcement during this period. Yet as Figure 10.11 illustrates, the qualitative patterns for these nations closely match the Italian trends up until 1995. The downturn in Italian drug deaths during 1991 and 1993 appears to have had little to do with repenalization, though possibly Italy's upturn in 1995 was an effect of the reinstatement of depenalization.

The paucity of relevant data preclude strong inferences about the efficacy of Italy's changing drug laws. Solivetti (1994) argued that "the intervention of the criminal law has had a very limited effect on a phenomenon whose evolution can be linked with the far more powerful pressure exerted by structural forces that lie at the very heart of the way in which society is organised" (p. 47), specifically, the postwar shift from an poor agricultural economy, organized around

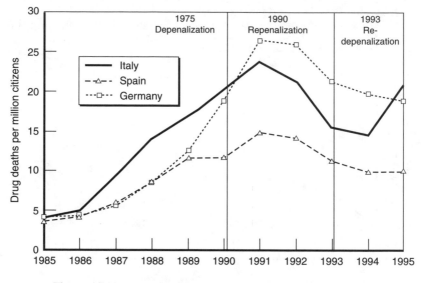

Figure 10.11 Drug deaths per million citizens, 1985–95

family enterprises, to a thriving consumer culture permitting "vocational integration" and "a phase of juvenile hedonism" (p. 51). Solivetti's socioeconomic account is plausible, but speculative. Nevertheless, we share his skepticism about the role of formal drug laws in shaping the severity and dynamics of Italian drug problems. The fact that repenalization was in place for only 3 years is also relevant; major policy changes take longer to implement. But we conclude that changes in the consequences of Italian heroin addiction probably have little to do with Italy's ever-changing drug laws and most likely reflect broader trends in epidemiology and drug trafficking beyond Italy's borders.

CONCLUSIONS

European experiences can indeed inform U.S. policy debates, partly by showing that variations in enforcement going well beyond (mostly below) recent American fluctuations can have surprisingly little measurable consequence. But that says more about the alternative possibilities for enforcing drug laws than about what might happen if those laws or their interpretation were significantly changed. To inform that larger question, we turn to a more radical European alternative, the Dutch de facto legalization of cannabis.

11   Cannabis Policies in The Netherlands

The first author was born in Michigan, where Dutch American communities carefully cultivate a tourist culture of wooden shoes, tulips, and windmills. Perhaps less intentionally, they have also cultivated a reputation for political and religious conservatism, if not intolerance. Thus, the walk down the Damrak from Amsterdam's "Centraal" train station still comes as a shock, even after numerous visits over two decades (and several years of residence in Berkeley). Large clusters of unkempt, scrawny junkies of indeterminate age sport dreadlocks and red-eyed, vacant stares. Sidewalk racks of postcards display lewd cartoons, full frontal nudity, prize strains of "Nederweed," or hands extending lit joints with the phrase "Holland Has It!" Within a few blocks, there's a Sex Museum. Posters advertise a Hash Museum, a HempWorks Store, and the Annual Cannabis Cup trade fair. Not far away, churches and bakeries share city blocks with partially clothed prostitutes displaying their wares in storefront windows. It is easy to understand why many Americans return home to tell anyone who'll listen that "Holland is out of control." Such impressions are further sensationalized by titillating accounts in the American media: most notoriously in Jonathan Blank's 1994 documentary film, *Sex, Drugs, and Democracy*.

It is true that Dutch drug policy is more explicitly tolerant than that of any other Western industrial nation, though few Americans realize that drugs are depenalized in both Italy and Spain. The Dutch impose no penalties for the possession of small amounts of cannabis, allow a number of coffeeshops to openly sell that drug, and were

238

among the first to pioneer needle exchange and other policies to reduce the harms that drug users pose to themselves and others (Ministry of Foreign Affairs; Ministry of Health, Welfare, and Sport; Ministry of Justice; & Ministry of the Interior, 1995). The Dutch dilemma is that a remarkably subtle and nuanced set of vice policies has produced visible manifestations that are remarkably unsubtle. Such vivid first impressions are hard to overcome, but we urge readers to try, because the visibility of drug use in the Netherlands gives an exaggerated impression of the true magnitude of Dutch drug problems.[1] The next chapter examines Dutch policies in a survey of European harm reduction interventions. This chapter examines the Dutch cannabis policy.

CHARACTERIZING DUTCH CANNABIS POLICY

The Netherlands legalized marijuana in 1978. Use among 13- to 25-year-olds fell from 15 percent in 1976 to 2 percent in 1983 . . . (Editorial in the *Oakland Tribune*, June 24, 1988, reprinted in Boaz, 1990, p. 151).

Despite easy availability, marijuana prevalence among 12 to 18 year olds in Holland is only 13.6 percent – well below the 38 percent use-rate for American high school seniors. More Dutch teenagers use marijuana now than in the past; indeed, lifetime prevalence increased nearly three-fold between 1984 and 1992, from 4.8 to 13.6 percent (Zimmer & Morgan, 1997).

The lifetime prevalence of marijuana use among Dutch adolescents is 30.2 percent; the U.S. prevalence is 10.6 percent (Letter to the *Los Angeles Times* by Robert Housman, Chief Policy Advisor, Office of National Drug Control Policy, July 26, 1998).

Assertions about Dutch cannabis policy and its effects have become commonplace in the U.S. drug debate. Needless to say, the preceding quotes tell very different stories. It is clear on their face that they cannot all be correct; in fact, none of them is correct. The available evidence suggests a complex story providing support to

---

1. One key tenet of Dutch policy is "normalization" – the goal of integrating users and addicts into the community rather than marginalizing them, in the hope that this will discourage antisocial behavior and facilitate treatment and rehabilitation. A necessary consequence of normalization is that drug users are more visible in the Netherlands than they are in most Western nations. This leads many visitors to an understandable but mistaken conclusion that drug use is more prevalent in the Netherlands than in the United States or neighboring nations. As discussed in the previous chapter, the evidence contradicts this view.

both reformers and prohibitionists. The most important lesson of the story is that, as hinted in Chapter 5, the term *legalization* confounds two very different interventions that are in principle separable: depenalization and commercialization.

Have the Dutch legalized marijuana? No. Well, yes and no. Sort of. Dutch law, in compliance with international treaty obligations, states unequivocally that cannabis is illegal. Savvy Americans understand that the law on the books does not always match the law as it is practiced. But the Dutch authorities do not simply wink at drug use and look the other way as in the American tradition of ignoring minor traffic violations, casual gambling, or (sometimes) prostitution.

In 1976 the Dutch adopted a formal written policy of nonenforcement for violations involving possession or sale of up to 30 grams of cannabis – a sizeable quantity, since few users consume more than 10 grams a month (probably twenty-five to thirty-five joints) (Peter Cohen, University of Amsterdam, personal communication). In late 1995, this threshold was lowered to 5 grams in response to domestic and international pressures.[2] A formal written policy regulates the technically illicit sale of those small amounts in open commercial establishments; as of late 1995, a 500-gram limit on trade stocks was established. Enforcement against those supplying larger amounts is aggressive; in 1995 the Dutch government seized 332 metric tons of cannabis, about 44 percent of the total for the European Union as a whole (Ministry of Foreign Affairs et al., 1995).

The complexity of the Dutch regime points to the danger of "Policy Platonism" – treating policy regimes as ideal types. This unusual cannabis regime falls partway between the depenalization of possession and the complete legalization of sales. Neither *legalization* nor *decriminalization* accurately describes this unusual system. We prefer the term *de facto legalization* (the qualifier making it clear that de jure, cannabis is illegal). The Dutch have concluded that this system of quasi-legal commercial availability not only avoids excessive punishment of casual users but also weakens hard-drug markets, a point we examine later.

Between 1976 and 1986, a set of guidelines emerged stipulating that coffeeshop owners could avoid prosecution by complying with five

---

2. The 1995 revisions to the policy were announced in a press release on September 18, 1996, by the Public Prosecution Service; see *www.om.nl.com/OM/engels/pressreleases/ pres1809.htm*.

rules: (i) no advertising, (ii) no hard-drug sales on the premises, (iii) no sales to minors, (iv) no sales transactions exceeding the quantity threshold, and (v) no public disturbances (Ministry of Foreign Affairs et al., 1995; Horstink-Von Meyenfeldt, 1996). In 1980, Ministry of Justice guidelines decentralized implementation, providing greater local discretion. As a result, enforcement became more lenient in Dutch cities and somewhat stricter in smaller towns (Jansen, 1991). The effect is illustrated graphically in Dutch geographer A. C. M. Jansen's (1991) maps plotting cannabis coffeeshop locations in Amsterdam. He depicts 9 locations in 1980, 71 in 1985, and 102 by 1988 – an astonishing rate of growth.[3] Jansen notes that "the first coffee shops were usually situated in unattractive buildings in backstreets . . ." (p. 69) but that, over the course of the 1980s, the shops spread to more prominent and accessible locations in the central city; they also began to promote the drug more openly.

The cumulative effect of these formal, quasi-formal, and informal policies is to make cannabis readily available at minimal legal risk to interested Dutch adults. Somewhere between 1,200 and 1,500 coffeeshops (about 1 per 12,000 inhabitants) now sell cannabis products in the Netherlands (Ministry of Foreign Affairs et al., 1995). Amsterdam alone now has somewhere between 350 and 450 coffeeshops and bars that sell cannabis (Flynn, 1994; Morais, 1996; *The Economist*, 1996). Two, the Bulldog and Coffeeshop Rusland, date back to 1975.[4]

Most offer an international variety of marijuana and hash strains of varying potency levels. A typical coffeeshop menu lists anywhere from five to twenty different "flavors," along with coffees, teas, and baked goods both laced ("space cakes") and unlaced. Gram prices are 5 to 25 guilders ($2.50 to $12.50) (Kraan, 1994) compared to U.S. figures of $1.50 to $15.00.[5] The continued high price of marijuana in the Netherlands probably reflects the aggressive enforcement against large-scale growers and distributors. The clientele appear to be predominantly young adults from a wide range of social backgrounds, including tourists – a point of contention in

3. Some locations may correspond to more than one coffeeshop.
4. There is some dispute over which is the oldest – the Bulldog or the Coffeeshop Rusland – with competing claims in media accounts, in travel guides, and on the shops' own "Web" pages (*www.bulldog.nl*; *channels.nl/amsterdam/rusland.html*).
5. Dutch marijuana may be of higher potency and "quality," a much less well-defined term used by experienced smokers. No data are available on either dimension.

Holland's relations with France, Germany, and Belgium (Horstink-Von Meyenfeldt, 1996).

The setting is considerably less lurid than one might imagine. Sales are low key; customers are more than welcome to simply sip coffee and eat a sandwich. Chess, backgammon, newspapers, and laptops occupy most customers' attention. Music varies in style (and volume) from bebop to blues to punk to reggae – the latter is especially popular – and many shops are readily identifiable by the Rastafarian imagery in their windows. They are also by the language on their signs; a coffeeshop is often the only establishment on the block with an English name, showing how important tourism is for their sales. The customers are mostly adults; surprisingly many of them in the 30 to 50 age range. Many are aging hippies; others belong to the burgher class, complete with suits and briefcases. For a visitor who prefers to remain "unaltered," the clientele is certainly less menacing than that at the many open-air pubs where tourist youth imbibe large quantities of beer on summer evenings.

Aggregate sales figures are hard to come by for this quasi-legal industry: annual sales "estimates" – really only guesses – range from 650 million guilders (about $360 million; Kaye, 1992) to 2 billion guilders (about $1.1 billion; NIAD, 1995). Morais (1996) asserted that foreigners "buy an estimated $180 million in cannabis a year directly from coffee shops – and spend a lot more staying in three- and four-star hotels, eating at expensive restaurants and visiting Holland's other tourist sites. Narco-tourism may account for as much as 25 percent of Holland's $5.3 billion tourist income." Though such estimates are of dubious provenance, it does seem likely that so-called "narco-tourism" plays a nontrivial role in the Dutch economy.

An increasing share of sales involves a high-potency domestic sinsemilla (seedless) strain called *nederwiet* (Netherweed). One story attributes *nederwiet* to an entrepreneurial coffeeshop owner named Wernard and some American backers (Morais, 1996); another traces it to the grassroots "Sinsemilla guerilla" movement, which sought to undermine large-scale traffickers (Jansen, 1994). At any rate, home production of cannabis has become widespread. Technically, Dutch law forbids the growth of anything but industrial- or agricultural-grade hemp, a law that has recently become somewhat more enforceable through the use of a permit system (Silvis, 1994; Horstink-Von Meyenfeldt, 1996). As discussed later, the Netherlands' neighbors increasingly fear that nederwiet is becoming an export product.

History

Holland is a small nation plagued by a precarious geography, and the Dutch were quick to take to the sea before it could overtake them. As a result, they have been long known for their entrepreneurialism and the pragmatism that supports it. Soon after the founding of the Dutch East Indies Company in 1602, Holland had a thriving business trading in opium and later, in coca leaves. By one estimate (de Kort, 1994), about 10 percent of the income the Dutch earned from their colonies between 1816 and 1915 came from the opium trade. In response to international pressures, the Dutch passed the 1919 Opium Act, banning opium trade, with a maximum penalty of only 3 months. The Opium Act of 1928 increased the maximum to 1 year. But cannabis trade was not formally banned until 1953.

Early Dutch experiences with the drug trade in Indonesia antici-pate many features of the current drug policy debate. For example, a Dutch source in 1929 rejected as "unenforceable" the so-called American position – then, as now – that drug smuggling could be completely eliminated (de Kort, 1994). And the Dutch were perhaps the first to implement the notion of user licenses advocated more recently by Mark Kleiman (1992a, 1992b; see Chapter 13). The government established an opium monopoly in the late nineteenth century and began licensing addicts in the late 1910s, a system that ended in 1944 (de Kort, 1994; van Luijk, 1991). Consumption and seizure data from Java and Madoera show steep declines from 1890 to 1940, leading van Luijk (1991) to proclaim the opium regime a "great success" relative to more repressive late twentieth-century approaches. Finally, the Dutch allowed physicians to prescribe opiates and cocaine late in the nineteenth century, before the so-called British model was established (de Kort, 1994; Silvis, 1994). Silvis noted that prior to the 1919 opium prohibition, an 1885 law limited physician prescriptions to fewer than 50 grams, having the ironic effect of "allowing everybody else to deal in larger portions"!

The emerging drug subculture. In 1961, the Netherlands signed the UN's Single Convention of New York, which remains today the core document in international drug control (Blom & van Mastrigt, 1994). Signatory nations agreed to take necessary steps to limit ". . . the production, manufacture, export, import, distribution of, trade in, use and possession of drugs"; compliance would be monitored by the International Narcotic Control Board. At the time, this Dutch commitment was uncontroversial because drug policy itself had too little salience to be controversial. As in the United States, Dutch drug problems only emerged as a pressing national priority with the growth of the youth counterculture of the mid-to-late 1960s. In Amsterdam, the Provos emerged as a prominent cultural force with an agenda blending communal politics and avant-garde art, not unlike their American counterparts the Diggers, the Hog Farm, and the Merry Pranksters. The Provos "playfully provoked the Amsterdam city administration and police" with happenings that prominently featured pot smoking (Leuw, 1994). Unfortunately, little is known about the actual prevalence of marijuana prior to the mid-1970s.

The rapid expansion of a youth drug culture provoked the formation of two expert commissions, one private and one governmental (Leuw, 1994). The private group was formed by the National Federation of Mental Health Organizations and is now known as the Hulsman Committee, after its chair Loak Hulsman, a law professor known for his skeptical views about the efficacy of penal enforcement. The public group was established by the Ministry of Health and chaired by Pieter Baan, a mental health official. The Hulsman Committee was radical, ideological, and academic; the Baan Commission was more moderate and pragmatic.

But the conclusions of the two groups (published in 1971 and 1972, respectively) were fairly similar, perhaps because of overlapping membership. A particularly influential member of both groups was the sociologist Herman Cohen. Cohen's (1972) study of 958 users in seventeen Dutch towns questioned several conventional beliefs about drugs, in particular the notion that users were pathological deviants and the so-called stepping-stone or gateway theory that soft drug use encourages hard drug use. Thus, each commission stressed the need to distinguish the causes of drug supply and drug demand and to address the two sides differently. Each noted the many unintended consequences of attempts to prevent illicit drug sales. Each viewed cannabis use as a relatively benign practice, generally limited to an adolescent phase of casual experimentation. And each rejected the version of the stepping-stone model holding that cannabis use creates an appetite for harder drugs; instead, they each adopted a second interpretation – that cannabis prohibition puts soft-drug experimenters into contact with the hard-drug black markets. If so, separating the cannabis and hard-drug markets should eliminate any "gateway" (see Chapter 13). Both commissions stopped somewhat short of the logic of this theory. The Hulsman Committee endorsed marijuana decriminalization but argued that distribution should remain criminalized. The Baan Commission supported legal cannabis in theory but argued that prohibition had valuable symbolic benefits; it also noted that legalization would be inconsistent with Holland's international legal commitment – the Single Convention of 1961 (Leuw, 1994).

The Revised Opium Act of 1976. A few years later, the influence of the Hulsman and Baan reports became clear with the introduction of a bill by a coalition of Social Democrats and Christian Democrats. Endorsed by the Ministers of Health and of Justice, the bill was signed into law as the Revised Opium Act of 1976, with only modest opposition by some members of the Conservative Party (VVD). The bill introduced an explicit drug-scheduling system (Leuw, 1994; Silvis, 1994). Schedule 1 included heroin and cocaine; these were labeled "unacceptable risks." Schedule 2 included "acceptable risks" – originally, cannabis and the barbiturates. (Some barbiturates were moved to Schedule 1 in 1988.) Possession (but not use per se) of Schedule 2 drugs was criminalized, but with a modest maximum criminal penalty of 1 month for amounts up to 30 grams – an amount intended to "allow a personal supply sufficient for two weeks that would also enable users to share some stuff with their friends" (Leuw, 1994).

By themselves, these revisions to the formal law were already sufficient to make the Dutch drug regime one of the most tolerant in Europe, but they are not dramatically different from the decriminalization laws adopted in Spain and Italy around the same time. What makes the Dutch regime truly distinct is not its written drug laws but rather the guidelines developed by the Public Prosecutions Department for the Act's enforcement – and more to the point, its *nonen-forcement*. The Anglo-American legal tradition has a long history of informal, discretionary nonenforcement of criminal laws, including jury nullification, the informal police regulation of prostitution and gambling, or the implicit (in many cities) and sometimes explicit (e.g., Berkeley) municipal decision to make marijuana offenses a low police priority. The Dutch system goes well beyond these examples; the Dutch have a system of *formal* nonenforcement of their cannabis laws. It is a particularly salient example of a more general Dutch legal principle, *gedoogbeleid* – the formal, systematic application of discretion, in this context usually translated as the *expediency principle*. Silvis (1994, p. 44) noted that "contrary to the principle of legality, which for example is incorporated into the German Code of Criminal Procedure, the Dutch have committed themselves to the principle of expediency (or opportunity) which formally allows discretionary powers to the police and prosecution."

Thus the guidelines stated that prosecutors and police would generally refrain from enforcing the act in cases involving 30 grams or less of cannabis; more importantly, they recommended that the police tolerate the selling of such quantities by house dealers in youth clubs and coffeeshops (Leuw, 1994; Horstink-Von Meyenfeldt, 1996). These sales remained technically illegal. Moreover, they remained technically unregulated, in the formal sense that alcohol and tobacco products are regulated in this country.

By creating a quasi-legal status for sales of modest quantities of soft drugs, these guidelines essentially created a system of de facto *legalization*. In both public settings and private conversations, some Dutch officials have taken issue with our use of that term; some prefer the term *de facto decriminalization*. The latter term captures the Dutch policy toward users but ignores the more notable fact that the Dutch have informally decriminalized *sales* as well as possession, which in our view constitutes de facto legalization by definition. (At least two Dutch addiction specialists agree, using the same phrase; see Mol & Trautmann, 1991, p. 17).

Why didn't the Dutch simply legalize cannabis, de jure? One answer is that their 1961 participation in the UN's Single Convention forbids it; recall that signatories were required to limit the "distribution of, trade in, [and] use and possession" of cannabis and other banned substances. But the Dutch contend that the Convention permits their law and implementation strategy in its Article 36, paragraph 4: "Nothing contained in this article shall affect the principle that the offenses to which it refers shall be defined, prosecuted and punished in conformity with the domestic law of a Party" (quoted in Blom & van Mastrigt, 1994). As Silvis (1994, p. 49) explained, "The Single Convention . . . [does] demand criminalization of possession, trafficking, dealing, cultivating, and producing of soft drugs as well as hard drugs. This obligation is met in Dutch legislation in the Opium Act. But there are no clauses in the relevant UN conventions that concern the actual *enforcement* of the legislation."

This kind of slippery legal thinking strikes many Americans as eccentric, even duplicitous. But a more charitable interpretation is possible, and perhaps even justified. *The Economist* (1996) linked it to Dutch tradition: "One quality that suffuses Dutch political and social mores is the notion of *gedogen*, a nigh-untranslatable term that means looking the other way when you must. It seems to feed a national need to compromise at all costs. It is often translated as 'tolerance,' but could also come close to mean something pretty close to sogginess, fudge, or even hypocrisy." In our view, this is far too cynical an appraisal. In fact, Dutch officials have been impressively candid, clear, and consistent in discussing their rationale for the policy.

Recent developments. Since 1990, the Dutch policy has gone through some important modifications, though more of an evolution than a revolution since the central principles remain unchanged. Indeed, the degree of consensus about drugs among Dutch politicians, academicians, journalists, physicians, judges, and lawyers provides a stark contrast to the rancor and name-calling that passes for a policy debate in the United States. In our perusal of over a decade of Dutch media coverage of drug policy, we have found scant evidence of fundamental challenges to the basic approach; debates mostly involve reforms at the margin. As recently as 1989, a Dutch newspaper essay confidently predicted that Dutch drug policy would be further liberalized in the future (Metz, 1989). But in fact, the Dutch regime has steadily tightened over the course of the 1990s in response to pressures on two fronts: local residents calling for less noise and disorder near coffeeshops, and neighboring nations calling for less drug tourism and soft-drug trafficking (Horstink-Von Meyenfeldt, 1996; Mol & Trautmann, 1991). Residents' concerns were dealt with fairly successfully by formalizing and tightening the regulations governing coffeeshop conduct. But Holland's neighbors have proved more difficult to mollify.

European unification has focused unwanted attention on the Dutch drug policy; what was once a matter of local culture has become a source of international brinkmanship. At the heart of the tensions is the 1992 Maastricht Treaty, and the earlier Schengen Treaty of 1985. These international treaties are intended to eventually eliminate the formal borders (and manned checkpoints) between signatory nations (Blom & van Mastrigt, 1994). In varying degrees, Holland's neighbors – Belgium, Luxembourg, Germany, and France – raised concerns about the ease with which Dutch cannabis and other drugs might flow across their borders. From the start, the French were particularly piqued by this prospect. *The Economist* (1996) quoted one French official as calling Holland "An airport surrounded by coffee-shops." A French legislator called Holland "a narcostate" (*MacLean's*, 1996).

The 1990 Schengen Implementation Agreement explicitly requires the Dutch to ensure that their drug policies have no effects on consumption and trafficking in neighboring countries (Blom & van Mastrigt, 1994). In December of 1992, the President of the UN's International Narcotics Control Board in Vienna wrote to Holland's Prime Minister, stating that some aspects of Dutch drug policy "are not in conformity with the Conventions" and that the Dutch distinction between soft and hard drugs is "somewhat artificial and arbitrary and might lead to misunderstandings which in turn carries the risk of undermining the Conventions." Specifically, the letter asserted that the Dutch policy of tolerating cannabis sales "constitutes a violation of the 1961 Convention (article 4, subparagraph c and article 33)." Prime Minister Lubbers wrote back in February of 1993, defending Dutch policy and explaining that Dutch officials consider it to be in complete compliance with their international obligations, and necessary for breaking the link between soft- and hard-drug markets.

In response to these pressures, the government began a crackdown on coffeeshops, proposing to close up to half of them for violations of the regulations. Coffeeshops are now licensed. The license is for operating a coffeeshop, not selling cannabis, but it is understood by all that this allows cities to keep owners on a tighter leash. More importantly, the 30-gram limit was reduced to 5 grams in late 1995, an amount that is ample for personal consumption but intended to discourage stockpiling by European tourists. A 1993 proposal would even have banned sales to foreigners, but it was clearly unenforceable – a "silly idea" according to one EU commissioner (Flynn, 1994).

Despite these measures, the Dutch have shown little intention of abandoning their course. In 1993, the Lower House of Parliament encouraged tighter regulation, but all parties largely agreed on the basic principles of the 1976 law and its guidelines. According to one official, "coffee shops are tolerated but they are, nevertheless, illegal. We have no intention of closing them all, but we want just enough to cater for our own citizens, not the drug tourists" (*CJ Europe*, 1993, p. 4). The Dutch recently resisted an attempt by Jacques Chirac and the French government to strong-arm them into adopting a universal European model of drug enforcement. The dispute started with the French decision to postpone implementation of the Schengen agreement. Tensions were heightened when media reports revealed that Dutch police allowed informants to traffic in drugs in order to infiltrate a high-level dealer network. Although a public commission condemned this practice, the Justice Minister defended it, and the Foreign Minister was quick to side with the Justice Ministry. The Prime Minister publicly rejected the French use of the epithet "narcostate"; a Dutch newspaper editorial concurred, finding that the term was "not only denigrating in itself, but it also appears to be the overture to a proposal to virtually place the Netherlands under the guardianship of its neighbors."[6] By the end of 1996, the drug policy dispute had brought all Dutch-French relations to a standoff. In February 1997, a face-saving agreement was finally reached – involving cooperation among customs officials, a crackdown on drug use in prisons, and cooperation against East European trafficking. According to the Reuters news agency (February 6, 1997), "France and the Netherlands literally kissed and made up" when Jacques Toubon, the French Justice Minister, "gave his Dutch counterpart, Winnie Sordrager, a kiss on the cheek."

6. The French-Dutch debate is documented in the Foreign Broadcast Information Service's (FBIS) *JPRS Reports: Narcotics*, issues 96-007, pp. 69–71; 96-008, p. 78; 96-103, p. 83; and 96-014, p. 67.

The problems of regulation when a drug is only de facto legal

The Dutch regime has had difficulties attempting to regulate an industry that is not legal. No document issued by the municipal licensing authorities actually mentions that marijuana is permitted on the premises. At one time the Amsterdam government inserted that word in a document they were using for licensing and were required by the national government to delete it (Dutch drug researcher, personal communication).

More seriously, the government cannot levy specific taxes on marijuana, following a ruling by the European tax court. Even the general sales tax (VAT) cannot be levied. This is also true for prostitution, another activity in the netherworld of de facto legalization. The government can collect income taxes on cannabis but must rely on shop estimates for that purpose.

The difficulty of regulation is best exemplified by the problems faced in trying to reduce the number of coffeeshops since 1995. Because regulation is at the local level and is not entirely open, there is no official count of the number of coffeeshops in existence nationally. The national government formed a Task Force, composed of national and local government officials, to develop a plan for reducing the (unknown) number by 50 percent. It aimed to restrict the number in each community to no more than 1 per 10,000 to 15,000 inhabitants but then it faced two problems, one of procedure and the other of substance.

The procedural problem was that the owners of the coffeeshops who were threatened with the loss of license went to court to retain it. The courts ruled that the owners had invested in the development of good will and had violated no terms of licensure; thus withdrawal of a license was arbitrary deprivation of property by the government. Even coffeeshop owners who were about to retire were successful in their suit to be allowed to sell the premises with the license, for the same reason; withdrawal of the license would greatly reduce the value of their principal retirement asset. It appears that this largely explains the fact that the number of coffeeshops in Amsterdam has only fallen from a peak of 400 to about 350 in mid-1998.

The second problem involves border towns, a particular concern to neighboring countries whose interests were taken seriously by the

Dutch government. Thus, the Task Force aimed at a border town (Venlo), which had 20 coffeeshops instead of the 4 that its population justified. However, the municipality pointed out that it was a regional center for the neighboring part of Germany. Germans came to Venlo not just to buy cannabis but also to purchase groceries and gasoline; prices in stores were regularly posted in German marks as well as Dutch guilders. The coffeeshops were not attracting tourists but servicing a well-developed regional legal market. The task force backed down.

Regulation always involves a sort of guerilla warfare between the regulated and the state. In this case, the state has few of its usual weapons available.

OUTCOMES

This chapter aims not to evaluate Dutch cannabis policy on its own terms but rather to help anticipate the possible effects of adopting a similar policy in the United States. Thus, we make no effort to assess the savings the Dutch have achieved by such a limited enforcement of cannabis prohibition. Instead, our principal goal is to assess the influence of Dutch policy change on the prevalence of drug use. A secondary concern is with the harms caused by cannabis use in the Netherlands, but as later explained such harms are either rare or difficult to document.

With respect to prevalence, we address three key policy questions. First, are levels of cannabis use higher in the Netherlands than in other Western nations? Second, did levels of cannabis use in the Netherlands increase following the 1976 depenalization and subsequent de facto legalization? Third, has the policy change weakened the statistical association between marijuana and use of other drugs?

This section examines the available cross-sectional and longitudinal data on cannabis use in the Netherlands, the United States, and several nations in Western Europe. Note at the outset, however, that no study has assessed cannabis use in the Netherlands and other nations using the same survey design and backtranslated survey instruments. As a result, the surveys being compared vary with respect to question wording, sampling design, and so forth.

The available surveys provide much better coverage of youth than of adult use. The coffeeshop regulations ban sales to minors, currently defined as youth under 18, although until recently some communities set the threshold at 16. Nonetheless, the Dutch adult regime has probably led to increased youth availability in much the same way that persistent teenage Americans can eventually find adult Americans (mostly in their early twenties) to purchase alcohol for them. (Of course, despite a much stricter cannabis regime, almost 90 percent of American high school seniors say that marijuana is somewhat or very easy to obtain.)

Prevalence of cannabis use in the Netherlands, United States, Denmark, and Germany

Are levels of cannabis use higher in the Netherlands than those of other Western nations? At the very least, meaningful cross-sectional comparisons of drug use should be matched for survey year, measure of prevalence (lifetime use, past-year use, or past-month use), and age groups covered in the estimate. Failure to meet these criteria has led to the grossly discordant comparisons quoted at the start of this article.

We have identified twenty-eight comparisons that meet these criteria (Table 11.1): sixteen comparisons to the United States, three to Denmark, two to West Germany, one to Sweden, one to Helsinki, one to France, and four to Great Britain.[7] All but two occur in the 1990s, during the period we have characterized as de facto legalization, not just depenalization, in the Netherlands.

Four contrasts compare national estimates from the Netherlands and the United States; three show negligible differences between the two countries (within sampling error), while the newest estimate (CEDRO, 1999) suggests that U.S. prevalence is much higher. This

---

7. MacCoun and Reuter (1997) identified fifteen comparisons. Here we add thirteen additional comparisons. Some of these predate that paper but were unknown to us at the time that paper was written. Two others (lifetime use among those 12 and older in Tilburg and Utrecht in 1995) were omitted from that study by an oversight. Including the latter increases the amount by which the U.S. rates exceed those in Utrecht (from a 0.3% difference to a 1.4% difference) and especially Tilburg (from a 3.4% difference to a 7.9% difference). This does not change our substantive conclusion that "U.S. rates are . . . similar to that of Utrecht, and higher than that of Tilburg" (MacCoun & Reuter, 1997, p. 49).

Table 11.1. *Comparing cannabis use in the Netherlands and other nations*

Age group	Year	Prevalence type	Dutch location	Dutch prevalence (%)	Contrast location	Contrast prevalence (%)	Difference (%)
Netherlands[c] vs. United States[b]							
12 to 17	1992	Lifetime	Netherlands	12.6	U.S.	10.6	2.0
Approx. 18	1992	Lifetime	Netherlands	34.5	U.S.	32.6	1.9
Approx. 18	1996	Lifetime	Netherlands	44.0	U.S.	44.9	-0.9
12 and older	1997	Lifetime	Netherlands	15.6	U.S.	32.9	-17.3
Tilburg[c] (population 165,000) vs. United States[b]							
12 and older	1995	Past month	Tilburg	2.4	U.S.	4.7	-2.3
12 and older	1995	Past year	Tilburg	4.0	U.S.	8.4	-4.4
12 and older	1995	Lifetime	Tilburg	13.9	U.S.	31.0	-17.1
Utrecht[c] (population 235,000) vs. United States[b]							
12 and older	1995	Past month	Utrecht	4.3	U.S.	4.7	-0.4
12 and older	1995	Past year	Utrecht	8.2	U.S.	8.4	-0.2
12 and older	1995	Lifetime	Utrecht	27.4	U.S.	31.0	-3.6
Amsterdam[d] (population 700,000) vs. United States[b]							
12 and older	1994	Past month	Amsterdam	6.7	U.S.	4.8	2.0
12 and older	1994	Past year	Amsterdam	10.5	U.S.	8.9	1.7
12 and older	1994	Lifetime	Amsterdam	29.1	U.S.	32.6	-3.5
35 and older	1994	Past month	Amsterdam	3.5	U.S.	2.3	1.2
35 and older	1994	Past year	Amsterdam	5.8	U.S.	4.1	1.7
35 and older	1994	Lifetime	Amsterdam	22.0	U.S.	25.4	-3.4

Table 11.1. (cont.)

Age group	Year	Prevalence type	Dutch location	Dutch prevalence (%)	Contrast location	Contrast prevalence (%)	Difference (%)
Netherlands vs. other European nations							
Approx. 18	1990	Lifetime	Netherlands[e]	28.0	Copenhagen[f]	52.0	-24.0
20 to 24	1994	Past year	Amsterdam[d]	25.0	Denmark[g]	16.0	9.0
25 to 29	1994	Past year	Amsterdam[d]	18.2	Denmark[g]	7.0	11.2
12 to 29	1990	Lifetime	Amsterdam[d]	33.0	W. Germany[f]	16.0	17.0
25 to 29	1994	Past year	Amsterdam[d]	18.2	W. Germany[g]	5.6	12.6
15	1996	Lifetime	Netherlands[h]	29.0	Sweden[i]	7.2	21.8
15	1992	Lifetime	Netherlands[h]	18.1	Helsinki[f]	10.0	8.1
16–59	1994	Past year	Amsterdam[d]	13.7	UK[i]	13.0	0.7
16–39	1994	Past year	Amsterdam[d]	17.8	UK[i]	8.0	9.8
15–16	1995–96	Lifetime	Netherlands[j]	29.3	UK[k]	41.0	-11.8
15–16	1995–96	Past month	Netherlands[j]	15.3	UK[k]	24.0	-8.8
Approx. 18	1994	Lifetime	Netherlands[l]	39.3	France[m]	29.0	10.3

[a] de Zwart, Stam, & Kuipers (1997), except 1997 data from CEDRO (1999).
[b] National Household Survey on Drug Abuse (SAMHSA, various years). In 1994, two different questionnaires were used; we have averaged the two sets of estimates, which were quite similar.
[c] Langemeijer (1997).
[d] Sandwijk et al. (1995).
[e] 1990 figure interpolated from 1988 and 1992 estimates in de Zwart et al. (1997).
[f] Hartnoll (1994).
[g] EMCDDA (1996).
[h] Unpublished estimate provided to us by Wil de Zwart of the Trimbos Institute (August 1998).
[i] EMCDDA (1997).
[j] The Independent (British Youth are "biggest users in Europe," 1997), confirmed for us by Wil de Zwart of the Trimbos Institute (August 1998).
[k] 1995 European School Survey Project on Alcohol and Other Drugs (Hibell et al., 1997).
[l] 1994 figure interpolated from 1992 and 1996 estimates in de Zwart et al. (1997).
[m] Boekhout van Solinge (1997).

discrepant result may be attributable to the inclusion of older adults in the latter comparison or due to some difference between the CEDRO (household) and Trimbos (school-based) national survey methodologies. Twelve comparisons involve U.S. national data and a Dutch city. Six contrasts pair the United States with an estimate from Amsterdam – a large urban setting with a highly visible drug culture. American surveys indicate little difference on average between large metropolitan samples and the United States as a whole (SAMHSA, various years), but the estimates in Table 11.1 suggest that Amsterdam has a higher fraction of marijuana users than smaller Dutch communities. U.S. rates are basically identical to those in Amsterdam and Utrecht, and higher than those in Tilburg (Langemeijer, 1997).

Many of the contrasts between the Netherlands and her European neighbors suffer from the same weakness, comparing rates for an entire nation to those in the largest city of another nation. In 1990, 18 year olds in the city of Copenhagen (Hartnoll, 1994) had considerably higher rates of cannabis use than their counterparts throughout the Netherlands. On the other hand, two contrasts suggest higher rates in Amsterdam than in Denmark as a whole (Hartnoll, 1994). Two contrasts indicate considerably lower rates of cannabis use in West Germany (Hartnoll, 1994) than in the city of Amsterdam. Comparisons of Dutch 15 year olds to those in Sweden and Helsinki show higher Dutch rates; the Swedish rate is considerably lower than the Dutch rate. A comparison of 16 to 59 year olds in Amsterdam and the United Kingdom shows quite comparable levels of monthly use. But when those aged 40 to 59 are dropped from the estimate (next row of Table 11.1), the Dutch rate is almost 10 percent higher, though this city vs. nation comparison is biased because rates are higher in Amsterdam than in other Dutch communities. On the other hand, the prevalence of cannabis among 15 to 16 year olds was 9 to 12 percent lower in the Netherlands in 1996 than in the United Kingdom in 1995. The 1995 British estimate of lifetime prevalence of cannabis among 15 to 16 year olds (41 percent) is also higher than the U.S. rate that same year (34 percent; Hibell et al., 1997). School surveys in the Netherlands and France suggest higher Dutch use levels. Finally, additional evidence presented later suggests that in recent years the Netherlands has had higher rates than Oslo, Norway.

We conclude that Dutch national rates now are somewhat lower than those in the United States but somewhat higher than those of many of its neighbors. The City of Amsterdam's level of marijuana use is comparable to that in the United States, and higher than in the Netherlands as a whole.

Trends in the prevalence of cannabis use

Did levels of cannabis use in the Netherlands increase following the 1976 depenalization and subsequent de facto legalization? Figure 11.1 plots estimates from 1970 to 1996 of the percentage of the Dutch population in various age groups who have ever used cannabis.[8]

Since the mid-1980s, there have been two periodic surveys of drug use in the Netherlands: (i) the Trimbos Institute national school-based survey covering the years 1984, 1988, 1992, and 1996 (de Zwart et al., 1997) and (ii) the University of Amsterdam's general population survey in Amsterdam, covering the years 1987, 1990, and 1994 (Sandwijk, Cohen, & Musterd, 1991; Sandwijk et al., 1995). In the period 1970–83, the Netherlands lacked repeated, standardized drug surveys, so the existing data are piecemeal across time, geography, and question-wording. Two Dutch-language publications (Korf, 1988; Driessen, Van Dam, & Olsson, 1989) systematically review earlier surveys. Driessen and colleagues (1989) conducted a multivariate analysis of data from twenty earlier surveys, statistically controlling for differences in age ranges, region, and survey characteristics. Figure 11.1 plots their estimated trend line for lifetime cannabis use among 18 year olds, 1970–86. The trend line reasonably characterizes the available data, but these estimates do not form a coherent time series like the Trimbos and University of Amsterdam data.

These early survey estimates are the only window into the effects of the 1976 policy change on cannabis use. The trend line implies that among Dutch adolescents, cannabis use was actually declining somewhat in the years prior to the 1976 change and that the change had little if any effect on levels of use during the first 7 years of the new regime. This impression is attenuated rather than

---

8. Past month or past year prevalence estimates would be more informative but are scarce, especially prior to 1986.

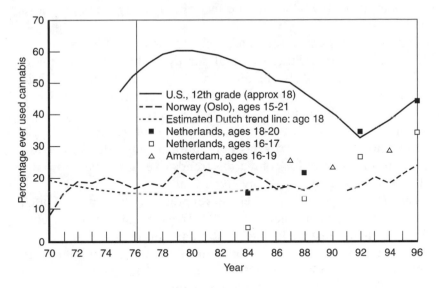

Figure 11.1 Lifetime prevalence of cannabis, 1970–96

enhanced by the multivariate analysis that produced the trend line in Figure 11.1. If anything, the individual survey points depict a more dramatic decline, apparently attributable in part to methodological differences across surveys over time. Unfortunately, there are no data on the stringency of enforcement in the years immediately prior to the change in law,[9] even though the trend lines are declining for at least 6 years prior to 1976, making it unlikely that some significant policy effect predating the formal 1976 change is being overlooked.

From the mid-1980s to the early 1990s, the period we characterize as a progression from depenalization to de facto legalization, these surveys reveal that the lifetime prevalence of cannabis in Holland increased consistently and sharply. For the age group 18 to 20, the increase is from 15 percent in 1984 to 44 percent in 1996; past-month prevalence for the same group rose from 8.5 percent to 18.5 percent

9. In the Second United Nations Survey of Crime Trends, the Dutch government re-ported 2,782 drug arrests in 1975, 3,643 in 1976, and 3,585 in 1977 (Crime Prevention and Criminal Justice Branch, 1981). These figures do not distinguish type of arrests (cannabis vs. other drugs, possession vs. distribution) and reflect both changes in enforcement and changes in drug prevalence.

(de Zwart et al., 1997). Is this an effect of the emergence of de facto legalization?

Only two comparison series are long enough to offer insight: the U.S. Monitoring the Future annual survey of high school seniors (Johnston, O'Malley, & Bachman, 1995) and an annual survey of Oslo youth aged 15 to 21 (Norwegian Ministry of Health and Social Affairs, 1997). The United States and Norway both strictly forbid cannabis sales and possession and aggressively enforce that ban. Note that because the Oslo survey has a broader age range, these estimates are more meaningful for comparing trends over time than absolute differences in prevalence in any given year.

The two comparison series behave very differently from the Dutch series, and from each other until 1992. The U.S. rates increase until 1979 and then fall steadily and substantially until 1992, whereas the Oslo figures increase sharply only until 1972 and then fluctuate around a flat trend until 1992. Interestingly, during 1992 to 1996, all three nations have seen similar large increases, as has Canada (e.g., Adlaf et al., 1995). This weakens the hypothesis that the Dutch increases from 1992 to 1996 are attributable to Dutch policies per se, though the parallel nature of the increases might be coincidental. But survey data do indicate that a variety of individual and social risk factors influence marijuana use; policy variations may play a fairly minor role (see Chapter 5).

The increases in Dutch prevalence from 1984 to 1992 provide the strongest evidence that the Dutch regime might have increased cannabis use among youth. As seen in Figure 11.1, this was a period in which use levels were flat in Oslo and declining in the United States. Available estimates also suggest flat or declining use during this period in Catalunya, Stockholm, Hamburg, and Denmark (Hartnoll, 1994), Germany as a whole (Reuband, 1992b), Canada (e.g., Adlaf et al., 1995), and Australia (Mugford, 1992). Thus, unlike the widespread post-1992 rises, the 1984–92 escalation seems (almost) uniquely Dutch. In fact, we have identified only one other location where cannabis use was clearly increasing during this period – Helsinki, where lifetime prevalence doubled among 15 year olds between 1988 (5 percent) and 1992 (10 percent, see Hartnoll, 1994).

Could the removal of criminal penalties for possession and small-scale sales require 8 years to have an effect? We hypothesize that the dramatic mid-1980s escalation in Dutch cannabis use is the consequence of the gradual progression from a passive depenalization regime to the broader de facto legalization, which allowed for greater access and increasing levels of promotion, at least until 1995 when the policy was revised. In short, it reflects a shift from a depenalization era to a commercialization era.

The Trimbos Institute, which provided much of the key Dutch data documenting escalating use, challenges such an interpretation[10] in their 1996 *Fact Sheet 7: Cannabis Policy:*

> The increase in cannabis use among young people is often linked to coffee shops, but this is highly unlikely. Not only are coffee shops responsible for a mere one-third of the total distribution, but the increase in use also started well before the rise in the number of coffee shops, and coffee shops are not allowed to sell to school pupils. The main argument against this connection, however, is that soft drug use among young people is on the increase in a large number of (western) countries, and in some these more strongly than in the Netherlands, while these countries do not have coffee shops and often have a more repressive policy.

As already seen, the argument – that use is on the rise everywhere – is accurate for the 1992–6 period but is not correct for the 1984–92 period where we hypothesize that commercialization had its effect. The Trimbos fact sheet does not cite any documentation for their other argument, that coffeeshops only account for one-third of total distribution, but it is inconsistent with other estimates. In 1996 the Trimbos school survey asked students who used cannabis in the past 30 days where they usually obtained it; 41 percent cited coffeeshops, 41 percent cited friends, and 19 percent cited dealers or other sources (Wil de Zwart, personal communication, Trimbos Institute, August 21, 1998). The rule banning minors from coffeeshops is difficult to enforce, but one would expect adolescent users to rely less heavily on coffeeshops than do adult users. In his intensive longitudinal study of the Amsterdam cannabis market, Jansen (1994, p. 172) claimed that the shops account for over 95 percent of Amsterdam cannabis sales. In their more recent study of 216 experienced Amsterdam cannabis users, Cohen and Sas (1998, p. 63) reported that 75 percent of those still using cannabis reported one or more coffeeshops as their primary source of

---

10. This statement predates our 1997 *Science* article and was not written as a critique of that article, but it clearly challenges our interpretation of the Trimbos data.

cannabis. Given the accessibility of coffeeshops in cities and the fact that one can buy enough for a few days (or weeks) each time, there is hardly more reason to make street purchases of cannabis than of instant coffee. And indeed, none of the users in the Cohen and Sas (1998) study reported purchasing cannabis from street dealers. But the 30-gram limit (or even the 5-gram limit) surely facilitates plenty of secondary transactions in which coffeeshop clients share or provide cannabis for their (sometimes younger) friends.

We should be clear about what we are and are not claiming. First, we are not claiming that the increases circa 1984–92 are solely attributable to coffeeshop commercialization. Second, we are not claiming that commercialization is synonymous with coffeeshop transactions; commercialization also involves the heightened salience and glamorization (in the youth-cultural sense) that results from widespread, highly visible promotion – in shop signs and advertisements but also in countercultural media ads, postcards, and posters.

Using somewhat different evidence (e.g., local comparisons between Amsterdam and Hamburg), Korf (1995) reaches conclusions quite similar to those offered here[11]:

> I find no indications that any real change occurred in the years following statutory decriminalization. Not until several years later was an increase in evidence, and then mainly in the cities. I have argued that this is due to the more open availability as de facto decriminalization of cannabis increasingly found concrete expression in the form of coffee shops.

In the final paragraph of his book, he argued

> To conclude, the forecasts of the prototypical prohibitionists appear to be borne out in the Netherlands, as decriminalization of cannabis has been accompanied by more users and longer term use. However, the deciding factor is evidently not so much the statutory decriminalization itself, as the form which actual decriminalization takes. Many other forms are conceivable than the coffee shop. That the prohibitionists are right doesn't inevitably mean the anti-prohibitionists are wrong.

Unfortunately, Korf's use of the term "decriminalization" obscures what an essential distinction between depenalization and commer-

---

11. Korf's book was called to our attention after the publication of our 1997 analysis of Dutch statistics.

cialization. Perhaps for this reason, Korf's analysis overlooks the possibility that the depenalization component of the Dutch policy is itself a success, in the sense that the Dutch have significantly reduced the monetary and human costs of incarcerating cannabis offenders with no apparent effect on levels of use.

Other effects

The gateway association. Has the policy change influenced the statistical association between marijuana and use of other drugs? An association between soft- and hard-drug use is necessary but not sufficient to establish a causal "gateway" mechanism (Kaplan, 1970), a point discussed in more detail in Chapter 14. Though American hawks argue that more lenient cannabis policies might lead to greater levels of hard-drug use, a central rationale for the 1976 Dutch legal change was the notion that separating the soft- and hard-drug markets might actually weaken any gateway effect (Ministry of Foreign Affairs et al., 1995). The Dutch appear to have had some success in separating these markets. As noted earlier, most Dutch cannabis users obtain that drug through either coffeeshops or friends; few buy from street dealers. According to the 216 experienced Amsterdam cannabis users interviewed by Cohen and Sas (1998), hard-drug sales at coffeeshops are quite rare; only four reported that cocaine could be purchased, and only one knew of heroin sales at a shop.

In Amsterdam, as in the United States, almost all hard-drug users have used cannabis, but the vast majority of cannabis users have not used hard drugs.[13] Only 22 percent of those aged 12 and over who have ever used cannabis have also used cocaine (Cohen & Sas, 1996). This compares to a figure of 33 percent for the United States. For heroin, the corresponding figures are 4 percent

---

13. In both countries, the surveys underestimate the number who frequently use cocaine or heroin and who almost certainly used marijuana. This reduces the denominator and numerator for calculating the percentage of marijuana users who went on to these other drugs; since the numerator is much smaller, this reduces the estimated rate below the true value. However, the problem holds in both nations, and since the Dutch are seen as doing a better job of integrating their addicts into the household population, it may be less severe for the Netherlands than for the United States.

for Amsterdam and 3 percent for the United States – statistically identical.[14]

Thus, though the Dutch have failed to eliminate the statistical association between cannabis and hard-drug use – the probability of cocaine or heroin use among those in Amsterdam who've never tried cannabis is essentially zero[15] – it is possible that they have weakened it, at least for cocaine. Also, only 6 percent of cannabis users had used cocaine more than twenty-five times; only 2 percent were current (past-month) users. Just 2 percent of cannabis users had used heroin more than twenty-five times; less than 1 percent were current users. But the probability of hard-drug use among cannabis users might vary across nations for a variety of reasons unrelated to policy. Also, even if the Dutch have a lower probability of hard-drug use among cannabis users, any increase in the probability of cannabis use due to coffeeshop sales might easily offset that benefit.

Other harms. It is difficult to assess the effects of Dutch policies on cannabis-related harms because such harms generally go unmeasured everywhere. They go unmeasured in part because the average harm per user is so modest and in part because those harms that do result from marijuana use are less tangible and less dramatic than the harms of crack or heroin.

One indicator is the need for treatment. The Trimbos Institute (1997) suggested that "there has been a rise in the number of requests for professional help over the years," noting that about 5 percent of all clients at Dutch government outpatient drug-and-alcohol clinics have cannabis listed as their primary problem as compared to approximately 18 percent among U.S. treatment centers (Gustafson, 1995). But such comparisons are inherently ambiguous. Cannabis treatment statistics reflect a complex mix of different factors – the prevalence of heavy cannabis use, the prevalence of polydrug (including alcohol) use, the intensity of law enforcement (in the United States) to coerce users to obtain treatment, and the

---

14. This unpublished estimate is from analysis of the 1993 National Household Survey on Drug Abuse, provided by Susan Everingham and Elsa Chen of the RAND Corporation.
15. Specifically, $p(\text{Cocaine}|{\sim}\text{Marijuana}) = [p(\text{Cocaine}) - p(\text{Cocaine}|\text{Marijuana}) * p(\text{Marijuana})]/p({\sim}\text{Marijuana}) = (0.06 - 0.22 * 0.28)/0.72 = 0.00$ within rounding error. Similarly, $p(\text{Heroin}|{\sim}\text{Marijuana}) = (0.01 - 0.04 * 0.28)/0.72 = 0.00$ within rounding error.

use of drug dependence as a reimbursable diagnosis for insurance purposes.

Another indicator of harm, qualitative rather than quantitative, has been the growing level of citizen complaints about certain coffeeshops. In part, the complaints involved violations of the five rules mentioned earlier (especially hard-drug sales and sales to minors), and the government has largely eliminated the violators. A second kind of complaint has been more difficult to address. In the same way that the Platzspitz failed in part because of its uniqueness (Chapter 12), the Dutch suffer from the novelty of their policy. Some of the tourists that Amsterdam now attracts are a chamber of commerce member's nightmare: they are young and unkempt in appearance, with limited funds that are earmarked mostly for getting stoned. Given the political and legal if not logistical difficulty of banning sales to foreign visitors, this problem is unlikely to go away unless Holland's neighbors ease their own cannabis laws; such a relaxation has begun in Germany and Belgium but seems unlikely in France.

INTERPRETING THE DUTCH EXPERIENCE AND OTHER ANALOGIES

There is no evidence that the depenalization component of the 1976 policy per se increased levels of cannabis use. On the other hand, the later growth in commercial access to cannabis, following de facto legalization, was accompanied by steep increases in use, even among youth. In interpreting that association, three points deserve emphasis. First, the association may not be causal; recent increases have occurred in the United States and Oslo despite very different policies. Second, throughout two decades of the 1976 policy, Dutch use levels have remained at or below those in the United States. And third, it remains to be seen whether prevalence levels will drop again in response to the reduction to a 5-gram limit, and to recent government efforts to close down coffeeshops and more aggressively enforce the regulations. But we are skeptical that much will change; very few purchases prior to 1995 were more than 5 grams, the efforts to reduce the number of coffeeshops are going slowly, and observers suggest that compliance with the regulations was already fairly high.

A complete assessment of the success of the Dutch model of cannabis regulation requires a consideration of other complications not discussed in this chapter, including potential tradeoffs between harm reduction and use reduction, the harms of drug use and the harms of drug control, and potential shifts in the distributions of those harms across social groups. This discussion comes in Chapters 14 and 15.

12 Harm Reduction in Europe

Western Europe is the original home of the harm reduction movement, the view that drug policy can have goals other than reducing prevalence and that it may be appropriate to sacrifice some reduction in use so as to lower the adverse consequences of that use. The slogan might be "tough on drugs, soft on users" in those countries that have explicitly implemented harm reduction. Aggressive hostility to this notion is almost peculiarly American, though Sweden has a history of skepticism as well. How well has it worked in those countries that have tried it?

NEEDLE EXCHANGE AND TREATMENT PROGRAMS IN EUROPE

HIV and drug use

In contrast to the United States, intravenous drug use rather than homosexual intercourse has been the principal risk factor for HIV in a number of Western European nations since the beginning of the epidemic in the early 1980s. For example, in Spain 64 percent of all AIDS cases have IVDU as the principal risk factor (Farrell, 1996, p. 124). Even in those countries that have not experienced a major outbreak of HIV, such as Britain, the IVDU vector has been viewed as the potentially most dangerous. Indeed, in Britain, the principal expert committee reporting to the Ministry of Health, stated in 1988:

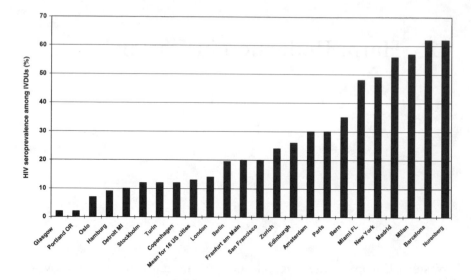

Figure 12.1 HIV seroprevalence among IVDUs, circa 1990–3

"HIV is a greater threat to public and individual health than drug misuse" (Advisory Council on the Misuse of Drugs, 1988).

For those interested in drug policy and its outcomes, the prevalence of HIV among intravenous drug users is one of the most relevant indicator of policy success. Figure 12.1 presents data on rates of HIV infection among IVDUs (around 1990–3) for a number of cities in Western Europe and the United States. These point to the importance of local variation. For example, Hamburg is among the cities with the lowest rates (less than 10 percent), whereas another German city, Nuremberg, has the highest rate (over 60 percent). Famously, Edinburgh (where the police aggressively enforced laws against needle possession in the early 1980s) has a very high rate (Pearson, 1991), whereas nearby Glasgow has the lowest rate among all the cities in the sample. The same variation can be observed for U.S. cities; New York City has rates at least five times those found in Los Angeles.

We do not present HIV rates among IVDUs nationally because good data have been gathered only for a few cities in most countries. At the national level, though, good data are available on per capita

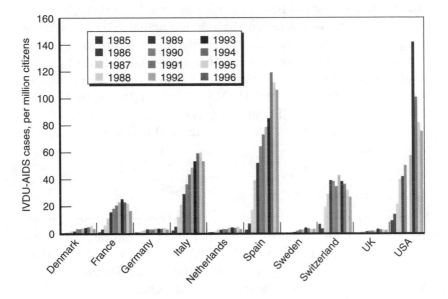

Figure 12.2 AIDs cases among IVDUs, per million citizens, 1985–96

AIDS cases with intravenous drug use as the primary risk factor. These data are shown in Figure 12.2 for the period 1985–96. Italy, Spain, and France stand out among European nations: we suspect that Switzerland would be close to them but have not been able to obtain appropriate data. Even the lowest of the leading three (France) has rates that are five to ten times those of other nations, such as Denmark, Sweden, and the United Kingdom. Given that French HIV has been heavily concentrated in the South (with a smaller pocket around Paris), the three worst affected countries have been referred to as the Mediterranean belt of AIDS in Western Europe.[1]

Until recently, U.S. rates have been higher than those of even the worst affected Western European nation. In the mid-1990s, however, the U.S. rates started to decline and now are a little lower than those for Spain, partly reflecting the fact that the epidemic started earlier

1. At least one observer has suggested that close family ties may be a risk factor for these societies. Young adult males are more likely to live with their parents in these societies, and concealing needles (incriminating evidence of a heroin habit) is particularly important in that setting.

in the United States and peaked earlier as well. Note that, given the long lead time between needle sharing and actual AIDS onset, the timing of the AIDS figures cannot readily be related to policy measures – except in the reverse sense that rising AIDS figures clearly stimulated new policies in many nations. We present the figures simply to make the point that IVDU-related AIDS has been a significant problem in some European nations. This has driven policies in many of their neighbors who are concerned about picking up the regional disease.

Needle exchange

The program most directly targeting the AIDS risk of intravenous drug use is needle exchange. Western European nations that have implemented such programs with little debate include Britain, Denmark, the Netherlands, and Switzerland. The Dutch, as in so many other spheres, have taken the most aggressive approach to needle exchange. Special programs provide needles to street prostitutes in larger cities, and outreach workers provide syringes for street users and even deliver to private homes of isolated addicts (Ministry of Foreign Affairs et al., 1995).

In Italy and Spain, where possession of syringes is not a criminal offense and where they are readily available at low prices from pharmacies, more aggressive distribution of such needles has come about only slowly. For example, a Spanish official said in 1992 that the national government had been trying to persuade provincial authorities to install syringe vending machines in convenient locations and had met considerable resistance (project interview). Only after the national government argued that these machines would reduce the incidence of needles in the street had there been any interest in adopting the measure.

Sweden has explicitly and consistently rejected needle exchange, except for two programs in Lund and Malmö, which are regarded as "outposts of a market focused on Copenhagen, Denmark, a short ferry trip away" (EMCDDA, 1997, p. 56). The programs also remain controversial in France and parts of Germany.[2]

---

2. On the other hand, some German regions have introduced needle exchange programs even in prisons (EMCDDA, 1997).

Other measures are also designed to promote use of clean needles. A number of cities in Switzerland have created *Fixer Stubli*, places in which addicts may inject drugs in the presence of public health workers, so as to minimize the risks associated with the activity. Consistent with this is the reported policy of the Geneva police department; if the police search an arrestee and find a needle, they replace it with a new one (Swiss Health Department, 1997).

Methadone treatment

Opiate addiction, principally addiction to heroin, dominates treatment populations in most of Europe.[3] Though methadone was developed in the United States and has become the mainstay of heroin treatment here, some Western European nations have made even more extensive use of methadone maintenance. Its acceptance has been driven in large part by AIDS concerns.

We have already noted the great variation in the availability of methadone as a maintenance substitute for heroin. Figure 12.3 quantifies these impressions around 1993; here we are able to estimate per-addict rates using the heroin prevalence estimates described in Chapter 10. Britain, the Netherlands, and Switzerland rely heavily on methadone as the principal modality for treatment of heroin addicts. The Dutch figures are particularly striking; about 60 percent of the estimated addict population are in methadone treatment. The Netherlands has a distinctive approach to treatment, with an emphasis on maximizing the extent of addict contact with health and social services. The most prominent instance of this is the "low-threshold" methadone programs, which provide the drug without imposing any compliance requirements on the patients,[4] in the hope that they will in fact take up the offer of other services and gradually move toward more intensive treatment; there is considerable controversy about their success (Ball & van de Wijngaart, 1994). Elsewhere the requirements for entering a methadone program are more familiar;

3. EMCDDA (1997) provided data on primary drug of abuse for seven of our sample nations. Only for Sweden was the percentage less than 68 percent.
4. On a project visit, one of the authors was taken aback to see a needle exchange facility immediately next to a methadone-dispensing window in the bus; the guide explained that at least methadone enabled active heroin addicts to start the day without anxiety about finding a fix immediately.

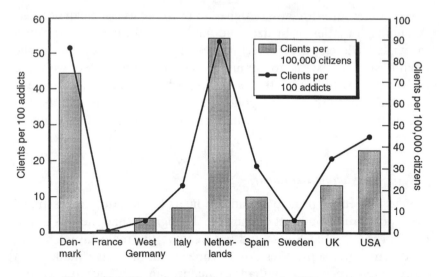

Figure 12.3 Methadone clients by nation in 1993

occasional urine testing (with erratic sanctioning) to back up a promise to end use of heroin.

Denmark, whose liberal dispensation of methadone has made that drug the principal cause of drug overdose deaths, is the only country that comes close to the Dutch penetration level. Note that the U.S. rate is moderately high by European standards, probably reflecting the intense pressure the criminal justice system imposes on heroin addicts to seek treatment.

Some nations (notably France, Germany, and Sweden) were long resistant to substituting one opiate for another. In France, where public health is a weak professional field (Steffen, 1992), the various psychiatric techniques were the dominant mode of treatment, whereas in Germany most treatment was delivered by general practitioners. Methadone availability has increased sharply in a number of countries, including France and Germany, since 1993; we nonetheless report on the 1993 numbers in the table because if policy determines outcomes, it is policy of earlier years. Overall, the European Monitoring Center on Drugs and Drug Abuse reported nearly a tripling in the number of methadone slots in the European Union between 1993 and 1996 (EMCDDA, 1997).

France and Germany are among those nations that have seen particularly large increases. Having been finally convinced of the need to act more aggressively in controlling HIV among intravenous drug users, in 1995 the French government changed policy radically. Private practitioners were now allowed to prescribe Buprenorphine (called Subutex in France), a longer acting opiate agonist in minor use in Britain, Australia, and the United States. Public health clinics were permitted to provide methadone. Within two years of the change, it is believed that about 30,000 patients wcre receiving Buprenorphine (from approximately zero in 1993), and 5,000 were receiving methadone (500 received it in 1993). Sweden remains a much noted exception to the trend to increasing methadone in Western Europe.

There is so little treatment evaluation research in Western Europe, apart from methadone in Britain (e.g., Bennett & Wright, 1986; Gossop et al., 1997) and the Netherlands (e.g., Grapendaal, Leuw, & Nelen, 1995), that it is impossible to make any statements about how well treatment serves the clients, but the British and Dutch literatures do report high drop-out rates and high criminality of patients, as in the United States.[5] In most of Western Europe, there is strong emphasis on the integration of treatment and other social services. Methadone treatment is not isolated from the rest of the health care system by a highly restrictive set of regulations specific to substitution therapies, as in the United States (Rettig & Yarmolinsky, 1995). In some countries, general practitioners can provide methadone to stabilized clients.

Treatment is offered as an alternative to incarceration in most nations. Sweden, a nation that has been perhaps the most consistently opposed to weakening of the criminal sanction against all drug offenses, has also adopted the most aggressive policy toward treatment. Most notorious is their use of compulsory short-term treatment. Boekhout van Solinge (1997, p. 123) argued that "contrary to popular belief (especially outside of Sweden) the compulsory treatment of drug addicts in Sweden is on thc whole quite uncommon." He notes that in 1994 there were approximately 900 people in compulsory treatment (accounting for about 7 percent of those in treatment that year), more of them for alcohol than for illicit drug use.

---

5. For example, Hartnoll et al. (1980) reported that 81 percent of methadone patients in their sample had at least one arrest in the year following treatment admission.

EVALUATING THE HARM REDUCTION
APPROACH: THE NETHERLANDS

Numerous evaluations are available at the programmatic level for methadone maintenance and needle exchange programs.[6] Indeed, harm reduction needs to be evaluated program by program. We also recognize, however, that it is more than a series of programs; it is indeed an approach to drug policy. It would be desirable to evaluate the overall approach rigorously, but there are numerous methodological barriers to doing so. Here we offer some observations on the Netherlands' policy with respect to heroin and take the risk of relating it to that nation's heroin problem.

Though none of its programs is unique, the Dutch government has adopted harm reduction more explicitly and broadly than any other. It is the lens through which the government reviews each programmatic and legal decision. This is particularly clear in the 1995 version of the government document, *The Drugs Policy in the Netherlands* (Ministry of Foreign Affairs et al., 1995):

> Given previous international experience of tackling markets in illegal products or services it seemed likely that government intervention would only have a limited effect. It is partly for this reason that the policy pursued in the Netherlands has always had the more modest objective of bringing or keeping the use of dangerous drugs, as a health and social problem, under control. ... On the basis of scientific criteria, legislation in the Netherlands distinguishes between drugs which present an unacceptable risk to health and cannabis products, the risks arising from which are considered less serious (i.e., between hard and soft drugs). The Dutch view is that the interests which have to be protected by the criminal law are primarily health interests. In the Netherlands drugs policy is therefore differentiated according to the seriousness of the potential damage to health which may be caused by the use or abuse of the drug in question (pp. 5–6).

An earlier version of the document declared that "Although the risks to society must of course be taken into account the government tries to ensure that drug users are not caused more harm by prosecution and imprisonment than by the use of drugs themselves" (Ministry of Welfare, Health and Cultural Affairs & Ministry of Justice, 1992, p. 8). In bold letters the same document adds "**Drug consumption is not prohibited by law.**" This would appear to be of primarily rhetor-

---

6. See Ward, Mattick, and Hall (1992) for a review of methadone treatment research and Normand, Vlahov, and Moses (1995) on needle exchange programs.

ical interest, since the previous sentence states that *possession* is prohibited by law. However, it then goes on to say "drugs are confiscated but an addict is not thrown in jail if he has less than half a gramme in his possession" (p. 10); half a gramme is a few days' supply for most heroin addicts.

This is not simply government posturing; independent researchers make similar statements. For example, "Law enforcement is viewed as an unsuitable means to regulate the demand side of drugs, as this instrument for control tends to aggravate rather than alleviate the public health and public order problems of illegal drug use" (Leuw & Marshall, 1994, p. xv). In concrete policy terms, that has led the Dutch to minimize enforcement against drug users, focusing instead on drug traffickers (see Chapter 10). Similarly policy toward drug use in prison "is consistent with the pragmatism typical for Dutch drug policy in general: one learns by doing from experience, fully aware of the fact that striving for a drug-free environment at all costs is an unrealistic goal" (Erkelens & van Alem, 1994, pp. 92–3). Thus methadone is provided, mostly for limited detoxification, to prisoners who need it. A small number receive methadone on a long-term maintenance basis, but the decision is left to individual prison doctors who may take into account the effect on drug-seeking behavior in prison in making their decision. Abstinence is sought (and lapses monitored), but it is recognized that some prisoners will continue to use and attempts are made to minimize the adverse consequences of that use.

Reference has already been made to Dutch efforts to ensure high access to treatment for the drug dependent. Income support for those whose poverty results from addiction is also generous. Grapendaal et al. (1995) reported that welfare payments provided nearly 30 percent of total income for heroin addicts in Amsterdam, much higher than the figures reported for Liverpool (Parker, Bakx, & Newcombe, 1988) and Oslo (Bretteville-Jensen & Sutton, 1996), let alone New York City in the mid-1980s (Johnson et al., 1985). The state also provides the drug dependent with access to numerous social services.

Prevention includes messages about safe use, as well as about the inherent dangers of drugs. "Measures to prevent occasional users from becoming addicted are . . . [e]xtremely important and preventing problems is accordingly given at least equal emphasis as preventing the use of drugs" (Ministry of Welfare, Health and Cultural Affairs & Ministry of Justice, 1992, p. 14).

Evaluating the success of Dutch drug policy

In its own terms, Dutch drug policy asks to be evaluated principally in terms of harms rather than prevalence. Given the paucity of harm measures in any nation, it is difficult to do so with any precision; we offer here the few available indicators.

Mortality. Almost all European nations publish annual figures on drug overdoses. Unfortunately it turns out that definitional differences are so great as to make cross-country comparison almost impossible except for subgroups of nations that have roughly comparable definitions and data collections processes. It has been said, for example, that French authorities will only record a death as drug-related if a needle is still sticking in the arm, whereas the Germans will include a driving fatality of a one-time client of a drug treatment clinic. Notwithstanding these differences, it is possible to make comparisons over time, since the recording systems in most countries seem to have been reasonably stable over the 15 years. These data, presented in Figure 12.4, show extremely rapid increases for a number of countries (Denmark, France, Germany, Italy, Norway, Spain, and Switzerland) along with reasonably stable figures for others (Britain, Netherlands, and Sweden). It is difficult to provide a fine interpretation of the movements in drug-related deaths over time, which are occasionally quite erratic. For example, German rates rose sixfold between 1986 and 1991 and then started to drop; the 1995 figure was about 25 percent lower than 1991, and then it started to rise again.[7] The initial drop after 1991 was extremely uneven geographically within Germany, with some states showing substantial declines even while others showed larger increases (Erling, 1993). For example, the city of Frankfurt, a national leader in harm reduction, witnessed a decline from 183 to 44 deaths between 1991 and 1995 (Associated Press, 1999).

---

7. The 1996 German figure was 1,712, up 9 percent from 1995 (Foreign Broadcast Information Service, February 17, 1997). In the first half of 1999, the number of deaths had risen 10 percent from the 1998 figure (Associated Press, 1999).

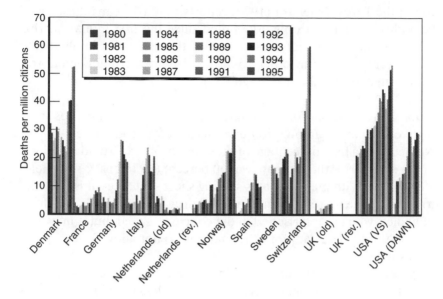

Figure 12.4 Drug-related deaths by nation, 1980–95 (see *Data Sources for Figures* for explication of alternative estimates)

The Dutch rate is notable for two reasons; it is comparatively low, and it was declining or flat when many other nation's rates were escalating dramatically. There is ambiguity about the absolute numbers, relating to the question of whether deaths of foreigners are included.[8] However, even under the broader definition, the Dutch figures are very low compared to its neighbors. We judge the Dutch monitoring system for drug-related deaths to be as comprehensive as its neighbors, though we are not expert enough in these matters to be very confident on this. But taking the national figures at face value, the Dutch death rate is 4–5 per million, compared to Germany's 20–25 per million.

Some additional support for the lower mortality of Dutch addicts comes from a long-term study of heroin users who initiated heroin

8. Remarkably, the published numbers for deaths in Amsterdam from one source show higher absolute numbers than official figures for the whole of Netherlands, clearly an impossibility. It appears that the older national series excluded deaths of non-Dutch citizens, a curiously parochial view. Amsterdam data show that a substantial number of heroin-related deaths are of citizens of other nations; in some years, more Germans than Dutch die of heroin overdose in Amsterdam (Korf, 1994, p. 134). Between 1980 and 1994, the Amsterdam overdose death rate fluctuated between 100 percent and 180 percent of its 1980 level with no apparent trend.

use in the 1970s. Swierstra (1994) reports that a 7-year follow-up of 90 addicts found that only 6 had died since the first interview. This rate (6.6 percent) is only about half of the estimated implied rate from twenty studies in other countries. This is a crude comparison with a small sample.[9]

Crime. In all nations for which information is available, studies show high crime rates among frequent users of heroin. Even in the Netherlands a high percentage of those in prison are drug-dependent; in the early 1990s the estimate was 50 percent (Erkelens & van Alem, 1994, p. 75). With many inmates serving short sentences, it is not easy to estimate the more relevant figure for drug policy, namely the share of addicts who are imprisoned in the course of a year, but it may well be one-third.[10] The data for other nations do not allow for comparable estimates.

A few studies of Dutch heroin addicts have found high self-reported rates of criminal activity as well but less than in other countries. For example, Grapendaal et al. (1995) report that in a sample of 150 "hard drug users" (mostly heroin but also including 59 who used cocaine regularly), only 24 percent of income came from property crime, compared to 43 percent for a New York sample (Johnson et al., 1985) and 65 percent for a Liverpool sample (Parker et al., 1988). The differences in sampling and data collection are so great that these should be regarded as broadly indicative figures rather than estimates of relative dependence on crime for income but they are consistent with the fact that Dutch addicts receive much more income from the state and have less need to engage in other income-generating activities, either criminal or legal.[11] On the other hand, a more recent study found that property crime accounted for only 18

9. For example, mortality rates are dependent both on the age and length of heroin career when first interviewed. If the Dutch sample were younger and less experienced than those in the studies from other countries, that might account for much of the difference. Dutch heroin may be less subject to fluctuations in purity, a potentially important contributor to mortality.
10. Erkelens and van Alem (1994) reported 10,745 drug users passing through the penal system in 1991. If 90 percent of those are heroin-dependent and 20 percent pass through twice in the course of one year, then approximately 7500 separate heroin users are imprisoned for at least part of the year. These are just pro forma figures to provide a sense of what is plausible. The estimated number of heroin addicts in the early 1990s was 20,000 to 25,000.
11. Jonathan Caulkins (personal communication) observed that in a setting where heroin use is effectively not subject to criminal penalty, the added risk of being criminally active may be greater.

percent of income among addicts in Oslo, a city much less tolerant than Amsterdam (Bretteville-Jensen & Sutton, 1996). Harm reduction has not then prevented high offending and involvement in a criminal subculture among those who become regular heroin users. Swierstra (1994) points to evidence that desistance from criminal activity occurs earlier in the criminal career than in other nations, with addicts in their mid-30s moving to a more conventional life-style though continuing to use heroin. This conclusion is based on a small sample, and again methodological and sample differences in studies done in the different countries make for weak comparisons.

Injecting vs. smoking. A distinctive feature of Dutch heroin use is the dominance of smoking ("chasing the dragon" or "Chinesing") rather than injecting (Grund & Blanken, 1993). It is estimated that only about one-third of Dutch heroin users inject as the primary route of administration (Farrell, 1996). Given that smoking dramatically reduces risks of HIV and other blood-borne diseases, this might be regarded as an indicator of harm reduction policy success. Alas, the evidence suggests that policy interventions played little direct role. Instead, the emergence of a heroin-smoking norm in Holland probably resulted from a complex configuration of historical factors (the growth of interacting Chinese, Surinamese, and Moroccan heroin subcultures during a period of widespread, and stable, availability of high purity Southeast Asian heroin; Grund & Blanken, 1993).

Conclusion. This evaluation focuses just on hard drugs, principally heroin, since Chapter 11 dealt so extensively with the other harm reduction policy, that for cannabis.

It is hard to make a case that the Netherlands' liberal policies have worsened the nation's heroin problem. In the 1970s and early 1980s, numerous foreign addicts moved to Amsterdam; it's not clear that this influx of addicts should be seen as a Dutch failure, since if Germany adopted Dutch policies both nations might see a decline in heroin-related problems. Initiation into heroin since the first epidemic of the 1970s has been low, as shown by the stable estimates of addiction prevalence and the rapid aging of the addict population. It is a criminally active population at much elevated risk of death or serious illness, but apparently it is less criminal and sick than its counterparts in other European nations.

Harm reduction policies generate less intrusion into the daily lives and activities of citizens; there is little concern about equity in enforcement, an issue that has bedeviled other Western European nations with large immigrant populations, such as Britain. Open drug scenes have sometimes been a public order problem in large Dutch cities, as they have in some other cities, such as Frankfurt and Copenhagen. Whether these tolerant policies lead to more dangerous patterns of use, for example in the workplace, cannot be determined, but there is a noticeable lack of articulated concerns about the problem in Holland itself.

Dutch drug policy appears to be expensive. The addict population receives numerous health and social services and still generates a substantial fraction of Holland's small but growing corrections budget. Drug use, including heroin consumption,[12] is more visible than in other European cities – a fact that can foster the mistaken impression that heroin addiction is more prevalent there. These are not minor matters.

But the Dutch can make a good case that they have probably reduced serious drug problems while maintaining a humane relationship with their drug addicts – a good case though not an unassailable one. For further insight on harm reduction we now consider the Swiss response to heroin.

SWISS EXPERIMENTATION

Switzerland has been much damaged by heroin addiction. As shown in Chapter 10, it is among the leaders, perhaps indeed the leader, of the European nations in the prevalence of heroin addiction and the extent of HIV among its heroin addicts.

No explanation has been offered as to why this has occurred; the epidemic of initiation appears to have occurred by the early 1980s before the policies described here were put in place.[13] What is inter-

---

12. One of us, being taken around Amsterdam by a Dutch drugs researcher, saw two people sharing a heroin pipe on a tram. It generated no interest among the other passengers and the smoke was less intrusive than that from a joint.

13. A sophisticated analysis of the pattern of incidence of new heroin/cocaine use in Switzerland is provided by Knolle (1997). He found the peak incidence in the early 1980s but detected a possible second epidemic in the early 1990s, which might be associated with the Platzspitz policies described later.

esting is the governmental response, particularly in Zurich. Without declaring an overriding principle with respect to drug control, as the Dutch government did, Switzerland[14] has been willing to try important harm reduction programs aimed specifically at reducing the severity of harms associated with heroin addiction. Neither of the innovations described here required formal legal change; both were very targeted changes in the implementation of heroin prohibition.

Background

Switzerland represents the federal form of government par excellence. The twenty-three cantons that make up the nation of Switzerland have great autonomy and power; for example, they have principal responsibility with respect to such matters as criminal law and welfare provision (Segalman, 1986). Even citizenship is conferred by the canton rather than the national government, and the welfare of a citizen is the continuing responsibility of the specific canton from which he or she comes. Cantons can choose their own social policies within fairly broad parameters. In general, they provide a high and broad safety net for their own citizens; addicts are frequently eligible for government benefits because addiction is classified as a disability. However, there are definite limits to the help provided. One official described the Swiss social service system as fairly passive, at least when contrasted to those in Scandinavia; case workers had large case loads and few rights to intervene in the lives of clients or their families. Foreign citizens, who play a significant role in the Swiss drug problem as users and, more prominently, sellers have little access to support.

A second distinctive feature of Switzerland is the extensive use of the referendum process. Even for Americans inured to the spectacle of California citizens voting on a wide array of regulatory and tax proposals, Switzerland represents almost a carnival of direct democracy. Minor tax changes and the establishment of a small number of facilities for injecting are all grist for the referendum mill. The requirements for getting a proposition on the ballot for a national

---

14. See, for example, the statement "Principles for the Future of Swiss Drug Policy" in *Spectra* (Swiss Health Department, 1995), an English-language quarterly newsletter on substance abuse policy in Switzerland. It is indistinguishable in content from recent U.S. government statements of principles for drug control.

vote are quite modest; only 100,000 signatures are needed, representing about 2 percent of the voting age population. A well-educated and active citizenry is eager to make use of this right. In the canton of Zurich, there are usually four referenda a year, with about five items on each referendum.[15] Given the severity of the Swiss drug problem, it is hardly surprising that referenda have been held on the general drug policy stance, both locally and nationally.

Third, the Swiss (as the conventional wisdom suggests) are a conformist people, with little tolerance for deviant life-styles. Certainly drug treatment officials see Swiss families as highly judgmental of their addicted adult children, unlikely to provide long-term support in dealing with their problems.[16] Addicts frequently migrate from their own communities at a fairly early stage of their careers, in part to avoid the disapproval of family and neighborhoods. Though the nation has a tradition of political tolerance, necessary for its continued survival with two large religious groupings (Calvinist and Catholic) and three language groupings (French, German, and Italian), that does not appear to extend to tolerance of what would now be called life-style differences. What is tolerated is community rather than individual differences.

Finally, the innovations described here have taken place in the context of a very intrusive overall drug policy. Switzerland has the highest rates of arrests for drug offenses in Europe[17] and a high rate for methadone treatment, which is part of a comprehensive health care system. Almost half of the nation's estimated 30,000 heroin addicts are in some form of treatment, with methadone maintenance as the principal modality (12,000 places). The innovations reported here are not a consequence of ignoring the usual responses but rather represent a belief that those responses do not go far enough, in

15. See *The Economist* (1998). Even the Swiss have their limits in political involvement; turnout for referenda is usually only about 20 to 30 percent.
16. Project interview with Zurich official. He also suggested that this disapproval was substantially more severe in German cantons.
17. Despite excellent documentation in the English language (as well as even more in French and German), it is still difficult to obtain a complete description of either formal or actual policies in Switzerland. For example, we were informed by some experts that the Swiss courts had ruled that incarceration for possession of even quite large amounts of marijuana (over 1 pound) was overly harsh, so that there was little effort at marijuana enforcement. Other experts maintained that the police and courts continued to treat marijuana offenses quite harshly. Data specific to marijuana arrest dispositions were not available.

particular with respect to reducing the consequences of heroin addiction both for addicts and for society generally.

Zones of tolerance: the Platzspitz

In 1987, the Zurich city government decided to end years of chasing an active heroin scene around its neighborhoods and let it settle in the Platzspitz (PS), a beautiful park tucked behind the central station of the city.[18] Up to that time the police had, with support from the health authorities, pursued an aggressive arrest policy, partly responding to concerns generated by youth riots in the late 1970s and early 1980s, which had revealed high levels of youth drug use. The police had also intervened against efforts to move the scene indoors (e.g., closing down some injecting rooms that had been established in a youth center).[19]

In the PS the police refrained from arresting drug users or small time retailers or from confiscating their drugs; open selling and injecting were tolerated, though the police still sought high-level traffickers there. In a city lacking slums, the park (surrounded on three sides by water and on the other by a high wall) offered one of the few locations in which the unsightly aspects of drug dealing and injecting would not be visible to residents. This toleration of drug selling and use was not embodied in any legislative change; it simply reflected a policy decision by the very active city council and the police department, implemented by the police department.

The initial purpose of the PS was to minimize the impact of drug selling on the quality of life of nonusers. Drug selling had been associated with disorder and petty crime, particularly in areas frequented by tourists. Later the PS was seen as a means for providing a central location for the provision of health services to addicts, a matter of urgency because of the high prevalence of AIDS in Switzerland, most of it associated with intravenous drug use. Facilities were set up for exchanging needles, dispensing methadone, promoting safe sex, and a variety of social services either in the park or in buses around it. Indeed, the exits to the park were literally surrounded by these facilities.

---

18. A brief history of the Platzspitz can be found in Eisner (1992). Some additional information is provided by Huber (1994).
19. Project interview with Zurich official, 1993.

By 1990 the park had started to attract large numbers of drug users from outside of the city of Zurich, hardly surprising, given that the market was located adjacent to the principal train station of a nation with one of the world's best rail systems. It was estimated that less than one-third of those using the park were Zurich city residents, with another third coming from the extensive suburbs of the canton, and most of the rest coming from other parts of Switzerland.[20] By the summer of 1989, an estimated 1,500 persons used the park each day, a figure that rose to over 2,000 by the summer of 1991 (Grob, 1992, p. 48). Most of those who patronized the park may well have been occasional drug users, but a hard core of addicted heroin users determined its character.

It constituted a gruesome sight. A visit near the end of its existence, when the numbers were already down, provided a Hieronymous Bosch vision of a drug hell. In an early winter's dusk, over flickering candles throwing eerie shadows, addicts sought to find a workable injection site in unseemly places (groin, neck), assisted by other addicts who made money by selling syringes or providing injection services in the park.[21] The grassed areas were now brown and filled with rubbish, a very un-Swiss sight, as were the apparently shrunken trees. Improvised soup kitchens and emergency care facilities did not make it any more attractive a scene, no matter what they did to protect the welfare of the users. Police patrolled, mostly to keep the nonusers out,[22] but that added to the air of a death camp, the addicts being the scripted, emaciated victims waiting for delivery as they shivered in the cold winds.

New ethnic groups, mostly from the Balkans, perhaps driven by the break-up of Yugoslavia at the end of the 1980s, flooded into selling in the park. The prices of cocaine and heroin fell dramatically during the period of its operation.[23] The park may have contributed to this by providing first a location for transactions without arrest risk to either buyer or seller and second a setting that allowed for more

20. Many of these were recorded as foreigners, not Swiss citizens. It appears, however, that most of them were domiciled in Switzerland before patronizing the park; they may have been children of guest workers or guest workers themselves.
21. Notes from a project visit in December 1991.
22. The project visit was conducted in the company of a Swiss medical researcher who had to vouch for the visitor when challenged by patrolling police; mere curiosity was insufficient reason for strolling through the park, at least at that late stage.
23. One researcher claimed that heroin prices fell from 600 francs per gram to 100 francs.

efficient selling; dealers needed to wait less time to find customers for their wares.

The park – dubbed "Needle Park" by the international media – quickly attracted attention throughout the Western world. For example, on January 14, 1990, CBS's *60 Minutes* aired a segment on the park, highlighting the contrast between the intense respectability of the famous Bahnhof Strasse shopping area on the other side of the train station and the syringe-scattered, urine-soaked park full of persons in various states of intoxication and ill health. The hypocrisy of it was the main point of the program's concluding comments: "The bankers in the Bauhaus [sic] Strasse are comfortably appalled by all this, not noticing perhaps the smell of some of their own money. But they do their bit. They see to it that the city keeps the place clean, so when the time comes for the victims to die, they will die in a neat and tidy place."

In January 1992, the Zurich city government closed the Platzspitz. The police announced that they would no longer tolerate open buying, selling, or injecting in the park; the whole area was sealed off with steel fences. This process, of course, was a somewhat protracted process, as the government tried to make provision for addicts who no longer would be able to access services through use of the park. However the citizenry, which had tolerated the park with relatively little complaint in its early years, demanded a prompt end to the affair.[24]

Having closed the Platzspitz and attempted to send the nonresident addicts back to their hometowns, Zurich police found themselves facing essentially the same problem as before the park had been opened, only on a larger scale. The addicts did not leave town; surveys continued to show that the great majority of addicts in contact with Zurich health services were still from the suburbs or other parts of Switzerland.[25] The drug scene was strung out along streets around the PS; driving into the city on a Saturday morning, addicts could be seen openly injecting.[26] The police continued to receive complaints from residential neighborhoods reporting the

24. Project interview with Zurich medical researcher.
25. Klingemann (1996) reported an estimate of 250 to 300 heavy users and up to 2,500 "passing clients" at the new location and said that this was not much different from the Platzspitz. Others suggest that the Platzspitz was home to many more addicts.
26. Personal observation, July 1992.

presence of addicts and sellers.[27] By mid-1993 the city was forced to allow a new zone of tolerance (never formalized) to operate in another, smaller area with few residents nearby. Continuing the train-spotter theme, this was near a bridge over the tracks, which allowed for rapid disposal of incriminating evidence when police approached. Needle exchange continued at roughly the 1991 rates, and new facilities opened up to allow for supervised injecting. The only demonstrable health gain, an important and surprising one, was an immediate precipitate decline in the number of recorded heroin-related deaths, from ten in November 1991 to a total of five in January and February 1992 (Huber, 1994, citing Krista, 1992, 1993).

What lessons can be drawn? The closing of the park also attracted a great deal of attention both from Swiss and international media. It was said to represent the acknowledgment of the failure of a toler-ant policy toward drug use. The *New York Times* had much to say on the topic in articles, editorials, and letters. "The park . . . is now a mon-ument to vain utopian hope and sordid devastation" (*New York Times*, February 11, 1992, A11). The criminologist head of John Jay College (Gerald Lynch) wrote to say that "[t]he case against [sic] decriminalizing drugs was dealt a mortal blow . . ." (*New York Times*, Letters, March 13, 1992, A30). In response, the head of the reformist Drug Policy Foundation wrote that "[w]hat developed at Needle Park was the worst of both worlds. The park was an island of limited decriminalization in the midst of one of the most harshly prohibi-tionist societies in Europe" (*New York Times*, Letters, March 27, 1992, A34).

Certainly the citizenry of Zurich believed that the PS experiment was a failure; the closing of the park happened rapidly and with little local controversy. The number of robberies and muggings almost doubled in the downtown areas around the Platzspitz as the popula-tion of addicts in the park expanded (Eisner, 1992). There had been a small number of gruesome homicides, apparently the result of battles between rival drug-dealing gangs, mostly from Eastern

27. During an interview with a Zurich drug squad official in July 1992, a phone call came in to the office from another part of the police force: could the drug squad chase the drug users and sellers out of a neighborhood of the caller's friends? The drug squad officer replied that they had so many calls of this kind that they couldn't keep respond-ing; anyway, the citizens could do it themselves, the users being a pretty harmless lot (Project interview, July 1992)!

Europe and the Mideast. The visibility of the PS, its notoriety, and the relatively modest elevation of crime, along with claims about the high cost of providing services to nonresidents, dominated local considerations. As already suggested, the international press applauded the decision.

Yet there was another side to the argument. The AIDS outreach efforts had shown considerable success; HIV-positive rates, adjusted for years of drug use, had fallen (Grob, 1992, Table 2). Given the numbers using the park, crime rates were surprisingly low[28]; if Zurich were drawing addicts from the rest of the nation, then the impact on national crime rates needed to be taken into consideration. The addicts were not visible in residential areas, though they spilled over into the underground shopping area adjacent to the train station. Medical emergencies had been handled very efficiently, precisely because there were numerous addicts and medical services in the area; an addict experiencing a problem would be immediately brought to one of the services. True, Zurich was bearing the burden of paying for services used by residents of other cities, but overall there was no evidence that the total number of addicts or problems for Switzerland was increasing.

What then are the criteria by which the success of the Platzspitz should be judged? Whose interests should be taken into account; just the citizens of the city of Zurich or those of Switzerland; what about the welfare of drug users? How should AIDS control be weighted against crime control? For the citizens of Zurich, AIDS control, for example, seems to have been a relatively minor consideration. It figured scarcely at all in the short debate accompanying the decision to close the park, though the professionals operating there saw reduced spread of HIV as the primary gain from the Platzspitz; instead, as already suggested, crime and visibility were the principal issues discussed publicly. Yet one local researcher and AIDS services provider concluded that "Neither the opening, existence nor the closure of the park affected the number of drug users, the quantity or the mode of the drugs used. . . . It also neither changed the

---

28. A senior police official in late 1991 provided a list of all the serious crimes in the PS for the previous 12 months; the list had thirty-one items on it, including one homicide but also two instances of resisting arrest. To an observer from Washington, DC, this looked like something less than a horrible indictment of the major drug addict congregating area in a metropolitan area of 750,000.

criminal acts of drug users nor their death toll. However, [the closing] shifted the visibility of the drug problem resulting in an element of relief to the commercial center of Zurich and to the battered image of 'beautiful' Switzerland" (Grob, 1992, p. 59).

Though no other city went so far as to set up a zone of tolerance for buying and selling, Zurich was not the only Swiss city to experiment with harm reduction measures. Others, primarily in the German-speaking region of the country, allowed injecting facilities, called either *Gastzimmer* or *Fixer Stubli*. Aimed at controlling the spread of HIV, these places, where addicts could inject under the supervision of medically trained personnel, attracted little attention. Bern also permitted a zone of tolerance, near the parliament building, known as the Kocher Park.

This helped provide national support for the next major innovative in Switzerland, the launching of national heroin maintenance trials. Innovation though it was, such a program had already acquired a history and some notoriety, starting with the clinics for heroin addicts in the early post-Harrison Act period in the United States (Musto, 1987).

HEROIN MAINTENANCE

The British experience

In a 1926 report, the blue-ribbon Rolleston Committee concluded "that morphine and heroin addiction . . . must be regarded as a manifestation of disease and not as a mere form of vicious indulgence." Thus, if repeated attempts to withdraw a patient from cocaine or heroin were unsuccessful, "the indefinitely prolonged administration of morphine and heroin [might] be necessary [for] those [patients] who are capable of leading a useful and normal life so long as they take a certain quantity, usually small, of their drug of addiction, but not otherwise" (as quoted in Stears, 1997, p. 123). This led the British to adopt (or at least formalize) a system in which physicians could prescribe heroin to addicted patients for maintenance purposes (Judson, 1974). With a small population of iatrogenically addicted opiate users (numbering in the hundreds), the system muddled along for four decades with few problems.

The system was not very controversial through most of that period. When the government in 1955 considered banning heroin completely, in response to international pressures rather than because of any domestic complaints about the system, the British medical establishment fought back effectively, and the government eventually abandoned the effort. The incident seems to say more about the power of the medical establishment and its dedication to physician autonomy than about the success of heroin maintenance (Judson, 1974, pp. 29–34).

Then in the early 1960s, a very small number of physicians began to prescribe irresponsibly, and a few heroin users began using the drug purely for recreational purposes, recruiting others like themselves. The result was a sharp proportionate increase in heroin addiction in the mid-1960s, still leaving the nation with a very small heroin problem; there were only about 1,500 known addicts in 1967 (Johnson, 1975). In response to the increase, the *Dangerous Drugs Act of 1967* greatly curtailed access to heroin maintenance, limiting it to a small number of specially licensed drug-treatment specialists.[29]

Addicts now were required to seek treatment, maintenance or otherwise, from specialized clinics. At the same time, oral methadone became available as a substitute pharmacotherapy. British specialists proved as enthusiastic about this alternative as did their U.S. counterparts. The fraction of maintained addicts receiving heroin fell rapidly. By 1975 only 4 percent of maintained opiate addicts were receiving heroin alone; another 8 percent were receiving both methadone and heroin (Johnson, 1977). That reluctance to prescribe heroin remains true today; fewer than 1 percent of those being maintained on an opiate receive heroin (Stears, 1997). The strong and continued antipathy of British addiction specialists to provision of heroin is a curious and troubling phenomenon for those who advocate its use for maintenance.

British research on the efficacy of heroin maintenance is quite limited. One classic study (Hartnoll et al., 1980) found that those being maintained on heroin did only moderately better than

---

29. It is difficult to obtain a precise description of the change in regime, which actually involved a number of changes over a period of years. Physicians retained the right to prescribe heroin for pain control purposes but not to maintain an addicted patient.

those receiving oral methadone. "[W]hile heroin-prescribed patients attended the clinic more regularly and showed some reduction in the extent of their criminal activities, nevertheless they showed no change in their other social activities such as work, stable accommodation or diet, nor did they differ significantly in the physical complications of drug use from those denied such a prescription" (Mitcheson, 1994, p. 182). There was moderate leakage of heroin from the trial; 37 percent of those receiving heroin admitted that they at least occasionally sold some of their supply on the black market. An important factor in explaining the relatively weak results for heroin maintenance may have been the effort to limit doses; the average dose received by the patients, who had to bargain aggressively with their doctors, was 60 milligrams of pure heroin daily.[30] Mostly though there was indifference in Britain; the claims of one British practitioner (John Marks, operating in the Liverpool metropolitan area) as to the efficacy of heroin in reducing criminal involvement aroused controversy but little curiosity in the British establishment. Observers from other nations, including Switzerland, were more interested (Ulrigh-Votglin, 1997).

The Swiss heroin maintenance trials

Having closed the Platzspitz, Zurich authorities still sought an innovative approach to controlling their severe heroin problem. In January 1994, they opened the first heroin maintenance clinics, part of a 3-year national trial of heroin maintenance as a supplement to the large methadone maintenance program that had been operating for at least a decade. In late 1997, the federal government approved a large-scale expansion, potentially accommodating 15 percent of the nation's estimated 30,000 heroin addicts (Leuthardt, 1997).

The motivation for these trials was complex. Two federal officials suggested that it was partly an effort to forestall a strong legalization movement. They believed that the Swiss citizenry are unwilling to be very tough about enforcement but are also offended by the unsightliness of the drug scene. Heroin maintenance was likely to reduce the visibility of the problem, an important element in

---

30. On the struggles between patient and doctor, see Edwards (1969).

Switzerland. A 1991 survey found that only about 10 percent favored police action against all drug users, but 57 percent favored suppression of open drug scenes (Gutzwiller & Uchtenhagen, 1997). For other policy makers, it was an obvious next step in reducing the risk of AIDS.

The decision was taken after very public consultations at the highest levels. An unusual "summit meeting" was held, at which the Swiss president[31] and the heads of the cantonal governments approved an experiment to test whether heroin maintenance would reduce heroin problems. Public opinion was generally supportive; in a 1991 poll, 72 percent expressed approval of controlled prescription of heroin (Gutzwiller & Uchtenhagen, 1997).[32] The experiment was widely discussed in the media before implementation. An elaborate governance structure was established, including very detailed ethical scrutiny by regional ethics officers (Uchtenhagen, Gutzwiller, & Dobler-Mikola, 1997). As an example of the care that was taken to protect the public health, enrollees were required to surrender their drivers licenses, thus reducing the risk of their driving while heroin-intoxicated. Similarly, it was decided that once the government has provided heroin addicts with the drug, it incurred a continuing obligation to maintain those addicts as long as they sought heroin.

The original design involved three groups of patients receiving different injectable opiates: 250 received heroin, 250 received morphine, and 200 received methadone. The early experience with morphine was that it caused discomfort to the patients and it was abandoned. Patients were reluctant to accept injectable methadone. As a consequence, the final report focused on injectable heroin.

Participants in the trials were required to be at least 20 years old, to have had two years of intravenous injecting, and to have failed at two other treatment attempts. These are hardly very tight screens. In fact, most of those admitted had extensive careers both in heroin addiction and in treatment; for example, in the Geneva site, the

31. The Swiss presidency is not such an august position, being occupied in 6-month rotations by each member of the seven-person cabinet elected by parliament. Nonetheless, the president does represent, at least temporarily, the leadership of the federal government.
32. Interestingly, the same survey found a noticeable increase in the percentage opposing this between 1991 and 1994 (from 24 to 30 percent); this was a period when the trials were being debated publicly.

average age was 33, with 12 years of injecting heroin and eight prior treatment episodes.[33]

A decision to allow addicts to choose the dose they needed was critical; it removed any incentive to supplement the clinic provision with black market purchases and removed an important source of tension in the relationship with clinic personnel. A patient could receive heroin three times daily, 365 days of the year.[34] The average daily dose was 500–600 milligrams of pure heroin, a massive amount by the standards of U.S. street addicts.[35] At the very beginning, patients, faced with no constraint with respect to the drug that had dominated their lives and that had always been very difficult and expensive to obtain, sought rapidly increasing doses; they soon plateaued at levels that still permitted many of than a high level of social functioning.[36]

The patient self-injected with equipment prepared by the staff, who could also provide advice about injecting practices as they supervised the injection. Participants paid 15 francs (ca. $10) daily; many paid out of their state welfare income. No heroin could be taken off the premises, thus minimizing the risk of leakage into the black market.

Initially, enrollment in the trials lagged behind schedule, but after the first year enthusiasm among local officials increased sharply; consequently, the trials ended up enlisting more than the initial targets and in a greater variety of settings than expected. Small towns (e.g., St. Gallen, population 70,000) and prisons volunteered to be sites and were able to enroll clients. Nonetheless, some sites, such as Geneva, were never able to reach their enrollment targets (Perneger et al., 1998). The project certainly demonstrated the feasibility of heroin maintenance. By the end of the trials, over 800 patients had

---

33. As of this writing, only one document describing the full 3-year multisite evaluation has been published in English. It is an 11-page "Summary of the Synthesis Report," which provides little quantitative detail. Hence, we use here more detailed data from specific sites.
34. Some patients were permitted to inject more than once in a single session.
35. At $1 per milligram, a low street price in recent years outside of New York, that would amount to $500–600 per day in heroin expenditures alone. The actual figure is about one-tenth of that (Riley, 1997).
36. Interesting comments on these dynamics are provided by Haemmig (1995), commenting on early experiences: "People in the project tend to take too much of the drug. Many seem to have a concept that their only real problem in life is to get enough drugs. In the projects, for the first time in their lives, they can have as much as they need. In the course of time, it gets depressing for them to realize that they have problems other than just getting enough drugs" (p. 377).

received heroin on a regular basis without leakage into the illicit market.[37] No overdoses were reported among participants while they stayed in the program. They had ended up choosing dosage levels that allowed them as a group to improve their social and economic functioning.[38] A large majority of participants had maintained the regime that was imposed on them, requiring daily attendance at the clinic. For example, in Geneva twenty out of twenty five patients received heroin on more than 80 percent of treatment days (Perneger et al., 1998).

Outcomes were generally very positive. Retention in treatment, a standard measure of success, was high relative to those found in methadone programs generally;[39] 69 percent were in treatment 18 months after admission.[40] About half of those recorded as dropouts in fact moved to other treatment modalities, some choosing methadone and others abstinence-based modalities. One observer suggested that these patients, having discovered the limitations of untrammeled access to heroin, were now ready to attempt quitting. Crime rates were much reduced as compared to treatment entry; self-reported rates fell by 60 percent during the first 6 months, and this was supported by data from official arrest records. Self-reported use of nonprescribed heroin fell sharply, and the percentage with jobs that were described as "permanent" increased from 14 to 32 percent and unemployment fell from 44 to 20 percent. Self-reported mental health improved substantially. Only three new HIV infections, probably related to cocaine use outside of the clinics, were detected. One interesting finding is that though many addicts were able to detach themselves from the heroin subculture, they were unable to develop other attachments. Given their weak labor force performance and estrangement over previous decade from nonaddicts, this isolation in retrospect is hardly surprising but points to the long-term psychosocial challenge.

37. This statement is uncontroversial, but, absent use of some marker on the clinic heroin, we do not know how it can be demonstrated.
38. The Geneva site reported that they reached stable dosages within the first month.
39. Wayne Hall (personal communication) noted that, given well-known problems of large-scale implementation, the more appropriate comparison is to retention in the early, experimental methadone programs involving researchers. See, for example, Gearing and Schweitzer (1974).
40. Eighteen months was used as the length of time for assessing success because only a modest fraction had entered treatment more than 18 months before the agreed-upon termination date for the trials as such.

The evaluation carried out by the Swiss government was led by Ambros Uchtenhagen, a leading Swiss drug treatment researcher. The trial design, primarily a comparison of before-and-after behavior of the patients without a well-specified control group (Killias & Uchtenhagen, 1996), limited the power of its findings. In the absence of a control group or random assignment, the natural metric for assessing the program was comparing the success of methadone programs with similar patients, yet the heroin maintenance trial participants also were targeted with substantially more psychosocial services than the typical methadone patient. Was the claimed success a function of the heroin or the additional services (Farrell & Hall, 1998)? The evaluation relied primarily on self-reports by patients, with few objective measures.

Only at the Geneva site was there random assignment between heroin and other modalities.[41] Experimental subjects were substantially less involved in the street heroin markets, were less criminally active generally, and showed improved social functioning and mental health compared to the controls. On a number of other dimensions (drug overdoses, precautions against AIDS, and overall health status), the two groups did not differ, though both improved. Unfortunately, the meticulous evaluation of that site was limited by small sample size (twenty-five in the experimental group and twenty-two controls) and a lack of detail on the treatments received by the controls.

Unsurprisingly, heroin maintenance is far more expensive than methadone maintenance. It requires three-times-daily attendance and provision of injecting equipment, while methadone is dispensed typically on a three-times-a-week basis, with take-homes being allowed to most experienced patients. Moreover, the Swiss researchers report that it has, so far, been expensive to provide sufficient quantities of pure heroin, given that there has previously been only a tiny legitimate market for the injectable form. The evaluators estimated total daily cost per patient per day at about 50 francs ($35), roughly twice the daily cost for a standard methadone program. Though the initial estimates are that the benefits per day of enrollment are 96 Swiss francs (including only savings on criminal investigations, jail stays,

---

41. Two sites apparently ran double-blind studies, but no results have yet been reported for those sites.

and health care costs), this hardly settles the matter of whether these additional costs are justified, particularly since most of the benefits are borne by a different government sector.

The response. Domestically, the trials became the focus of the two wings of Swiss opinion, which used the very open referenda process. One group (Youth Without Drugs) obtained enough signatures to place on the ballot a measure that would "exclude further controlled prescription experiments and methadone, end attempts to differenti-ate between soft and hard drugs and focus prevention programmes on deterrence only" (Klingemann, 1996, p. 733). Shortly after the launching of the Youth Without Drugs initiative, an opposing group with the ungainly name For a Reasonable Drug Policy – Tabula Rasa with the Drug Mafia was created, advocating a new Constitutional article stating that "the consumption, production, possession and pur-chase of narcotics for individual use only is not prohibited." They also obtained the 100,000 signatures necessary for putting their proposal on the ballot.

The federal government opposed both initiatives. In the vote on the abstinence initiative in September 1997, almost 4 years after the Youth Without Drugs initiative had gathered their signatures, 70 percent voted against the proposition.[42] This strong majority provided important support for the government in its decision as to whether to extend the trials into a second phase. The second referendum on the legalization initiative was held in 1998 and was handily defeated.

The heroin trials have also been internationally controversial. The International Narcotics Control Board (INCB), a UN agency that inter alia regulates the international trade in legal opiates, very reluc-tantly authorized the importation of the heroin required for the trials (Klingemann, 1996). The INCB required, when approving the initial importation of heroin, that the Swiss government agree to an inde-pendent evaluation by the World Health Organization that only appeared in March 1999, even though the trials themselves were com-pleted in December 1996 (McGregor, 1998). The evaluation was crit-ical of the research design but concluded that the trials showed the

---

42. An earlier referendum confined to Zurich and focused merely on the continuation of funding for the pilot scheme was also approved by over 60 percent of the vote (Associated Press, 1996).

feasibility of heroin maintenance and improvements in health and social functioning (Ali et al., 1999[43]).

The INCB expressed its concern about the proposed expansion of the trials (INCB, 1997). Its officials used unusually strong language for a UN agency, especially when dealing not with a pariah country such as Afghanistan or Burma but a veritable bulwark of international respectability, the home of the World Health Organization among many UN agencies. The Secretary of the INCB said "Anyone who plays with fire loses control over it." He also claimed that it would send "a disastrous signal to countries in which drugs were produced." They were asking why they should cut back cultivation "when the same drugs were being given out legally in Europe." The Board's annual report more diplomatically regretted the proposed expansion of the scheme before the completion of the WHO evaluation.

Whether that was correct or not, the Swiss trials sparked interest in other wealthy nations. The Dutch government committed itself to launch a trial of injectable heroin for purposes of addiction maintenance (Central Committee on the Treatment of Heroin Addicts, 1997). This followed almost 15 years of inconclusive discussions about such trials, after a rather murky episode in which the Amsterdam municipal health authority had attempted to maintain about forty addicts on morphine (Derks, 1997). That Switzerland was willing to take on the disapproval of the international community was undoubtedly helpful in pushing the Dutch government to launch a trial involving 750 addicts.[44]

In Australia, the trials also helped spark interest in the mounting of a feasibility study in Canberra (Bammer & McDonald, 1994), which has a substantial heroin addiction problem. Only the personal intervention of the prime minister in 1997, overriding a decision by a council of state and federal ministers, prevented the study from moving to the next pilot stage. There have been expressions of interest from Denmark as well.[45]

---

43. The concluding sentence of the summary points to the limited enthusiasm of the panel for the experiment: "There is need for continued skepticism about the specific benefits of one short-acting opioid over others and there is a need for further studies to establish objectively the differences in the effect of these different opioids."
44. The Dutch design was much tighter than that used in the Swiss trial, with random assignment initially to heroin versus methadone and then a cross-over after 6 months.
45. Bammer et al. (1999) provided a discussion of international experiences and design problems in heroin maintenance.

In the United States the official reaction was also hostile. We discuss this briefly in Chapter 15.

Implications. Perhaps the principal accomplishment of the trials was simply to show that heroin maintenance is possible, a matter that previously had been in question. For example, Kaplan (1983) doubted the feasibility of even an experiment in heroin maintenance, raising a host of possible objections, from community rejection of sites at which addicts could be found nodding off to heroin diversion by employees. At least in the context of a wealthy, well-ordered society, the Swiss have shown that it is possible to maintain large numbers of otherwise chaotic addicts on this drug in a way that the community finds acceptable and without any dire consequences to the health and safety of the community or participants. Indeed, the addicts' ability to operate in society appears to have been enhanced.

Feasibility is not desirability. Heroin maintenance has a contradiction at its heart. Having chosen to prohibit the drug, society then makes an exception for those who cause sufficient damage, to themselves and to society, as a consequence of their violation of the prohibition. Society's decision is setting the damage level that entitles a user to access. It can require that an addict cause a lot of damage to gain access, which is expensive (in terms of crime and health risks) and inhumane. However, if it sets the barrier low, then access to heroin becomes too easy, and the basic prohibition is substantially weakened. That contradiction alone does not make maintenance bad public policy, but it does raise a fundamental ethical concern.

There are other inherent problems. Providing heroin in accord with the desires of the patient may allow for the delivery of psychosocial services that do indeed assist the addict in dealing with his or her problem. However, heroin maintenance itself is clearly social policy not medicine; indeed, the INCB's objections to authorizing the shipments of opiates to Switzerland emphasized just that. Social policy should not be dressed up as a therapeutic activity.

Moreover, even if the evaluation results hold up on tighter inspection and heroin outperforms methadone, some important questions remain unanswered. The Swiss evaluation was patient-focused. This elides one of the basic concerns of opponents, namely that broad availability of heroin maintenance will increase the attractiveness of heroin use or even more generally of drug use. Answering that question requires more than pilot programs, since it is a function of scale. It is worth noting though that large-scale expansion of this maintenance, if it substantially reduces addict involvement in heroin use and selling, may also have the benign effect of making heroin less accessible to new users. Markets are now primarily supplied at the retail level by committed addicts; if they withdraw, the efficiency of markets supplying only nonaddicted users is likely to be much lower. Evaluations of small-scale pilot projects have their inherent limits for policy skeptics, a point made by Vincent Dole (1972).

The harshness of reactions in the international community illustrates the difficulty faced by nations interested in testing harm reduction innovations. Whereas Dutch coffeeshops could arguably be viewed as undercutting the sovereignty of neighboring countries because of drug tourism, the Swiss heroin maintenance programs were clearly restricted to that nation's own citizens. Rather than enthusiasm about the promising findings of the trials, the undoubted weaknesses of the evaluation were seized on for accusations of irresponsibility. There was no recognition that current policies, in particular the tough enforcement of prohibitions, have a much thinner research base supporting them. High drug-incarceration rates, even if they have no demonstrable benefits and highly visible harms in terms of increased violence, get no such international condemnation.

Finally, it is not even clear that heroin maintenance is an important policy innovation (Farrell & Hall, 1998). That depends on how many addicts will seek it. The Swiss recruitment difficulties suggest that few addicts will enter such programs, no matter how attractive they sound in theory. For example, the Geneva site found that only one of the control group entered the heroin program when access was provided. The regime, with its highly routinized provision of the mythologized drug in a sterile environment, may fall betwixt and between for most heroin addicts; it takes the glamor from the drug that has dominated their lives without providing any cure for their addiction. It may do little more than improve the performance of a small fraction of those who would otherwise choose methadone but prove erratic participants in that modality.

LEARNING FROM EUROPE

As so often with cross-national comparisons, one learns first what is feasible. The Dutch have shown that harm reduction can be used as a principle to guide decisions consistently and have some successes to show and no disasters to hide. Italy has removed criminal sanctions for possession of small quantities of cocaine and heroin without experiencing much greater problems than their neighbors. The Swiss trials show that heroin maintenance programs can operate in an orderly and systematic fashion for the benefit of a substantial fraction of the clients. These are important facts for drug policy debates in the United States.

Chapters 13 through 15 present a discussion of how European experiences contribute to the legalization debate. This section simply examines what leads each nation to adopt its particular policies, for this may be helpful in understanding the political dynamics of legalization in the United States.

The values that inform drug policy

Choices of drug policies are not determined so much by examination of alternatives but largely by political values and definition of what constitutes the drug problem. Spain and Sweden provide two useful polar extremes of the influence of values. Spain, notwithstanding a heroin problem almost as severe as that of any other European nation, and one that has had notable criminal consequences (both in terms of disorder and organized crime[46]), has refused to apply the criminal sanction against drug possession itself. Two factors are cited by observers to explain this apparent paradox: (1) the Anarchist traditions of Spanish politics from the late nineteenth century, emphasizing the rights of the individual over those of the state, and (2) the recent experience with an authoritarian state under General Franco, which has ensured that even right-wing political parties emphasize the importance of restraining police powers.[47]

46. Spain is the only nation for which the Foreign Broadcast Information Service regularly contains reports of community actions against drug-dealing disorder.
47. For example, the right-wing parties voted against extending electronic surveillance authority for the police in 1992 (interviews in Madrid, 1992).

At the other extreme, Swedish law allows local authorities to mandate treatment for an individual suspected of being a drug abuser. No criminal conviction, or even arrest, is required. Such a level of intervention in individual life, without the pretext of a criminal act, strikes non-Swedes as extreme. Yet it appears quite noncontroversial in Sweden (Gould, 1989), constituting a natural extension of a long-standing policy with respect to alcohol abuse.[48] "From an Anglo-Saxon point of view, we may shrink from the coercive measures and illiberal controls the Swedes are prepared to adopt, but on the positive side it can be said that they show more concern than we do over the damage people do to themselves through the consumption of alcohol and the taking of drugs" (Gould 1988, p. 127). It is also consistent with the tradition of a benign and paternalistic state, where for example citizens have long been required to provide the local police with address information when they move. The Swedish passion for abstinence and adamant rejection of harm reduction (more forceful than that of any other European nation) probably reflects the severity of alcohol problems associated with drunkenness and their efforts to control it, involving state monopolies that limit alcohol production and distribution. Oddly though, their alcohol policies are very much oriented toward quantity and harm reduction; their hostility to harm reduction in the field of illicit drugs has different origins from that of the United States.

Policy differences may also represent differences in the conception of the drug problem. The use of illicit drugs can be seen as constituting a public health, individual control, social order, or crime problem. Of course, in most societies, it is seen as some mix of these elements, but the weight assigned to each varies. We believe that the British see heroin use as principally a problem of individual health; the primary reason for providing treatment is to help the addict solve his own health problem, though the reduction in social costs is most welcome. The Swedish give more weight to the threat of the addict to expand drug use generally and perhaps also the unseemliness of the intoxication. For France we suggest, even more speculatively, that it is the connection to an underworld that has long been seen as a threat to the power of the state that is the dominant element of the

48. Local temperance boards had the power to decide on compulsory treatment in a public institution for alcoholics (Gould, 1988, p. 125).

drug problem. Each of these conceptions of the drug problem leads to a different assessment of alternative policies.

Drug policy at the broadest level then is not determined in the abstract but very much in the context of the political and cultural traditions of the state. Similar idiosyncratic factors can affect lower-level decisions. The long-time German resistance to methadone seems to have had its origins in the medical profession's concerns about its behavior during the Nazi regime, when the medical association agreed to practices that served the interests of the state rather than the patient. Methadone has been seen by many as addiction maintenance on behalf of the state, and the medical association until recently was strongly opposed to allowing its members to provide that drug. In Britain the relative power of the medical profession and its determination to allow physicians full autonomy has probably been the principal explanation for the continuation of the right to prescribe heroin to addicted patients. Even hard-line Sweden imposes odd restrictions on its police who have limited rights ability to search an apartment after 9 P.M. (Bolling, 1989), hardly compatible with effective investigation of drug users but representing the limits that a basically bourgeois citizenry might impose on its authorities.

There is then likely to be continuing differences in drug policy among the nations of Western Europe, even as the forces of integration strengthen. For those interested in learning about the effects of different approaches, it will continue to be a laboratory. However, given the resistance of even near neighbors to learn from each other, we must not be surprised if the laboratory results have little impact on U.S. policy making.

PART IV: ASSESSING THE ALTERNATIVES

13 Summary of the Evidence and a Framework for Assessment

This book's goal is to understand and assess the likely consequences of major change in the laws governing drug use and sale in America. Having described a wide array of related experiences and identified a large number of outcomes that ought to be taken into account, the final three chapters try to give a more precise guide for the interested citizen. This chapter summarizes what is known empirically and describes a way of assessing different drug control regimes. Chapter 14 attempts to project what would happen if, for example, heroin were available for maintenance of experienced addicts or marijuana could be legally sold. The final chapter explores why it is so hard to obtain a serious public discussion of change, even of a modest nature, in drug laws.

INTERPRETING THE ANALOGIES

Table 13.1 presents the analogies considered in this book, summarizing their relevant features, lessons, and inferential limitations. Most of the analogies fall into two categories: Legal relaxations and legal tightenings. Since the aim is to project the consequence of loosening current legal restrictions, more attention is given to relaxations.

Each analogy is seriously flawed for our purposes, but this does not mean that they are inherently uninformative. The principle of triangulation suggests that flawed sources of data are more informative when their lessons converge rather than diverge, provided that the

Table 13.1. *Case studies in the legal control of drugs and other vices*

Analogy	Drug (vice)	Availability?	User sanctions?	Policy change?	Major lesson	Inferential limitations[a]
Dutch cannabis policy since 1976	Cannabis	Commercially available (quasi legal)	None if under 30 g (5 g as of 1996)	Relaxation	Reduced user sanctions had little effect; commercialization may have increased prevalence	Cannabis only; different country
Repeal of Prohibition, 1933	Alcohol	Commercially available	Little change	Relaxation	Little short-term increase in use: long-term growth possibly due to commercialization	Alcohol only, different era
Marijuana depenalization in United States and Australia	Cannabis	Remained illegal	None or minor for small quantities	Relaxation	Little or no effect on use or harms	Cannabis only, weak policy change
Italian depenalization, 1975–90, 1993–present	All street drugs	Remained illegal	None or minor for small quantities	Relaxation	Possible effect on heroin use, but probably spurious	Different country; limited data
Creation of state lotteries	Gambling	Legal participation	None	Relaxation	Aggressive promotion led to steep increases in gambling	Nondrug vice

Table 13.1. (cont.)

Analogy	Drug (vice)	Availability?	User sanctions?	Policy change?	Major lesson	Inferential limitations[a]
Harrison Act (1914)	Heroin, cocaine, other drugs	Became illegal	Yes	Tightening	Decline in use; growth of black markets	Different era
Prohibition	Alcohol	Became illegal	Only if in commercial setting	Tightening	Decline in use; growth of black markets	Alcohol only, different era
Tightening British heroin prescribing	Heroin	Less available from doctors	Unchanged	Tightening	Increase (spurious?) in use and black markets	Different country
Legal cocaine, 1885–1914	Cocaine	Available in tonics and by prescription	None	Pre-prohibition period	?	Different era
Prostitution enforcement, contemporary United States	Prostitution	No legal access	Yes (misdemeanor)	No major recent change	Feasibility of less harmful enforcement of prohibition	Nondrug vice
Tobacco and alcohol regulation, contemporary United States	Tobacco, alcohol	Regulated adult access	Only for minors	No major recent change	Obstacles to effective regulation; harmfulness under legal regime	Tobacco nonintoxicating; alcohol better integrated into culture than cocaine, heroin, cannabis

[a] All analogies share one major inferential limitation: lack of controlled experimentation.

flaws are heterogeneous rather than homogeneous (Cook & Campbell, 1979). There is indeed some convergence; none of the "relaxations" per se appears to have led to dramatic escalation in drug use or drug problems, even though commercialization has led to sharp increases.

Relaxations

Dutch cannabis regime. The Dutch experience provides the richest data. How should inferences be drawn for the U.S. legalization debate? There are two classes of inferential problems: correctly identifying the effects of the Dutch policy on Dutch drug outcomes (internal validity) and determining whether any such effects would generalize to the U.S. context and/or to other drugs like cocaine or heroin (external validity). Both problems are daunting. Chapter 11 showed that the initial depenalization was not followed by increases in cannabis use rates for almost a decade. However, there was then a sharp and sustained increase in marijuana prevalence from 1984 to 1992, plausibly attributable to increased access and promotion through the coffeeshops. Dutch treatment statistics suggest an increase in patients seeking treatment for cannabis-related problems, and the Dutch media report occasional complaints from retail and residential neighbors about certain coffeeshops. Beyond that, we are unable to document any significant social harms accompanying increased cannabis use (e.g., the increase in cannabis use was not followed by rising rates of hard-drug use or drug-related crime).

Can the Dutch cannabis experience be generalized to the United States and to other drugs? Dutch society differs in important ways from American society. With less income disparity and a stronger social safety net, the Dutch poor face less bleak prospects than their U.S. counterparts, though this appears less relevant for marijuana than for hard drugs. The Netherlands does have minority groups (Surinamese and Moluccans) that have experienced discrimination and marginalization, but there is less alienation in Dutch society than in America.[1] It is impossible to state systematically how important each effect is individually, but it is probably their joint influence that is most significant. They are enough to weaken the claim that conse-

---

1. On the economic status of minorities in the Netherlands, see Veenman (1995).

quences of legal change in the Netherlands should be projected to the United States in any direct fashion.

Compared to other drugs, cannabis is less addictive, less criminogenic, and less health-threatening than cocaine and heroin. Careers of dependence seem to be shorter and less intense than those of heroin addicts (certainly) and cocaine addicts (probably). Though it is reasonable to classify marijuana along with cocaine and heroin as a psychoactive drug used primarily for pleasurable sensations, the differences are far more salient than the similarities. Yet none of these specific differences seem to threaten the generalizability of the finding that depenalization did not increase the prevalence of cannabis use.

The finding that commercial access raised experimentation levels also generalizes but only in a narrow sense because of the consequences of that increase. The higher dependence potential of cocaine and heroin implies that increased experimentation might have much larger effects on current prevalence and dependence rates. Public reaction for these drugs might be much greater, and this would threaten the political acceptability of the regime. The Dutch reaction to the rising prevalence of marijuana (as opposed to their neighbor's pressures) has been somewhere between indifference and insouciance.[2] That would surely not be the case if rates were to rise similarly sharply to increased legal access for cocaine and heroin.

Each of the other analogies is similarly problematic.

Repeal. This is the cleanest case, both in terms of regime change and internal validity. What had been prohibited and subject to moderately serious enforcement (arrests for Prohibition violations being higher in 1932 than any previous year) became a full-scale legal regime in most states. The most sophisticated estimates suggest barely any increase in total consumption in the 5 years following Repeal (Chapter 8). None of the principal indicators (e.g., cirrhosis, alcohol-related mortality) changed much during the period 1933–8.

The problems here are mostly of external validity but because of history rather than the nature of the drug itself. Repeal involved a substance that had been widely used previously and whose use in

---

2. This reflects impressions from conversations with Dutch citizens and the absence of any mention in the popular press about this phenomenon.

moderation was perceived as safe, certainly causing far fewer harms than, for example, those associated with cocaine today. There was probably little popular curiosity about the effects of alcohol post-Repeal. Moreover, the immediate post-Repeal regime for liquor sales involved strict regulation of promotion and distribution; indeed, some states and counties maintained local prohibition on liquor sales. Liquor consumption and related problems started to rise only after World War II. A plausible interpretation is that these increases stemmed from the gradual erosion of tight restrictions as the alcohol industry gained political and commercial influence. But other possibilities – increasing wealth, a more hedonistic society, and demographic changes – cannot be dismissed.[3]

Depenalization of marijuana in the United States and Australia. There is reasonable evidence that depenalization in American states produced no increase in marijuana use. This conclusion has been supported by similar findings in several new studies of marijuana depenalization in Australia. These findings are not incontrovertible. Findings of "no difference" are sometimes an artifact of weak interventions, and it is not clear that depenalization made much difference to users. The probability of being arrested for using marijuana was low before the change in those states that did depenalize, and few of those arrested received anything more than a term of probation or a fine. Nor is it clear that the most directly affected population (adolescents) remained aware of the regime change after the initial publicity. These concerns also threaten external validity; if the change was minor and unobserved, then it provides little information for the consequences of much more substantial and salient change (e.g., depenalization of cocaine). Still, the lack of a measurable response to depenalization is consistent with the deterrence literature (Chapter 5); variations in sanction severity rarely have sizeable effects on crime rates.

Moreover, some aspects of implementation are quite puzzling. In particular, possession arrest rates for the depenalization states are identical to those in states that retained the full criminal prohibition and have been so since 1985. The arrests in the decriminalization

---

3. Miron (1997) claims to be able to explain alcohol consumption largely in terms of changing age structure, though in Chapter 8 we raised concerns about this inference.

states include many that are the equivalent of traffic citations but not all are in that category. For example, in California only one-third of reported marijuana possession arrests were under the ordinance rather than subject to criminal penalties. Further, note that depenalization in the United States generally left a penalty for possession. Specifically, six states made possession of small amounts a civil offense, and five made it a misdemeanor or violation with no permanent criminal record (Schroeder, 1980). That the penalty was fairly trivial is important but society still expressed its disapproval through the law. Also, most states retained criminal penalties for possession of larger amounts, even if for personal use, and for offenses other than the first. True depenalization would presumably mean the removal of all penalties for possession for personal use.

Italian depenalization of all drugs. The tale here is a tangled one (Chapter 10). Heroin-related deaths did rise in Italy from during the first depenalization (1975–90) and less dramatically during the second (from 1993 to 1995). But similar time patterns are observed in Spain (consistent depenalization over the period) and Germany (consistent penalization over the period), suggesting that these trends probably had nothing to do with changes in Italian drug laws. No other relevant data are available.

The creation of state lotteries. Prior to the state lotteries, purchase of an illegal lottery (numbers) ticket was not a criminal offense; a negligibly enforced depenalization accompanied a moderately tough regime against promotion. The introduction of legal lotteries appears to have substantially increased participation in regular betting, and massively increased the amount wagered.[4] The states aggressively promoted the game without any notable federal restrictions. The regime change and effects are both clear.

Generalizing from gambling, particularly lottery play, to drugs is problematic. Lottery participation per se has minimal stigma, either in the earlier regime or presently. Nor are others harmed by the behavior itself, as opposed to the loss of money; there is no counter-

---

4. Interestingly, some legal games were more expensive than their illicit counterparts. The state usually offered the same odds, but federal income taxes were levied on those winning more than $600. However, the states offered a much wider array of related games, so the pure legalization effect cannot be estimated.

part to intoxication or the aggression associated with some drugs. Community attitudes toward lottery play are thus not hardened by increased exposure. Lotteries illustrate how legalization and promotion can dramatically increase a risky behavior in the absence of strong regulatory counterpressures or informal social controls.

Summary: Relaxations. Following a strategy of triangulation, we now consider the relaxations jointly. Three of the relaxations are strikingly consistent: Repeal, marijuana depenalization in the United States and Australia, and Dutch cannabis depenalization prior to the expansion of the coffeeshop market. None of these changes, involving three countries, two drugs, and two widely separated historical periods, led to a substantial increase in prevalence of use within 5 years. The Italian case is simply ambiguous; the indicators turn out to be too weak to draw any clear inference. Later increases in alcohol consumption (Repeal) and cannabis prevalence (the Netherlands) are consistent with the hypothesis that increased access and commercial promotion led to the observed rises. Because Dutch cannabis commercialization has not involved steep price declines, it arguably understates the increases that might occur under true legalization – but price effects are unlikely to be important for depenalization. Despite a different target behavior (gambling), there is a similar pattern for the aggressive promotion of unregulated state lotteries.

Tightenings

There are three instances of invoking criminal sanction or of substantially tightening legal availability: The Harrison Act (cocaine and heroin), Prohibition, and the British shift to tighter control of heroin prescribing. Since our principal interest is in the consequences of a relaxation, we treat these more briefly.

The Harrison Act. The Harrison Act in 1914, following enactment of various state-level prohibitions, accelerated the decline in opiate use that had begun by 1900. The regime change was clearly substantial, particularly after the Treasury Department obtained rulings from the Supreme Court against clinics maintaining addicts. A substantial black market developed, primarily serving those who had become dependent before 1914. For cocaine, the decline in use seems to have been sharper, notwithstanding continued manufacture by legitimate firms both in Europe and the United States, and re-import from Canada for another decade. Opiate use remained low for 50 years; cocaine use, for 60 years.

Prohibition. Alcohol consumption appears to have fallen only moderately during Prohibition. Without rigorous enforcement, prices may not have risen much, but promotion was eliminated and accessibility was somewhat restricted. The limits on generalizability are similar to those for Repeal.

Tightening British heroin prescribing. British heroin maintenance prior to 1965 treated a small number of patients, most of whom had became addicted in the course of medical treatment. The black market for opiates was modest. The tightening was followed, with a lag, by a substantial growth in total use and black market sales. This growth in use may have been unrelated to the tightening; a variety of social changes can as readily account for the growth of these markets in Britain and comparable heroin epidemics occurred in other Western European countries at about the same time. Nor is it clear that the regime change was major; heroin availability for addicts may have been only modestly affected by the shift to methadone.

Summary: Tightenings. The tightenings show less consistency than the relaxations. British heroin prescription is the outlier here. There is no evidence that the 1967 shift to centralized clinics reduced the prevalence of heroin use; indeed there is a plausible case that it contributed something to the increase that occurred in the 1970s. But it was most likely simply not a major policy change.

With so few case studies of relaxations or tightenings available, conclusions must be cautious. Relaxation, with tightly controlled commercial promotion, seems to have moderate effects on prevalence and consumption. The evidence on tightening is simply ambiguous.

None of the analogies speaks directly to cocaine and heroin legalization. Not only are there both evidence and argument against confident generalization across substances, but there is also an asymmetry in reasoning from strong to weak regime changes or vice versa. If a weak regime change (e.g., U.S. cannabis depenalization) has a strong effect on levels of use, then a strong regime change (full legalization) should have an even stronger effect. And if a strong regime change (Dutch cannabis de facto legalization) has a weak effect, a weak regime change should also have little consequence. But the opposite results are unhelpful (i.e., weak effects of depenalization reveal little about legalization, and strong effects of legalization reveal little about depenalization).

Other relevant analogies

Several other analogies are relevant, although they do not involve legal change per se. First, the experience with legal cocaine from 1885 to 1914 gives a glimpse of what a commercial cocaine regime in America actually looked like, albeit one that existed over 80 years ago. In support of the legalization case, during a period of easy commercial access, cocaine consumption was far below 1990s levels. On the other hand, consumption was much lower in the decades after the Harrison Act and immediately preceding the recent cocaine epidemic. The historical evidence also suggests the need to be wary of glib assumptions that drug control can be handed over from the police to physicians and pharmacists. Second, American experiences with the enforcement of prostitution laws suggest that the harms that theoretically follow from vice prohibition can be mitigated – though not eliminated – by discretionary enforcement. Arrests can be reserved for particularly harmful or disruptive behavior and need not be triggered automatically by law violations per se. Indeed, despite America's moralistic views about prostitution and adultery, policing of prostitution has much in common with the discretionary policing of drug use in many European cities. Finally, recent experiences with alcohol and tobacco illustrate the power of commercial marketing, and the difficulty of maintaining or tightening regulatory controls in the face of that power. Moreover, the evidence for both of those licit substances shows quite clearly that while prohibition may cause considerable harm, eliminating prohibition does not mean eliminating drug-related harm.

THE SPECTRUM OF REGIMES[5]

With the exception of some libertarians (e.g., Szasz, 1974), no one seriously advocates relaxing the drug laws so that the currently illicit substances would be as freely available as peanut butter or gasoline, regulated only for purity, quality, or safety. Everyone seems to agree that children, at least, should not be able to buy cocaine at the local candy store.[6] Thus, "legalization," taken literally, is not under discussion. Indeed, even for the presently legal drugs, except for caffeine (with high dependency potential but very modest stimulant effect and negligible adverse health consequences), there is some age restriction.

One way to differentiate among regimes, simply as a set of laws, is the extent of justification a user has to provide to obtain the drug. As seen in Figure 13.1, plausible control models, both existing and theoretical, can be arrayed along a spectrum of *legal access* with respect to who may legally use and administer the drug. The following subsections briefly describe eight distinct control models falling into three broad and overlapping categories – prohibitory regimes, prescription regimes, and regulatory regimes – each of which provides a distinctive set of policy levers.[7]

Restrictiveness is the principal, or at least most salient, dimension of drug control policy, but drug policy is inherently multidimensional. A second relevant dimension (not shown in the figure) is the *sanctioning severity* of enforcement. For this reason, the concept of depenalization does not appear in our spectrum. Depenalization differs from conventional prohibition with respect to sanctioning severity, not the restrictiveness of access (at least not by law), since it only replaces criminal with civil penalties. In principle, every regime short of complete legal access can be implemented in a high-severity or a low-severity version.

5. This section is adapted from MacCoun, Reuter, & Schelling (1996).
6. "If there is a universal proposition that is accepted by all parties to the debate on drugs, it is that children and youth should not have unregulated access to potentially harmful psychoactive substances. Even the most ardent libertarians assent to this" (Zimring & Hawkins, 1992, p. 115). Note though that some access may be allowed.
7. We are most grateful to Jonathan Caulkins for his suggestions on ordering the models.

Regime   Model

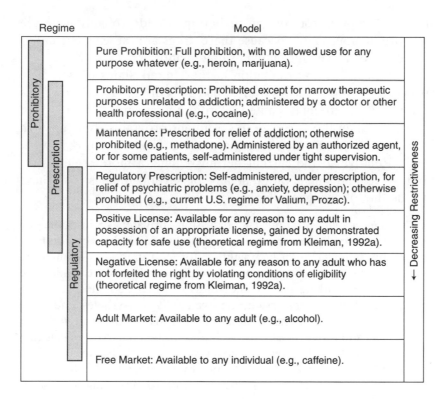

Figure 13.1 The spectrum of drug control regimes

Prohibition regimes

At least for possessing and using, the Alaska marijuana regime from 1975–90 and the current U.S. heroin regime may represent the least and most restrictive forms of prohibition. Alaska's regime is notable because it not only substitutes civil for criminal penalties for marijuana possession (low sanction severity) but also applies similarly modest civil penalties to home cultivation for personal consumption, including gifts to others (reduced restrictiveness of access).[8] Given the ease of home cultivation, the latter change had the effect of making the drug highly accessible for those willing to grow it. A

---

8. The status of the Alaska marijuana regime is somewhat murky currently. The 1990 marijuana criminalization referendum was held unconstitutional by a Superior Court judge in Ketchikan (Rinehart, 1993).

similar exemption for cocaine or heroin would probably generate little production, simply because these drugs are (at least currently) difficult to produce efficiently in small quantities.

In contrast, heroin prohibition in the United States is extremely stringent; the retail price is over $1,000 per pure gram in many cities and access is extremely limited. Heroin addicts are at high risk of arrest; certainly those known to treatment programs show up with long histories of arrests on drug charges (e.g., Hser, Anglin, & Powers, 1993). Relative to the current heroin regime, a more lenient prohibitory regime might differ in any of several dimensions. These include the following standards:

1. *The activity prohibited* – possession (privately or in public, by adults or by minors), using (privately or in public, by adults or by minors), offering facilities for consumption. Though all nations prohibit sale and production, there is considerable variety with respect to the status of other activities, including penalties for possession, the availability of syringes, and "safe injection" locations (Chapters 10–12). Within the United States, an example of an activity exemption, albeit a narrow one, is that granted by the federal government (through the Religious Freedom Restoration Act) and by many states to the Native American Church of North America for the religious use of peyote.

2. *The severity of sanctions for the prohibited activities.* Suggestions are frequently made for use of sanctions other than incarceration for first-time offenders or those convicted of possession or use offenses; such sanctions include loss of driving licenses (encouraged in the United States by the 1988 Anti Drug Abuse Control Act[9]) and loss of passports (Italy, since 1990). The very harsh mandatory penalties for drug selling, at the federal level and also in some states, can be reduced.

3. *Lessening the intensity of enforcement against each activity, for each drug.* It is a truism of contemporary American policing that in large cities the police may make as many drug possession or retail sales arrests as they wish.[10] The decision to intensify

---

9. According to the Department of Transportation as of October 1, 1994, twenty-one states had enacted a law imposing a 6-month suspension of drivers license for anyone convicted of a drug offense (Marijuana Policy Project, 1995).

10. For example, the number of marijuana possession arrests doubled between 1992 and 1996, a period in which the NHSDA shows no change in total prevalence of marijuana use.

enforcement against drug markets was a policy decision; it can be reversed.

4. *The selectivity or discretion with which enforcement is pursued.* For example, the nation could move to a policy like that adopted for prostitution, implicitly tolerating drug traffic and use provided that it did not involve other harms, such as violence, disorder, and advertising. Zurich's Platzspitz (Chapter 12) offers an instance of such a policy focused in one geographic area.

Prescription regimes

As seen in Figure 13.1, prescription regimes occupy a gray area overlapping prohibition and regulation. The first model, designated *prohibitory prescription*, seems a trivial deviation from pure prohibition. Under prohibitory prescription, psychoactive substances are administered by medical professionals in narrowly specified ways; those treated receive no positive pleasure from consumption and the medical use provides a trivial source of the drug for the illicit market. For example, cocaine is available for use as a topical anesthetic, and PCP (phencyclidine) is used as an anesthetic for large-animal veterinary surgical procedures. Most opiates that were once widely used for recreational purposes, such as morphine and codeine, remain available for medicinal uses as analgesics. Heroin, not widely used recreationally until criminal prohibitions against opiates were imposed in many states (Musto, 1987), is unusual in the totality of the prohibition; even for heroin there have been proposals to permit its use for pain control in terminally ill cancer patients (e.g., Trachtenberg, 1994).

Altogether different is permitted use, under a physician's care, of an addictive drug for *maintenance* (i.e., cessation of withdrawal symptoms). Chapter 12 discussed two kinds of maintenance regimes for heroin. The first is methadone maintenance – the medical provision of a substitute for heroin. About 100,000 addicts are currently in methadone treatment in the United States (Rettig & Yarmolinsky, 1995). There are at least two acknowledged purposes: to reduce the client's discomfort when abstinent from heroin and to keep the client out of trouble. *Trouble* would be illegally attempting to acquire heroin or to acquire money with which to buy heroin (e.g., Hser et al., 1993). The second is heroin maintenance – the medical provision of heroin, rather than a substitute – as practiced at a very low scale by British specialists since 1925[11] and as recently field tested by the Swiss (Chapter 12).

The third prescription model is *regulatory prescription*. This model currently applies to psychoactives (e.g., Valium) that are useful for treating anxiety, depression, or other conditions but require careful quantity or safety regulation. The drug may be potentially habit-forming; there may be danger of overdose; or any dose may be dangerous, but benefits outweigh risks if the dose is controlled. The distinction is that the purpose of the prescription is not purely hedonic pleasure (though we recognize the difficulty of making that distinction) but to treat some underlying condition. Marijuana has been legally available to a handful of patients for the relief of symptoms of glaucoma, the nausea of cancer chemotherapy, and several other indications. The FDA and DEA have recently approved controlled trials involving human subjects for several drugs in the currently prohibited psychedelic category (MDMA, LSD, DMT, ibogaine). The aim is to identify health risks posed by recreational use and also to assess their therapeutic potential for individual and marital psychotherapy and treatment of opiate and cocaine addiction (Strassman, 1995). Significant positive results could conceivably lead to a rescheduling of these substances and a new class of medical exceptions to the prohibition of drugs.

Regulatory regimes

A regulatory regime recognizes some nonmedical use as legal but stipulates who may use, sell, or purchase a substance, where or when or in what activities, and so on. The two regulated nonmedicinal dependency-creating substances for human consumption that are most widely used in this country are alcohol and tobacco. Where prescription regimes involve selective provision, regulatory regimes essentially involve selective prohibition, although sanctions may differ from those under prohibitory regimes. For example, selling liquor to minors may be punished by an alcoholic beverages control agency through withdrawal of license. Not all regulation is selectively prohibitory; labeling of purity or concentration – tar, nicotine, alcohol

---

11. Indeed, these specialists may also provide cocaine or amphetamines to addicted patients; again, few do (Strang et al., 1994).

– may be required without any regulation of the purity or concentration. Regulatory regimes also facilitate the use of common law controls (e.g., tort liability) that are difficult to apply under strict prohibition.

The Dutch cannabis regime may be considered a form of regulation, albeit one that is conducted in a netherworld of conflicting laws and regulations. By retaining the basic criminal prohibition against sale, the government has managed to control the powers of the distributors, even while sacrificing certain powers (notably taxation) itself.

Just as a prohibitory regime may be one that opposes all use, or alternatively one that denies some legitimate use because selective prohibition is infeasible ("reluctant denial"), a regulatory regime may be one that "grudgingly tolerates" the allowed consumption (Kleiman, 1992a, 1992b) – perhaps because full prohibition is politically unachievable or because enforcement of full prohibition would be infeasible. Alternatively, it may be one that recognizes a right to consume and even the benefits of consumption, as long as consumption is within certain limits. Current regulation of alcohol appears to represent a majority (but not unanimous) opinion of the latter type.

Regulatory regimes share many features with prescription regimes. One major difference involves their scope of restriction; prescription regimes are a form of selective provision, not selective prohibition. A second is that medical regimes rely on the physician and the pharmacist as the primary agents of enforcement; their stakes in compliance with licensing requirements, because of their substantial profession-specific human capital investment, is much greater than those of alcohol vendors.

One attraction of regulatory regimes is that, with respect to both statutory restrictions and enforcement mechanisms, they are typically more multidimensional and more detailed than prohibitory or prescription regimes. Consider the following description of the alcohol regime in this country,[12] probably the most lenient regulatory model that would ever be proposed for any of the currently illicit drugs. It is instructive to see along how many dimensions the various alcohol

12. For a survey of controls used throughout North America and Western Europe, along with a summary of the evidence on effects of each control, see Edwards et al. (1994).

beverages (beer, wine, and distilled spirits) are regulated. The following elements are subject to regulation:

1. *Who* may purchase, possess, or consume alcohol. Currently the only prohibition is on age, though other dimensions (e.g., military status, health status, criminal record, or history of alcohol abuse) could be invoked.
2. *Where* the possession, consumption, or sale of alcohol is permitted or prohibited. Every state licenses package stores, bars, and restaurants or has a state-operated retail alcoholic beverage system. "Zones of intolerance" include public buildings, public areas, military bases, school grounds, and some sports events.
3. *When* alcohol may be sold. Sales and service are often prohibited for certain hours of the day, days of the week, and days of the year (e.g., election day).
4. *What* activities may not be associated with consumption of alcohol (e.g., driving a car, piloting a commercial aircraft).
5. *Purity and concentration* of the substance.
6. *Mandatory labeling* of content (e.g., on distilled spirits and wine but not beer) and health hazards (e.g., risks of alcohol for pregnant women).
7. *Promotional restrictions.* Advertising of distilled spirits on television has been discontinued as the result of voluntary restrictions. There has been discussion of banning beer and wine ads on television; such ads are already subject to certain voluntary restrictions (e.g., the act of drinking cannot be shown).
8. *Taxation.* So-called sin taxes are now regarded as a major control mechanism for both alcohol and tobacco (e.g., Manning et al., 1991).
9. *Quantity restrictions.* No effort has been made in the United States to regulate alcohol quantity for individuals directly except as it applies to certain conduct in which high levels of consumption engender risk; in many states the statutory definition of driving while intoxicated relies on some threshold level of blood alcohol. Sweden had quantity limits on adult monthly retail purchases from 1920 to 1955 (Edwards et al., 1994).

The existing tobacco and alcohol regimes do not exhaust the possibilities for regulatory drug control. Kleiman (1992a, 1992b) suggests *licensing* purchase or use (see Figure 13.1). A negative license would be a default condition, which could be revoked in response to any violation of certain eligibility conditions. Alternatively, a positive license model would require the holder to complete a course on drug safety, or otherwise demonstrate a capability for safe use. Kleiman's license proposal for tobacco is perhaps more closely analogous to a maintenance scheme; tobacco would only be available via ration cards to those who are current users at the time rationing is implemented, and access to ration cards would be gradually phased out.

Regulatory regimes provide a much greater array (not simply number) of explicit levers to achieve specific policy goals. Among many attributes that distinguish liquor vendors from retailers of illicit drugs is the visibility – and hence ease of monitoring – of their operation. Consider time-of-sale control. Police can no doubt intensify enforcement against drug dealing that occurs at particular times of day (e.g., end of the school day) but such enforcement will be effective only against the visible transactions which, for some drugs (e.g., marijuana and MDMA), constitute a small share of all transactions. After-hours provision of liquor by licensed vendors occurs, but certainly the vast majority of alcohol outlets do in fact comply with hours of sale regulations. Police enforcement against illegal distribution can be selective and aimed at specific harms but provides a far blunter instrument than regulation.

That argument is clearly not sufficient to demonstrate the superiority of regulation to prohibition or prescription. But it is a useful reminder that the three classes of regimes are labels for bundles of programs and laws that make the array by level of restrictiveness only a rough heuristic.

OUTCOMES: TOTAL HARM AND ITS COMPONENTS

Chapter 6 provided a detailed taxonomy of drug-related harms. Some categories of harm are primarily attributable to drug prohibition and its enforcement (e.g., criminal justice system costs, intrusiveness, black-market violence). Other harms appear to be intrinsic properties of a drug and its psychopharmacological effects on the user, irrespective of the regime in which the drug is used. Thus, everything else being equal, a move toward a less restrictive drug control regime will reduce or eliminate harms attributable to prohibition, while retaining the more intrinsic harms of drug use.

But, of course, everything else isn't likely to be equal. Chapter 5 examined seven ways in which drug laws influence drug use. Some of those mechanisms discourage drug use (e.g., the fear of legal sanctions), and others inadvertently encourage drug use (e.g., the forbidden fruit effect), but the conventional wisdom is probably correct: the cumulative effect of drug prohibitions is to reduce levels of use. Thus, a regime change might reduce the harmfulness of drug use yet increase the prevalence and intensity of drug use. This section examines this tradeoff by invoking the notion of *total harm*. To understand the dynamic relationship between drug use and drug harms, it is helpful to decompose total drug-related harm into its components. This begins with the notion of *macro harm* – the aggregate level of any given category of harm. For any given type of drug harm,

Macro Harm = Number of Users × Average Units Used per User
× Average Harm per Unit

or, more conveniently,

Macro Harm = Prevalence × Intensity × Micro Harm

(see MacCoun, 1996, 1998a; MacCoun & Caulkins, 1996; Reuter & MacCoun, 1995). Total harm is then the sum of these macro harms, across each category of harm listed in Chapter 6.

This formulation is not a hypothesis; it is true by definition for any category of harm that has a risk of occurring each time a drug is used or a drug law is enforced – what might be called *frequency-based harms*. The few exceptions to this principle might be called *invariant harms*, harms created by policy decisions that don't increase as a function of drug use; examples include the loss of liberty inherent in prohibition, any ban on beneficial uses of the drug, and the effect of U.S. policies on source countries and international relations.

The distinction between macro and micro harm is enormously helpful for thinking through the tradeoffs involved in drug control. Surprisingly, this distinction has been largely overlooked in the legalization and harm reduction debates, resulting in enormous confusion.[13] Each side of the legalization debate tends to focus on part of macro harm while neglecting or ignoring other components. The

13. It is at least implicit in some of the more sophisticated analyses of drug policy (Hall, Room, & Bondy, 1995; Kleiman, 1992a).

content analysis in Chapter 3 showed that advocates of legal change make their case by describing the ways in which prohibition makes drug use harmful and the ways in which an alternative regime might mitigate or eliminate those harms. On the other hand, prohibitionists almost exclusively couch their rejection of these alternatives in terms of the risk of increased drug use under a more relaxed regime. Rather than disputing that claim, reformers frequently ignore it; similarly prohibitionists never take up the hard question of whether significant reductions in harm might in fact make some increase in drug use an acceptable tradeoff.

THE NECESSITY OF VALUE JUDGMENTS

The notion that drug policies should be evaluated by their consequences does *not* imply that values and moral judgments have no place in the rational assessment of drug policies. Our framework explicitly allows values to enter the analysis in four different ways: (1) in the identification of the types of harms that should matter, (2) in the relative weight given to each category of harm, (3) in the standard of proof used to judge whether the evidence regarding an alternative regime is sufficient to justify a change in policy, and (4) in the burden of proof that applies when the evidence is ambiguous or incomplete. We discuss each in turn.

The identification of harms (and benefits)

Table 13.2 offers a more manageable abbreviation of the complete list of harms that appeared in Chapter 6. As explained in Chapter 6, only some harms are quantifiable on a dollar metric; indeed many cannot be quantified at all, except perhaps by invoking subjective personal judgments of utility or disutility. (Modern psychometric methods make it possible to achieve the latter, but for over a century philosophers, economists, and political scientists have contested the notion that such judgments could be aggregated across individuals; see Broome, 1995). With no convincing way of conducting such calculations, at best we can list categories of harm and attempt to project qualitative changes in those harms (increase, decrease, or no change) under an alternative regime. But

Table 13.2. *Abbreviated list of drug-related harms*

1. Suffering due to physical/mental illnesses	16. Property/acquisitive crime victimization
2. Addiction	17. Violence, psychopharmacological
3. Health care costs (treatment)	18. Violence, economically motivated
4. Health care costs (illness)	19. Reduced property values near markets
5. Disease transmission	20. Criminal justice costs (including opportunity costs)
6. Loss of incentives to seek treatment	21. Punishment and its consequences for user and family
7. Restriction on medicinal uses of drug	22. Corruption, demoralization of legal authorities
8. Reduced performance, school	23. Interference in source countries
9. Reduced performance, workplace	24. Violation of the law as intrinsic harm
10. Poor parenting, child abuse	25. Devaluation of arrest as moral sanction
11. Harmful effects of stigma due to use	26. Infringement on liberty and privacy
12. Accruing criminal experience	27. Prevention/restriction of benefits of use
13. Elevated dollar price of substance	
14. Accident victimization	
15. Fear, sense of disorder	

listing these harms ensures that no important values are missed; examples include the critical responsibility of parenting, the loss of volition and autonomy inherent in addiction (no matter what its consequences), the toll taken by a sense of fear and disorder (even when exaggerated), the fact that punishment (even when justified) creates suffering, and the symbolic loss when people disobey laws for even trivial offenses.

Though the list consists of adverse effects, recall that the loss of any benefits of drug use is a type of harm. This may seem a back-handed way of including benefits in the analysis, but we take seriously the notion that there can be benefits for the user – certainly in the eyes of the user, but possibly in a broader more objective sense (e.g., as means for personal growth, spiritual experience, and possibly even medical or psychiatric treatment, though such uses are not yet established). Consider alcohol. Alcohol harms some users; in aggregate, it may indeed do more damage than good. There is, however, no doubt that many people derive pleasure from alcohol consumption and that most segments of Western society believe such pleasure no less legitimate than that derived from food or sex. Those pleasures are essential to society's decision to allow the legal distribution of the substance; the fear of Prohibition's corruption is not enough. It may well be that after 100 years of legal availability, moderate use of cocaine or heroin would be seen as no less legitimate.

Weighing the harms

Values enter into the analysis in a second way, through the weight that the assessor gives to each category of harm. For some readers, the fact that a given drug regime might be less intrusive is nearly decisive in its favor; for others, intrusion into the lives of drug users may be an acceptable (or even desirable) attribute of the status quo. These weights are usually implicit in advocates' arguments, obscuring the crucial source of disagreement. Even for strict pragmatists, the choice of weights across types of harm is vexing. Assume a new regime dramatically reduces criminality and violence but increases the psychological and physical toll of drug dependence; is that a reasonable tradeoff? Several alternative regimes pose just this sort of choice.

Another weighting dilemma involves the sociodemographic distribution of harms across the lines of social class, race, ethnicity, and age. The gains and losses resulting from a major change in drug laws will be unevenly distributed across segments of society. Many, including ourselves, would weight changes that benefit the poor and vulnerable much more heavily than those that benefit the middle class. The harms in the current regime are grossly disproportionately borne by inner-city minorities in the form of crime, disorder, and involvement in drug selling as well as using. Those regime changes that promise substantial reduction in black markets confer large gross benefits on these communities, even if they may also increase the level of drug use and addiction. The per capita gains for these groups may be very high indeed. The elimination of the black market confers smaller aggregate benefits on the middle class and quite modest benefits per capita; those benefits may look very small in comparison to the costs of increased risk of drug involvement of other family members, particularly adolescent children. This issue is taken up in more detail in Chapter 14.

Perhaps the most fundamental weighting decisions involve changes in drug use vs. changes in average harm, and changes in harms to users vs. harms to others. The distinctions made in Chapter 4 suggest that weightings will vary across philosophical positions. The two deontological positions are simplest. For legal moralists, the decisive factor is drug use itself; the policy that most reduces drug use is to be preferred. For strict libertarians, neither use nor harms matter, except one particular harm – the loss of liberty that occurs when the state prevents citizens from freely choosing whether or not to use drugs. But, of course, few people fall into these extreme categories; if pushed to deliberate on the matter, most Americans people would probably evaluate drug policies more broadly, in a more consequentialist manner. Some would lean toward Millian liberalism: harms to nonusers are what matter, and if users choose to risk harm, that's their business. Others would lean toward legal paternalism, giving weight to harms to users as well as nonusers. Though this is a crucial philosophical distinction, it turns out that the regime changes considered in Chapter 14 all involve changes in harm for both users and for others, so that this distinction is less significant than expected.

For those with a consequentialist perspective, the relationship between macro and micro harm is of enormous significance. But what is less clear is whether the harms that should matter are *average* harms (per user) or *total* harms. It is easier for most people to think in terms of personal narratives than aggregate statistics; as Stalin put it, "the death of a single Russian soldier is a tragedy; a million deaths is a statistic" (cited in Nisbett & Ross, 1980, p. 43). In that sense, average harm more naturally describes the life of an individual user, and the effect of his use on those around him. But the macro perspective is arguably more relevant for public policy making; if the choice were made explicit, we suspect most citizens would pick total harm as the bottom line.

Total harm is not always more important than average harm. Consider the philosophical debate about utility maximization (Parfit, 1984). In many situations, total utility is equivalent to average utility as a guide to policy, and in some situations it is actually less preferable (Harsanyi, 1990). Consider, for example, a hypothetical policy that doubles the population size, thereby increasing total utility while making each individual worse off. Whenever a policy moves average and total utility (or average and total harm) in opposite directions, there will be a tradeoff.[14]

The choice between average and total harm minimization depends on the weight one gives to harms to current users vs. harms to nonusers (and potential users in the future). For current users (and perhaps their loved ones), reforms that reduce average harm will reduce personal risk, irrespective of what happens to anyone else. More generally, when average harm reduction and total harm reduction are in conflict, the choice of a criterion has costs that the chooser should acknowledge. To endorse policies that might lower average harm and raise total harm, one should believe that the current users' reduction in suffering will justify the harm to be suffered by new users and those around them. To endorse policies that might lower total harm and raise average harm, one should accept that some users (and those near them) will suffer harms that could have been prevented.

Burdens and standards of proof

The final way that values enter into the analysis involves two questions: How much evidence is needed to make a policy change? And if the evidence is ambiguous, who wins? These questions identify the applicable *standard of proof* and *burden of proof*. When Carl Sagan proclaimed that "Evolution is a *fact*," many scientists squirmed with discomfort. Though he was fighting the good fight against creationism, most scientists view evolution as a theory, not a "fact." It is one of the better supported theories in the natural sciences, but as philosophers from Hume to Popper have shown, one can never definitively prove a theory – there is always the possibility that discomfirming evidence is just around the corner. The evidence seems solid for evolution, yet it remains a matter of cultural dispute. Thus, it is little surprise that policy research, vastly less precise and more ambiguous, rarely decides issues once and for all. Precise theories and measures are lacking, social causation is statistical rather than deterministic, research designs are weak, data are sparse and often indirect, and findings are open to alternative explanations.

---

14. Note, however, that while drug-related harms may influence utility, they are clearly not synonymous with it.

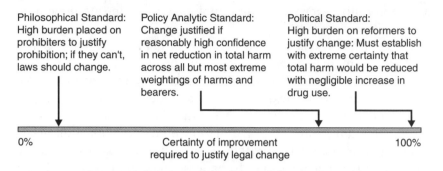

Figure 13.2 Alternative standards of proof

Inevitably, consumers of policy research will differ in their interpretation of the available facts. These differences of opinion are indefensible when facts are selectively chosen or distorted to support a preferred position; such selective biases are pervasive (see review in MacCoun, 1998b). On the other hand, in the policy domain (unlike a trial court or statistical journal), it is perfectly defensible for two readers to hold the same evidence to different (more stringent vs. more lax) standards of proof.

The legalization debate can be subjected to three different standards of proof (Figure 13.2). The first is *philosophical.* If a society were starting from scratch (as in John Rawls' 1971 "original position"), the burden might well be placed on those who would prohibit drug use – at least according to the Western liberal tradition of Locke, Mill, Rawls, and Nozick (irrespective of their differences). If this standard were applied today, the current laws would be changed unless prohibiters could make a convincing case for the current laws. Though some reformers write as if this were the applicable standard, they are mostly talking to themselves, since it is seems unlikely that the American public is ready to accept this standard.

Our own previous writings have implicitly adopted an intermediate standard, one which many (but by no means all) in the policy analytic community would probably endorse. According to this *policy analytic* standard, a change in laws is justified if (a) theory and available evidence provide reasonable confidence that the change would yield (b) a net reduction in total drug-related harm (c) across all but the most extreme weightings of types of harm (morbidity vs. crime vs. lost liberty) and bearers (users vs. nonusers, the middle class vs. the urban poor). "Reasonable confidence" means something stronger than a preponderance of the evidence (too unstable) but weaker than beyond a reasonable doubt (unattainable for real-world policy problems). Even if applied neutrally, in practice this standard gives the edge to the status quo (whatever it may be). The reason is epistemological rather than ideological; high standards of evidence are difficult to meet in policy research, so the reasonable confidence criterion is actually quite demanding.[15]

The third standard is *political* and falls at the high end of the continuum. In the United States at the end of the twentieth century, public opinion (and the almost complete absence of drug reform rhetoric among elected officials) makes it clear that the political burden lies on those who would advocate significant relaxations in our current drug laws. To carry the day politically, any projected net gains from an unpopular legal change must have high certainty, and the projected changes should not offend fundamental values, such as substantially increasing the extent of intoxication or use, particularly among the young.

This means that politically, the burden of proof seems to fall on reformers to explain why their proposals are preferable to the status quo, no matter how dismal it is. (This may be one reason why reform advocates use more complex arguments; see Chapter 3.) Proponents must rely on a disgust with policies that have vast faults; that is unlikely to be enough to carry the day. This is an uncomfortably conservative mode of assessing the issue; the devil we know should not always prevail over its competitors. Any policy innovation requires some risk taking, even if the contemplated change has been implemented some time previously; societies cannot step into the same river twice.

SUMMARY PROPOSITIONS

Using the analytical framework to integrate the available theory (Chapters 4–6) and evidence (Chapters 7–12) results in eleven

---

15. The policy analytic standard is "risk neutral" – focusing on average or expected values rather than worst-case scenarios. This is defensible for descriptive policy analysis, not necessarily for prescriptive policy making.

propositions. They are presented without elaboration because there is nothing new here; each point has been discussed earlier and will be further developed in Chapter 14 in the context of particular drug regimes.

A. Elimination of criminal sanctions for drug possession (i.e., depenalization)

A1. Reductions in criminal sanctioning have little or no effect on the prevalence of drug use (i.e., the number of users), at least relative to existing levels of enforcement. The basis for this proposition is stronger for cannabis than for cocaine or heroin.

A2. It seems plausible that reductions in criminal sanctioning might produce minor increases in intensity (units consumed per user), though direct evidence on this point is limited.

A3. Reductions in criminal sanctioning, almost by definition, produce significant reductions in the criminal justice costs, burdens, and intrusiveness associated with those sanctions.

A4. Reductions in criminal sanctioning per se have little effect on drug-related harms involving health and impaired functioning.

B. Increases in legal access to a drug (partial or total legalization)

B1. Allowing some form of legal access to a drug increases the prevalence and intensity of its use. (In the terms of Chapter 5, the combined impact of price reductions, increased availability, decreased legal risks, and reduced symbolic threshold outweighs the reduced impact of the forbidden fruit and stigmatization effects.)

B2. Allowing some form of legal access to a drug eliminates some types of harm (those entirely attributable to prohibition, including criminal sanctioning costs, loss of liberty, and so on), and substantially reduces some other types of harm (income-generating crimes, needle sharing, and some overdoses).

B3. Legal access to a drug may curtail, but will not eliminate, those harms per use attributable to the psychoactive properties or behavioral effects of a drug (e.g., addictive potential, intoxication, impaired functioning, and drug side effects). Any increase in prevalence or intensity of consumption will increase the aggregate impact of these harms.

B4. Commercial promotion leads to a greater expansion in drug use than mere legal accessibility.

B5. Growth in drug use under expanded legal access can be limited or prevented by sufficiently strict regulatory or prescription barriers, but commercial providers will aggressively resist most such barriers.

B6. Strict regulatory or prescription barriers within a regime of legal access will reproduce many of the harms of a prohibition regime (B2), unless they can selectively target the heaviest users (addicts).

B7. If relaxed drug laws increase the prevalence of use (B1), the additional users will, on average, use less heavily and less harmfully than those who would have also have used drugs under prohibition (*composition effect*). (This proposition is purely theoretical; there is little direct evidence.)

14 Projecting the Consequences of Alternative Regimes

In this chapter, we attempt to project the most likely consequences of various alternative regimes for cocaine, heroin, and cannabis – the three drugs most central to the drug legalization debate. Doing so is hazardous given the limitations of the available evidence, but using the analytical framework to make projections helps to illustrate the kinds of tradeoffs involved in choosing among drug control models.

We consider alternative cocaine and heroin models together because many of the issues are similar, but the differences are such that in the end we are more sanguine about changes in heroin control than reform of cocaine laws. Like many previous authors, we consider cannabis separately because the prospects for change and the plausibility of change seem more promising. To justify our arguments, we briefly review the evidence on the harms of cannabis use and on its alleged role as a gateway to hard-drug use.

PROJECTIONS FOR COCAINE AND HEROIN

We now use the framework outlined in Chapter 13 to offer what we believe are the most plausible projections as to the likely consequences of changing legal control regimes for cocaine, heroin, and cannabis. In addition to the possibility of relaxing user sanctions (i.e., depenalization), our spectrum of regimes suggests at least six different alternatives to strictly prohibited access (prohibitory prescription, maintenance, regulatory prescription, user licenses, regulated adult market, and a free market).

Even limiting ourselves to the three most important illicit drugs (cocaine, heroin, and cannabis) leaves at least twenty-one different scenarios – an unmanageable number. We can safely ignore completely unregulated free markets, which have few serious advocates among legalization proponents. With more regret, we also ignore licensing models, which have some attractive theoretical properties but little currency in the debate. This leaves depenalization (a modest legal change), a regulated adult market (a more dramatic change), and intermediate alternatives that seem plausible for heroin (heroin maintenance) and cannabis (depenalization of home cultivation in small quantities). Our projections are summarized in Table 14.1; Tables 14.2 to 14.4 in the chapter appendix present detailed projections for three heroin regimes (adult market, maintenance, depenalization) to illustrate the complexity of the assessments. Although the text discusses the most important issues, it is not feasible to provide a detailed justification for each of the almost 400 specific projections (56 per regime) across the seven regimes we analyzed – depenalization of cocaine and heroin, adult market for cocaine, adult market for heroin, heroin maintenance, cannabis depenalization, adult market for cannabis, and an Alaska-type version of cannabis depenalization allowing home cultivation.

For each regime, we offer projections with respect to *prevalence* (number of users), *intensity* (average consumption per user), and *harmfulness* (harm per unit consumed, or micro harm) for a list of twenty-seven different harms – abbreviated from our more extensive listing in Chapter 6. Some reductions in harm are attributable to the regime change itself, either directly (e.g., reduction in prison cell-years for drug offenses) or via changed patterns of drug use (less needle sharing) or drug sales (fewer dealer homicides). Other reductions are *composition effects* (Proposition B7) – statistical reductions in the average level of harm that would occur if new users were more cautious and less impulsive than previous users. Why? These are users who would not have used the drug in question under a prohibition regime, and prohibition is likely to filter out the more cautious and risk averse (Chapter 5).

Table 14.1. *Summary of projections*

Drug	Regime	Changes relative to status quo		Distributive issues	Major uncertainties
		Use	Harms		
Cocaine	Depenalization	Little or no increase in prevalence; minor increase in intensity	Possible increases in impaired functioning and crime; decreases in criminal justice costs	Users benefit more than nonusers	Little directly relevant evidence
	Adult market	Increased prevalence; increased intensity	Increases in addiction, health care costs, impaired functioning; decreases in economic crime, criminal justice costs/harms, and intrusiveness	Users benefit more than nonusers; inner cities may benefit more than middle class	Little directly relevant evidence
Heroin	Depenalization	Same as cocaine depenalization	Same as cocaine depenalization	Same as cocaine depenalization	Same as cocaine depenalization
	Adult market	Increased prevalence; decrease in intensity (?)	Similar to cocaine adult market, but also decreases in drug-related illness and disease transmission	Similar to cocaine adult market	Little directly relevant evidence
	Maintenance (if significant diversion from black market)	No change in prevalence; possible increase in intensity	Increased treatment costs (maintenance), but decreases in illness, impaired functioning, crime, and intrusiveness	Similar to cocaine adult market	Logistics of implementation; will many addicts participate?
Cannabis	Depenalization	No change in prevalence; little or no increase in intensity	Reduced intrusiveness and criminal justice costs/harms	Users benefit more than nonusers	Much less uncertainty than other regimes
	Alaska model	No change in prevalence; possible increase in intensity	Possible increases in harmful effects of use (which are modest); decreases in criminal justice costs/harms and intrusiveness	Users benefit more than nonusers; might reduce alcohol (and even hard drug) intoxication	Effect on black market? Effect on gateway?
	Adult market	Increased prevalence and intensity	Some increase in harmful effects of use (which are modest); decreases in criminal justice costs/harms and intrusiveness	Same as Alaska model	Effect on black market? Effect on gateway? Substitution away from alcohol?

We generally assume that macro harm is the product of prevalence × intensity × micro harm.[1] Thus, if a micro harm is reduced without increasing prevalence, macro harm will also drop. If a reduction in average harm is accompanied by an increase in prevalence or intensity of use, we generally lack a firm basis for predicting the net effect at the macro level. Our projections in such instances reflect our judgment about the most likely net effect. All our projections are uncertain; projections that are *particularly* uncertain – "educated guesses" in the absence of any direct evidence – are flagged in the tables with question marks.

Regulated adult market for cocaine and heroin

Here we assess a regime that makes cocaine and heroin accessible to adults at a price that is lower than current black market prices but that includes substantial taxes both to correct for externalities and to moderate use for its own sake (or the sake of addiction reduction). For the moment, we also assume that promotion is kept at modest levels, though we have little faith that such limits can be maintained. Adolescents are not completely locked out, just as is the case for alcohol. They purchase illicitly, mostly through young adult friends, and hence at a somewhat higher price and lesser convenience. We assume that other drugs are no more or less available than in the current prohibition regime; possible substitution and gateway effects of cannabis legalization are discussed later in the chapter.

Effects on prevalence of use. We are confident that legalization would increase heroin prevalence (i.e., the total number of persons who would use the drugs). Our prediction of some nontrivial increase is based on the analysis presented in Chapter 5 and won't be repeated here. However, the magnitude of that increase is quite uncertain. Unlike other authors quoted in Table 5.1, we see no credible basis for predicting the magnitude of the increase in prevalence. Anything between 50 percent and 500 percent seems possible.

One might argue that this increase would be temporary – a brief period of experimentation by those currently abstaining, drawn out

---

1. In the terminology of Chapter 13, this is true of frequency-based harms but not invariant harms (e.g., restrictions on medicinal use) that are not a function of consumption per se.

of curiosity to taste the once forbidden fruit. But this is a short-term argument that ignores the multiple ways in which drug laws discourage use, and the potential for an increase in initiation rates among later cohorts. The cumulative consequence of the deterrent, price, availability, and symbolic threshold effects (ways that prohibition reduces use) are likely to be collectively stronger than forbidden fruit and labeling effects (ways that prohibition increases use).

Effects on intensity of use. It is less clear that escalation rates (the fraction of light users who become frequent users) would increase. One can identify effects working in opposing directions. Several lines of argument suggested a reduction in average intensity of use. First, there is the aforementioned composition effect; the new users are probably less risky users on average. Indeed, there is even the possibility of what has been observed in the alcohol literature under the rubric of the "Ledermann" hypothesis, that there is a fixed relationship between the consumption levels of the average drinker and the heaviest drinkers at the right tail of the consumption distribution (e.g., Edwards et al., 1994).[2] If so, an increase in the fraction of moderate cocaine users might lead to less extreme consumption by heavy users.

Second, though cocaine and heroin are expensive and difficult to obtain under the current regime, current addicts may find themselves trapped in that state as a result of the criminal career and stigma that are their fate. In a regime where heroin use was compatible with a more normal life, in which the user might have the option of developing social and family ties unrelated to heroin, careers of those who do become dependent might well become shorter. Preliminary findings from the Swiss heroin maintenance trials provide evidence that some long-term addicts having been able to detach themselves from the drug scene have sought to end their use of the drug altogether. And third, less potent forms may be available in the legal market, and safe use campaigns might reduce escalation. (Such campaigns

2. Under current circumstances, there are important differences in the shapes of the distribution of use for alcohol on the one hand and cocaine and heroin on the other. Most of those who drink, drink moderate amounts; very heavy drinking is rare. A larger fraction of those who use cocaine and heroin do so very frequently. The extent to which this is a consequence of the substances themselves, as opposed to the settings that have been created, remains unclear.

are a staple of contemporary efforts to socialize young adults into "sensible drinking.")

On the other hand, several other considerations predict increased intensity of use. The lower price and easier access would facilitate heavier use of these attractive drugs; this may be particularly important early in drug-using careers. These are very rewarding drugs for the first few episodes; even if new users are less risk prone, the "capture rate" into heavy use may be substantial.[3] With a large increase in experimentation, capture rates do not have to be high to produce a substantial rise in the number of regular users. A second argument is more subtle. Under the current regime, the criminal justice system plays a major role in bringing heavy users into treatment (Anglin & Hser, 1990; Kleiman, 1997); legalization would greatly weaken if not eliminate this source of influence. On the other hand, the fear of legal sanctions probably discourages some users from seeking treatment, and these two effects might offset each other.

We see no clear basis for determining the relative importance of these effects. In the end, we are inclined to predict – with little confidence – that the average intensity of use would increase slightly for both cocaine and heroin. We expect the combined result to be an increase because some of the new users are likely to slip into heavier use over time.

Effects on total consumption (prevalence × intensity). Because we expect a sharp increase in prevalence and at least some increase in intensity of use, we are confident that *total* consumption would increase substantially. Whether *substantially* means 50 percent or 1,000 percent is impossible to determine from existing evidence. We suspect that it will be closer to the high end, but that is little more than intuition. None of the analogies provides strong evidence on intensity of use.

In a prohibition regime, total consumption is an important measure since so many of the crime-related harms are a consequence of consumption and/or expenditures. In a legal regime, the consequences are less clear, so we turn to harms.

---

3. For example a recent national survey estimated that 23 percent of those who had tried heroin had been dependent on it at some stage of their lives (Anthony et al., 1994).

Effects on harmfulness (average harm per use). We hypothesize that legalization will reduce average harm per dose consumed. That is a message from Chapter 6, where we argued that the principal source of many categories of drug-related harm is either illegality or enforcement. Prohibition increases harm via black market (systemic) violence, economic-compulsive criminality, the deleterious effects on the criminal justice system (opportunity costs, corruption), STD transmission due to needle sharing, stigmatization of users, and so on. The number of harms related to use alone is much smaller and they seem qualitatively less serious. We see no reason why legal markets would increase psychopharmacological harms per dose; indeed, such harms might decline significantly. In addition, the composition effect will change the pool of users. Under legalization, it is likely that the *average* user would be a safer user.

Effects on total harm. We can offer tentative predictions about the effects of legalization on total harm (i.e., harmfulness × prevalence × intensity) per category of harm, but these predictions are necessarily less confident – if our predictions about harmfulness, prevalence, and intensity are uncertain, predicting the multiplicative product of those effects is tenuous indeed. A further complication is endogeneity; the reduction in average harm might itself increase use, irrespective of direct effects of legalization on use. If so, ceteris paribus, total harm would increase. This is a concern not only for legalization but also for any intervention designed to reduce harmfulness per use. In Chapter 15, we take up these arguments in detail and argue that even though they cannot be ignored, there are reasons to believe that reduced harmfulness is probably not "self-extinguishing."

A related argument is that there is a self-limiting aspect to the spread of dependent drug use, indeed exactly what would be expected from a phenomenon for which the term epidemic is used (Johnston, 1991; Musto, 1987). Drug use is behavior learned from other users. The previous heroin and crack epidemics burned themselves out in part because the adverse consequences of these drugs manifested themselves clearly enough over time that they served as strong negative role models for potential users in the neighborhoods in which they were so heavily concentrated. In effect, there was a developed immunity within the community. We hypothesize that the heroin and crack epidemics burned out more rapidly than that for powder cocaine because the user population was more concentrated and the ill-effects of frequent use were so conspicuous, particularly for crack. If cocaine and heroin prove very destructive to self under a legal regime, then initiation will decline substantially. It may, however, turn out that precisely because they are legal, the adverse consequences are sufficiently reduced and/or delayed that the immunity develops much more slowly. But while we would expect some harms to decline on average under legalization (e.g., AIDS transmission), others that are also highly visible would not (dependence, intoxication, impaired functioning). At any rate, any substantial increase in prevalence is more likely to be a direct effect of legal access than an indirect effect of reduced harmfulness.

One thing we can predict with certainty: Legalization would produce major changes in the composition of harms. Legalization would reduce those criminality and criminal justice costs associated with drug-law enforcement and black-market activity but increase the direct ill effects of drug use on health and responsible functioning. The state will be less intrusive; more individuals will be addicted. The tradeoff is somewhat more favorable for heroin than for cocaine; cocaine is less strongly implicated in AIDS transmission (and then, usually in conjunction with heroin), and overdoses are less strongly related to adulterants. Still, identifying the net effect across harms for either drug is daunting. Thus, we are sure there would be tradeoffs; the exact nature of those tradeoffs is harder to predict.

Redistributive effects. Various authors have attempted to predict the redistributive effects of hard-drug legalization across age, region, income, and race/ethnicity (e.g., Kornblum, 1991; MacCoun & Caulkins, 1996).

The urban poor. Most authors agree that the minority poor bear a disproportionate share of the harms of drug prohibition (e.g., Miller, 1996; Tonry, 1995). Legalization of cocaine and heroin would benefit those communities by reducing these forms of crime. A principal path would be through reductions in incarceration of young males, which are at an extraordinary level currently.

But those gains are no guarantee that the minority poor would be better off in a legal drug regime; that would depend on whether consumption rates in their neighborhoods increased and by how much. In conversations, we have heard the argument, sotto voce, that drug use is already rampant among the minority poor and couldn't get any worse. This is stereotyping. First, until recently, most surveys showed lower levels of self-reported drug use among minorities. And even though the minority poor do have disproportionately high levels of heroin and crack dependence, these levels are nowhere any kind of "ceiling" on potential addiction. Thus, some prominent minority leaders argue that legalization is "the moral equivalent of genocide" (Cockburn, 1993). Inner-city neighborhoods lack the treatment and prevention resources of the middle class, and the experience with alcohol promotion (liquor store locations, the marketing of higher potency wines and beers) is hardly reassuring.[4] Moreover, according to economic theory, the price elasticity of demand is generally higher for goods that consume a large fraction of disposable income. Current poor users spend most of their disposable income on cocaine and heroin (see Chapters 2 and 5). They may greatly expand consumption (i.e., their price elasticity of demand may be particularly high). On the other hand, the people for whom availability would change the least under legalization are precisely those for whom availability is not currently a problem: residents in neighborhoods with open-air drug markets, college students, people who frequent bars and night clubs where drugs are sold, and so on. Hence, the increased availability of legalized drugs would probably have a greater impact on consumption in rural areas than in large cities (MacCoun & Caulkins, 1996).

Age. Irrespective of ethnicity and income, we would expect legalization to produce a redistribution across age groups. Adults are more influenced by deterrence and symbolic threshold and less influenced by forbidden fruit and price. The proposed regime should also increase adult availability more than youth availability. Longer careers of use among those who did use would also raise the average age.

Users vs. nonusers. Perhaps the most important dimension of redistribution involves users and nonusers. In the current regime, the

---

4. State lottery advertising patterns, though less well documented, are similarly disturbing in this regard.

harms of drug use, particularly dependence, are borne heavily by nonusers through crime and, to a lesser extent, disease. One way to see this is to compare the components of the estimated costs of alcohol abuse and drug abuse (Rice et al., 1991). The estimated economic costs of alcohol are primarily health-related and are borne mostly by the user and intimates; auto accidents and the pooling of health costs through insurance are the principal mechanisms by which damages are inflicted on the broader community. The economic costs of illicit drugs come primarily from crime – not just criminal justice costs (including the opportunity costs of incarcerating drug offenders) but also victimization costs and fear. We hypothesize that the distribution of costs associated with cocaine and heroin would become similar to that for alcohol under legalization. A higher share would be incurred by the user and his or her intimates. With health costs much larger and crime costs substantially less, the broader community would bear a lower share. It might still be the case that current nonusers would be harmed and that current users as a group would benefit. Nonusers would be at higher risk of becoming users themselves or seeing their children become users.

Summary. In the end, we see no easy verdict for cocaine or heroin legalization, surely not the open-and-shut case implied by some proponents. Cocaine and heroin legalization would produce some immediate, tangible gains, and for that reason, it has real appeal. But the risk that those gains would later be swamped by dramatic increases in hard-drug use (and its direct health and behavioral effects) is also very real.

Depenalization of cocaine and/or heroin

If a regulated adult legal market is too risky, perhaps a less dramatic change is an easier sell. Our propositions suggest that even though prevalence increases with legal access, possibly substantially (Proposition B1), it is little affected by depenalization or weaker reductions in user sanctions (Proposition A1). Alas, though depenalization does reduce criminal justice costs and intrusiveness (Proposition A3), it offers few of the more significant harm-reducing benefits of increased legal access (Propositions A4, B2). Moreover, most of our evidence regarding the effects of depenalization on prevalence involves cannabis, so we have less confidence predicting little effect on cocaine or heroin use.

Specific projections for heroin depenalization are depicted in Table 14.2; in essence, they are just a watered-down version of our predictions for the legal adult market. The same projections can also be applied for cocaine. There are fewer risks due to increased prevalence, but few of the most dramatic reductions in harm are produced by legalization. For example, depenalization does little to address AIDS transmission, black-market violence, income-generating crime, or accident victimization. It does reduce criminal justice costs associated with heroin and cocaine possession, but not those associated with the distribution of those drugs, and many heavy users would continue to be drug sellers. Additionally, depenalization would reduce one set of incentives for seeking treatment.

Proposition A2 suggests that depenalization produces stronger effects on intensity (average consumption per user) than on prevalence (the number of users). This is somewhat speculative; there is little direct evidence, and we suspect that the legal barrier between use and nonuse is stronger than that between light use and heavy use. One way to offset increases in intensity is to limit depenalization to first offenses and/or offenses for small amounts, with steeply rising sanctions thereafter. But the tradeoff is that many of the cost-saving benefits of depenalization are then lost. Surprisingly, we find that this logic leads to a rather counterintuitive prediction: depenalizing heroin or cocaine could actually result in greater harm than legalizing them. Again, the reason is that even though both options would likely raise total consumption (depenalization less so than legalization), legalization would reduce a greater number of drug-related harms, reducing some of them more dramatically. We aren't suggesting hard-drug depenalization is even riskier than opponents imply; rather, we are suggesting that hard-drug legalization (relative to depenalization) offers substantial benefits in addition to its substantial risks.

In the end, given substantial psychopharmacological hazards associated with cocaine and heroin use, the risk that such use might increase, and the inapplicability of many of the strongest legalization arguments, it is hard to make a strong case for cocaine or heroin depenalization. For cocaine, a more prudent strategy would be to retain user sanctions, but at substantially reduced levels, perhaps starting quite low and rising more steeply with repeated offending (see Kleiman, 1997). As we argued in Chapter 5, variations in penalty levels that do not cross the nonpenalty boundary appear to have little effect on criminality. A good start would be to abolish the federal mandatory minimums. These are patently unfair to minorities, and don't even offer effective crime control: Caulkins and colleagues (1997) strongly argue that a return to traditional sentencing would be substantially more cost-effective. For heroin, we now turn to an alternative prospect that seems more promising.

Heroin maintenance regime

Is there a way to retain the substantial benefits of legalization (e.g., the elimination of the black market and its attendant harms) while curtailing the risk of increased drug use? Proposition B4 suggests that commercialization is the biggest culprit – a notion that finds some support in our examination of the repeal of Prohibition, the Dutch cannabis coffeeshops, state lotteries, and contemporary tobacco and alcohol marketing. Thus, one temptation is to seek out a halfway model, one that provides selective access under strict prescriptive or regulatory controls. Alas, Propositions B5 and B6 suggest the difficulty of restricting the growth in drug use without also restricting some of the reductions in harmfulness. Take taxation, for example. There are compelling reasons for using a tax to offset some of the risks of legal commercial access to heroin (Grinspoon & Bakalar, 1990). But as we noted in Chapter 5, a tax large enough to discourage consumption is likely to reproduce the kind of black markets that legalization was intended to eliminate. (Witness Canada's abandoned effort to reduce tobacco consumption through a steep increase in their cigarette tax; Gunby, 1994.)

One way to soften this tradeoff is to very selectively target access so that those most likely to utilize the black market have no need to do so. Heroin maintenance attempts such a strategy. We examined heroin maintenance at considerable length in Chapter 12 and won't repeat that discussion. Here we attempt to project the likely effects of heroin maintenance, *conditional upon the assumption that the program is implemented widely and is successful in diverting addicts from the black market.* That rather large caveat reflects our conviction that for heroin maintenance, the major empirical uncertainties involve implementation, not program effects. (We discuss another source of uncertainty, moral rather than empirical, later.) In fact, if a heroin maintenance program succeeds in diverting addicts from the black market, we believe that it offers significant gains by almost any consequentialist's standards. Almost every category of harmfulness (per use) should be reduced, and none should increase.

Of course, a sizeable increase in heroin use might swamp these gains. But heroin maintenance seems much less likely than legalization to generate increases in prevalence, and there are reasons to believe any increases in intensity of use (per user) would generate little offsetting increases in average harm. With respect to intensity of use, the Swiss trials found that given the ability to choose their own dose, experienced users chose a stable daily level. In addition, we hypothesize that the dose-response curve for those behavioral harms intrinsic to heroin use (i.e., not caused by prohibition per se) rises sharply but quickly reaches a plateau. If so, higher doses may have little behavioral impact.

With respect to prevalence, the reduction in harmfulness might make heroin use more attractive. In particular, someone who tinkers with black market heroin might reason that if she does become dependent, her habit will be supported by government-provided doses of predictable purity and potency, at a modest price, from a reliable and safe source. Though this is plausible, it is hard to imagine someone with the foresightedness to reason this way who would knowingly choose to become "enslaved" to a drug, no matter the source. Moreover, such a person would have to knowingly accept the substantial risks of using black-market heroin for years before becoming eligible for a maintenance program. One might also argue that heroin maintenance would reduce the likelihood that an addict would come clean. We find this compelling in the abstract, but the argument loses a great deal of force when one considers the remarkably long duration of heroin "careers" in the current regime (e.g., Hser et al., 1993). At any rate, such prevalence-increasing effects would almost surely be counterbalanced by the substantial reduction in black-market access that would result when current addicts stop frequenting (and running) those markets.[5]

---

5. The risk of diversion from maintenance to the black market can be mitigated by following the Swiss approach in which participants are not allowed any "take-home" doses.

Thus, if a substantial percentage of current heroin addicts were to participate, which is by no means certain, heroin maintenance would result in large gains in health, social functioning, and criminal justice costs. It is worth emphasizing that although the Swiss results add to our confidence in these conclusions, our projections for heroin maintenance don't require those results – we think that we would have reached similar conclusions even in the absence of the Swiss trials, just based on our understanding of how illicit drug markets work (Reuter et al., 1990). But we should reiterate that these projections are conditional; they are contingent upon the assumption that a heroin maintenance regime successfully diverts a sizeable fraction of eligible addicts from the black market. If that diversion fails to occur, or if that diversion is temporary, heroin maintenance still offers benefits, though whether those benefits outweigh its costs (or the benefits of expanded methadone maintenance) is less clear.

Our projections are, of course, consequential, but we cannot ignore the nonconsequentialist moral issues posed by heroin maintenance. Though it is not precisely a slippery slope, heroin maintenance goes further down a path started by methadone maintenance and needle exchange, two programs we endorse heartily. We confess to some squeamishness about heroin maintenance. It is easier to feel the qualitative breakpoint between them than to articulate it. Needle exchange and methadone maintenance each help the addict meet his need in a safer way; methadone maintenance does so in a way that is less pleasurable than heroin. One can object to facilitating that pleasure on either consequentialist or deontological grounds. In Chapter 15, we examine both kinds of objections to heroin maintenance and other harm-reducing interventions.

CANNABIS: BACKGROUND

For purposes of the legalization debate, marijuana is the cutting edge drug, the only politically plausible candidate for major legal change, at least depenalization and perhaps even outright legalization. Compared to other drugs, the harms, physiological or behavioral, are less severe, and the drug is better integrated into the culture. It has been used by a large share of the population at some time in their lives.

Thus, we give substantial space to policy options for a drug that otherwise would have less claim to special attention than either heroin or cocaine, which cause so much more damage to society. However, we note a comment by a British observer that marijuana, though perhaps a relatively harmless drug, causes great harm to policy commissions (Woodcock, 1995). The plausibility of relaxing the stringency of America's marijuana prohibition regime has been obvious for a quarter century; yet those bodies that have endorsed such relaxation have suffered only calumny as a consequence. Though less distinctively a cultural symbol than in the 1960s and 1970s, if only because so many prominent political figures have admitted youthful experiences with the substance,[6] marijuana retains a symbolic role in continuing culture wars. The obstacles to a fair hearing for marijuana policy reform are formidable.

Current usage patterns and policy

The drug is used by very large numbers of persons, mostly aged between 15 and 30, and that use is not concentrated in a single social class. Considering only those born after 1960, a majority of Americans over the age of 17 have tried the drug; see Chapter 2. Most persons using marijuana in the last year used it only about once a month, and less than a third used it more than once a week. Most persons use marijuana for relatively short periods of time. Among 26 to 34 year olds who had used the drug daily at some time in their life in 1994, only 22 percent reported that they had used it in the past year.[7]

Yet prolonged use is not uncommon. The one published long-term study of a cohort of American youth shows long periods of daily marijuana use (defined as 20 days in the previous month) for a large share of the sample. Kandel and Davies (1992) reported on a cohort of tenth and eleventh graders recruited from New York State high schools in 1971. When the respondents were re-interviewed in 1984, at age 28 or 29, over one-quarter (26.2 percent) had been daily users

6. For example, Vice President Al Gore, during the 1988 presidential campaign, admitted to use of marijuana as a young man. Indeed, for a while it became a ritual event for national political figures to admit to use as an adolescent, accompanying that with a statement of regret about youthful indiscretion. Even the hawkish William Bennett asserted that such use was no basis for political disgrace.
7. All statements about use, unless otherwise noted, are from the 1995 National Household Survey on Drug Abuse.

of marijuana for at least some 1-month period in their life. Even more striking, the mean duration of spells of near-daily use was over 3.5 years. The much greater involvement of this sample in marijuana use may be cohort and location specific[8]; this was a group that went through the high-risk years near the peak of the counterculture movement and many were from New York City, which was particularly influenced by that movement.

In other surveys, relatively few of those who tried marijuana have experienced problems as a consequence, but about 10 percent of users were classified as dependent, a matter we take up more fully later. Few go on to use more dangerous illicit drugs; only 23 percent of 26 to 34 year olds who had used marijuana at some time had also used cocaine during their lives.

The drug's illegal status imposes only modest direct harms on the average user. Impurities are not a concern. Though there are instances of egregiously harsh sentences for those caught, particularly in the federal system, for any activity related to production or distribution (see e.g., Schlosser, 1994), the overwhelming majority of the annual 500,000 recorded possession arrests each year probably result in either a fine or probation[9]; many of the arrests are expunged from the record within a year.[10] The 500,000 arrests also have to be put in the context of the size of the user population of approximately 20 million.[11] Each year an average user faces a 1 in 40 chance of being arrested; per use episode the risk is only about 1 in 4,000.[12]

---

8. The differences with national data sets are less striking than we expected initially. For example, in the Kandel study, over 70 percent reported use at some time prior to the interview. The closest comparison we were able to make was with the 1979 NHSDA, 18 to 25 year olds (i.e., born between 1954 and 1961). This comparison is appropriate because most initiation occurs before age 20. The NHSDA figure for lifetime use of marijuana was 68 percent; no data are available for just the two-year birth cohort of 1955–6.

9. This statement is a conjecture, since no data sets allow the tracking of misdemeanor arrests to sentence. It accords with impressions of officials and researchers in many jurisdictions.

10. For example, in the District of Columbia, a person can apply to the court for removal of a criminal record if his marijuana possession conviction is not followed by any other offense within 12 months.

11. The 1994 NHSDA estimated 18 million used in the previous year. We have chosen to round up to reflect evidence of underreporting, even in household surveys, as compared to in-school surveys, which provide greater anonymity (Gfroerer et al., 1997).

12. The starting point for this calculation is 750 tons consumption (Rhodes et al., 1995). If the average joint has 0.4 grams, this yields a total of almost 2 billion joints. Assuming one joint per session yields 1 arrest per 4,000 sessions. Note though that many arrests occur at time of possession, as for example in a car, rather than use.

Enforcement against cannabis sellers is only moderately vigorous. Selling arrests, which also encompass growing and importation, have totaled between 65,000 and 85,000 for a decade. This led in 1994 to 16,000 felony convictions in state courts (*Sourcebook of Criminal Justice Statistics*, annual). At the federal level, about 4,000 received prison sentences for marijuana offenses annually between 1990 and 1995. For states, we estimate the figure at 11,000 in 1994.[13]

The drug is extraordinarily expensive relative to its production cost or what it might cost if legal. A tobacco cigarette, even with tax, costs about 10 cents in most states. At current prices a marijuana joint, with only 0.4–0.5 grams of cannabis in it, costs about $4, a tribute to the harshness of the nation's effort at interdiction (which has cut off low-cost Colombian sources), aggressive domestic eradication campaigns (a continuing federal and state priority), and perhaps long federal sentences for growing. However, in terms of the cost of intoxication, marijuana still provides a very cheap high. Kleiman (1992a, Chapter 9) estimated that two persons sharing a single joint would probably get two hours of intoxication each; a person-hour of intoxication is thus about $1, much below the cost of even cheap alcohol.

As discussed in Chapters 3 and 5, depenalization of marijuana was the major target of drug policy reform in the 1970s and twelve states adopted changes that at least removed criminal penalties for first offenses involving simple possession of small amounts (usually less than 1 ounce) for personal consumption. However, as concern about illegal drugs in general rose in the 1980s, support for changing marijuana's legal status weakened, even among those who used the drug. For the total household population, the percent favoring marijuana legalization went from a high of 30 percent in 1978 to a low of 16 percent in 1987, 1989, and 1990; by 1996 it had crept up to 26 percent.

Even among the young there is little support for legalization; the percentage of high school seniors who believed that marijuana should be entirely legal peaked in 1977 at 34 percent and fell to

---

13. In 1994, 872,000 persons were convicted of a felony. Of these convictions, 1.3 percent were for marijuana possession (11,336) and 1.8 percent for marijuana trafficking (15,696), giving a total of 27,032 for marijuana offenses. For all drug offenses, 42 percent received prison sentences; 27 percent went to jail, and 31 percent received probation. Though marijuana offenders may be treated more leniently by sentencing judges, applying these figures gives an approximate total of 11,000 persons sent to state prison for marijuana offenses.

27 percent by 1994. The percent in favor of depenalization fell from 31 percent in 1977 to 19 percent in 1994 (Johnston et al., 1995).

One interesting aspect of the depenalization movement was the brevity and intensity of its success. All changes occurred between October 5, 1973, and July 1, 1978. South Dakota quickly reversed itself, but that is the only definite reversal. A voter initiative over-turned Alaska's 1975 referendum in November 1990, but a 1993 court interpretation voided the initiative, ruling that it conflicted with the state constitution (D'oro, 1997; Pitler, 1996). Oregon's legislature voted to reverse depenalization in 1997. However, sufficient signa-tures were gathered for a referendum endorsing depenalization that the legislative action was suspended (Green, 1997). No state has decriminalized since 1978, but depenalization is not generally seen as a failure.

The gateway mechanism[14]

The case for continued prohibition of nonmedical uses of marijuana rests primarily on four possible harms: (1) marijuana's role as a gateway to other drugs of known dangerousness, a role believed to be unrelated to its legal status; (2) its health consequences and impact on adolescent development; (3) user behavior when intoxicated; and (4) the difficulty of quitting. We explore each of these before con-sidering the strength of the case for legal change.

Though cannabis use is not without harm, especially for adoles-cents, as a source of danger it is surely trumped by alcohol, tobacco, reckless driving, criminality, and unsafe sexual behavior, unless, of course, it actually promotes subsequent hard-drug addiction. Hence the concern with the gateway. It is devilishly difficult to establish a causal role for cannabis; the surest test would be a controlled exper-iment, a prospect that cannot be pursued ethically. But even if one were to stipulate that cannabis plays a causal role in hard-drug use, the policy implications are less clear than generally imagined; much depends on the nature of the linkage.

---

14. Zimmer and Morgan (1997) provided a detailed analysis of this and other claims about the effects of marijuana use. We believe that they do a better job of critiquing the claims of hawks than of establishing that the harms of marijuana are modest; the same judg-ment is reached by Hall (1997a).

In summary, we believe that there is little evidence that expanding marijuana use does increase the use of other, more harmful drugs. Our belief is less than certainty. Nor is the gateway insensitive to legal status; the transition probability may be higher or lower in a harsh prohibition regime than in one which treats marijuana as distinct from other illicit drugs. The available data simply do not speak to this.

The notion that cannabis use is a gateway to hard-drug use is a time-honored staple of the drug policy debate. Given the relative subtlety of marijuana's direct harms, the gateway notion has served as a major rationale for sustaining (or escalating) cannabis prohibition since the mid-1960s. For at least as long, doves have dismissed the evidence for the gateway as spurious, trivial in magnitude, or both. The lack of agreement may have less to do with self-serving interpretations of the data than with considerable confusion about the meaning of the gateway concept. We suggest that there are at least seven coherent (though not necessarily credible) interpretations of the evidence; some support hawkish views, some support quite dovish alternatives, and one even suggests the whole issue might have little policy relevance.

Version 1: The first step. The most simplistic version is that (a) almost all heroin and cocaine users first used cannabis, and so (b) cannabis must be a stepping stone toward hard-drug use. The evidence for the first proposition is overwhelming, at least in this country and many other Western nations. But, of course, the second proposition is a non sequitur; temporal precedence is necessary but not sufficient to establish causality. Thus, doves frequently dismiss the gateway notion as a classic post hoc, ergo propter hoc fallacy: "Yes, but before cannabis, they started with milk; is milk a gateway substance?" This retort demolishes Version 1, but leaves the other interpretations untouched.

In addition to temporal precedence, causal claims require evidence of correlation or statistical association. One way of thinking about statistical association is in terms of conditional probabilities, or relative risk. Is the probability of trying cocaine higher for those who have tried cannabis than for those who have not? Do cannabis triers face a higher statistical risk of hard-drug addiction? Yes. The evidence for a correlation between cannabis use and hard-drug use is also overwhelming (e.g., Kandel, Yamaguchi, & Chen, 1992). Here's where the milk argument falters; although all cocaine users (except a few lactose-intolerants) have tried milk, there is surely no correlation between milk and cocaine use.

Version 2: The spurious correlation. Like temporal precedence, correlation is necessary but not sufficient to establish causality. It is plausible that the correlation between pot and cocaine (or heroin, or LSD) is spurious, reflecting some third factor that puts people at risk for use of both cannabis and hard drugs. Generating good candidates isn't hard; it has long been known that behaviors like smoking, drinking, and using illicit drugs tends to cluster in adolescence (e.g., Ferguson & Horwood, 1997), along with other problem behaviors like truancy, poor grades, fighting, property crime, teenage pregnancy, and depression. It is likely that for most problem youth, these are all manifestations of an unfortunate interaction of dispositional factors (poor self-control and socialization skills, hyperactivity, and sometimes even neurological deficits) and bad situations (economic deprivation, limited or inappropriate adult supervision, neighborhood disorder). Nevertheless, analyses that statistically control for a lengthy list of known risk factors find that the link between marijuana and hard drug use is reduced, but not eliminated (Fergusson & Horwood, 2000).

Version 3: The early warning. Of course, even if the link between cannabis use and hard drugs isn't causal, early cannabis use might serve as an early warning signal. From this perspective, even if cannabis doesn't cause hard-drug use, it reliably precedes it and predicts it. The data support this interpretation, but they also show that the diagnostic value is limited. As a signal, cannabis mostly generates false alarms. The majority of cannabis triers never try harder drugs, and of those who do, few become regular users, much less addicts. A brief adolescent phase of "acting out" in delinquency and casual drug experimentation is well within the range of statistical normality in the United States and many other nations and has been for generations.

Among those who do proceed from pot to harder drug use (especially heavy use), one finds some statistical clustering of other problem indicators – a higher propensity toward criminality, joblessness, and so on. But adolescents who casually experiment with cannabis appear to function quite well with respect to schooling and mental health (Shedler & Block, 1990). Acknowledging these facts doesn't condone such experimentation; low risks in the aggregate can have big effects for some individuals, and minute harms at the individual level might sum up to important aggregate effects. But it does complicate one's interpretation of the cannabis signal. On the other hand, longitudinal research does indicate that some patterns of cannabis use – early onset and/or high frequency – are more reliable signals of subsequent problems with other drugs and other risky behaviors (e.g., Ferguson & Horwood, 1997).

Version 4: The trap. Version 4 is a straw man argument; we are unaware of any hawks that seriously endorse it, but doves knock it down with great relish. The notion is that cannabis use inexorably (with high probability) yanks one into the trap of hard-drug use. Thus, one recent analysis argued that a gateway would exist if 75 percent or more of cannabis users went on to hard drugs. Since they didn't, and don't in any sample we know of, one can argue that the gateway has been refuted. This purely deterministic notion of causality may work for billiard balls and other inanimate objects (at least above the subatomic level), but surely no one believes it applies to cause and effect in human actions. Thus, the fact that most cannabis triers never try hard drugs is not sufficient to exonerate cannabis from a causal role.

Version 5: The tantalizer. Version 5 appears to be what most hawks actually have in mind. In this version, cannabis isn't a trap so much as a tease, tantalizing unwitting (and stoned) young minds with the prospect of experimentation with ever more intriguing varieties of intoxication. The idea is hardly preposterous on its face. Few go straight to Miro without passing through Magritte, and the same applies to complexity in music, food, wine, and literature. Still, plausibility isn't evidence; where's the beef? Until recently, one was hard-pressed to find any expert endorsement of this version (see critiques by Kaplan, 1970; Kleiman, 1992a). But much was made of new research demonstrating that cannabis activates neurochemical processes that respond in qualitatively similar ways to cocaine, heroin, tobacco, and alcohol (see Wickelgren, 1997). Popular media coverage suggested a "smoking gun" – hard scientific evidence for a neurological basis for the gateway effect, an impression the source articles did little to discourage.

Naturally, few drew the equally plausible (or implausible) interpretation that alcohol is a gateway drug. In fact, alcohol is a bit of a red herring here. With respect to temporal precedence, the evidence that almost all hard-drug users first tried alcohol is also overwhelming; moreover, for most of them, alcohol preceded cannabis. But experience with alcohol is so common in our culture that as a statistical correlate of hard-drug use, having tried alcohol is more akin to having tried milk than having tried cannabis. (Prolonged heavy drinking is another matter altogether. Under any theory, the gateway notion is more credible when the gateway substance is used heavily and frequently rather than lightly and sporadically.)

Arguably, the new research captured popular attention because of the widespread belief that if scientists in lab coats can observe effects of cannabis on brain chemicals, then the locus of causation must be biological rather than psychological or sociological. Yet no serious psychologist rejects the notion that neurochemical processes are involved in everything psychological and everything sociological; our attitudes toward Monica Lewinsky and Kenneth Starr have neurochemical signatures, and some day we may know how to read them. Identifying those neurochemical processes is of tremendous value, but establishing their existence hardly settles the issue of causality. Neither study actually examined the relationship between rats' cannabis consumption and their motivation to use harder drugs. And several critics have pointed out that rats won't even self-administer cannabis, raising questions about the applicability of the "rat model" to human behavior (see Coffin, 1997; also, the exchange of letters in the August 8, 1997, issue of *Science*). This latter point is particularly troubling, because one's interpretation of these new studies depends on how one translates the rat doses to human equivalents – equivalents with respect to relevant psychological and physiological effects, and not just body weight. At one extreme, the rat doses might only compare to extremely heavy human consumption. If so, their generalizability to typical cannabis experience is rather remote. At the other extreme, the rat doses might be comparable to fairly typical human doses.

If so, then given what we know about the epidemiology of drug use in this country over the past 20 years, these new studies actually imply that the neurochemical processes in question obviously have a much weaker hold on human behavior than many had previously assumed, since it is known the dependence is relatively uncommon among typical human users. The evidence (reviewed later in this section) suggests 10 percent as an upper-bound figure.

Version 6: The toe in the water. Alternatively, a causal link between cannabis and later hard-drug use might be more sociological than physiological (Kaplan, 1970; MacCoun et al., 1996). For example, seemingly safe experiences with marijuana might reduce the perceived riskiness of harder drugs – the health risks, the legal risks, or both. Indeed, if one's experiences fail to confirm the dire predictions of prevention programs, one might discredit warning messages about the dangers of cocaine or heroin. If so, perhaps public information campaigns should draw a clearer distinction between marijuana and more dangerous drugs. Or experience with marijuana use without getting caught (as is true of the vast majority of such experiences) may challenge one's view of the omnipotence of law enforcement (Parker & Grasmick, 1979). If so, a gateway might result from a reduction in the perceived legal risks of using harder drugs. One solution might be to drastically enhance the probability of detection of marijuana use (e.g., through mandatory drug testing); this approach is hard to justify absent more compelling risk evidence, and might well backfire politically. Alternatively, one might undermine the gateway by largely or completely depenalizing marijuana, to take it out of the realm of illicit behavior.

Version 7: The foot in the door. Finally, cannabis experience might cause hard-drug experience indirectly, by bringing experimenters into contact with hard-drug sellers. Indeed, sociologist Herman Cohen's (1972) articulation of this theory was instrumental in persuading the Dutch to permit low-level cannabis sales in coffeeshops and night-clubs; the Dutch argue that this approach separates the soft-and hard-drug markets, weakening the gateway. In Amsterdam, as in the United States, almost all hard-drug users have used cannabis, but the vast majority of cannabis users have not used hard drugs (P. Cohen & Sas, 1996). Evidence in Chapter 11 indicates that U.S. cannabis users are more likely than Dutch cannabis users to also try cocaine. Though the Dutch have failed to eliminate the statistical association between cannabis and hard-drug use, it is possible that they have weakened it, at least for heroin. But since the alleged gateway is a function of both the number of people who have tried marijuana and the probability of cocaine use given marijuana use, any increase in the former component (the prevalence of marijuana use) might offset reductions in the latter component (the probability of moving on to cocaine use). Because there are reasons to believe the Dutch commercialization of cannabis may have increased marijuana prevalence (Chapter 11), the net result of the two components is difficult to estimate.

Conclusion. Given the current state of knowledge, one can coherently argue that (a) the gateway is a myth – it doesn't exist; (b) the gateway is very real and it shows why we must sustain or strengthen our ban on marijuana; or (c) the gateway is very real and shows why we should depenalize or even legalize marijuana. It all comes down to which interpretation of the available evidence one favors. But this isn't an argument for nihilism, radical deconstructivism, or the like. Rather, it suggests the need for more focused studies of potential gateway mechanisms. For example, animal experiments might directly test the effects of cannabis exposure (frequency, duration, setting) to the propensity to self-administer harder drugs or the willingness to work (bar pressing) to earn doses of heroin or cocaine. Existing panel survey data sets might permit more careful statistical control for background factors common to both marijuana use and harder drug use. New longitudinal studies might focus on marijuana experience and its effects on the transition to hard-drug use, examining the relative influence of changes in peer associations, drug-dealing sources, and perceived health risks and legal sanctioning risks. In the absence of better causal evidence, a strong allegiance to any particular gateway theory would seem to reflect ideology or politics rather than science.

Health consequences of cannabis

Views about the health consequences of marijuana are highly polarized, reflecting the thin research base that, in turn, reflects the generally low level of interest in the drug. A recent editorial in the

premier British medical journal, *Lancet* (1995), began with the strong
declarative statement, "The smoking of cannabis, even long term, is
not harmful to health." In contrast, a very careful Australian review
of health effects, summarized by Hall (1994), concluded much more
cautiously, "There probably are adverse health and psychological
effects of cannabis use" (p. 219). The Australian review found that
acute effects included "anxiety, dysphoria, panic and paranoia, especially in naïve users" and "an increased risk of low birthweight babies
if cannabis is used during pregnancy" (Hall, Solwij, & Lemon, 1994).
The same report, while asserting that chronic effects were ill understood, said that *probable* chronic effects included "respiratory diseases associated with smoking as the method of administration,"
dependence, and "subtle forms of cognitive impairment."

Three earlier reviews (from Britain, the United States, and WHO),
mostly examining the same literature as Hall et al., came to similarly
cautious conclusions. "[T]he verdict in each case has been that the
available evidence is not nearly complete enough to permit an identification of the full range and frequency of occurrence of adverse
effects from cannabis use" (Kalant, 1982; p. 343). One may be struck
by how modest are the effects cited, given the prevalence of sustained
marijuana use in modern Western society. Or one may be struck by
how long it took to identify the full range and severity of effects of
cigarette smoking; marijuana has surely generated less than 1 percent
of the research on the health effects of cigarettes.

The possible impact on cognitive development is another health
harm. There is no doubt that heavy cannabis use has acute effects on
attention and memory, thus the fear that it constitutes a particular
problem for adolescents. However, the longitudinal evidence is
mixed. For example, Kandel et al. (1986) found that the relationship
between adolescent marijuana use and years of education completed
disappeared when they controlled for the lower educational aspira-
tions of the marijuana users. Newcomb and Bentler (1988) in the
other major longitudinal study that has investigated this issue, found
again that other factors explain the correlation between marijuana
use and educational attainment.

There is a growing interest, outside the United States, in the relationship between cannabis and psychosis. Hall (1998) suggests that
though there is evidence that the drug can trigger schizophrenia
in the most susceptible individuals, the evidence also suggests that

cannabis contributes little to the prevalence of schizophrenia at the population level.

Cannabis intoxication

Marijuana use impairs judgment and motor skills. Accidents resulting from marijuana intoxication may cause harm to users and others, and a controversy rages over the extent to which marijuana is a source of automobile accidents and fatalities. Until recently the summaries were fairly skeptical; for example, Hollister (1988) reviewing four studies on drugs detected in the bodies of drivers involved in fatal accidents found that 13 percent of those tested positive for marijuana, but the vast majority of those also tested positive for alcohol. Only 2.2 percent tested positive for marijuana alone and that was hardly dispositive of marijuana's role in the accidents since the drug has such a long half-life and can be detected for up to 30 days after use. More recent findings are less sanguine. Brookoff et al. (1994) tested drivers arrested for reckless driving who were not alcohol impaired and found that half tested positive for marijuana.

A small body of laboratory simulation research does not resolve matters. Though drivers are more likely to make errors under the influence of marijuana, such as departing from their lane, they also drive more slowly and keep a greater distance from the car in front (Smiley, 1986).[15]

The evidence is thus quite mixed. It is plausible that marijuana contributes nontrivially to auto injuries and fatalities, but it is unlikely that it is a major source of injury and mortality to marijuana users as a group.

Cannabis dependence

The dependence potential of marijuana has been only weakly studied, but the evidence is generally consistent. Self-report data

---

15. Pat Paulsen, who sadly died of cancer in 1997, was a great American comedian and comedy writer, best known for his poker-faced delivery and his periodic runs for the U.S. presidency. In 1996, the first author asked then-candidate Paulsen to clarify his position on the legalization debate. His reply: "I'm definitely in favor of people being able to legally obtain drugs for medical purposes, but otherwise, I don't want to be driving on the freeway with everyone driving at 30 mph" (e-mail correspondence, April 22, 1996).

suggest that about 10 percent of cannabis users become dependent at some time; perhaps half of those who use daily become dependent for some period of time. Cannabis users constitute a substantial fraction of all those dependent on illicit drugs; however, this dependence seems to be very much less harmful to the user than alcohol, cocaine, or heroin dependence. The major recent research reports on long-term cannabis dependence have come from an Australian research group (Swift, Hall, & Copeland, 1997; Reilly et al., 1998). They reported populations that have moderate problems of social and psychological adjustment, rarely seek treatment, and are not much involved with crime.

We note that there is a danger of reifying the term *dependence* here. The surveys that we report defined it in terms of the DSM (Diagnostic and Statistical Manual of the American Psychiatric Association) and ICD (International Classification of Disease) categorizations. Each involves a check list of symptoms and scoring "3" or more leads to classification as dependent. This classification creates a very heterogeneous group of people, some of them with what might be regarded as quite ambiguous collections of symptoms. For example, the Sydney (Australia) study of long-term users (Swift et al., 1997) found that under ICD, the most common symptom was "strong urge to use marijuana." Under DSM's version III-R, the most common symptom was "intoxication during daily activities." Using either diagnostic system, only half this sample of long-term users met the tolerance criterion, and only a small minority met the withdrawal criterion. Thus this notion of dependence is qualitatively different from what we usually think of as cocaine or heroin dependence.

The Epidemiologic Catchment Area study of mental disorders and substance abuse found that of those classified as having experienced drug dependence in their lifetimes, about half reported only marijuana use; 4.4 percent of the American population in the early 1980s was estimated to meet the diagnostic criteria for cannabis abuse or dependence (Anthony & Helzer, 1991). The National Comorbidity Study, a 1993 national survey of mental health and substance abuse estimated that 9 percent of those who reported trying marijuana reported dependence at some stage (Anthony et al., 1994). In the 1989 High School Senior Survey, 7.4 percent of past-year marijuana users reported that they had attempted to quit but failed. Similarly, of those classified as clearly in need of treatment for drug abuse/dependence in the 1990 National Household Survey, 45 percent reported the use of marijuana only (Ebener et al., 1994).

These percentages may appear modest but the population bases are large. If 10 percent of the estimated 70 million Americans who have tried marijuana have been cannabis-dependent at some stage, the number in need of treatment at some time would amount to about 7 million, comparable to the totals in need of treatment for cocaine and/or heroin at some stage in the last two decades. Kandel et al. (1997) estimated that only 0.7 percent of Americans over age 12 in 1992 had been marijuana-dependent in the previous 12 months (compared to 0.3 percent for cocaine), but that produced a total of almost 1.5 million individuals.[16]

On the other hand, the clinical literature reports very little on the phenomenon, or treatment, of cannabis dependence. It may be that dependence is common but not very severe. There is a paucity of clinical evidence of a dependence syndrome. A leading marijuana researcher noted that physical withdrawal symptoms for marijuana were mild and typically passed in a few days (Jones, 1987). The same author noted that "In some experiments, patients smoked cannabis, as many as 20 cigarettes daily for two or three weeks, and showed only minimal tolerance and no abstinence syndrome" (Jones, 1992, p. 112). Another trio of experienced marijuana researchers concluded that in light of the large population of marijuana users and the infrequent reports of medical problems following marijuana abstinence, tolerance and dependence are not major issues: "If one considers the present existence of a large population of marijuana users, and the infrequent reports of medical problems following marijuana abstinence, then it is apparent that tolerance

16. We note that this estimate, like all those using the National Household Survey on Drug Abuse (in this case combining the surveys of 1991–3), resolutely ignores that survey's well-known limitations. Thus, it underestimates cocaine and heroin dependence by approximately 1 million; much higher and more credible estimates come from drug test data on those who are arrested. Most of those who are dependent on those two drugs are also marijuana-dependent. Further, the estimates do not include the 1.2 million currently imprisoned, a population for which reported drug-dependence rates may be over 50 percent. A recent study of Cook County using more sophisticated modeling techniques estimated the total number of regular heroin/cocaine users (eight or more times in the previous 2 months) at approximately three times the figure generated from NHSDA data (Simeone et al., 1997). Though the undercount for frequent marijuana use is unlikely to be similarly large, it may nonetheless be substantial.

and dependence are not major issues" (Compton, Dewey, & Martin, 1990).

Further evidence for that view comes, oddly enough, from the observation that over 10 percent of all treatment episodes annually, as reported in the Treatment Episode Data Set, are for persons reporting only marijuana use (SAMHSA, 1997b). This annual flow of about 200,000 patients, many of them not poor, would surely engender an active research literature if their problems were significant.

The treatment population figure has other implications. When patients are categorized by primary drug of abuse, it appears that the drug for which legal coercion is the most significant source of referral is marijuana. A substantial fraction of those being treated for marijuana may not be dependent but in treatment to avoid more confining alternative dispositions. If the survey-based estimates of the prevalence of marijuana dependence are correct, it is likely that fewer than 10 percent of currently dependent users are in treatment.

In summary, dependence occurs frequently, almost as frequently as for alcohol amongst those who start using the drug. However, dependence seems to have modest adverse consequences.

THE BASIS FOR CONTINUED CANNABIS PROHIBITION

Penalties against a drug should not be more dangerous to an individual than use of the drug itself; and where they are they should be changed. Nowhere is this more clear than in the laws against the possession of marijuana (President Jimmy Carter, 1977 cited in D. F. Musto, 1987, p. 267).

Like President Carter our judgment is that at present the primary harms of marijuana use (including those borne by nonusers, a group apparently ignored in his statement) come from criminalization, expensive and intrusive enforcement, inequity, shock to the conscience from disproportionate sentence, and a substantial (though generally nonviolent) black market. This is not to ignore that the drug itself causes damage: it generates accidents causing harm to both the user and others; regular use by adolescents may adversely affect development; it may have some substantial impact on the prevalence of cancer among frequent users; and a nontrivial share of users have difficulty quitting when they wish to and see their lives as somewhat harmed because of their dependence. But the adverse consequences of criminalization, with current U.S. enforcement, seem more substantial.

Reminding the reader once again that we are giving no policy weight to the pleasures that cannabis provides its users, we now consider whether the harms that arise from the drug itself are sufficient to justify continued prohibition of possession and sale. The available evidence suggests that simply removing the prohibition against possession (depenalization) does not increase cannabis use. This prohibition inflicts harms directly and is costly. Unless it can be shown that the removal of criminal penalties will increase use of other more harmful drugs, perhaps because of signal of lessened disapproval, it is difficult to see what society gains. The removal of the sales prohibition has more complex effects.

Can cannabis prohibition be reconciled with legal alcohol and tobacco?

Alcohol and tobacco are for most purposes appropriately thought of as drugs; however, an analysis of alternatives to the current alcohol and tobacco regimes would take us too far afield. But their regulation does bear on the justifiability of regimes for cocaine, heroin, and especially marijuana. Reformers frequently note that tobacco and alcohol are vastly more harmful in the aggregate than any of the illicits – or even all the illicits put together. Kleiman (1992a) noted that this comparison confounds harmfulness with prevalence – it may be that the licits cause more damage because more people use them. This argument still works for cannabis, but with less force. Though pot smoking never approached the level of aggregate alcohol consumption, we do know what happens when a sizeable fraction of the population uses cannabis because it happened in the late 1970s. As a result, there's now a sizeable fraction of the population struggling to reconcile cannabis prohibition with legal alcohol and tobacco – a moral problem that troubles even supporters of our drug laws. Logically, it would seem that if tobacco causes greater harm than cannabis (putting aside who bears those harms), a regime should treat tobacco more restrictively than cannabis.

There may indeed be principled reasons to justify less stringent regimes for alcohol and tobacco despite their steep social costs, though we have strained to come up with examples. One could argue that alcohol merits a legal status because it is easier than other drugs to use without intoxication (though not always and not for everyone). One might also argue that tobacco, though not harmless to non-smokers, merits a legal status because it imposes a smaller share of its vast harms on nonusers than do other drugs. We find neither argument fully convincing. A more persuasive argument is purely pragmatic. There are enormous political obstacles to prohibition of these substances; alcohol and tobacco have much larger and better organized constituencies than do cannabis, cocaine, or heroin. The divisiveness of such prohibitions would be enormous.

This begs the question: why not remove the inconsistency by changing the pot laws?

Cannabis depenalization

Here we assess a regime that eliminates criminal penalties for possession of small quantities of cannabis. We are agnostic about the definition of *small quantity*; we also ignore the question of whether repeated offenses are criminalized. In our view, these variations have little impact on our projections so long as the thresholds reasonably distinguish possession from dealing.

Depenalization has no consequence for the prevalence of cannabis use. Moreover, it will not increase the use of other drugs for several reasons. First, under the "tantalizer" gateway theory, increases in cannabis use might lead to increases in hard-drug experimentation – but depenalization won't increase cannabis use in the first place. Second, under the "toe in the water" gateway theory, depenalization might actually reduce hard-drug use by discouraging any inference that hard drugs are as safe as cannabis. Under the "foot in the door" version, depenalization would fail to yield this benefit because cannabis sales would still take place in illicit drug markets. Note that depenalization also fails to provide any benefits of substitution; if cannabis use doesn't increase, use of more dangerous substances can't decrease.

Cannabis depenalization would reduce those criminal justice costs associated with cannabis enforcement. It will significantly reduce the government's intrusiveness and infringements on liberty and privacy, no small matter in an era of drug testing of student athletes. It should significantly enhance the perceived legitimacy and credibility of the government's control efforts against other illicit drugs. We see two risks, one minor and the other quite speculative. The minor risk is that depenalization might reduce incentives to seek treatment; we view that as a minor harm given the small fraction of the dependent that seek treatment now, the modest harms of dependence itself, and the lack of documented effectiveness of marijuana treatment. The speculative risk is that depenalization might expand the duration of cannabis-using careers, by reducing the stigma and legal risks of cannabis use.[17]

This is surely the strongest of our regime projections, for we have more relevant (and recent) evidence than for any other regime (summarized in Chapter 13). The American experience with depenalization in 12 states in the 1970s and the Dutch experience (prior to expansive commercialization) each suggest no discernable impact on prevalence levels.

Supporting evidence is also available from Australia where South Australia and the Australian Capital Territory (ACT) have adopted various depenalization schemes.[18] The national survey of cannabis use found no difference between South Australia and other states in the prevalence of cannabis use (Donnelly et al., 1995). Though small sample size limits the strength of that finding (Hall, 1997b), a longitudinal comparison of cannabis use among 421 students at the Australian National University (in the ACT, a depenalization territory), and 470 students from the University of Melbourne (in Victoria, a nondepenalization territory) also found no changes in use for either group (McGeorge & Aitken, 1997). The data on Spain, where marijuana and other psychoactive drugs have been depenalized for a generation, provide some support in that the Spanish rates are comparable to those for other Western European nations (Chapter 10).[19]

There is also no evidence that the probability of using cocaine or heroin conditional on using cannabis increased as the result

---

17. One piece of relevant evidence comes from Amsterdam, where past-month use escalated among those 30 and older between 1987 and 1994 (Sandwijk et al., 1995; *http://www.frw.uva.nl/cedro/stats/asd/cannabis.html*). But this evidence is ambiguous; we've argued that Dutch increases in the 1990s probably reflect unexplained secular trends common to nations with very different drug policies.
18. One irony of the South Australian expiation scheme, as it is called, is that more marijuana users have been imprisoned for nonpayment of fines than were previously incarcerated for marijuana possession offenses (MacDonald & Atkinson, 1995).
19. Italy, the other depenalization nation, provides no data.

of depenalization. The evidence from the Netherlands weakly supports the hypothesis that the gateway effect is mediated by legal status (i.e., that removing the criminal prohibition on marijuana possession may lower the probability of going on to use cocaine).

Thus there is reasonable, though not indisputable, evidence that the removal of criminal penalties for personal possession does not increase use of marijuana or more dangerous drugs. In particular, it does not seem to affect adolescent use rates. That may be enough to make the case for depenalization, since criminalization causes harms to many and increases the intrusiveness of the state and the powers of the police.

One way of approaching this is to consider the implications if these same findings about impacts of criminal sanctions applied to methamphetamine, a drug known to cause considerable harm to its users. Even if there were no evidence that continued criminalization of possession increased consumption, one might still favor retention of those criminal sanctions. This involves the appropriateness of the state's expressing its clear disapproval of behavior that endangers others in substantial ways, even if that disapproval does not actually reduce the extent of the harms. But these more symbolic benefits of prohibition need to be weighed against the harms imposed by criminal sanctions if they were retained – though those could be reduced by low levels of enforcement.

We reject the argument that marijuana raises the same symbolic disapproval issues with the same force. The harms of cannabis are clearly no greater than those of alcohol, at the individual level.[20] That is, if we were to reverse the status of alcohol and cannabis – prohibiting alcohol while making cannabis as available as alcohol is now – the health and behavioral consequences (accidents, long-term physiological damage, aggression) from cannabis use would still fall short of those currently attributable to alcohol. It is a mistake to believe that depenalization of cannabis somehow introduces into the legal marketplace a uniquely noxious substance.

Also relevant is the extent of substitution between alcohol and marijuana. Heavy drinking by young males is an enormously important source of damage, particularly automobile accidents and related

---

20. This is also the conclusion reached by Hall et al. (1995) in their review of relative and population attributable risk associated with marijuana, tobacco, and alcohol.

fatalities.[21] There is some evidence that for high school seniors decreased availability of legal alcohol increased the use of marijuana (DiNardo & Lemieux, 1992); if the relationship is symmetric, then increased accessibility for marijuana might reduce alcohol consumption. Another study found that higher marijuana prices were positively associated with drinking frequency and heavy drinking episodes (Chaloupka & Laixuthai, 1994), again suggesting that the two psychoactive substances are substitutes rather than complements. On the other hand, an econometric study by Pacula (1998) estimated that marijuana consumption fell in response to increased beer taxes, suggesting that marijuana and alcohol use might be complements, not substitutes. Future research will hopefully reconcile these conflicting findings.

There is also evidence that marijuana might substitute for hard-drug use. Model (1993) analyzed data from the Drug Abuse Warning Network (DAWN) for the years 1975–8 in states that either did or did not depenalize marijuana. She found that depenalization was associated with an increase in marijuana mentions in Emergency Room records, which nevertheless remained a low-frequency event. (Note that this doesn't necessarily contradict the previously cited research; depenalization might influence the intensity of use among users rather the prevalence of use; see Chapter 14). But Model also found a decrease in total illicit drug mentions other than marijuana. Model interprets this as evidence for a substitution effect, in which users shifted from harder drugs to marijuana after its legal risks decreased. Recent laboratory studies of hypothetical drug purchase choices by heroin addicts also suggested that marijuana and heroin are substitutes (Petry & Bickel, 1998).

Thus, in addition to the gains from elimination of unwarranted intrusion of the criminal law into private lives, there is the potential gain from reductions in harms from another psychoactive substance. The evidence on the latter point is far too speculative for strong policy recommendations – substitution is one topic on which it is plausible that further research could provide substantial reductions in uncertainty.[22] But even without invoking the benefits of

---

21. According to the Fatality Analysis Reporting Scheme, about 600 males aged 16 to 20 died in alcohol-related automobile accidents in 1995 (*www-fars.nhtsa.dot.gov/fars/fars.cfm*).
22. Such research would include more analysis of the impact of marijuana enforcement and prices on alcohol-using careers. This might be accomplished with the longitudinal panels from Monitoring the Future.

substitution effects, the consequentialist case for cannabis depenalization seems compelling.

Cannabis legalization

James Q. Wilson (1990) has offered the most elegant case against the legalization of cocaine and heroin, but even he carefully notes (in the paper's only footnote) that his arguments do not apply to marijuana:

> I do not here take up the question of marijuana. For a variety of reasons – its widespread use and its lesser tendency to addict – it presents a different problem from cocaine or heroin (p. 23).

Wilson decidedly does not argue in favor of marijuana legalization; he simply exempts it from his case, presumably because the arguments have less force. In an absolute sense, cannabis legalization seems less risky because cannabis itself is less risky. But relative to the status quo, cannabis legalization is not without risk.

As with similar market models for cocaine or heroin, we would expect an adult legal market for cannabis to produce significant increases in prevalence, and possibly intensity of use. The increase in prevalence is the result of promotion by the legal suppliers, for we do not see how promotion could be effectively limited in the American commercial marketplace. We are skeptical that tight controls could be maintained for products that, with no therapeutic goal, would be provided in conventional commerce rather than through doctors and pharmacies. Recent experience with legalized gambling, as well as the difficulty of suppressing cigarette promotion, added to the post-World War II erosion of Repeal's liquor controls all suggest that legal commercial interests are likely to weaken regulatory efforts. This is especially plausible for marijuana, whose harms are relatively slight, hence complicating the task of defending stringent regulation against the efforts of a legal industry. There are only modest additional gains to counterbalance the increase in prevalence under the commercialization induced by legalization.

Ironically, because cannabis is less dangerous, legalization is more plausible for cannabis than cocaine or heroin; yet for the same reason, cannabis legalization offers fewer major reductions in harm than legalization of the harder drugs. Cannabis is sold in black markets, but those markets are less violent. Cannabis creates dependence, yet there is little evidence of users committing crimes to pay for their habits. And any link between cannabis and HIV transmission is trivial in comparison to the role played by heroin (and even cocaine). For one category – fear and the sense of disorder – we even predict a greater increase following cannabis legalization than the legalization of harder drugs. That kind of fear has two sources: the intoxication of others and the criminality of others. For cocaine and heroin, legalization increases intoxication, but it almost certainly reduces the total criminality. For cannabis, legalization increases intoxication, but there is little drug-induced criminality for it to reduce.

Extrapolating from relatively minor variations within a prohibition regime (as occurred with depenalization in the United States) to the consequences of major changes in the accessibility and legal status of the drug is hazardous. The ability to consume openly and to obtain the drug readily may have quite different effects. The only directly relevant evidence is the Dutch experience with commercialization under de facto legalization since the mid-1980s. This commercialization, by U.S. standards, retains extraordinarily stringent restrictions on sales and promotion of the drug. Not only is there an effective prohibition on use of the airwaves, but no newspaper or mainstream magazine or billboard carries ads. It strains credulity that U.S. producers of a legal commodity, subject to no FDA regulation, could be subject to such stringent restraints in their efforts to expand markets. Chapter 8 explored how difficult it has been to obtain effective regulation of the notoriously dangerous legal substances, alcohol and tobacco. The voluntary agreement by distillers against television advertising of hard liquor sales is the only major restraint until the recent promotional restrictions in the tobacco settlement with the states. Aggressive promotion of legal cannabis is at least a major risk; we think it is a near certainty. The history of alcohol and tobacco also suggests that a legal marijuana industry would be able to keep tax rates modest and thus establish, in the long-run, a price well below current levels.

Even with substantial control, the Dutch experienced large increases in the prevalence of cannabis use that are plausibly attributable to commercialization, as suggested by our earlier analysis of cocaine and heroin. That is, not enough to justify prohibition or even to establish that depenalization is preferable. It does strongly suggest that promotion and access can have a large effect, hardly a surprising conclusion in modern times.

The Alaska model

Kleiman (1992a, Chapter 9) provides the tightest analysis of the issue of marijuana policy, building on his earlier book devoted entirely to that drug (Kleiman, 1989). He argues that legalization, with tight regulatory restrictions well beyond what currently applies to alcohol, is probably preferable to our current regime. However, he considers it a close call, indeed noting that in the earlier book he narrowly came out against legal availability. Kleiman's shift is the consequence of his development of a rationing scheme, which he thinks permits effective regulation. Apart from elimination of black markets and reduced enforcement intrusions, he emphasizes the added credibility of prevention efforts aimed at more dangerous drugs arising from a clear legal distinction between cannabis and those drugs for which messages about acute harms have a much better basis. He thinks that the 1980s Alaska regime, allowing home growing, provides a possible alternative with a less cumbersome regulatory apparatus. (South Australia offers a similar regime; see Donnelly et al., 1995.)

We do not believe that Kleiman's rationing scheme is feasible, on political economic grounds (i.e., the industry once formed would effectively work to undermine a regulatory scheme that is simply inconsistent with American views of the role of government). If marijuana is legal but is not medicine, then how can the government interfere in consumption decisions? After all, the dangers of excess alcohol consumption have provided no basis for considering liquor rationing in times of peace.

We do concur that the earlier Alaska regime offers an attractive option. Depenalization, with removal of all sanctions against possession of small quantities and production for own consumption and gifts, but with retention of penalties for sales, is our preferred option. The gains from continued prohibition of possession are too insubstantial to justify the retention of the criminal sanction. The current U.S. depenalization regimes, which retain civil fines and retain criminal penalties for offenses other than the first, are confused and confusing. The civil fine to control harm to self lacks any parallel in existing U.S. regulations. Similarly, it is hard to find a justification for invoking the criminal sanction for second offenses.

The move to commercialization is clearly riskier. With commercialization, American style, we would project a large increase in marijuana use; the possibility that this might lead to substitution of cannabis for heavy alcohol consumption is not strong enough for us to think this a desirable outcome. Home production is an important element of the regime, which gets around the fact that simple depenalization of possession is normatively inconsistent. Permitting consumption is a barren right without a legitimate source of supply, and continued illegality of all production generates large black markets. Home production, which is accessible to any committed user, provides that source without incurring the risk of commercialization. Home producers would be allowed to give drugs to friends but not to sell. No doubt that last restriction would be difficult to enforce, but it would at least drive out the large commercial operations that are the source of most of the current black-market harms. And if the "foot-in-the-door" interpretation of the gateway is indeed correct – the verdict is not yet in – then allowing home production of cannabis ought to discourage involvement with hard-drug sellers.

This model is very much that used by the state of Alaska during 1975–90. The evidence about its effects is modest and ambiguous. Segal (1990) found that levels of alcohol, tobacco, cocaine, and stimulant use were higher in Alaska than other states; his study was strictly cross-sectional and omitted any time series analyses of the 1975 and 1990 legal changes. For these and other reasons, Segal explicitly rejects any inference that his Alaskan research informs the depenalization debate. Nevertheless, since we are choosing among possible regimes, it seems prudent to push these data a bit further and see what they might plausibly tell us.

Segal compared cannabis prevalence in 1988 in Alaska, the lower 48 states (via the NHSDA and Monitoring the Future senior survey), and state-specific surveys in Oregon and Texas. Aggregating across Segal's many comparisons (by site, question, and age group), cannabis prevalence in 1988 was on average 38 percent higher in Alaska than in other states. If we restrict the comparison to estimates for ages 12 to 17 and the eleventh grade, it is possible to compare rates across substances. Alaska exceeded the comparison sites by 74 percent for cannabis, 16 percent for tobacco and 13 percent for alcohol.

Conservatively, this pattern might indeed suggest that, controlling for the specific Alaska community influences common to all three substances, the Alaska regime is indeed associated with higher levels of use. But Alaska exceeds the other sites by an average of 121 percent for cocaine – almost twice the excess marijuana rate. It is difficult to plausibly attribute the latter gap to the Alaskan cannabis regime (e.g., no plausible gateway mechanism would predict a cocaine increase exceeding the marijuana increase). Thus, the Alaskan data are quite ambiguous. These comparisons are crude, but if we take them at face value, it does suggest some risk of increased marijuana use under the Alaska model, as Kleiman (1992a) acknowledged. But we share his assessment that "it seems more likely than not that some form of restricted licit availability represents our least-bad alternative for dealing with the most widely used illicit drug" (p. 280).

Curiously, the current depenalization regimes do not distinguish between adult and adolescent use, notwithstanding general agreement that adolescent use of the drug has distinctive potential harms. We would retain penalties of the same kind applicable to underage drinking and distribution of alcohol to those under the legal age. No doubt that restriction would merely reduce adolescent usage slightly but would at least retain the proper message about who should be allowed to use the drug.

For some readers, the mere fact that a regime allowing legal or quasi-legal (tolerated) access to cannabis might increase its use provides definitive proof that the regime would be a failure – and perhaps even immoral. Implicit in that reasoning is the sole adherence to a use-reduction criterion for drug policy – a position that we examine in the final Chapter.

APPENDIX

The following tables illustrate our attempt to project the net consequences of an alternative drug-control regime, relative to the status quo. We provide three examples, each involving heroin: heroin depenalization (Table 14.2), an adult legal market for heroin (Table 14.3), and heroin maintenance (Table 14.4).

The tables are organized around the following dimensions: (a) predictions: use (effects on prevalence, effects on intensity of use); (b) predictions: harms (category of harm, type of harm, effect on average harm per unit of consumption, effect on macro harm – generally the product of average harm, prevalence, and intensity); (c) distributional implications; (d) major uncertainties; and (e) other considerations. The ≈ symbol denotes little or no change relative to the status quo; the ▲ and ▽ symbols denote increases or decreases relative to the status quo.

The general formulation

$$\text{Macro Harm} = \text{Prevalence (\# users)} \times \text{Intensity (units/user)} \times \text{Harmfulness (harm/unit)}$$

should not be taken literally as a formal mathematical calculation or algorithm. The table entries reflect our judgments, based on our review of the available evidence as well as speculation based on limited theory and some intuition. But that formulation, and these tables, represent an effort to discipline such judgments and encourage a full recognition of tradeoffs. We encourage skeptical readers to follow the same exercise and see where it leads them.

Table 14.2. *Heroin depenalization (no criminal penalties for possession of small quantities)*

Predictions: Use

      Effect on prevalence (# users): None or minor increase (via duration, reduced treatment)

      Effect on intensity (units/user): Minor increase?

Predictions: Harms

Category	Harm	Effect on harmfulness (harm per unit)[a]	Effect on macro harm[b]
Health	Suffering due to physical/mental illnesses	≈	≈
	Addiction	≈	≈
	Health care costs (treatment)	≈	≈
	Health care costs (illness)	≈	≈
	Disease transmission	na	na
	Loss of incentives to seek treatment	∇	▲
	Restriction on medicinal uses of drug	na	∇
Social and economic functioning	Reduced performance, school	≈	▲?
	Reduced performance, workplace	≈	▲?
	Poor parenting, child abuse	≈	▲?
	Harmful effects of stigma due to use	≈	≈
	Accruing criminal experience	∇	∇
	Elevated dollar price of substance	∇	∇
Safety and public order	Accident victimization	≈	▲?
	Fear, sense of disorder	≈	▲?
	Property/acquisitive crime victimization	≈	▲?
	Violence, psychopharmacological	≈	▲?
	Violence, economically motivated	≈	▲?
	Reduced property values near markets	≈	▲?
Criminal justice	Criminal justice costs (inc. opportunity costs)	∇	∇
	Punishment and its consequences for user	∇	∇
	Corruption, demoralization of legal authorities	∇	∇
	Interference in source countries	≈	≈
Symbolic/ intangible harms	Violation of the law as intrinsic harm	≈	≈
	Devaluation of arrest as moral sanction	∇	∇
	Infringement on liberty and privacy	∇	∇
	Prevention/restriction of benefits of use	∇	∇

[a] Arrows without subscripts refer to direct effect of regime change; na = not applicable.

[b] For most harms, Macro Harm = Prevalence (# users) × Intensity (units/user) × Harmfulness (harm/unit).

Distributional implications: Benefits users more than others.

Major uncertainties: Little directly relevant data.

Other considerations: If only first offense is targeted, less risk of increased intensity, but fewer gains on other dimensions.

Table 14.3. *Heroin adult market (strictly regulated legal market for adults)*

Predictions: use

    Effect on Prevalence (# users): Increase
    Effect on Intensity (units/user): Slight increase (net effect; see text)

Predictions: Harms

Category	Harm	Effect on harmfulness (harm per unit)[a]	Effect on macro harm[b]
Health	Suffering due to physical/mental illnesses	∇	?
	Addiction	∇_c	▲?
	Health care costs (treatment)	∇_c	▲?
	Health care costs (illness)	∇	∇
	Disease transmission	∇	∇
	Loss of incentives to seek treatment	▲	▲
	Restriction on medicinal uses of drug	na	∇
Social and economic functioning	Reduced performance, school	≈	▲
	Reduced performance, workplace	≈	▲
	Poor parenting, child abuse	≈	▲
	Harmful effects of stigma due to use	∇_c	∇
	Accruing criminal experience	∇	∇
	Elevated dollar price of substance	∇	∇
Safety and public order	Accident victimization	≈	▲
	Fear, sense of disorder	∇	∇
	Property/acquisitive crime victimization	∇	∇
	Violence, psychopharmacological	∇	?
	Violence, economically motivated	∇	∇
	Reduced property values near markets	∇	∇
Criminal justice	Criminal justice costs (inc. opportunity costs)	∇	∇
	Punishment and its consequences for user	∇	∇
	Corruption, demoralization of legal authorities	∇	∇
	Interference in source countries	∇	∇
Symbolic/ intangible harms	Violation of the law as intrinsic harm	∇	∇
	Devaluation of arrest as moral sanction	∇	∇
	Infringement on liberty and privacy	∇	∇
	Prevention/restriction of benefits of use	∇	∇

[a] Arrows without subscripts refer to direct effect of regime change; c = indirect effect due to changed composition of user pool; na = not applicable.
[b] For most harms, Macro Harm = Prevalence (# users) × Intensity (units/user) × Harmfulness (harm/unit).

Distributional implications: May benefit inner-city residents more than others.
Major uncertainties: Theoretically plausible predictions, but little direct evidence.
Other considerations: Tight controls would reduce prevalence but might restore black markets.

Table 14.4. *Heroin maintenance (government provision to substantial fraction of registered addicts not in methadone treatment)*

Predictions: use

Effect on Prevalence (# users): No change (supply effect vs. Musto effect)

Effect on Intensity (units/user): Increase

Predictions: harms

Category	Harm	Effect on harmfulness (harm per unit)[a]	Effect on macro harm[b]
Health	Suffering due to physical/mental illnesses	▽	▽
	Addiction	▽	▽
	Health care costs (treatment)	▽c	▲
	Health care costs (illness)	▽	▽
	Disease transmission	▽	▽
	Loss of incentives to seek treatment	?	?
	Restriction on medicinal uses of drug	na	▽
Social and economic functioning	Reduced performance, school	≈	≈
	Reduced performance, workplace	?	?
	Poor parenting, child abuse	?	?
	Harmful effects of stigma due to use	▽	▽
	Accruing criminal experience	▽	▽
	Elevated dollar price of substance	▽	▽
Safety and public order	Accident victimization	▽	?
	Fear, sense of disorder	▽	▽
	Property/acquisitive crime victimization	▽	▽
	Violence, psychopharmacological	▽	▽
	Violence, economically motivated	▽	▽
	Reduced property values near markets	▽	▽
Criminal justice	Criminal justice costs (inc. opportunity costs)	▽	▽
	Punishment and its consequences for user	▽	▽
	Corruption, demoralization of legal authorities	▽	▽
	Interference in source countries	▽	▽
Symbolic/ intangible harms	Violation of the law as intrinsic harm	▽	▽
	Devaluation of arrest as moral sanction	▽	▽
	Infringement on liberty and privacy	▽	▽
	Prevention/restriction of benefits of use	≈	≈

[a] Arrows without subscripts refer to direct effect of regime change; c = indirect effect due to changed composition of user pool; na = not applicable.

[b] For most harms, Macro Harm = Prevalence (# users) × Intensity (units/user) × Harmfulness (harm/unit).

Distributional implications: May benefit inner-city residents more than others.

Major uncertainties: Will it divert users from heroin black market?

Other considerations: Tight controls reduce prevalence but might restore black markets.

15 Obstacles to Moving Beyond the Drug War

In this final chapter, we step back from the details and assess the prospects for significant change in American drug laws. On the surface, those prospects appear slim for cocaine, slight for heroin, and slender for cannabis. A more balanced assessment suggests that at least for cannabis, there is a small but real chance that public views might support significant change. But the uncertainty and complexity of the case for legal change tends to support adherence to the status quo, putting reformers at a significant disadvantage. An examination of the politics surrounding marijuana reform, medical marijuana, needle exchange, and heroin maintenance – each far more incremental than cocaine or heroin legalization – suggests that the most crucial barrier to change is the unwillingness to consider tolerating increases in drug use to achieve reductions in drug-related harm.

The next sections of the chapter examine two types of explanations for this attitude. One is consequentialist; the notion that, in fact, society would be worse off in the end. We confront this view by examining the argument that harm reduction and other drug reforms "send the wrong message." Our analysis suggests that even though this fear isn't groundless, there are good reasons to believe that micro harm reduction (programs that protect the average user) can produce macro harm reduction (net benefits for society as a whole). Harm reduction as a philosophy might significantly improve all aspects of American drug policy. Still, harm reduction in its present form, as a set of specific new interventions, seems rather limited. Arguably, a

371

strategy of quantity reduction (focusing on consumption levels rather than prevalence rates) might fare better, having broader applicability but also serving both use reduction and harm reduction ends. Unfortunately, the alcohol literature suggests that quantity reduction has also encountered strong political opposition, leading us to consider a second, more symbolic class of explanations for the passion for prevalence reduction. There are a variety of reasons why harm reduction and related strategies might be threatening at a more symbolic level, irrespective of their benefits.

Even without contemplating major legal change, there are good reasons to reject the current war on drug users and scale back the more aggressive aspects of prohibition. A call for "nonzero tolerance" is tantamount to treason in some circles, but such a call might encourage more humane, less intrusive, less damaging ways of coping with drugs and their harms.

UNCERTAINTY AND THE LEGALIZATION DEBATE

A close look at the relevant evidence suggests that there is much greater uncertainty about the likely consequences of alternative regimes than is suggested by most previous works on drug legalization – on either side. And to the extent that one can make predictions, it is clear that there are difficult tradeoffs among outcome criteria: reductions in average harm but increases in use, reductions in crime but increases in addiction and intoxication, and gains for some citizens but losses for others.

The lack of experience with alternative policies has favored the reformers in one sense. Fair comparisons of prohibition and legalization should not be of ideal types, if the implementation of those ideals is likely to be undermined by their predictable political/administrative consequences. Yet reformers get to compare the actual administration of prohibition, with all its ineptness, brutality, and corruption, to an idealized form of legalization, in which tough regulation is maintained against rule-compliant companies.

Experience with markets that involve direct provision to customers, as opposed to mediation through medical professionals, points to the dangers of such assumptions. Cigarettes are the most dramatic example of the ability of a legal industry to thwart regulation through (mostly) legal means. Restrictions on promotion, product regulation, and taxation have all been greatly attenuated by the industry's strategic use of political contributions and reframing of legal issues (e.g., promotion of a dangerous product becomes an issue of free speech). Even what once seemed a significant victory, the acceptance of a ban on television advertising that ended broadcast of mandatory anticigarette statements under an "equal time" doctrine, turned out to be in the interests of the current industry leaders; rather than decreasing industry sales, it merely allowed them to reduce marketing costs through a legal restraint of trade (Warner, 1979). The alcoholic beverage industry has also been aggressive and frequently successful in its efforts to fight restrictions. The tight restraints of the early post-Repeal era have been substantially eroded. State alcohol control boards have often ruled in favor of the industry with respect to promotional restrictions, use of credit, and so on.

The rhetorical advantage of vagueness is more than offset by the fear of the unknown. Chapter 13 outlined three different standards of proof for change. Reformers would prefer a philosophical standard that puts the burden of proof on those who would reduce liberty. Scholars and analysts apply a more neutral standard of expected value that would risk some uncertainty for reasonable promise of improvement. But surely the operative standard of proof in the policy arena is political, not philosophical or analytic. And that standard is quite protective of the status quo. The combination of high uncertainty about the outcome of a change, the partial irreversibility of any bad outcomes, and a pervasive tendency for decision makers to favor the status quo (Kahneman, Knetsch, & Thaler, 1991) pose steep barriers for reformers.

Legal markets for cocaine or heroin might meet the philosophical standard, but not the analytic and surely not the political. Our projections are very uncertain but there is clearly a substantial risk of increasing total harm to society, notwithstanding large reductions in crime-related harms. We view this risk with regret, not relief. The legalizers are almost certainly correct that these regimes would significantly reduce average harm on most dimensions – especially those most salient in the current regime. One would like to believe that a simple, sweeping solution might be found. But even under relaxed standards of evidence, there are striking and difficult tradeoffs and expected losers as well as winners. There seems little basis for consensus.

Depenalization of cocaine or heroin, often viewed as a halfway step toward legalization, falls well short of the political standard and possibly the analytic standard, depending on how one weighs reductions in intrusiveness and criminal justice costs against the risk of increased consumption. For these drugs, depenalization does little to reduce the harms caused by prohibition of sale and production, so reformers lose their strongest arguments. Those harms arise largely from high drug prices and the resulting crime, disorder, and poverty of dependent users, which exacerbate the isolation and sociopathy created by frequent drug use itself. Removing the criminal penalty for possession of small amounts, as Italy and Spain have done, does little to alter these matters, though addicts will benefit from reduced police harassment.

Heroin maintenance might, with more experimentation, soon meet the policy analytic standard but almost certainly not the political. The projections do not have sufficiently high credibility, and it is too difficult to explain why the state should provide a drug that has been the source of so much actual damage (albeit mostly because of conditions created by policy). Of course, methadone maintenance once overcame similar (but weaker) objections. The Swiss trials provide reassurance but will never substitute for a U.S. counterpart, and the prospects for such a trial seem almost as remote as those for the policy change itself.

In principle, cannabis depenalization can meet all three standards of proof. It generates important gains and no losses, unless one believes, against the weight of the evidence and compelling theoretical arguments, that initiation of cannabis use will rise and that this will in turn lead to a higher prevalence of more dangerous drugs. It violates no deeply held norms with respect to government role or allowing a much more harmful substance into permitted use. Permitting home production and gifts may not meet the political standard, given that the Alaska data are weak and that there is a potential for increased consumption among users, but we think it can meet the analytic standard. A legal market for adult cannabis purchases falls well short of the political standard; whether it meets the analytical standard depends crucially on the effects that increased cannabis use would have on the use of other, more dangerous, intoxicants. If legal cannabis reduced alcohol or cocaine intoxication, the risk of increased cannabis use would seem well worth incurring. Further research on substitution effects could resolve this question.

With adequate political stewardship, national depenalization of cannabis possession (and possibly home cultivation) could meet the political standard and deserves to do so. Widespread acceptance of heroin maintenance seems less plausible without better evidence; what's needed is political leadership on the research and testing side. Is that kind of leadership forthcoming? A closer look at the politics of marijuana reform, medical marijuana, needle exchange, and heroin maintenance suggests major obstacles.[1]

POLITICS

Marijuana reform

We cast our lot with the reformers. In so doing, we suspect we side with the inevitable; but more important we believe that these laws are indefensible and therefore *ought* to be changed. We are convinced that logic, science and philosophy have had almost nothing to do with the evolution of drug policy. The social structure will ultimately adjust to the realities of drug-using behavior. America will become comfortable with marihuana and the laws will vanish in practice if not form (Bonnie & Whitebread, 1974; pp. 298–9).

Thus began the conclusion of a careful history of marijuana policy, written just after the report of the National Commission on Marihuana and Drug Abuse (1972). Twenty-five years later what is striking is how optimistic this statement seems. There has been a hardening of American marijuana policy, at least since the early 1980s, perhaps reflecting the growth of other drug problems and the increasing tendency of the policy process to blur distinctions among illicit drugs. Statements of President Nixon about the dangers of marijuana are indistinguishable from those of General McCaffrey (except for the spelling of the drug). "[L]egalizing marihuana would simply encourage more and more of our young people to start down the long dismal road that leads to hard drugs and eventually self-destruction." (Richard Nixon, as cited in Bonnie & Whitebread, 1974). "Clearly, if we want to reduce the rate of teenage drug use and prevent American youth from using dangerous drugs like

1. See the review of these issues by Bertram et al. (1996).

cocaine, we must continue to oppose efforts to legalize marijuana" (McCaffrey, 1997).

There is no basis for believing that reform is close now. The arguments for reform seem fairly compelling, and the downside risks seem modest. But that has been true for a quarter century. Moreover there is no "ripeness" that might generate change. Marijuana has been low on the American policy and political agenda since the late 1970s, when the decriminalization movement effectively ended. The harms from the current prohibition are themselves serious; some 50,000 persons currently incarcerated for marijuana offenses (Chapter 14) is an affront to a liberal society's belief in the benevolence of government, as well as a waste of (even now) scarce penal resources. Yet the figures do not reach the threshold of public discomfort that encourages a political candidate for major office to take the risks involved in promoting any change that can plausibly be interpreted as increasing the use of illegal drugs in the United States.

This reluctance is particularly a pity because major changes in the United States would be consistent with a general international trend toward less aggressive use of the criminal sanction against marijuana. In some nations the change has already occurred (e.g., Italy, Spain, and the Netherlands), and other countries are exploring it (e.g., Belgium and Australia). In yet others (e.g., Germany and Switzerland), court rulings have dramatically reduced penalties. In Britain in 1998, there were large-scale public demonstrations in favor of formal depenalization.

Calls for fundamental change in marijuana prohibition have been frequent and have come from highly respectable institutions as well as individuals. President Nixon's Commission on Marihuana and Drug Abuse proposed the repeal of criminal sanctions for the use of the drug (National Commission on Marihuana and Drug Abuse, 1972). Its recommendation received strong endorsements from the most respectable professional associations, such as the American Medical Association and the American Bar Association. Nonetheless, President Nixon disowned the report, even before its actual publication.[2]

Five years later, President Carter spoke out against criminal sanctions for marijuana possession (Chapter 14). However, a scandal

---

2. A law enforcement official of that time reported to us that President Nixon in an informal conversation said that he thought marijuana no more dangerous than the drink that he had in his hand at that moment, but he did not wish to "send the wrong signal."

involving his principal drug policy advisor meant that his voice carried little weight (Bertram et al., 1996).

A National Academy of Sciences (NAS) panel (National Research Council, 1982) suggested that the existing policies merited reexamination and that decriminalization should be considered. Even that questioning of the status quo was enough to lead Frank Press, the head of the National Academy of Sciences, to disown the report in his introduction to it. "My own view is that the data available to the Committee were insufficient to justify on scientific or analytical grounds changes in current policies dealing with the use of marijuana" (National Research Council, 1982, p. 2). It is almost unheard-of for the President of the NAS to write such a letter, let alone require that it be included in the published report itself. Moreover, Press insisted that only 300 copies of the report be printed. His statement may have simply reflected a concern that the report endangered funding for the NAS, at least with respect to drug policy and perhaps a bit more broadly. Certainly he had received a visit from senior officials giving him reason for concern.[3] In any case, the report, issued near the beginning of the Reagan administration's launch of the war on drugs, attracted attention only briefly, perhaps reflecting the lack of copies.

The federal government actively disseminates information about the dangers of marijuana use. The intensity of the campaign has picked up since 1994 with the rise in adolescent marijuana use. It has usually taken the form of aggressive promotion of findings of adverse effects in quite limited studies. For example, a 1993 paper found that heavy marijuana users (daily for an average of 7 years) scored lower than nonusers on several tests of cognitive performance (Block & Ghoneim, 1993). Government bulletins stressed this and ignored the finding that those who smoked marijuana regularly but less than daily were indistinguishable from nonusers on those same tests. *NIDA Notes*, the official bulletin of the National Institute on Drug Abuse (a scientific research institution), often features strong statements of this kind. For example, one issue recently declared that "Marijuana use impairs driving-related functions and is linked to a pattern of behaviors that leads to poor job performance" (Mathias, 1996). This article was based on series of earlier studies that found that only a moderate percentage of drivers in serious accidents (4–16 percent for

---

3. This account is based on conversation with an NRC official of the period.

fatal and 6–12 for nonfatal) tested positive for marijuana and made no effort to adjust for background rates of marijuana use among the relevant age groups, predominantly young males. Moreover, a large share of the drivers also tested positive for recent alcohol consumption. This evidence is indeed a slender basis for the assertion.

Beyond medical marijuana, there is little political activity targeting marijuana specifically. Though William Bennett campaigned for reversal of decriminalization in a few states, his successors as Drug Czar have not actively pursued that path. On the other hand, there has been little campaign for depenalization in those states that did not do so in the 1970s. A punitive stasis prevails.

Medical marijuana

Marijuana policy became more salient nationally when in November 1996 California and Arizona voters approved referenda measures that allowed medical use of marijuana. Proposition 215 in California (passed with 56 percent of the vote) permits cultivation, possession, and use of marijuana to relieve the symptoms associated with AIDS, cancer, and other illnesses, provided a person has "written or oral permission" from a physician. Arizona's Proposition 200 (passed with 65 percent of the vote) allows doctors to prescribe marijuana or any controlled substance to terminally and seriously ill patients. The Arizona bill requires doctors to show that scientific research justifies the prescription and to obtain a second opinion from another doctor. The Arizona legislature promptly repealed the referendum proposition, but it passed again in 1998; five other states passed related referenda in the 1998 elections.

Both the California and Arizona propositions are at best sloppy (because of vague language and the lack of medical research) and at worst deceptive (because the positions being advanced serve other drug policy interests). Both propositions require doctors to make a judgment about the appropriateness of marijuana as a medicine with only limited scientific evidence.[4] It will be impossible to defend

---

4. Lynn Zimmer points out (personal communication, 1998) that much of the current pharmacopoeia has never been subject to rigorous testing because it was included before the FDA imposed that requirement. Thus, one might argue that the requirement of a research base is inappropriately stringent given that marijuana is already being recommended by some doctors.

decisions consistently, even though many oncologists already recommend that at least some of their patients obtain marijuana to ameliorate the nausea associated with chemotherapy (Doblin & Kleiman, 1991[5]).

Senior federal officials initially responded to these initiatives with strong condemnation of the legislation and threats of counteractive measures. Federal officials and other drug policy hawks (Califano, 1997) argued not simply that there was no scientific base for the claims of therapeutic efficacy but that the passage of these referenda would increase marijuana use generally. General Barry McCaffrey, director of the Office of National Drug Control Policy, said that "By our judgment, increased drug abuse in every category will be the inevitable result." There is no evidence bearing on the latter proposition,[6] and it has hardly enough face plausibility for the bold declarative statement.

Attorney General Reno threatened prosecution of any physician who recommended marijuana to a patient. DEA promised to step in where a state or local agency was unable to bring a case or seize marijuana because of the referenda; the case would then go to a federal prosecutor.

These reactions are partly explained by the auspices of the initiatives. The advocates were heavily financed by George Soros, a supporter of major reforms to drug policy,[7] who provided over $500,000 for the California initiative alone. The chief spokesman for Proposition 215 in California was explicit about his hope that this was merely the first step toward broader legalization; indeed, he flaunted his enthusiasm for the drug by smoking a celebratory (and presumably nonmedicinal) joint in the presence of a *San Francisco Chronicle* reporter the night Proposition 215 passed (Epstein, 1996). Half of

5. The Doblin and Kleiman study has attracted a vigorous critique (e.g., Plasse, 1991), but its central finding that a substantial fraction of oncologists at least occasionally recommend that chemotherapy patients use marijuana still stands unrefuted.
6. Results of the NHSDA in California in 1997, the year following passage of Proposition 215, showed no impact on use of marijuana or any other drug, but this is not dispositive of the matter.
7. "Since 1993, Soros has committed about $15 million to changing the nation's drug policies. He has also made personal political contributions to marijuana-related initiative campaigns, including $550,000 to California's Proposition 215, $530,000 to Arizona's Proposition 200, $335,000 to Washington's Proposition 685, and $40,000 to the Oregon referendum that will appear as Measure 57 on the November 1998 ballot" (Green, 1997). Soros has expressed himself as quite unsure about the wisdom of legalization but certain that current policies are far too harsh (Soros, 1997).

those who reported in the month before the referendum that they planned to vote in favor said that they did so because they wanted more liberal polices toward marijuana, not because they believed in the medical claims (CASA, 1996). Medical marijuana could easily be portrayed as a Trojan horse for broader liberalization.

Over the following 6 months, federal officials' passions cooled. No prosecutions or even license suspensions have been reported, at least in part because federal judges have provided rulings that emphasize free speech considerations over drug control objectives ("U.S. threat over drug is lifted in California," 1997).[8] The National Institutes of Health held a conference on the potential therapeutic effects of marijuana. The resulting conference report by prominent scientists identified a number of areas of promise, and it recommended that NIH begin a research program to explore the matter (*Workshop on the Medical Utility of Marijuana*, 1997).[9] In 1999, the Institute of Medicine released a highly publicized expert assessment (Joy, Watson, & Benson, 1999) that generated surprisingly little controversy; it was a very balanced report that seemed to have quieted the debate.

The sensible separation of the issue of marijuana's therapeutic potential and the recreational use of the drug seems now to be accepted by the federal leadership. This has provided a firmer stance for fighting the efforts to allow medicinal use before results of the research tests of clinical anecdote and folk beliefs are available.

Needle exchange

With remarkable consistency, the U.S. government has aggressively resisted needle exchange (Kirp & Bayer, 1993; Reuter & MacCoun, 1995). There are probably more than 1 million injecting drug users in this country, and injection drug use accounts for about one-third of all AIDS cases.

8. Note however that in February 1998 the California Supreme Court let stand a lower court finding that Proposition 215 does not allow commercial cannabis sales, a decision that could shut down cannabis-buying clubs throughout the state (Rojas, 1998).
9. An earlier Dutch report on the matter has had no currency in the U.S. debate. A Dutch medical advisory committee "concluded that evidence is insufficient to justify the medical use of marijuana" (Health Council of the Netherlands: Standing Committee on Medicine, 1996, p. 10). Though it did not directly address the issue of whether research was justified, the tone of the report was generally negative.

There is considerable empirical backing for claims that needle exchange programs can bring about significant reductions in HIV transmission. Favorable assessments of the evidence have been provided by a variety of expert groups, including Des Jarlais, Friedman, and Ward (1993), the General Accounting Office (1993), the Institute of Medicine/National Academy of Sciences (Normand et al., 1995), and a consortium of University of California researchers (Lurie & Reingold, 1993). A comparison of eighty-one U.S. cities estimated a 5.9 percent increase in HIV seroprevalence in fifty-two cities without needle exchange, and a 5.8 percent decrease in twenty-nine cities with needle exchange during the period 1988–93 (Hurley, Jolley, & Kaldor, 1997). Lurie and Drucker (1997) recently estimated that between 4,394 and 9,666 HIV infections could have been prevented in the U.S. between 1987 and 1995 if a national needle exchange program had been in place.

Yet fewer than 100 needle exchange programs operate in the United States. Why? Because prescription laws, paraphernalia laws, and local "drug-free zone" ordinances ban needle exchange programs in most of the country. Indeed, almost half of the existing programs are operating illicitly or quasi-legally. Despite endorsement of these programs by the Centers for Disease Control, the National Academy of Sciences, and various leading medical journals and health organizations, drug policy officials in the federal government and most state governments have actively opposed needle exchange. Indeed, even in late 1997, Congress reaffirmed its hostility to needle exchange by including in the Department of Health and Human Services (DHHS) appropriations bill a total ban on federal funding of needle exchange. This bill strengthened previous language which had allowed the Secretary of Health and Human Services to fund research on the topic.

In 1998, Secretary Shalala publicly endorsed the scientific basis for the claim that needle exchange did not increase drug use, a statutory preliminary to allow federal funding, but she announced that the administration had decided that such funding would be unwise. A *Washington Post* story claimed that DHHS officials had already arranged a press conference in the belief that the President would support funding needle exchange programs; Secretary Shalala's memo of talking points was reported to say "the evidence is airtight" and "from the beginning of this effort, it has been about science,

science, science" (Harris & Goldstein, 1998). General Barry McCaffrey had apparently been the key figure in persuading President Clinton that funding needle exchange programs would be a major blow to federal drug control efforts.

During the 1998 debate, critics of needle exchange made much of two studies associating participation in needle exchanges with elevated HIV risk in Vancouver (Strathdee et al., 1997) and Montreal (Bruneau et al., 1997). The studies' authors cautioned that this association might reflect features that distinguish these evaluations from others in the literature. For example, they were conducted at the peak of the HIV epidemic, their clients were heavily involved in cocaine injection, and the number of needles dispersed fell well short of the amount needed to prevent needle sharing (Bruneau & Schechter, 1998). New results and analyses (Schechter et al., 1999) indicated that the Vancouver result was spurious; the program simply attracts many of the city's highest-risk users – the young, the homeless, cocaine injectors, and sex-trade workers. This is surely a desirable selection effect and brings those results back in line with the rest of the empirical literature.

Heroin maintenance

In the early 1970s, near the height of the U.S. heroin epidemic, serious consideration was given to a trial of heroin maintenance in New York City. Though the incident occurred twenty-five years ago, it is worth briefly describing because it illustrates the continuity of drug policy debates.[10]

The Vera Institute, then a young but already well-respected social policy research institution with its roots primarily in criminal justice, initiated plans to test heroin maintenance in the United States. It had been impressed by the apparent success of Britain in keeping the heroin addict population to manageable numbers.[11] It proposed a pilot program for New York City in which heroin would be provided to addicts for an initial period of perhaps 3 months, before

10. A lengthy informal description, emphasizing the politics, can be found in Judson (1974; pp. 126–40).
11. Judson reports that originally a Vera research group had viewed the British maintenance regimes as unsuccessful and had projected very large increases in the number of addicts. When those increases were not realized, they changed their view of the British programs.

switching them to methadone or an abstinence regime. The rationale was that providing heroin could entice recalcitrant addicts to enter programs. If a first batch of 30 patients performed well in this regime, then a second set of 200 patients would be selected and randomly assigned to either the same regime or to methadone maintenance. Only then would large-scale implementation be tried.

Though far from a heroin maintenance scheme (being purely transitional in form), the proposal generated extremely hostile reactions from all quarters. Harlem's Congressman Charles Rangel said, "[I]t is imperative that we dispel some of the myths about the British system of drug treatment so that the American people will open up their eyes and recognize heroin for what it is – a killer, not a drug on which a human being should be maintained. . . ." The head of the predecessor agency to DEA asserted, "[I]t would be a virtual announcement of medical surrender on the treatment of addiction and would amount to consigning hundreds of thousands of our citizens to the slavery of heroin addiction forever." Vincent Dole, one of the two developers of methadone, published a *Journal of the American Medical Association* editorial attacking the notion on many grounds, such as the impossibility of finding stable doses or the implausibility that a small-scale demonstration could establish the feasibility of providing services to 250,000 heroin users. Even the generally liberal *New York Times* published negative stories; for example, it cited a Swedish psychiatric epidemiologist as suggesting "you could easily get up to three or four million addicts in five years. Heroin maintenance? Only those who don't know anything about addiction can discuss it."[12]

Each of these critics could be discounted on grounds of prior positions. Rangel represented the most hard-hit population group, African-Americans, who had a deep suspicion that drugs were being employed to reduce black anger following the urban riots of the late 1960s. Law enforcement agencies are notoriously conservative. The researcher responsible for developing a substitute medication for heroin was hardly likely to be an enthusiast for returning to the original drug. Sweden was, as a nation, harshly antimaintenance, even opposing methadone. But with so many different enemies and no prominent friends, the proposal quickly disappeared.

12. All cites taken from Judson (1974, pp. 131–2).

A few years later, the National League of Cities considered endorsing trials of heroin maintenance in several cities. After much debate, the NLC reaffirmed its support for such trials, but as Senay, Lewis, and Millar (1996) reported "thereafter the topic receded into obscurity" (p. 192). They also reported that later research proposals died either because of scientific review, which David Lewis (a participant in the original Vera proposal) thought was correct or, in one case, because the NIDA National Council (intended to advise the institute on policy issues) overruled a scientific panel.

In the United States, official reaction to the recent Swiss trials (Chapter 12) was illustrated in hearings held by a House subcommittee.[13] The subcommittee called as witnesses from Switzerland two doctors with long records of hostility to both needle exchange and heroin maintenance. One doctor (Ernst Aeschbach) was on the board of the Youth Without Drugs group, the principal group responsible for an initiative to end heroin prescribing. The other doctor (Erne Mathias) asserted that there was a conspiracy, initially supported by the East German or Soviet intelligence agencies, to create narco states in Europe; Switzerland had been targeted when the Netherlands acquired too controversial a reputation. Most members, both Democratic and Republican, were delighted with the Swiss witnesses, whose views were supported by two hawkish U.S. witnesses. Sample comments included: "Giving away free needles or doctor-injected heroin is simply . . . a fast track to moral corruption and the first step towards genuine disintegration of public security" (Shane, 1998).

Still the proposal recurs. David Vlahov, a professor at the Johns Hopkins School of Public Health proposed once again to undertake trials (Shane & Shields, 1998). The usual chorus of disapproval was instantaneous. Maryland's Democratic governor said, "It doesn't make any sense. It sends totally the wrong signal." The Lieutenant Governor expanded on this slightly. "It's much better to tell young people that heroin is bad. This undermines the whole effort." Even Baltimore Mayor Kurt Schmoke, a leader in liberal drug policy, distanced himself from the proposal and censured his health commissioner for endorsing it. It was also reported that "many addiction

---

13. The National Security, International Affairs and Criminal Justice Subcommittee of the House Government Reform and Oversight Committee.

experts say funding for traditional drug treatment falls far short of the demand, and heroin maintenance is a dubious distraction from proven remedies for drug abuse."[14]

It is striking that this impassioned hostility is engendered not by a policy proposal but simply by a proposal to conduct a demonstration or trial whose results could inform both sides of the debate. Clearly, government provision of a prohibited drug raises serious ethical issues, as discussed in the analysis of the Swiss trials in Chapter 12. Moreover, some of the empirical objections cannot readily be answered through a small-scale trial in a large city. For example, impact on initiation rates for injecting drug use of a program with 100 subjects will be hard to detect in New York City, with its 200,000 or more IVDUs. But the indignation and the willful misrepresentation of foreign experiences (Britain in the 1970s; Switzerland in the 1990s) are troubling.

THE STRICT ALLEGIANCE TO USE REDUCTION[15]

Harm reduction and use reduction

The ends of drug control. Table 15.1 lists and briefly defines four overlapping drug control strategies: Prevalence reduction, quantity reduction, micro harm reduction, and macro harm reduction. These should be distinguished from the budgetary debate over the appropriate balance between supply reduction (interdiction, source country control, domestic drug law enforcement) and demand reduction (treatment, prevention), which involves choices among programs, not strategic goals.

The alternative perspective offered by harm reduction can best be understood by recognizing that, despite their disagreements, demand-side and supply-side advocates share a common allegiance to what might be called the use reduction paradigm. This is the view that the highest, if not the exclusive, goal of drug policy should be to reduce (and, if possible, to eliminate) psychoactive drug use. In both practice and rhetoric, use reduction usually means *prevalence reduction.*

14. All quotes from Shane and Shields (1998).
15. This section is an updated version of an essay in *American Psychologist* by MacCoun (1998a).

Table 15.1. *Overlapping drug control strategies*

Strategy	Goal
Prevalence reduction	Reduce total number of drug users
Quantity reduction	Reduce total quantity consumed
Micro harm reduction	Reduce average harm per use of drugs
Macro harm reduction	Reduce total drug-related harm

That is, the goal has been to reduce the total number of users by discouraging initiation on the part of nonusers and by promoting abstinence for current users. Later, we will discuss *quantity reduction*, a second form of use reduction that receives less attention. The term *micro harm reduction* refers to harm reduction as it is generally conceptualized; the strategy of reducing average harm per incident of use. Finally, the notion of *macro harm reduction* follows from our observation that macro harm equals total use times average harm (Chapter 13).

The harm reduction critique of the enforcement-oriented U.S. drug strategy is twofold. First, it argues that prevalence reduction policies have failed to eliminate drug dependence, have at best only moderately reduced drug use, and have left its harms largely intact. Second, as argued in Chapter 6, these harsh enforcement policies are themselves a *source* of many drug-related harms, either directly or by exacerbating the harmful consequences of drug use (Nadelmann, 1989). Although many drug-related harms result from the psychopharmacologic effects of drug consumption, many others are primarily attributable to drug prohibition and its enforcement. These harms would be greatly reduced, if not eliminated, under a regime of legal availability. By almost exclusively relying on use reduction – primarily through drug law enforcement – as an indirect means of reducing harm, Americans are foregoing opportunities to reduce harm directly, and perhaps even increasing some aggregate harms in the process.

Opposition to harm reduction. These arguments have largely fallen on deaf ears. Yet harm reduction is the clearest lens through which to view the possibilities for change. This section explores the promises and pitfalls of harm reduction for the United

States, paying particular attention to the sources of hostility to its elements.

The slighting of the harms arising from drug use and policy is made particularly clear in a recent document from the Office of National Drug Control Policy (1998). Among five principal goals for drug policy, ONDCP lists reduction of the adverse crime and health consequences of drug use. Yet not a single program is directed specifically at that goal. It is accomplished only through reductions in drug use or availability. Thus, needle exchange, even bleach programs, get no mention, though AIDS reduction is identified as a performance target. No consideration is given to welfare policy with respect to drug dependence, even though such support may have a very substantial effect, positive or negative, on the behavior of drug addicts (Satel et al., 1997). Nor is there any listing of programs that might reduce the violence in drug markets, except by actually shrinking them.[16]

The almost exclusive emphasis on use reduction rather than harm reduction in the United States has many causes (Reuter & MacCoun, 1995). One is the fear that harm reduction is a Trojan horse for the drug legalization movement.[17] Another factor might be that whereas harm reduction focuses on harms to users, drug-related violence and other harms to nonusers are more salient in the United States than in Europe. Harm reduction programs may reduce violence, but that is not the effect that has been emphasized. In addition, prevalence is more readily measurable than harms, and few harm reduction programs, with the notable exception of needle exchange, have been rigorously evaluated – though ironically, political opposition to harm reduction is itself a major cause of the lack of relevant data.

Other objections, however, involve beliefs about behavior. For example, it may seem only logical that reducing use is the best way to reduce harm. But this logic holds only if the elimination of drug use is nearly complete, and if efforts to reduce use do not themselves

16. The one indication that harms might be reduced without lowering prevalence is indirect. One of the objectives under the goal of reducing harmful consequences is to lower drug use by those in treatment by 10 percent, thus accepting that treatment as implemented is not exclusively an abstinence program.

17. ONDCP Director McCaffrey (1998) was very explicit in making this claim; "the real intent of many harm reduction advocates is the legalization of drugs, which would be a mistake." His evidence for the general proposition was based on the statements of one advocate, Ethan Nadelmann.

cause harm. Unfortunately, many prevalence reduction policies fail on one or both counts. Although it is true that abstinence from drugs (or teenage sex, or drinking among alcoholics) is "100 percent effective" at reducing harm, the key policy question is whether it is possible to be 100 percent effective at convincing people to become abstinent. Finally, the most frequent objection to harm reduction is the claim that harm reduction programs will "send the wrong message." The logic by which harm reduction sends the wrong message is rarely articulated in any detail, suggesting that, for its proponents, the proposition is self-evident. It seems likely that harm reduction advocates will continue to face opposition in the United States until they successfully address this concern.

Harm reduction in other policy domains. The tension between preventing a behavior and reducing the harmfulness of that behavior is not unique to the debate about illicit drugs. Table 15.2 lists some intriguing parallels in other contemporary American policy debates. Despite many superficial differences, each domain involves a behavior that poses risks to both the actor and others. And each raises the question about the relative efficacy of policies that aim to reduce the harmful consequences of a risky behavior (harm reduction) versus policies designed to discourage the behavior itself (prevalence or quantity reduction).

The first row of Table 15.2 – safety standards for consumer products – is notable for its lack of controversy outside the Washington Beltway and a few industrial centers. Even though these safety regulations clearly have a harm reduction rationale – albeit one generally not recognized as such – recent Congressional efforts to scale them back have received a remarkably lukewarm public response.

But in the other domains listed in the table, a debate centers on the fear that an intervention to reduce harm – harm reduction in spirit if not in name – will in some way send the wrong message, encouraging the risky behavior. The parallels to drugs are particularly striking for the topic of condom distribution in schools (and to a lesser degree, sex education). Advocates argue that condom distribution is needed to reduce the risks of unplanned pregnancies and sexually transmitted diseases, while opponents vociferously

Table 15.2. *Policies aimed at reducing harms associated with risky behaviors*

Policy	Risky behavior	Harms that policy tries to reduce
Mandated safety standards for motor vehicles, toys, sports equipment, food, pharmaceuticals, etc.	Driving, participation in sports, consumption of products, etc.	Physical injury, illness, death
Needle exchange	Intravenous drug use	HIV transmission
Teaching of controlled drinking skills	Drinking by diagnosed alcoholics	Social, psychological, and physical harms of alcohol abuse
School condom programs	Unprotected sexual contact among teens	Sexually transmitted diseases, unwanted pregnancies
Welfare	Becoming and/or remaining unemployed	Poor quality of life (housing, health, education), especially for children
Provision of benefits for illegal immigrants	Illegal immigration to the United States	Poor quality of life (housing, health, education), especially for children

argue that distribution programs and other safe sex interventions actually promote sexual activity (Jemmott, Jemmott, & Fong, 1998; Mauldon & Luker, 1996). On the other hand, recent U.S. debates about welfare and immigration benefits may seem to have little to do with concepts like risk regulation or harm reduction. But at an abstract level, the issues are similar. Assertions are made that policies designed to mitigate the harmful consequences of being unemployed, or of immigrating to the United States, actually encourage people to become (or remain) unemployed, or to immigrate to the United States.

Does harm reduction send the wrong message?

Recall that Macro Harm = Harmfulness × Prevalence × Intensity, or more simply, Macro Harm = Micro Harm × Total Use. We can use this formulation to evaluate concerns that harm reduction sends the

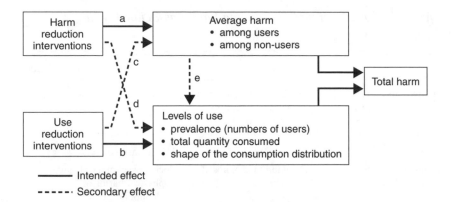

Figure 15.1 Use reduction and harm reduction: An integrative framework

wrong message. Figure 15.1 depicts this relationship graphically using a causal path diagram.

Links *a* and *b* depict the intended effects of harm reduction and use reduction policies, respectively. Links *c*, *d*, and *e* depict the ancillary harmful effects – unintended and often unanticipated – these policies might have. Link *c* denotes the unintended harms caused by prohibiting a risky behavior – the lack of clean needles, lack of drug quality control, violence associated with illicit markets, inflated prices that encourage income-generating crime, and so on (Nadelmann, 1989). This category of unintended harms is of central concern to any assessment of alternative legal regimes for drug control.

Here we focus on a second set of unintended consequences, those resulting from harm reduction policies, to see whether objections to harm reduction have merit. If a harm reduction strategy reduces harm per incident but leads to increases in drug use (links *d* and *e*), the policy might still achieve *net* harm reduction; on the other hand, a sufficiently large increase in use could actually result in an *increase* in total harm. There are two potential mechanisms for such an unintended consequence, one direct and one indirect. For reasons to be explained, link *d* can be conceptualized as the direct *rhetorical* effect (if any) of harm reduction on total use; link *e* is an indirect *compensatory behavior* effect. Either might be interpreted as sending the wrong message.

Direct version: Does harm reduction literally send the wrong message? The rhetorical hypothesis is that irrespective of their effectiveness in reducing harms, harm reduction programs literally communicate messages that encourage drug use. As noted earlier, those who espouse this rhetorical hypothesis rarely explain how it is supposed to work. The most plausible interpretation is that without intending to do so, harm reduction sends tacit messages that are construed as approval – or at least the absence of strong disapproval – of drug consumption.

If harm reduction service providers *intend* to send a message, it is something like this: "We view drugs as harmful. We discourage you from using them, and we are eager to help you to quit if you've started. But if you will not quit using drugs, we can help you to use them less harmfully." Is that the only message? Psycholinguistic theory and research do suggest that people readily draw additional inferences that are *pragmatically implied* by an actor's conduct, regardless of whether those inferences were intended, or even endorsed, by the actor (Harris & Monaco, 1978; Wyer & Gruenfeld, 1995). Thus, if heroin users are given clean needles, they might infer that authorities don't expect them to quit using heroin – otherwise, why give out needles? Arguably, this perception could undermine their motivation to quit.

But would nonusers infer that authorities think heroin use is *good*, or at least "not bad"? It is not obvious how harm reduction might actually imply *endorsement* of drug use. Ultimately, whether any such rhetorical effects occur is an empirical question. It would be useful to assess the kinds of unintended inferences that users and nonusers draw from harm reduction messages, and from the mere existence of harm reduction programs. But in the absence of such evidence, the rhetorical hypothesis that harm reduction conveys approval of drug use is largely speculative.

It is difficult to reconcile this notion with the secondary prevention and treatment efforts that frequently accompany actual harm reduction interventions. Through such efforts, users are informed that their behavior is dangerous to themselves and others, and that assistance and support are available to help them if they wish to quit drug use. Braithwaite's (1989) research on *reintegrative shaming* indicates that it is possible simultaneously to send a social message that certain acts are socially unacceptable while still helping the actors to repair their lives. Braithwaite suggests that this approach is integral to Japanese culture, but it is also reflected in the Christian tradition of "hating the sin but loving the sinner."

Indirect version: Does a reduction in harm make drugs more attractive? Even if no one took harm reduction to imply government endorsement of drugs, harm reduction might still influence levels of drug use *indirectly* through its intended effect – that is, by reducing the riskiness of drug use. This is a second interpretation of sending the wrong message. Though there are ample grounds for being skeptical of a pure "rational-choice" analysis of drug use (Chapter 5), the notion that reductions in risk might influence drug use is certainly plausible and would be consistent with a growing body of evidence of compensatory behavioral responses to safety interventions. Thus, one should be mindful of potential tradeoffs between harm reduction and use reduction.

Risk assessors have known for some time that engineers tend to overestimate the benefits of technological improvements in the safety of automobiles, cigarettes, and other products. The reason is that engineers often fail to anticipate that technological improvements lead to changes in behavior. When technological innovations successfully reduce the probability of harm given unsafe conduct, they make that conduct less risky. And if the perceived risks were motivating actors to behave somewhat self-protectively, a reduction in risk should lead them to take fewer precautions than before, raising the probability of their unsafe conduct to a higher level. This notion has been variously labeled *compensatory behavior, risk compensation, offsetting behavior*, or in its most extreme form, *risk homeostasis* – a term that implies efforts to maintain a constant level of risk (Wilde, 1982). While some find this general idea counterintuitive, one economist has noted that, on reflection, it is hardly surprising that "soldiers walk more gingerly when crossing minefields than when crossing wheat fields," and "circus performers take fewer chances when practicing without nets" (Hemenway, 1988).

Compensatory behavioral responses to risk reduction have been identified in a variety of settings. For example, everything else being equal, drivers have responded to seat belts and other improvements in the safety of automobiles by driving faster and more recklessly than they would in a less safe vehicle (Chirinko & Harper, 1993).

Similarly, filters and low-tar tobacco each reduce the harmfulness per unit of tobacco, yet numerous studies have demonstrated that smokers compensate by smoking more cigarettes, inhaling more deeply, or blocking the filter vents (Hughes, 1995). In both domains, some of the safety gains brought about by a reduction in the probability of harm given unsafe conduct have been offset by increases in the probability of that conduct. Though early correlational studies were criticized on methodological grounds, the compensatory behavioral hypothesis has received important support from recent controlled laboratory experiments (Stetzer & Hofman, 1996).

The compensatory behavioral mechanism suggests that if reductions in average drug-related harm were to motivate sufficiently large increases in drug use, micro harm reduction would actually increase macro harm. Blower and McLean (1994) offer a similar argument based on their recent epidemiological simulations, which suggests that an HIV vaccine, unless perfectly prophylactic, could actually exacerbate the San Francisco AIDS epidemic, provided that individuals behaved less cautiously in response to their increased sense of safety. But to date, research on compensatory responses to risk reduction provides little evidence that behavioral responses produce net increases in harm, or even the constant level of harm predicted by the "homeostatic" version of the theory. Instead, most studies find that when programs reduce the probability of harm given unsafe conduct, any increases in the probability of that conduct are slight, reducing, but not eliminating, the gains in safety (Chirinko & Harper, 1993; Hughes, 1995; Stetzer & Hofman, 1996). As a result, in our terms, micro harm reduction produces macro harm reduction.

Do drug interventions achieve macro harm reduction? It is clearly impossible to calculate total drug harm in any literal fashion, or to compare rigorously total harm across alternative policy regimes. Many of the harms are difficult to quantify, and observers will differ in their weighting of the various types of harm. Thus at the strategic level of national policy formation, macro harm reduction is not a rigid analytical test but rather a heuristic principle. Are existing policies reducing drug harms, and reducing drug use in ways that do not increase drug harm? But at the level of specific interventions, macro reduction of *specific* harms is a realistic evaluation criterion, as illustrated by the compensatory behavioral research just cited.

Unfortunately, few drug policy programs are evaluated with respect to both use reduction and harm reduction. Prevention and treatment programs are generally evaluated with respect to changes in abstinence or relapse rates, whereas harm reduction program evaluators tend to assess changes in crime, morbidity, and mortality rates. As a result, researchers are unable to determine whether many programs achieve macro harm reduction.

The empirical literature on needle exchange is a notable and exemplary exception. As already mentioned, there is now a fairly sizable body of evidence that needle exchange programs produce little or no measurable increase in injecting drug use (Lurie & Reingold, 1993; Watters et al., 1994). Because it significantly reduces average harm, needle exchange provides both micro and macro harm reduction. But the empirical success record for needle exchange does not constitute blanket support for the harm reduction movement. Each intervention must be assessed empirically on its own terms.

Let us offer three cautionary tales, two real and one hypothetical. One real example involves bongs and water pipes. Though these devices have been touted as a means of reducing the health risks of marijuana smoking, a recent test found that they actually increase the quantity of tars ingested. The apparent reason harkens back to the compensatory behavioral mechanism. Water pipes filter out more THC than tar, so users smoke more to achieve the same high, thereby increasing their risk (Gieringer, 1996). A second real example is the apparent failure of the zone of tolerance strategy in Zurich's Platzspitz (Chapter 12), where any gains in addict health were believed to have been outweighed by an increase in heroin consumption in and near the park. The Zurich case and the bong study suggest that harm reduction strategies can fail, but it is important to note that neither failure resulted from increasing rates of *initiation* to drug use. In the Zurich case, the prevalence of drug use rose primarily because the park attracted users from other Swiss cities and neighboring countries. Arguably, the program might have been successful had other European cities adopted the idea simultaneously. In the bong case, the filtering benefits were offset by increases in consumption levels among users, but it seems unlikely that bongs and water pipes have ever encouraged nonusers to start smoking marijuana.

One can imagine hypothetical examples of how a harm reduction strategy might plausibly attract new users. For example, from a public health perspective, it is better if current heroin injectors switch to smoking their drug. Imagine a public information campaign designed to highlight the relative health benefits of smoking. If some fraction of nonusers have resisted heroin because of an aversion to needles, the campaign might indeed end up encouraging some of them to take up heroin smoking, despite our best intentions. Of course, no one has implemented such a campaign.[18] But the example demonstrates that concerns about increased use are plausible in principle.

Quantity reduction as a middle ground

American drug policy rhetoric is dominated by concerns about the number of users, drawing a bright line between users and nonusers. This is illustrated by U.S. national drug indicator data. Most available measures of drug use are *prevalence*-oriented: rates of lifetime use, use in the past year, or use in the past month. But drug-related harms may well be more sensitive to changes in the *total quantity consumed* than to changes in the total number of users. One million occasional drug users may pose fewer crime and health problems than 100,000 frequent users. Recent U.S. cocaine problems provide an illustration. After significant reductions in casual use in the 1980s, total consumption has become increasingly concentrated among a smaller number of heavy users. At an individual level, these heavy users are at much greater risk than casual users with respect to acute and chronic illness, accidents, job- and family-related problems, and participation in criminal activities. Thus while cocaine prevalence has declined, total cocaine consumption and its related harms have remained relatively stable (Everingham & Rydell, 1994).

This suggests that *quantity reduction* (reducing consumption levels) holds particular promise as a macro harm reduction strategy. Quantity reduction occupies a point halfway between prevalence reduction and micro harm reduction. Like prevalence reduction, quantity reduction targets use levels rather than harm levels. But like harm reduction, and unlike prevalence reduction, quantity reduction is based on the premise that when use cannot be prevented, we might at least be able to mitigate its harms.

---

18. In MacCoun (1998), we said, "no one has seriously proposed such a campaign"; a similar proposal by Wodak (1997) was later called to our attention.

Less clear is the optimal targeting strategy for quantity reduction. Consider the distribution of users across consumption levels, which for most psychoactive drugs (licit and illicit) is positively skewed, with a long right tail indicating a small fraction of very heavy users. One strategy is to target those heaviest users – to "pull in" the right tail of the distribution. The marginal gains in risk reduction should be greatest at the right tail, and only a small fraction of users need to be targeted.

This approach has received considerable attention – and notoriety – in the alcohol field under the rubric "controlled drinking." Few public health experts dispute the notion that problem drinkers are better off drinking lightly than drinking heavily. But there has been an extraordinary furor surrounding the notion of controlled drinking as a treatment goal. The evidence suggests that (1) even though abstinence-based treatment programs experience high relapse rates, many of the relapsing clients successfully reduce their drinking to relatively problem-free levels; (2) it is possible to *teach* controlled drinking skills to many, but not all, problem drinkers; (3) it is difficult to predict which problem drinkers will be able to control their drinking at moderate levels; and (4) most treated problem drinkers fail to achieve either abstinence or controlled levels of drinking (Marlatt et al., 1993). Opponents assert that, irrespective of any benefits to be derived from controlled drinking, the very notion undermines the goal of abstinence and discourages drinkers from achieving it. The small-scale studies conducted to date do not support that claim, but the evidence is not yet decisive.

In addition to the abstinence-moderation debate, a second quantity reduction debate has emerged among alcohol experts. Are problem drinkers even the appropriate intervention target? An alternative quantity reduction strategy targets the middle of the alcohol consumption distribution. For some years, many experts have argued that the total social costs of alcohol might be better reduced by lowering average consumption levels, rather than concentrating on the most problematic drinkers at the right tail (Rose, 1992; Skog, 1993). If so – and this is a matter of ongoing debate – broad-based efforts to reduce total drug use might indeed be the best way to achieve total harm reduction, at least for alcohol consumption. The controversy here has been more purely technical and less emotional than the controlled drinking debate, in part because few people still champion the notion of abstinence for casual drinkers. Many Americans seem quite willing to accept the notion of nonproblem alcohol consumption yet reject the notion of nonproblem marijuana or cocaine consumption.[19]

In fact, the viability of "lower risk" drug consumption, and the relative efficacy of the pull-in-the-tail and the lower-the-average strategies, will depend on a variety of factors. One consideration is the degree of skew of the consumption distribution: the greater the share of total consumption due to heavy users, the greater the efficacy of targeting them. A second is the dose-response curve for risks, which is usually S-shaped for those drug-risk combinations that have been studied. (A great deal more is known about dose-response functions for health and public safety risks involving licit drugs than for comparable risks involving illicit drugs.) When this function is very steep, even moderate consumption levels are risky, making the shift-the-distribution strategy more efficacious. A third factor involves the possibility that individuals with a higher propensity for danger self-select higher consumption levels. The latter effect will spuriously inflate the quantity-risk relationship. To the extent that this effect predominates, convincing right-tail users to cut back may yield fewer benefits than anticipated.

Psychological foundations of the strict allegiance to prevalence reduction

The consequentialist grounds for opposing harm reduction are the easiest to describe. They are characterized primarily by the belief that harm reduction will be counterproductive, either by failing to reduce average harm or by increasing drug use enough to increase total harm. Those who oppose harm reduction on truly consequentialist grounds should change their mind and support it if the best available facts suggest that an intervention reduces harm without producing offsetting increases in use. In recent years, the favorable evidence for needle exchange has received increasing publicity in the mass media.

19. One middle-aged Dutch researcher spoke of his irritation with a young American guest who took marijuana rapidly so as to get stoned, while the host and his Dutch guests smoked slowly (as they sipped cognac) in order to feel mellow over a 3-hour postdinner discussion. We have no data on how extensive is this more winelike consumption pattern for cannabis in the Netherlands.

This media coverage may explain why a 1996 poll found that 66 percent of Americans endorsed needle exchange as a means of preventing AIDS – a dramatic increase over earlier surveys (The Henry J. Kaiser Family Foundation, 1996). But the vehemence of the opposition to harm reduction suggests that attitudes toward these interventions are based on something more than purely instrumental beliefs about the effectiveness of alternative drug policies.

Attitudes toward the death penalty are instructive in this regard. Attitude research indicates that many citizens overtly endorse a *deterrence* rationale for the death penalty, believing that "it will prevent crimes." Yet most do not change their views when asked how they would feel if there were unequivocal evidence that execution provided no marginal deterrence above and beyond life imprisonment. The evidence suggests that ostensibly instrumental views are actually masking deeper retributive motives (Ellsworth & Gross, 1994). As a result, support for capital punishment is relatively impervious to research findings (Lord, Ross, & Lepper, 1979).

The nonconsequentialist grounds for opposing harm reduction are more complex than the consequentialist grounds. A number of distinct psychological processes might play a role in shaping these views. Note that these psychological accounts do not constitute evidence for or against the wisdom of opposition to harm reduction, nor are they meant to imply that such views are somehow pathological.

The need for predictability and control.   A central tenet of the social sciences is that harmonious social relations require a minimal level of predictability because we must routinely relinquish control to other people – automobile drivers, surgeons, airline pilots, our children's teachers, and so on. The notion that others are using drugs can be threatening because it suggests that they have lost some self-control. While harm reduction can minimize the consequences of diminished control, it may be more reassuring to believe that others are completely abstinent. When we are unable to control aversive stimuli, any signal that enables us reliably to anticipate danger will significantly reduce our anxiety (Miller, 1980). Perhaps the belief that others are completely abstinent from drugs works like a "safety signal" to free us from worrying about their conduct.

Fears about others' behavior are augmented by a robust bias in risk perceptions. Most people – adults as well as adolescents – perceive themselves to be less vulnerable than the average person to risks of injury or harm (e.g., Weinstein & Klein, 1995). An apparent corollary is that most of us believe we are surrounded by people less cautious or skillful than ourselves. We may think we can control our own use of intoxicants – most of us feel that way about alcohol – but we find it harder to believe that others will do the same. Indeed, this might explain why a sizeable minority of regular cannabis users opposes the complete legalization of that drug (Erickson, 1989).

Aversion to making value tradeoffs. Individual attitudes toward public policy involve more than simple judgments about effectiveness and outcomes. They are symbolic expressions of core values. Unfortunately, most difficult social problems bring core values into conflict. Drug problems are no exception; they bring personal liberty into conflict with public safety, compassion into conflict with moral accountability. Contemplating harm reduction brings these conflicts into strong relief. Acknowledging such conflicts is psychologically aversive, and so many people avoid explicit tradeoff reasoning, preferring simpler mental strategies (Tetlock, Peterson, & Lerner, 1996). The easiest is to deny that there is a conflict, by ignoring one value or the other. If that doesn't work, individuals may adopt a simple "lexicographic" ranking. Many of us engage in complex multidimensional tradeoff reasoning only when we can't avoid it, as when the conflicting values are each too salient to dismiss or ignore.

Recall that the content analysis of op-ed essays (Chapter 3) found that legalizers and decriminalizers (all of whom were harm reduction advocates, though the converse is not necessarily true) used significantly more complex arguments than prohibitionists. The reform advocates were less likely to view the drug problem in terms of a simple good-bad dichotomy; they identified multiple dimensions to the problem and were more likely to acknowledge tradeoffs and counterarguments to their own position. It may be hard to persuade others to acknowledge the full complexity of harm reduction logic unless the values that support it become more salient in drug policy discourse.

The propriety of helping drug users. Of course, there is little basis for value conflict if one feels that drug users *should* suffer harm when they use drugs. There are a number of reasons why some people might hold this view. One is authoritarianism, a complex trait defined as a chronic tendency to cope with anxiety by expressing hostility toward outgroup members; intolerance of unconventional behavior; and submissive, unquestioning support of authority figures. Authoritarianism is strongly correlated with support for punitive drug policies (Peterson, Doty, & Winter, 1993): indeed, several items from the Right Wing Authoritarianism Scale (R. Christie, 1991) – a leading research instrument for measuring this trait – seem to equate authoritarianism with opposition to harm reduction interventions almost by definition. According to item 7, "The facts on crime, sexual immorality, and the recent public disorders all show we have to crack down harder on deviant groups and troublemakers if we are going to save our moral standards and preserve law and order." Item 12 states, "Being kind to loafers or criminals will only encourage them to take advantage of your weakness, so it's best to use a firm, tough hand when dealing with them." Authoritarians are more likely to agree with these items and to disagree with item 19: "The courts are right in being easy on drug offenders. Punishment would not do any good in cases like these."

Scoring high in authoritarianism is probably not a prerequisite for hostility toward drug users. There is a general antagonism to hard-drug users among U.S. citizens, partly stemming from the strong association between drugs and street violence in American cities. It is much easier to see harshness as the appropriate response in the United State than in Europe, where drug use is more likely to be perceived as a health problem. Race and social distance may play a role here as well; arguably, Americans were more tolerant of drug users in the 1970s, when the mass media's prototypical drug user was an Anglo-American student in a college dorm instead of a young African-American male on a city street corner (Kirp & Bayer, 1993). But irrespective of race and class, the mere fact that someone uses drugs will often be sufficient to categorize them as "the other," particularly if we don't already know them. Citizens with a friend or family member who is an addict may embrace micro harm reduction, whatever its aggregate consequences, but those who don't know any addicts may prefer a strategy of isolation and containment.

Even in the absence of malice, many people may feel that addicts should suffer the consequences of their actions. Addiction is widely viewed as a voluntary state, regardless of many experts' views to the contrary (Weiner, Perry, & Magnusson, 1988). Many Americans, especially conservatives, are unwilling to extend help to actors who are responsible for their own suffering; such actors are seen as undeserving (Skitka & Tetlock, 1993). The retributive view that bad acts require punishment is deeply rooted in the Judeo-Christian tradition, particularly in Protestant fundamentalist traditions. In light of the possibility that opposition to harm reduction traces back to our nation's strong Puritan and Calvinist roots, it is ironic that the Dutch and the Swiss have championed such an approach in Europe.

Disgust and impurity. A final ground for opposing harm reduction might be the vague, spontaneous, and nonrational sense that drug use defiles the purity of the body, and hence that anything that comes in contact with drug users becomes disgusting through a process of contagion. Stated so bluntly, this may sound utterly implausible; such concepts are quite alien to Western moral discourse. Nevertheless, this kind of thinking is quite explicit in other cultures, and anthropologists argue that it often lurks below the surface of our own moral judgments (Douglas, 1966; Haidt et al., 1993; Rozin, 1999).

HOW FIRM IS THE RESISTANCE TO CHANGE?

This chapter provides ample evidence of resistance by high-level authorities to major change in drug policy. One might reasonably conclude that the public supports or even demands this resistance. For example, Chapter 3 showed that a strong majority opposes legalization (and less strongly, decriminalization) of cannabis, the least harmful and most prevalent of the major drugs under debate. Moreover, this opposition has been roughly constant for almost 25 years. In this sense, the political threshold of proof might look like a looming, impenetrable wall.

Nevertheless, there are several reasons to believe opinion could shift, perhaps even suddenly and dramatically. Indeed, that is how some interpreted the sweeping support for Proposition 215 in California and Proposition 200 in Arizona (a bastion of Republicanism). But surveys indicate that most supporters viewed their votes narrowly, as an endorsement of compassionate medical use rather than a stepping-stone to less restrictive recreational use (Blendon &

Young, 1998). We are more convinced by other, less direct forms of evidence. A growing literature documents swift, "nonlinear" reversals in public opinion toward various policy topics (Jones, 1994; Kuran, 1995; Noelle-Neumann, 1991). At least two mechanisms seem to be at work in these cases. They share the notion that people's policy preferences are often ill-formed and labile.

The first mechanism arises from the fact that many citizens mute their true sentiments about controversial topics, exaggerating or falsifying their support for whichever viewpoint seems safest and least controversial, leading to a "spiral of silence" (Noelle-Neumann, 1991), "spiral of prudence" (Kuran, 1995), or "pluralistic ignorance" (e.g., Miller & Prentice, 1994). As Kuran (1995, p. 113) put it,

> When large numbers of people conceal their misgivings about the status quo, individuals may consider their own disenchantments exceptional. They may think that they are in conflict with the rest of society and hence that by being truthful they would only invite trouble. Through preference falsification, they may thus hold in place structures that they could, if only they acted together, easily change.

Miller and Prentice (1994, p. 543) offer a particularly relevant illustration:

> An example [of pluralistic ignorance] is provided by the history of Prohibition. Though strongly advocated and enforced by various constituencies in America, Prohibition never had majority support. It *seemed* [their emphasis] to have public support, however, because people were reluctant to express their anti-Prohibition sentiment (Robinson, 1932). Once polls revealing the depth of private anti-Prohibition sentiment were made public, pluralistic ignorance was dissipated, and Prohibition swiftly ended (Katz & Schanck, 1938).

Of course, one difference between Repeal and the present situation is that private survey responses are now routinely publicized, and these responses show little evidence of any "private anti-Prohibition sentiment" for drugs in the 1990s. But it is well-known that people often distort their survey responses to appear socially acceptable (Kuran, 1995). For example, Fendrich and Vaughan (1994) found that about a third of respondents who in 1984 admitted having tried marijuana or cocaine denied having tried those drugs when asked again in 1988 – a period of increasing intolerance toward drug use. More to the point, White and Zimbardo (1980) demonstrated that college students evaluated marijuana decriminalization less favorably when they believed their views might be monitored.

A second mechanism also can produce sudden nonlinear shifts in opinion – even in the absence of any self-censorship. Jones (1994) reviewed evidence that public opinion responses are seldom fully considered and deliberative. He argued that, over time, people's views on important issues are multidimensional; but at any given moment in time responses are constructed "on the fly," based on whichever dimension is currently most salient. This harkens back to the discussion of rhetorical complexity in Chapter 3. Recall that those arguing for reform of drug laws (legalization or depenalization) tend to use significantly more complex arguments – more multidimensional, with greater integration across the dimensions – than prohibiters. For example, reformers recognize that even though drug use can cause serious harm, efforts to stop drug use can make some of those harms worse. For Americans who have given little thought to the issue – out of lack of interest, not simple-mindedness – the legalization agenda debate may seem to be prodrug vs. antidrug. Reformers try to reframe legalization, with such justification as prohealth, anticrime, anticorruption, and the like.

Chapter 3 found little evidence that such efforts have succeeded – yet. But staunch prohibition defenders appear to be worried about that prospect, judging from their willingness to squander a substantial portion of their "bully pulpit" efforts to denouncing the legalizers. It is baffling to find that the annual National Drug Control Strategy (NDCS) still spends a few paragraphs each year denouncing the danger of legalization, given how thin is the support for, or visibility of, legalization, absent these official attacks. Indeed, the NDCS even includes as a strategic objective showing that legalization is a mistake. Perhaps that fear is well-founded. Jones (1994, pp. 107–8) argued that the launching of the drug war itself created a radical swing in public opinion. After President George Bush announced his "war on drugs" on September 5, 1989, "television coverage of the problem increased eightfold"; within a month, polls indicated that the percentage of Americans naming drugs as "the most important problem facing the United States" jumped from about 27 percent to almost 65 percent. The Bush speech reinforced the simple "drugs are bad, so let's stop drug use" message. What would happen if a major public leader gave comparable salience to a more nuanced message; for example, that the cure shouldn't be worse than the disease, that we should get smart rather than getting tough, or that our war on drugs shouldn't be a war on drug users? It is impossible to guess.

CAN AMERICA TREAT AND PREVENT ITS WAY OUT OF DRUG PROBLEMS?

In the last few years, a number of groups have formed to press for change in American drug policy. For example, a prestigious committee of doctors formed the Physicians Leadership on National Drug Policy in 1997 to make public health the guiding principle of drug policy. Other medical bodies, including the College on Problems of Drug Dependence[20] and the American Academy of Pediatrics have issued formal statements espousing similar positions. We ourselves are members of an interdisciplinary group formed under the auspices of the Federation of American Scientists to press for a "third way" (Wren, 1997[21]). All accept, at least implicitly, the retention of prohibitions.

Most of these groups, and other reformers, contend that the nation's drug problems are exacerbated by current U.S. policies and can be ameliorated by changes in policies within the prohibitionist framework. It is the harshness of drug enforcement that has generated the disease and violent crime that surround drug use; that is the standard liberal critique (e.g., Skolnick, 1992). Yet this may give too much credit to the role of policy, a common fallacy in modern American discussions. Whether or not there is an epidemic of experimentation with a particular drug, what fraction of experimenters go on to become dependent, and the severity of health and crime consequences of dependence may all be mostly shaped by factors other than drug policy. Certainly, when comparing America's drug problems with those of Western European nations, most of the relevant differences appear to be rooted either (a) in broader features of societies (e.g., the United States is characterized by greater hedonism, weaker informal social controls, a higher propensity for risk taking,

20. Reuter was a member of the CPDD committee that drafted the organization's drug policy statement.
21. The Web address for the Principles is *http://www.fas.org/drugs/Principles.htm*

and a higher level of criminal violence generally) or (b) in broader policy characteristics (e.g., inadequate provision of health care for the poor and unequal income distribution). The United States also suffers from being more intimately connected with cocaine-and opium-growing regions, such as Colombia and Mexico. All these factors promote use of illicit psychoactive drugs and/or worsen the problems associated with that use.

That proposition about the marginality of drug policy is not as nihilistic as it might first appear. If policy is only moderately important in controlling drug use, then perhaps the United States can mitigate the harshness of its policies with little risk of seeing an expansion of drug use and related problems. Reducing the U.S. drug *policy* problem (i.e., the adverse consequences of the policies themselves) is worth a good deal, though it would obviously be even more desirable if the United States could also reduce the prevalence and adverse consequences of drug abuse and dependence themselves.

It is hard, however, to be highly prescriptive here, to say what good drug policy would look like, because one consequence of politicians treating drug control as a moral crusade has been an absolute uninterest, bordering on gross negligence, in assessing the consequences, good or bad, of the emphasis on punishment. It is impossible to say, even approximately, whether locking up more drug dealers or seizing lots of assets has any substantial effect on prices; similarly there is only tentative evidence concerning the effects that higher prices would have on American drug usage or related violence (Chapters 5 and 6). There is no credible basis for describing a policy that would reduce, in any important dimension, the extent of American drug problems by, say, one-third in the next 5 years.

At a minimum, it would be useful to say whether longer prison sentences, more drug seizures, or more intensive money laundering investigations can increase prices or reduce availability and what effect these changes would have on drug use by current and prospective users and on drug-related problems. Until quite recently, the only attempt to answer that question was a paper of 25 years ago which found that higher prices for heroin increased property crimes in Detroit (Silverman & Spruill, 1977). There has been some progress lately in estimating the price elasticity of demand for various drugs and various populations (e.g., Saffer & Chaloupka, 1995) but these are just initial steps. As noted in Chapter 2, we can say more about the effectiveness of treatment partly because it always needs to defend itself and partly because of its ties to the more research-oriented public health policy community.

One can usefully adapt a complaint of the public health research world to explain this situation. Prevention researchers object that whereas surgical procedures only have to be shown to be safe, and medicines safe and effective, prevention programs have to be demonstrated to be safe, effective, and cost-effective as well. The corollary for drug enforcement is that it doesn't even have to be shown to be safe, let alone effective or cost-effective. Drug enforcement has become a crusade, and crusaders scarcely need a map, let alone evaluation.

Clearly, we need a large research and analysis program that has the depth and durability to develop more credible measures of the intensity of enforcement and the size of the drug problem in a particular community. Analysts need to take account of the enormous variation that seems to exist across cities and states. For example, in Texas in 1992 the median prison sentence for those convicted of drug trafficking was 10 years, compared to only 2 years for those in Washington State. It should be possible to build on the improvements in the drug data indicators being developed by various federal agencies.[23]

Why is there so little research on drug enforcement? Surely part of the answer is simply that there is, as James Q. Wilson (1997) noted recently, shockingly little research on crime control generally. But another factor, we conjecture, is a curious confluence of liberal and conservative interests. Those who support tough drug enforcement see no gain in evaluation; Peter Rossi's oft-cited comment "if you don't like a program, evaluate it" is highly relevant. Liberals find the whole effort distasteful enough that they simply want nothing to do with it; in particular, they do not want to evaluate it for the purposes of making it work better. They would much rather focus on the pro-

23. For example, the National Institute of Justice has expanded and improved its Drug Use Forecasting system on drug use by arrestees. The expanded program, the Arrestee Drug Abuse Monitoring (ADAM) system, collects data in thirty-five counties. Similarly, the National Household Survey on Drug Abuse has been expanded to allow estimates of the prevalence of drug use in large states and major metropolitan areas.

grams in which they have faith and in which they passionately and rather naïvely believe, namely prevention and treatment. We use the term *naïve* with some hesitation, being firm advocates of large increases in treatment expenditures and improvement of the treatment system. But it is clear that treatment has sharp limits. Even with a large expansion in funding, sufficient to provide good-quality services for anyone who wants them, the nation will be left with a very large drug problem. Most addicts will drop out of treatment or relapse after completion of a program. Rydell and Everingham's (1994) work is mostly cited for its finding that treatment is more cost-effective than enforcement. Much less attention is paid to their finding that even if the United States provided treatment for every heavy user (which might not be possible), after 15 years cocaine consumption would decline by only about a third, from about 310 metric tons per year to about 210 metric tons per year. There is more to good policy than changes in funding priorities, and treatment can only soak up a modest share of the $20 to 25 billion that is spent on drug enforcement by different levels of government.

For prevention, the empirical base for advocacy is even weaker. (For a more sanguine view, see Caulkins et al., 1999.) Some programs have, in well-designed and executed experimental forms, shown modest effects (Chapter 2), but the implementation problems for school-based prevention programs are massive (Gottfredson, 1997). Worse, the schools with the populations at highest risk of drug abuse, those in poor urban communities, are generally the ones least able to effectively implement behaviorally subtle programs. The upturn in adolescent marijuana use between 1992 and 1996, at a time when prevention programs were getting increased funding and a stronger set of curriculum materials were being developed, is a reminder of how little is known about their ability to deal with large-scale cultural shifts.

None of this is to say that more treatment funding and development of better prevention programs would not be helpful. But there are clear limits to what they are likely to accomplish in the next decade. Making enforcement work better and reducing the damage it creates have to be at the front of any agenda for large-scale policy reform.

ON DOING LESS: DRUG POLICY IN MODERATION
AND SOME NONZERO TOLERANCE

Increased treatment and prevention, even under the most generous scenarios, will not solve the U.S. drug problem. It is doubtful that a complete "solution" exists. The pursuit of a drug-free society seems quixotic, and its nobility is tarnished by the associated hatred and contempt for drug users. Defenders of the current regime deliberately avert their eyes from an honest assessment of a massive and frequently cruel intervention that sacrifices so many other goals for the one desiderata of drug abstinence. Society is forgoing significant reductions in drug-related damage by its unwillingness to make policy changes that risk sending the wrong message.

Some of those changes involve doing more (e.g., needle exchange, safe-use campaigns targeted at addicts, and an expansion of methadone maintenance programs). And a whole range of nondrug policies – welfare rules and income support, public housing policies, health care provision, general education – may do more to affect drug abuse and related problems than those programs that claim to target them explicitly (Boyum & Reuter, in press). But other changes might involve doing less. The European experience (and U.S. experiences with policing prostitution and gambling) illustrate the breadth of possibilities for selective, targeted enforcement of a prohibition. Locking up drug offenders for shorter terms, worrying more about the racial disparities in sentencing policies, and giving up fewer civil liberties for unlikely reductions in drug problems may be the best one can do at the moment. Doing less (or doing differently) would mean less intrusive, divisive, and expensive policies, with little demonstrable risk of increasing drug use.

This chapter is more opinionated than the rest of the book. Throughout the book, we have attempted to be honest brokers – noting time and again the serious limitations and drawbacks of the reformers' arguments – but it is by now clear that our own sympathies are with the reform effort, at least in its best-intentioned, least dogmatic form. But our judgments are just that – our judgments. Others may reach quite different conclusions about specific changes, and we have tried to provide the evidence and conceptual principles to let readers reach (or reevaluate) their own conclusions. We earnestly believe that, ignoring specific proposals, the desirability of major reform has a reasonable empirical and ethical basis. To scorn discussion and analysis of such major change, in light of the extraordinary problems associated with current policies, is frivolous and uncaring.

Bibliography

1988 heroin addiction, treatment statistics analyzed. (1988, December 21). *Madrid Diario*, p. 14. Cited in *JPRS: Narcotics* (1989, February 28, p. 22).

A foolish proposal to legalize hookers. (1996, August 2). *San Francisco Chronicle*.

Aaron, P., & Musto, D. (1981). Temperance and prohibition in America: A historical overview. In M. Moore & D. Gerstein (Eds.), *Alcohol and public policy: Beyond the shadow of prohibition* (pp. 127–81). Washington, DC: National Academy Press.

Abbey, A., Scott, R. O., & Smith, M. J. (1993). Physical, subjective, and social availability: Their relationship to alcohol consumption in rural and urban areas. *Addiction, 88*, 489–99.

Adlaf, E. M., Ivis, F. J., Smart, R. G., & Walsh, G. W. (1995). *The Ontario student drug use survey: 1977–1995*. Toronto: Addiction Research Foundation. *http://www.arf.org/isd/stats/studdrug.html*.

Advisory Council on the Misuse of Drugs. (1988). *Drug Misuse and AIDS*. London: Advisory Council on the Misuse of Drugs.

Ajzen, I., & Fishbein, M. (1981). *Understanding attitudes and predicting social behavior*. Englewood Cliffs, NJ: Prentice Hall.

Albrecht, H. J. (1989). Drug policy in the Federal Republic of Germany. In H. J. Albrecht & A. Kalmthout (Eds.), *Drug policies in Western Europe* (pp. 189–94). Frieburg, Germany: Eigenverlag Max-Planck Institut.

Albrecht, H. J., & Kalmthout, A. (Eds.), (1989). *Drug policies in Western Europe*. Frieburg, Germany: Eigenverlag Max-Planck Institut.

Aldrich, M. R., & Mikuriya, T. (1988). Savings in California marijuana law enforcement costs attributable to the Moscone Act of 1976: A summary. *Journal of Psychoactive Drugs, 20*, 75–81.

Ali, R., Auriacombe, M., Casa, M., Cottler, L., Farrell, M., Kleiber, D., Kreuzer, A., Ogborne, A., Rehm, J., & Ward, P. (1999). *Report of the external panel on the evaluation of the Swiss scientific studies of medically prescribed narcotics*

410

to drug addicts (WHO/PSA/96.14). Unpublished report to the World Health Organization.

Allgemeine (Frankfurt/Main Frankfurter). (1996, March 2). Article. Cited in FBIS *Narcotics Bulletin*, FBIS-TDD-96-0110L.

Almost all heroin seized in Spain was confiscated from less than 10 percent of detainees. (1991, October 17). *Madrid El Pais*, p. 18. In *JPRS: Narcotics* (1991, November 19, p. 38).

Altschuler, D., & Brounstein, P. (1991). Patterns of drug use, drug trafficking and other delinquency among inner-city adolescent males. *Criminology, 29*, 589–622.

American Broadcasting Corporation. (1988, September 13). A national town meeting: The legalization of drugs. *The Koppel Report*. New York: ABC News.

American Broadcasting Corporation. (1998, June 22). The battle over how to fight the war on drugs. *Nightline* (Transcript 98062201-jo7).

American Heart Association. (1998). Cigarette/tobacco smoke. *Heart and stroke guide. http://www.amhrt.org/Heart_and_Stroke_A_Z_Guide/bioci.html.*

American Pharmaceutical Association. (1903). Report of the Committee on Acquirement of Drug Habits. *Proceedings of the American Pharmaceutical Association, 51,* 476.

American Psychiatric Association (APA). (1994). *Diagnostic and statistical manual for mental disorders: Fourth edition.* Washington, DC: American Psychiatric Association.

Anderson, P. (1995). Alcohol and risk of physical harm. In H. Holder & G. Edwards (Eds.), *Alcohol and public policy: Evidence and issues* (pp. 82–113). Oxford: Oxford University Press.

Anglin, M. D., & Hser, Y. (1990). Treatment of drug abuse. In M. Tonry & J. Q. Wilson (Eds.), *Drugs and crime* (pp. 393–460). Chicago: University of Chicago Press.

Anthony, J., & Helzer, J. (1991). Syndromes of drug abuse and dependence. In L. Robbins & D. Regier (Eds.), *Psychiatric disorders in America*. New York: The Free Press; London: Collier Macmillan Publishers.

Anthony, J., Warner, L., & Kessler, R. (1994). Comparative epidemiology of dependence on tobacco, alcohol, controlled substances and inhalants: Basic findings from the National Comorbidity Study. *Experimental and Clinical Psychopharmacology, 2,* 244–68.

Archer, C. M. (1995, January 8). Hooker heaven: How lax justice fuels DC's prostitution boom. *Washington Post*, p. C1.

Arnao, G. (1994). Italian referendum deletes criminal sanctions for drug users. *Journal of Drug Issues, 24,* 483–8.

Asbury, H. (1938). *Sucker's progress: An informal history of gambling in America from the colonies to Canfield.* New York: Dodd, Mead and Co.

Associated Press. (1988, September 29). Congress hears drug legalization arguments. The Associated Press.

Associated Press. (1996, December 1). Swiss voters approve heroin distribution programs. The Associated Press.

Associated Press. (1997, January 9). Government to spend $1 million studying marijuana as medicine. *New York Times*, p. B10.

Associated Press. (1999, July 28). German Cabinet approves plan for "junkie" centers. *AP Worldstream*.

Association of The Bar of The City of New York. (1977). *The nation's toughest drug law: Evaluating the New York experience*. New York: Association of The Bar of The City of New York.

Bachman, J. G., Johnston, L. D., & O'Malley, P. M. (1990). Explaining the recent decline in cocaine use among young adults: Further evidence that perceived risks and disapproval lead to reduced drug use. *Journal of Health and Social Behavior*, *31*, 173–84.

Bachman, J. G., Johnston, L. D., & O'Malley, P. M. (1998). Explaining recent increases in students' marijuana use: Impacts of perceived risks and disapproval, 1976 through 1996. *American Journal of Public Health*, *88*, 887–92.

Bachman, J. G., Johnston, L. D., O'Malley, P. M., & Humphrey, R. H. (1988). Explaining the recent decline in marijuana use among young adults: Differentiating the effects of perceived risks, disapproval, and general lifestyle factors. *Journal of Health and Social Behavior*, *31*, 173–84.

Bachman, J., Wadsworth, K., O'Malley, P., Johnston, L., & Schulenberg, J. (1997). *Smoking, drinking, and drug use in young adulthood: The impacts of new freedoms and new responsibilities*. Mahwah, NJ: Lawrence Erlbaum Associates.

Baker, T. B. (Ed.). (1988). Models of addiction (Special issue). *Journal of Abnormal Psychology*, *97*, 115–245.

Bal, D., & Lloyd, J. (1994). Advocacy and government action for cancer prevention in older persons. *Cancer*, *74*, 2067–70.

Ball, J., & Ross, A. (1991). *The effectiveness of methadone maintenance treatment: Patients, programs, services, and outcomes*. New York: Springer Verlag.

Ball, J., & van de Wijngaart, G. (1994). A Dutch addict's view of methadone maintenance: An American and Dutch appraisal. *Addiction*, *89*, 799–802.

Ball, J., Rosen, L., Flueck, J., & Nurco, D. (1982). Lifetime criminality of heroin addicts in the United States. *Journal of Drug Issues*, *3*, 225–39.

Bammer, G., & McDonald, D. (1994). Report on a workshop on trial evaluation. In *Issues for designing and evaluating a "heroin trial"* (Working paper 8). Canberra, Australia: National Center for Epidemiology and Population Health.

Bammer, G., Dobler-Mikola, A., Fleming, P., Strang, J., & Uchtenhagen, A. (1999). The heroin prescribing debate: Integrating science and politics. *Science*, *284*, 1277–8.

Bandura, A. (1986). *Social foundations of thought and action: A social cognitive theory*. Englewood Cliffs, NJ: Prentice-Hall.

Bartholow, R. (1900). *A practical treatise on materia medica and therapeutics* (10th ed.). New York: D. Appleton and Company.

Beaumont, J. F. (1989, July 18). Health Ministry will undertake a campaign against the consumption of cocaine and cpiates. *Madrid El Pais*, 25. In *JPRS: Narcotics* (1989, September 26, p. 51).

Beccaria, C. (1764/1963). *Essay on crimes and punishments*. Indianapolis: Bobbs-Merrill.

Beck, J., & Rosenbaum, M. (1994). *Pursuit of ecstasy: The MDMA experience*. Albany, NY: State University of New York Press.

Becker, G. S., & Murphy, K. M. (1988). A theory of rational addiction. *Journal of Political Economy, 96*, 675–701.

Becker, G. S., Grossman, M., & Murphy, K. M. (1992). Rational addiction and the effect of price on consumption. In G. Loewenstein & J. Elster (Eds.), *Choice over time* (pp. 361–70). New York: Russell Sage Foundation.

Beierer, M., & Rigotti, N. (1992). Public policy for the control of tobacco-related disease. *Medical Clinics of North America, 76*, 515–39.

Beigel, H., & Beigel, A. (1977). *Beneath the badge*. New York: Harper & Row.

Bell, R. (1976). Moral views on gambling promulgated by major American religious bodies. In Commission on the Review of the National Policy toward Gambling, *Gambling in America, Appendix 1* (pp. 161–239). Washington, DC: U.S. Government Printing Office.

Bennett, T., & Wright, R. (1986). The impact of prescribing on the crimes of opioid users. *British Journal of Addiction, 81*, 265–73.

Bennett, W. (1989). Introduction. In Office of National Drug Control Policy, *National Drug Control Strategy* (pp. 1–10). Washington, DC: U.S. Government Printing Office.

Bennett, W. (1995, April 6). *Nightline* (Transcript #3619). American Broadcasting Companies, Inc.

Benson, B. L., & Rasmussen, D. W. (1991). The relationship between illicit drug enforcement and property crimes. *Contemporary Policy Issues, 9*, 106–15.

Benson, B. L., Kim, I., Rasmussen, D. W., & Zuehlke, T. W. (1992). Is property crime caused by drug use or by drug enforcement policy? *Applied Economics, 24*, 679–92.

Bentham, J. (1789/1948). *An introduction to the principles of morals and legislation*. Oxford: Basil Blackwell.

Bertram, E., Blachman, M., Sharp, K., & Andreas, P. (1996). *Drug war politics: The price of denial*. Berkeley, CA: California University Press.

Bieleman, B., Diaz, A., Merlo, G., & Kaplan, C. (1993). *Lines across Europe: Nature and extent of cocaine use in Barcelona, Rotterdam and Turin*. Amsterdam: Swets & Zeitlinger.

Bild (Hamburg). (1995, July 31). Article. Cited in FBIS *Narcotics Bulletin*, FBIS-TDD-95-031-L.

Black, D. (1976). *The behavior of law*. New York: Academic Press.

Blendon, R. J., & Young, J. T. (1998). The public and the war on illicit drugs. *Journal of the American Medical Association, 279*, 827–32.

Bless, R., Korf, D., & Freeman, M. (1993). *Urban drug policies in Europe, 1993*. Amsterdam: O + S, The Amsterdam Bureau of Social Research and Statistics.

Block, R. I., & Ghoneim, M. M. (1993). Effects of chronic marijuana use on human cognition. *Psychopharmacology, 110*, 219–28.

Blom, T., & van Mastrigt, H. (1994). The future of the Dutch model in the context of the war on drugs. In E. Leuw & I. H. Marshall (Eds.), *Between prohibition and legalization: The Dutch experiment in drug policy* (pp. 255–82). Amsterdam: Kugler.

Blower, S. M., & McLean, A. R. (1994). Prophylactic vaccines, risk behavior change, and the probability of eradicating HIV in San Francisco. *Science*, *265*, 1451–4.

Blumstein, A. (1993). Making rationality relevant. *Criminology*, *31*, 1–16.

Blumstein, A., Cohen, J., & Nagin, D. (Eds.). (1978). *Deterrence and incapacitation: Estimating the effects of criminal sanctions on crime rates*. Washington, DC: National Research Council.

Boaz, D. (1990). The consequences of prohibition. In D. Boaz (Ed.), *The crisis in drug prohibition* (pp. 1–9). Washington, DC: CATO Institute.

Boekhout van Solinge, T. (1997). Cannabis in France. In L. Böllinger (Ed.), *Cannabis science: From prohibition to human right*. Frankfurt am Main: Peter Lang. *http://www.frw.uva/nl/cedro/library/bremen95/france.html*.

Boekhout van Solinge, T. (1997). *The Swedish drug control system*. Amsterdam: University of Amsterdam Centre for Drug Research (CEDRO).

Bolling, A. (1989, July 18). Reporter accompanies police on trip through drug underworld. *Dagens Nyheter*.

Bonnie, R. J. (1986). The efficacy of law as a paternalistic instrument. In G. B. Melton (Ed.), *The law as a behavioral instrument: Nebraska symposium on motivation, 1985* (pp. 131–211). Lincoln, NE: University of Nebraska Press.

Bonnie, R. J., & Whitebread, C. H. (1974). *The marihuana conviction: A history of marihuana prohibition in the United States*. Charlottesville, VA: University Press of Virginia.

Borio, G. (1998). *Tobacco timeline*. *http://www.tobacco.org/History/Tobacco_History.html*.

Bosworth, F. (1884). A new therapeutic use for cocaine. *Medical News*, *5*, 533–4.

Botvin, G. J., Baker, E., Dusenbury, L., Botvin, E. M., & Diaz, T. (1995). Long-term follow-up results of a randomized drug abuse prevention trial in a white middle-class population. *Journal of the American Medical Association*, *273*, 1106–12.

Botvin, G. J., Batson, H. W., Witts-Vitale, S., Bess, V., Baker, E., & Dusenbury, L. (1989). A psychosocial approach to smoking prevention for urban black youth. *Public Health Reports*, *104*, 573–82.

Bourgois, P. (1996). In search of masculinity: violence, respect and sexuality among Puerto Rican crack dealers in East Harlem. *British Journal of Criminology*, *36*, 412–28.

Boys who use cocaine. (1904, December 8). *Pharmaceutical Era*, p. 586.

Boyum, D., & Reuter, P. (In press). Drug policy and social policy. In P. Heymann (Ed.), *Drug policy without blinders*. Cambridge, MA: Harvard University Press.

Braithwaite, J. (1989). *Crime, shame, and reintegration*. Cambridge, England: Cambridge University Press.

Branch, T. (1988). Let Koop do it: A prescription for the drug war. *The New Republic, 199*, 22–5.

Bravo, G., & Grob, C. (1996). Psychedelic psychotherapy. In B. W. Scotton, A. B. Chinen, & J. R. Battista (Eds.), *Textbook of transpersonal psychiatry and psychology* (pp. 335–43). New York: Basic Books.

Brecher, E. (1972). *Licit and illicit drugs*. Boston: Little Brown and Company.

Brehm, S. S., & Brehm, J. W. (1981). *Psychological reactance*. New York: Academic Press.

Brehm, S. S., & Weintraub, M. (1977). Physical barriers and psychological reactance: Two-year-olds' responses to threats to freedom. *Journal of Personality and Social Psychology, 35*, 830–6.

Brenner, H., Hernando-Briongos, P., & Goos, C. (1991). AIDS among drug users in Europe. *Drug and Alcohol Dependence, 29*, 171–81.

Bretteville-Jensen, A. L., & Sutton, M. (1996). The income-generating behavior of injecting drug users in Oslo. *Addiction, 91*, 63–80.

British youth are "biggest users in Europe." (1997, November 30). *The Independent*. (Circulated by Hemp On-Line e-mail news service on December 2, 1997; see *www.hemp.on.net.au*).

Brookoff, D., Cook, C. S., Williams, C., & Mann, C. S. (1994). Testing reckless drivers for cocaine and marijuana. *New England Journal of Medicine, 331*, 518–22.

Broome, J. (1995). *Weighing goods*. Oxford: Blackwell.

Bruneau, J., & Schechter, M. T. (1998, April 9). The politics of needles and AIDS. *New York Times*, p. A11.

Bruneau, J., Lamoth, F., Franco, E., Lachance, N., Désy, M., Soto, J., & Vincelette, J. (1997). High rates of HIV infection among injection drug users participating in needle exchange programs in Montreal: Results of a cohort study. *American Journal of Epidemiology, 146*, 994–1002.

Bucholz, K. K., & Robins, L. N. (1989). Sociological research on alcohol use, problems, and policy. *Annual Review of Sociology, 15*, 163–86.

Bundesamt für Statistik. (1991). *Kriminalstatistik Nr. 10: Zwanzig jahre drogen und strafrecht* [Twenty years of drugs and the criminal law]. Bern: Bundesamt für Statistik.

Bundesamtes fur Gesundheitswesen. (1990). *Soziale und praventive aspekte des drogen problems unter deondere Berucksictigung der Schweiz*. Lausanne: Schweizerische Fachstelle fur Alkoholprobleme, Université de Lausanne.

Bureau of Justice Statistics (BJS). (1985). *The national survey of crime severity*. Washington, DC: U.S. Department of Justice.

Bureau of Justice Statistics (BJS). (1992). *Drugs, crime, and the justice system*. Washington, DC: U.S. Department of Justice.

Bureau of Justice Statistics (BJS). (1994). *Drugs and crime facts, 1993*. Washington, DC: U.S. Department of Justice.

Bureau of Justice Statistics (BJS). (Biannual). *Correctional populations in the United States*. Washington, DC: U.S. Department of Justice.

Bureau of Justice Statistics (BJS). (Biannual). *Felony sentences in state courts*. Washington, DC: U.S. Department of Justice.

Burnham, J. (1968–9). New perspectives on the prohibition "experiment" of the 1920s. *Journal of Social History*, 2, 51–68.

Bushman, B. J. (1993). Human aggression while under the influence of alcohol and other drugs: An integrative research review. *Current Directions in Psychological Science*, 2, 148–52.

Bushway, S., Nagin, D., & Taylor, L. (1995). *The stigmatic impact of criminal records on legitimate employment* (working paper). Pittsburgh: Heinz School of Public Policy and Management, Carnegie Mellon University.

Califano, Jr., J. A. (1997, September 30). Marijuana: It's a hard drug. *Washington Post*, p. A21.

California Assembly Committee on Criminal Procedure (1968). *Deterrent effects of criminal sanctions*. Sacramento: Assembly of the State of California.

Cami, J., & Barrio, G. (1991). *Drug consumption in Spain: Trends, implications and policies*. Presented at the International Conference on Drug Policies and Problems, RAND Drug Policy Research Center, Washington, DC, 1991.

Campbell, D. (1993, May 10). Arrests in sweep of London crack-dealing area. *The Guardian*, p. 6.

Cantor, J., Harrison, K., & Krcmar, M. (1995). Ratings and advisories for television programming: University of Wisconsin, Madison study. In *National television violence study: Executive summary, 1994–1995* (pp. 41–7). Studio City, CA: Mediascope, Inc.

Carlisle, J. (1976). Gambling in Detroit: An informal history. In Commission on the Review of the National Policy toward Gambling, *Gambling in America, Appendix 1* (pp. 144–60). Washington, DC: U.S. Government Printing Office.

Carroll, J. S. (1978). A psychological approach to deterrence: The evaluation of crime opportunities. *Journal of Personality and Social Psychology*, 36, 1512–20.

Casey, J. T., & Scholz, J. T. (1991). Boundary effects of vague risk information on tax payer decisions. *Organizational Behavior and Human Decision Processes*, 50, 360–94.

Caulkins, J. (1995). *Estimating the elasticities and cross elasticities of demand for cocaine and heroin* (working paper 95–13). Pittsburgh: Heinz School of Public Policy and Management, Carnegie Mellon University.

Caulkins, J. (1997). Is crack cheaper than (powder) cocaine? *Addiction*, 92, 1437–43.

Caulkins, J. (1999). Can supply factors suppress marijuana use by youth? *Drug Policy Analysis Bulletin*, 7, 3–5.

Caulkins, J., & McCaffrey, D. (1993). *Drug sellers in the household population* (unpublished manuscript). Santa Monica, CA: RAND.

Caulkins, J., & Reuter, P. (1998). What price data tell us about drug markets. *Journal of Drug Issues*, 28, 593–612.

Caulkins, J., Rydell, C. P., Everingham, S., Chiesa, J., & Bushway, S. (1999). *An ounce of prevention, a pound of uncertainty: The cost-effectiveness of school-based drug prevention programs*. Santa Monica, CA: RAND.

Caulkins, J., Rydell, C. P., Schwabe, W. L., & Chisea, J. (1997). *Mandatory minimum drug sentences: Throwing away the key or the taxpayers' money?* Santa Monica, CA: RAND.

Celarier, M. (1997). Privatization: A case study in corruption. *Journal of International Affairs, 50*, 531–44.

Center for Addiction and Substance Abuse (CASA). (1994). *The cost of substance abuse to America's health care system: Medicare.* New York: Center for Addiction and Substance Abuse.

Center for Addiction and Substance Abuse (CASA). (1995). *Legalization: Panacea or Pandora's box.* New York: Center on Addiction and Substance Abuse.

Center for Addiction and Substance Abuse (CASA). (1996). *Survey of California voters on Proposition 215 and marijuana legalization.* New York: Center on Addiction and Substance Abuse.

Centers for Disease Control (CDC). (1990). Cigarette advertising – United States, 1988. *Morbidity and Mortality Weekly Report, 39*, 261.

Centers for Disease Control (CDC). (1993). Cigarette smoking – Attributable mortality and years of potential life lost – United States, 1990. *Morbidity and Mortality Weekly Report, 42*, 645–9.

Centers for Disease Control (CDC). (1994). *Tobacco information and prevention sourcepage. http://www.cdc.gov/nccdphp/osh/adstat3.htm.*

Centers for Disease Control and Prevention. (1997). Update: Trends in AIDS Incidence – United States, 1996. *Morbidity and Mortality Weekly Report, 46. http://www.ama-assn.org/special/hiv/newsline/special/mmwr/mmwr4637/html.*

Central Committee on the Treatment of Heroin Addicts. (1997). *Investigating the Medical Prescription of Heroin.* No publisher identified.

Centre for Drug Research (CEDRO). (1999, January 5). *National estimates of drug use in the Netherlands available, for first time* (press release). Amsterdam: Centre for Drug Research.

Chaloupka, F. J., & Laixuthai, A. (1994). *Do youths substitute alcohol and marijuana? Some econometric evidence* (working paper 4662). Cambridge, MA: National Bureau of Economic Research.

Chirinko, R. S., & Harper, E. P. (1993). Buckle up or slow down? New estimates of offsetting behavior and their implications for automobile safety regulation. *Journal of Policy Analysis and Management, 12*, 270–96.

Christie, P. (1991). *The effects of cannabis legislation in South Australia on levels of cannabis use.* Adelaide: Drug and Alcohol Services Council.

Christie, R. (1991). Authoritarianism and related constructs. In J. P. Robinson, P. R. Shaver, & L. S. Wrightsman (Eds.), *Measures of personality and social psychological attitudes* (pp. 501–71). New York: Academic Press.

Cialdini, R. B. (1985). *Influence: Science and practice.* Glenview, IL: Scott, Foresman & Co.

Cialdini, R. B., Kallgren, C. A., & Reno, R. R. (1991). A focus theory of normative conduct: A theoretical refinement and reevaluation of the role of norms in human behavior. In M. Zanna (Ed.), *Advances in experimental social psychology, Vol. 24* (pp. 201–34). New York: Academic Press.

CJ Europe. (1993, May–June). AIDS success converts critics of Dutch drugs policy. *CJ Europe, 3,* 4.

CJ Europe. (1994). The Netherlands: Dutch drug policies changing in light of increasing criminality. *CJ Europe, 4,* 9–10.

Clark, N. H. (1976). *Deliver us from evil: An interpretation of American prohibition.* New York: Norton.

Clawson, P., & Rensellaer, L. (1996). *The Andean cocaine industry.* New York: St. Martin's Press.

Clotfelter, C., & Cook, P. (1989). *Selling hope: State lotteries in America.* Cambridge, MA: Harvard University Press.

Clotfelter, C., Cook, P., Edel, J., & Moore, M. (1999). *State Lotteries at the Turn of the Century: Report to the National Gambling Impact Study Commission.* Washington, DC: National Gambling Impact Study Commission (CD-ROM).

Coate, D., & Grossman, M. (1988). Effects of alcohol beverage prices and legal drinking ages on youth alcohol use. *Journal of Law and Economics, 31,* 145–71.

Cockburn, A. (1993). Beat the devil: A press conference by "drug czar" Lee Brown. *The Nation, 257,* 560–1.

Coffin, P. O. (1997, August 9). I smell a rat. *Slate. http://www.slate.com/HeyWait/97-08-09/HeyWait.asp.*

Cohen, H. (1972). Multiple drug use considered in the light of the stepping-stone hypothesis. *The International Journal of the Addictions, 7,* 27–55.

Cohen, P. (1989). *Cocaine use in Amsterdam in non-deviant subcultures.* Universiteit van Amsterdam: Instituut voor Sociale Geografie.

Cohen, P. D. A., & Sas, A. (1996). *Cannabis use, a stepping stone to other drugs? The case of Amsterdam.* Amsterdam: Department of Human Geography, University of Amsterdam. *http://www.frw.uva.nl/cedro/library/ASC95/ASC95.html.*

Cohen, P. D. A., & Sas, A. (1998). *Cannabis use in Amsterdam.* Amsterdam: Department of Human Geography, University of Amsterdam.

Cohn, E. S., & White, S. O. (1990). *Legal socialization: A study of norms and rules.* New York: Springer Verlag.

Collins, D. J., & Lapsley, H. M. (1992). Costs and benefits. *International Journal on Drug Policy, 3,* 153–9.

Commission of the European Communities. (1989). Europeans and the prevention of cancer. *Standard Eurobarometer, March–April.*

Committee on the Social and Economic Impact of Pathological Gambling. (1999). *Pathological Gambling.* Washington, DC: National Academy Press.

Common Cause. (1997, May 13). *Tobacco political giving hits record $9.9 million for '96 elections. http://www.commoncause.org/publications/051397_sdy.htm.*

Common Cause. (1998, April 16). *Under the influence: Congress backs down to big booze. http://www.commoncause.org/publications/booz_toc.htm.*

Compton, D. R., Dewey, W. L., & Martin, B. R. (1990). Cannabis dependence and tolerance production. *Advances in Alcohol & Substance Abuse, 9,* 129–47.

Connelly, M. T. (1980). *The response to prostitution in the Progressive era.* Chapel Hill, NC: University of North Carolina Press.

Cook, F. J. (1961). *A two dollar bet means murder.* New York: Dial Press.

Cook, P. (1980). Research in criminal deterrence: Laying the groundwork for the second decade. In N. Morris & M. Tonry (Eds.), *Crime and Justice: An Annual Review of Research, Vol. 2* (pp. 211–68). Chicago: University of Chicago Press.

Cook, T., & Campbell, D. (1979). *Quasi-experimentation: Design and analysis issues for field settings.* Boston: Houghton Mifflin.

Council on Compulsive Gambling. (1996, March 20). *1995 statistics for 1-800-GAMBLING helpline. http://www.800gambler.org/95stats.htm.*

Courtwright, D. (1982). *Dark paradise: Opiate addiction in America before 1940.* Cambridge, MA: Harvard University Press.

Courtwright, D., Joseph, H., & Des Jarlais, D. (1989). *Addicts who survived.* Knoxville, TN: University of Tennessee Press.

Crime Prevention and Criminal Justice Branch. (1981). *Second United Nations Survey of Crime Trends.* Vienna: United Nations.

Dawes, R. M. (1988). *Rational choice in an uncertain world.* San Diego: Harcourt Brace Jovanovich.

Decker, J. F. (1979). *Prostitution: Regulation and control.* Littleton, CO: Fred B. Rothman.

Degkwitz, P., Chorzelski, G., & Krausz, M. (1993). Five years of methadone prescription in Germany. In M. Reisinger (Ed.), *Aids and drug addiction in the European Community* (pp. 79–89). Lisbon, Portugal: European Monitoring Centre for Drugs and Drug Addiction.

de Kort, M. (1994). A short history of drugs in the Netherlands. In E. Leuw & I. H. Marshall (Eds.), *Between prohibition and legalization: The Dutch experiment in drug policy* (pp. 3–22). Amsterdam: Kugler.

Delegatión del Gobernio para el Plan Nacional Sobre Drogas. (1990). *Plan Nacional Sobre Drogas: Memoria 1990.* Madrid: Ministerio de Sanidad y Consumo.

Dennis, R. J. (1990). The economics of legalizing drugs. *The Atlantic, 266,* 126–31.

Derks, J. (1997). The dispensing of injectable morphine in Amsterdam: Experiences, results and implications for the Swiss project for the medical prescription of narcotics. In D. Lewis, C. Gear, L. M. Laubli, & D. Langenick-Cartwright (Eds.), *The medical prescription of narcotics: Scientific foundations and practical experiences* (pp. 167–79). Seattle: Hogrefe and Huber Publishers.

Dertouzos, J., Larson, E. V., & Ebener, P. (1999). *The economic costs and implication of high technology thefts.* Santa Monica, CA: RAND.

Des Jarlais, D. C., & Friedman, S. R. (1994). Aids and the use of injected drugs. *Scientific American, 270,* 82–6.

Des Jarlais, D. C., Friedman, S. R., & Ward, T. P. (1993). Harm reduction: A public health response to the AIDS epidemic among injecting drug users. *Annual Review of Public Health, 14*, 413–50.

Des Jarlais, D. C., Friedmann, P., Hagan, H., & Friedman, S. R. (1996). The protective effect of AIDS-related behavioral change among injection drug users: A cross-national study. *American Journal of Public Health, 86*, 1780–5.

Devlin, P. (1959/1965). *The enforcement of morals*. New York: Oxford University Press.

de Zwart, W. M., Stam, H., & Kuipers, S. B. M. (1997). *Kerngegevens: Roken, drinken, drugsgebruik en gokken onder scholieren vanaf 10 Jaar*. Utrecht: Trimbos-instituut.

Die Welt (Berlin). (1994, September 6). Article. Cited in FBIS *Narcotics Bulletin*, JPRS-TDD-94-040-L.

Die Welt (Berlin). (1996, October 9). Article. Cited in FBIS *Narcotics Bulletin*, FBIS-WEU96-197.

DiFranza, J., Richards, J., & Paulman, P. (1991). RJR Nabisco's cartoon camel promotes Camel cigarettes to children. *Journal of the American Medical Association, 266*, 3149–53.

DiNardo, H. (1993). Law enforcement, the price of cocaine, and cocaine use. *Mathematical and Computer Modeling, 17*, 53–64.

DiNardo, J., & Lemieux, T. (1992). *Alcohol, marijuana, and American youth: The unintended consequences of government regulation* (working draft WD-59220-DPRC). Santa Monica, CA: RAND.

Distilled Spirits Council of the United States (DISCUS). (1996). *Public revenues from alcohol beverages, 1995*. Washington, DC: DISCUS. *http://www.discus.health.org/govlev.htm*.

Distilled Spirits Council of the United States (DISCUS). (1997). *State gallonage excise tax rates on alcohol beverages, 1997*. Washington, DC: DISCUS.

Doblin, R. E., & Kleiman, M. (1991). Marijuana as antiemetic medicine: A survey of oncologists experiences and attitudes. *Journal of Clinical Oncology, 9*, 1314–19.

Dole, V. (1972). Editorial. *Journal of the American Medical Association, 220*, 1493.

Donnelly, N., Hall, W., & Christie, P. (1995). The effects of partial decriminalisation on cannabis use in South Australia 1985–1993. *Australian Journal of Public Health, 19*, 281–7.

Douglas, M. (1966). *Purity and danger: An analysis of concepts of pollution and taboo*. London: Routledge.

D'Oro, R. (1997, December 28). Alaska growers sport "very green thumbs." *Anchorage Daily News*, p. 1F.

Driessen, F. M., Van Dam, G., & Olsson, E. B. (1989). De ontwikkeling van het cannabisgebruik in Nederland, enkele Europese landen en de VS sinds 1969. *Tijdschrift voor Alcohol, Drugs en Andere Psychotrope Stoffen, 15*, 2–14.

Driscoll, R., Davis, K. E., & Lipetz, M. E. (1972). Parental interference and romantic love. *Journal of Personality and Social Psychology, 24*, 1–10.

Drug Enforcement Administration (DEA). (1992). *The illicit drug wholesale/retail price report*. Washington, DC: U.S. Department of Justice.

Drug Enforcement Administration (DEA). (1994). *Drug legalization: Myths and misconceptions*. Washington, DC: U.S. Department of Justice.

Drug Policy Foundation. (1993). *The Drug Policy Letter, November/December*, 1–3.

Duke, S., & Gross, A. (1993). *America's longest war: Rethinking our tragic crusade against drugs*. New York: G. P. Putnam.

Dukes, M. N. G. (Ed.). (1996). *Meyler's side effects of drugs, 13th edition*. Amsterdam: Elsevier Science.

Duncan, C. H. (1976). Federal gambling taxation. In Commission on the Review of the National Policy toward Gambling, *Gambling in America, Appendix 1* (pp. 887–917). Washington, DC: U.S. Government Printing Office.

Dworkin, R. (1978). *Taking rights seriously*. Cambridge, MA: Harvard University Press.

Ebener, P. A., Caulkins, J. P., Geschwind, S. A., McCaffrey, D., & Saner, H. L. (1994). *Improving data and analysis to support national substance abuse policy: Main report*. Santa Monica, CA: RAND.

The Economist. (1996, October 12). Drug dealers? What drug dealers? *The Economist*, p. 58.

The Economist. (1997, March 29). Neighbours. *The Economist*, p. 25.

The Economist. (1998, October 17). Swiss people power. *The Economist*, p. 58.

Edsall, T., & Edsall, M. (1991). *Chain reaction: The impact of race, rights and taxes on American politics*. New York: W. W. Norton.

Edwards, G. (1969). The British approach to the treatment of heroin addiction. *Lancet, 1*, 768–72.

Edwards, G., Anderson, P., Babor, T. F., Casswell, S., Ferrence, R., Giesbrecht, N., Godfrey, C., Holder, H. D., Lemmens, P., Mäkelä, K., Midanik, L. T., Norström, T., Österberg, E., Romesljö, A., Room, R., Simpura, J., & Skog, O. (1994). *Alcohol policy and the public good*. Oxford: Oxford University Press.

Eilperin, J., & Torry, S. (1998, August 8). Tobacco bill written off in House. *Washington Post*, p. A6.

Eisner, M. (1992). Policies towards open drug scenes and street crime: The case of the city of Zurich. *European Journal on Criminal Policy and Research, 1*, 61–75.

Ekland-Olsen, S., Lieb, J., & Zurcher, L. (1984). The paradoxical impact of criminal sanctions: Some microstructural findings. *Law and Society Review, 18*, 159–78.

Ellickson, P. L. (1995). Schools. In R. H. Coombs & D. M. Ziedonis (Eds.), *Handbook on drug abuse prevention* (pp. 93–120). Needham Heights, MA: Allyn & Bacon.

Ellickson, P. L. (1998). Preventing adolescent substance use: Lessons from Project ALERT program. In J. Crane (Ed.), *Social programs that work* (pp. 201–24). New York: Russell Sage.

Ellickson, P. L., Bell, R., & McGuigan, K. (1993). Preventing adolescent drug use: Long term results of a junior high program. *American Journal of Public Health, 83,* 856–61.

Ellickson, R. C. (1987). A critique of economic and sociological theories of social control. *Journal of Legal Studies, 16,* 67–99.

Elliott, D. S., Huizinga, D., & Ageton, S. S. (1985). *Explaining delinquency and drug use.* Beverly Hills, CA: Sage.

Ellsworth, P. C., & Gross, S. R. (1994). Hardening of the attitudes: Americans' views on the death penalty. *Journal of Social Issues, 50,* 19–52.

Elster, J. (1992). *Local justice.* New York: Russell Sage.

EMCDDA. (1996). *Annual report on the state of the drugs problem in the European Union, 1995.* Lisbon, Portugal: European Monitoring Centre for Drugs and Drug Addiction.

EMCDDA. (1997). *Annual report on the state of the drugs problem in the European Union, 1997.* Lisbon, Portugal: European Monitoring Centre for Drugs and Drug Addiction.

Environmental Protection Agency (EPA). (1993). *Respiratory health effects of passive smoking: Lung cancer and other disorders.* Washington, DC: U.S. Department of Health and Human Services.

Epoca (Madrid). (1989, January 2). Article. Cited in FBIS *Narcotics Bulletin* (7 February 1989, p. 18).

Epstein, E. (1996, November 6). Medicinal pot initiative rolls to an easy victory. *San Francisco Chronicle,* p. A1.

Epstein, E. J. (1978). *Agency of fear.* New York: Putnam.

Erickson, M. L., & Gibbs, J. P. (1978). Objective and perceptual properties of legal punishment and the deterrence doctrine. *Social Problems, 25,* 253–64.

Erickson, P. G. (1989). Living with prohibition: Regular cannabis users, legal sanctions, and informal controls. *International Journal of the Addictions, 24,* 175–88.

Erkelens, L. H., & van Alem, V. C. M. (1994). Dutch prison drug policy – Towards an intermediate connection. In E. Leuw & I. H. Marshall (Eds.), *Between prohibition and legalization: The Dutch experiment in drug policy* (pp. 75–94). Amsterdam: Kugler.

Erling, J. (1993, May 12). Experts rack their brains over decline in drug-related deaths. *Die Welt* (Hamburg), p. 2.

Ernst and Young (annual). *Compilation of Gaming Data.* [No city provided.]

Evans, R. L., & Berent, I. M. (Eds.). (1992). *Drug legalization: For and against.* La Salle, IL: Open Court Publishing.

Everingham, S. S., & Rydell, C. P. (1994). *Modeling the demand for cocaine.* Santa Monica, CA: RAND.

Ezell, J. (1960). *Fortune's merry wheel: The lottery in America.* Cambridge, MA: Harvard University Press.

Fact Research, Inc. (1976). Gambling in perspective. In Commission on the Review of the National Policy toward Gambling, *Gambling in America, Appendix 1* (pp. 1–101). Washington, DC: U.S. Government Printing Office.

Fagan, J. (1990). Intoxication and aggression. In M. Tonry & J. Q. Wilson (Eds.), *Drugs and crime: Crime and justice, a review of research, Vol. 13* (pp. 241–320). Chicago: University of Chicago Press.

Farr, K. A. (1990). Revitalizing the drug decriminalization debate. *Crime & Delinquency, 36,* 223–37.

Farrell, G., Mansur, K., & Tullis, M. (1996). Cocaine and heroin in Europe 1983–93: A cross-national comparison of trafficking and prices. *British Journal of Criminology, 36,* 255–81.

Farrell, M. (1996). *Drug prevention: A review of the legislation, regulation, and delivery of methadone in 12 member states of the European Union: Final report.* Luxembourg: Office for Official Publications of the European Communities.

Farrell, M., & Hall, W. (1998). The Swiss heroin trials: Testing alternative approaches. *British Medical Journal, 316,* 639.

Federal Bureau of Investigation (FBI). (Annual). *Uniform crime reports: Crime in America.* Washington, DC: U.S. Department of Justice.

Feinberg, J. (1984). *The moral limits of the criminal law, Volume 1: Harm to others.* New York: Oxford University Press.

Feinberg, J. (1985). *The moral limits of the criminal law, Volume 2: Offense to others.* New York: Oxford University Press.

Feinberg, J. (1986). *The moral limits of the criminal law, Volume 3: Harm to self.* New York: Oxford University Press.

Feinberg, J. (1988). *The moral limits of the criminal law, Volume 4: Harmless wrongdoing.* New York: Oxford University Press.

Fendrich, M., & Vaughn, C. M. (1994). Diminished lifetime substance use over time: An inquiry into differential underreporting. *Public Opinion Quarterly, 58,* 96–123.

Ferguson, D., & Horwood, K. (1997). Early onset cannabis use and psychosocial adjustment in young adults. *Addiction, 92,* 279–96.

Fergusson, D. M., & Horwood, L. J. (2000). Does cannabis use encourage other forms of illicit drug use? *Addiction, 95,* 505–20.

Fessier, Jr., M. (1993, August 26). Trail's End. *Los Angeles Times* (Magazine), p. 26.

Feucht, T., & Kyle, G. (1996). *Methamphetamine use among adult arrestees: Findings from the Drug Use Forecasting (DUF) program.* Washington, DC: National Institute of Justice.

Fish, J. M. (Ed.). (1998). *How to legalize drugs.* Northvale, NJ: Jason Aronson, Inc.

Fiske, A. J., & Tetlock, P. E. (1997). Taboo trade-offs: Reactions to transactions that transgress the spheres of justice. *Political Psychology, 18,* 255–97.

Fitzgerald, J. L., & Mulford, H. A. (1992). Consequences of increasing alcohol availability: The Iowa experience revisited. *British Journal of Addiction, 87,* 267–74.

Flanigan, T. J., & Maguire, K. (1984). *Sourcebook of criminal justice statistics.* Washington, DC: Bureau of Justice Statistics, U.S. Department of Justice.

Flexner, A. (1914). *Prostitution in Europe.* New York: Century Company.

Flynn, J. (1994, April 24). Letter from Amsterdam: Where the sixties keep on tokin. *Business Week*, pp. 26A–E.

Forte, R. (Ed.). (1997). *Entheogens and the future of religion.* San Francisco: Council on Spiritual Practices.

Freeman, J. (1989–90). The feminist debate over prostitution reform: Prostitutes' rights groups, radical feminists and the (im)possibility of consent. *Berkeley Women's Law Journal, 5,* 75–109.

Freeman, R. B. (1995). The labor market. In J. Q. Wilson & J. Petersilia (Eds.), *Crime.* San Francisco: ICS Press.

French, J. R. P., Jr., & Raven, B. (1959). The basis of social power. In D. Cartwright (Ed.), *Studies in social power* (pp. 150–67). Ann Arbor, MI: Institute for Social Research.

French Observatory of Drugs and Drug Addiction. (1996). *Drugs and drug addiction: Indicators and trends.* Paris: French Observatory of Drugs and Drug Addiction.

Friedman, M. (1991). The war we are losing. In M. Kraus & E. Lazear (Eds.), *Searching for alternatives: Drug control policies in the United States* (pp. 53–67). Stanford, CA: Hoover Institute Press.

Gable, R. S. (1993). Toward a comparative overview of dependence potential and acute toxicity of psychoactive substances used nonmedically. *American Journal of Drug & Alcohol Abuse, 19,* 263–81.

Gable, R. S. (1997). Opportunity costs of drug prohibition. *Addiction, 92,* 1179–82.

Gallup Organization. (1991, October). *The Gallup Poll Monthly,* p. 73.

Galston, W., & Wasserman, D. (1996). Gambling away our moral capital. *The Public Interest, Spring,* 58–71.

Gearing, F. R., & Schweitzer, M. D. (1974). An epidemiologic evaluation of long-term methadone maintenance treatment for heroin addiction. *American Journal of Epidemiology, 100,* 101–12.

Geerken, M. R., & Gove, W. R. (1975). Deterrence: Some theoretical considerations. *Law and Society Review, 9,* 497–513.

Geis, G. (1971). *Not the law's business? An examination of homosexuality, abortion, prostitution, narcotics and gambling in the United States.* Rockville, MD: National Institute of Mental Health.

Gendreau, P., & Goddard, M. (1991). *The realities of punishment: Implications for offender rehabilitation.* Presented at the Conference on the Interface Between Treatment and Punishment. Santa Monica, CA: Drug Policy Research Center, RAND.

General Accounting Office. (1993). *Needle exchange programs research suggests promise as an AIDS prevention strategy.* Report to the Chairman, Select Committee on Narcotics Abuse and Control, House of Representatives. Washington, DC: U.S. Government Printing Office.

General Accounting Office. (1997). *Drug courts: Overview of growth, characteristics, and results* (GAO/GGD-97-106). Washington, DC: U.S. Government Printing Office.

George, R. P. (1993). *Making men moral: Civil liberties and public morality.* New York: Oxford University Press.

Gerstein, D., & Green, L. (Eds.). (1993). *Preventing drug abuse.* Washington, DC: National Academy Press.

Gerstein, D., & Harwood, H. (1990). *Treating drug problems.* Washington, DC: National Academy Press.

Gerstein, D., Foote, M., & Ghadialy, R. (1997). *The prevalence and correlates of treatment for drug problems.* Rockville, MD: Substance Abuse and Mental Health Services Administration.

Gerstein, D., Harwood, H., Suter, N., & Malloy, K. (1994). *Evaluating recovery services: The California Drug and Alcohol Treatment Assessment (CALDATA).* Sacramento, CA: California Department of Alcohol and Drug Programs.

Gfrocrer, J., Wright, D., & Kopstein, A. (1997). Prevalence of youth substance use: The impact of methodological differences between two national surveys. *Drug & Alcohol Dependence, 47,* 19–30.

Gibbs, J. P. (1975). *Crime, punishment, and deterrence.* New York: Elsevier.

Gieringer, D. (1996). Marijuana research: Waterpipe study. *Multidisciplinary Association for Psychedelic Studies, 6,* 59–63.

Glantz, S., Barnes, D., Bero, L., Hanauer, P., & Slade, J. (1995). Looking through a keyhole at the tobacco industry. *Journal of the American Medical Association, 274,* 219–24.

Golden, T. (1997, July 11). Misreading Mexico: How Washington stumbled. *New York Times,* p. A1.

Golden, T. (1998, September 19). Swiss recount key drug role of Salinas kin. *New York Times,* p. A1.

Goldstein, A. (1994). *Addiction: From biology to drug policy.* New York: W. H. Freeman & Co.

Goldstein, A., & Kalant, H. (1990). Drug policy: Striking the right balance. *Science, 249,* 1513–21.

Goldstein, P. (1985). The drug/violence nexus: A tripartite conceptual framework. *Journal of Drug Issues, 14,* 493–506.

Goldstein, P., Brownstein, H. H., & Ryan, P. J. (1992). Drug-related homicide in New York: 1984 and 1988. *Crime & Delinquency, 38,* 459–76.

Goldstein, P., Brownstein, H. H., Ryan, P. J., & Bellucci, P. A. (1989). Crack and homicide in New York City, 1988: A conceptually based event analysis. *Contemporary Drug Problems, 16,* 651–87.

Goldstein, P., Lipton, D. S., Preble, E., Sobel, I., Miller, T., Abbot, W., Paige, W., & Soto, F. (1984). The marketing of street heroin in New York City. *Journal of Drug Issues, Summer,* 553–66.

Golub, A., & Johnson, B. (1997). Crack's decline: Some surprises across U.S. cities. *NIJ Research in Brief, July.*

Goode, E. (1989). *Drugs in American society* (3d ed.). New York: Alfred A. Knopf.

Goode, E. (1997). *Between politics and reason: The drug legalization debate.* New York: St. Martin's Press.

Goodman, R. (1995). *The luck business: The devastating consequences and broken promises of America's gambling explosion.* New York: Free Press.

Gossop, M., Marsden, J., Stewart, D., & Edwards, C. (1997). The National Treatment Outcome Research Study in the United Kingdom: Six-month follow-up outcomes. *Psychology of Addictive Behaviors, 11,* 324–37.

Gottfredson, D. (1997). School based crime prevention. In L. Sherman (Ed.), *Preventing crime: What works, what doesn't, what's promising.* Washington, DC: National Institute of Justice.

Gottfredson, M. R., & Hirschi, T. (1990). *A general theory of crime.* Stanford, CA: Stanford University Press.

Gould, A. (1988). *Conflict and control in welfare policy: The Swedish experience.* London: Longman.

Gould, A. (1989). Cleaning the people's home: Recent developments in Sweden's addiction policy. *British Journal of Addiction, 84,* 731–41.

Grapendaal, M., Leuw, E., & Nelen, H. (1995). A world of opportunities: Lifestyle and economic behavior of heroin addicts in Amsterdam. Albany, NY: State University of New York Press.

Grasmick, H. G., & Bryjak, G. J. (1980). The deterrent effect of perceived severity of punishment. *Social Forces, 59,* 471–91.

Grasmick, H. G., & Bursik, H. J., Jr. (1990). Conscience, significant others, and rational choice: Extending the deterrence model. *Law & Society Review, 24,* 837–61.

Grasmick, H. G., & Green, D. E. (1981). Deterrence and the morally committed. *The Sociological Quarterly, 22,* 1–14.

Green, A. S. (1997, October 21). Pot referendum get its money from out of state. *The Oregonian.*

Grinspoon, L., & Bakalar, J. B. (1990). Arguments for a harmfulness tax. *Journal of Drug Issues, 20,* 599–604.

Grob, P. J. (1992). The needle park in Zurich: The story and the lessons to be learned. *European Journal on Criminal Policy and Research, 1,* 48–60.

Grogger, J. (1992). Arrests, persistent youth joblessness and black-white employment differentials. *Review of Economics and Statistics, 74,* 100–6.

Grossman, M., Chaloupka, F. J., & Brown, C. C. (1995). *The demand for cocaine by young adults: A rational addiction approach* (working paper 5713). Cambridge, MA: National Bureau of Economic Research.

Grossman, M., Chaloupka, F. J., & Brown, C. C. (1998). The demand for cocaine by young adults: A rational addiction approach. *Journal of Health Economics, 17,* 427–74.

Grund, J. P. (1993). *Drug use as a social ritual: Functionality, symbolism, and determinants of self-regulation.* Rotterdam: Instituut vor Verslavingsonderzoek (IVO).

Grund, J. P., & Blanken, P. (1993). *From chasing the dragon to Chinezen.* The Hague, Netherlands: CIP-Gegevens Konninklijke Bibliotheek.

Gruson, L. (1986, November 9). Corruption is brotherly in Philadelphia. *New York Times,* p. A4.

GTECH Corporation. (1996). *The national gaming survey*. From a May 22, 1997 facsimile from the American Gaming Association.

Gunby, P. (1994). Canada reduces cigarette tax to fight smuggling. *Journal of the American Medical Association, 271*, 647.

Gusfield, J. (1963). *Symbolic crusade: Status politics and the American temperance movement*. Urbana, IL: University of Illinois Press.

Gusfield, J. (1993). The social symbolism of smoking and health. In R. Rabin & S. Sugarman (Eds.), *Smoking policy: Law, politics and culture* (pp. 49–68). New York: Oxford University Press.

Gustafson, J. S. (1995). *State resources and services related to alcohol and other drug problems, Fiscal year 1994*. Washington, DC: National Association of State Alcohol and Drug Abuse Directors.

Gutzwiller, F., & Uchtenhagen, A. (1997). Heroin substitution: Part of the fight against drug dependency. In D. Lewis, C. Gear, L. M. Laubli, & D. Langenick-Cartwright (Eds.), *The medical prescription of narcotics: Scientific foundations and practical experiences* (pp. 295–300). Seattle: Hogrefe and Huber Publishers.

Haaga, J., & Reuter, P. (1995). Prevention: The (lauded) orphan of drug policy. In R. Coombs & D. Ziedonis (Eds.), *Handbook on drug abuse prevention* (pp. 3–17). Englewood Cliffs, NJ: Allyn and Bacon.

Haemmig, R. B. (1995). Harm reduction in Bern: From outreach to heroin maintenance. *Bulletin of the New York Academy of Medicine, Winter*, 371–9.

Haidt, J., Koller, S. H., & Dias, M. G. (1993). Affect, culture, and morality, or is it wrong to eat your dog? *Journal of Personality & Social Psychology, 65*, 613–28.

Hair, W. I. (1976). *Carnival of fury: Robert Charles and the New Orleans race riot of 1900*. Baton Rouge, LA: Louisiana State University Press.

Hall, G. M. (1979). *Prostitution in the modern world*. New York: Garland Publishing.

Hall, W. (1994). The health and psychological effects of cannabis use. *Current Issues in Criminal Justice, 6*, 209–20.

Hall, W. (1997a). Marijuana, myths, marijuana fact. *Science, 278*, 75.

Hall, W. (1997b). The recent Australian debate about the prohibition on cannabis use. *Addiction, 92*, 1109–15.

Hall, W. (1998). Cannabis and psychosis. *Drug and Alcohol Review, 17*, 433–44.

Hall, W., Room, R., & Bondy, S. (1995). *A comparative appraisal of the health and psychological consequences of alcohol, cannabis, nicotine and opiate use* (unpublished document). Toronto: Addiction Research Foundation.

Hall, W., Solowij, N., & Lemon, J. (1994). *The health and psychological consequences of cannabis use*. Canberra, Australia: Government Printing Office.

Hammond, W. (1886). Cocaine and the so-called cocaine habit. *New York Medical Journal, 44*, 637–9.

Hansen, K. M. (1990, March 12). Police inspector declares addiction situation grim. *Oslo Aftenposten*, 3. In *JPRS: Narcotics* (1990 April 17, p. 23).

Harris, J. F., & Goldstein, A. (1998, April 23). Puncturing an AIDS initiative. *Washington Post*, p. A1.

Harris, R. J., & Monaco, G. E. (1978). Psychology of pragmatic implication: Information processing between the lines. *Journal of Experimental Psychology: General, 107,* 1–22.

Harsanyi, J. C. (1990). Interpersonal utility comparisons. In J. Eatwell, M. Milgate, & P. Newman (Eds.), *The new Palgrave: Utility and probability* (pp. 128–33). New York: W. W. Norton.

Hart, H. L. A. (1963). *Law, liberty, and morality.* Oxford: Oxford University Press.

Hartnoll, R. (1994). *Multi-city study: Drug misuse trends in thirteen European cities.* Co-operation Group to Combat Drug Abuse and Illicit Trafficking in Drugs (Pompidou Group). Strasbourg, France: Council of Europe Press.

Hartnoll, R., Mitcheson, M., Battersby, A., Brown, G., Ellis, M., Fleming, P., & Hedley, N. (1980). Evaluation of heroin maintenance in a controlled trial. *Archive of General Psychiatry, 37,* 877–84.

Harwood, H. J., Fountain, D., & Livermore, G. (1998). *The economic costs of alcohol and drug abuse in the United States, 1992.* Rockville, MD: National Institute on Drug Abuse.

Hauge, R. (1991). *Drug problems and drug policies in Norway.* Presented at the International Conference on Drug Policies and Problems. Washington, DC: RAND Drug Policy Research Center.

Health Council of the Netherlands: Standing Committee on Medicine (1996). *Marihuana as medicine.* Rijswijk: Health Council of Netherlands.

Healy, W. (1915). *The individual delinquent: A text-book of diagnosis and prognosis for all concerned in understanding offenders.* Boston: Little, Brown.

Heather, N., Wodak, A., Nadelmann, E., & O'Hare, P. (Eds.). (1993). *Psychoactive Drugs and Harm Reduction: From Faith to Science.* London: Whurr.

Hecht, B. (1991, July 15). Out of joint: The case for medicinal marijuana. *New Republic, 205,* 7–10.

Heckathorn, D. D. (1990). Collective sanctions and compliance norms: A formal theory of group-mediated social control. *American Sociological Review, 55,* 366–84.

Hemenway, D. (1988). *Prices and choices: Microeconomic vignettes* (2d ed.). Cambridge, MA: Ballinger.

The Henry J. Kaiser Family Foundation. (1996). *The Kaiser survey on Americans and AIDS/HIV.* Menlo Park, CA: The Henry J. Kaiser Family Foundation.

Hibell, B., Andersson, B., Bjarnason, T., Kokkevi, A., Morgan, M., & Narusk, A. (1997). *The 1995 ESPAD report: Alcohol and other drug use among students in 26 European countries.* Stockholm: Swedish Council for Information on Alcohol and Other Drugs, and the Council of Europe Pompidou Group.

Hilts, P. J. (1994, August 2). Is nicotine addictive? It depends on whose criteria you use. *New York Times,* p. B6.

Hirschi, T. (1969). *Causes of delinquency.* Berkeley, CA: University of California Press.

Hobson, B. M. (1987). *Uneasy virtue: The politics of prostitution and the American Reform Tradition.* New York: Basic Books.

Hogarth, R. M., & Reder, M. W. (1986). *Rational choice: The contrast between economics and psychology.* Chicago: University of Chicago Press.

Hollister, L. E. (1988). Cannabis – 1988. *Acta Psychiatrica Scandinavia, 78*, 108–18.

Home Office. (1991). *Statistics on the Misuse of Drugs: Addicts notified to the Home Office, 1990*. London: Home Office Statistical Bulletin.

Home Office. (1992). *Statistics of drug seizures and offenders dealt with, United Kingdom 1991*. London: Home Office Statistical Bulletin.

Homer, J. B. (1993a). A system dynamics model for cocaine prevalence estimation and trend projection. *Journal of Drug Issues, 23*, 251–79.

Homer, J. B. (1993b). Projecting the impact of law enforcement on cocaine prevalence: A system dynamics approach. *Journal of Drug Issues, 23*, 281–95.

Horney, J., & Marshall, I. H. (1992). Risk perceptions among serious offenders: The role of crime and punishment. *Criminology, 30*, 575–94.

Horstink-Von Meyenfeldt, L. (1996). The Netherlands: Tightening up the cafés policy. In N. Dorn, J. Jepsen, & E. Savona (Eds.), *European drug policies and enforcement*. London: MacMillan.

Housman, R. (1998, July 26). *Los Angeles Times* (Letter), p. M4.

Howe, E. S., & Brandau, C. J. (1988). Additive effects of certainty, severity, and celerity of punishment on judgments of crime deterrence scale value. *Journal of Applied Social Psychology, 18*, 796–812.

Hser, Y., Anglin, M. D., & Powers, K. (1993). A 24-Year follow-up of California narcotics addicts. *Archives of General Psychiatry, 50*, 577–84.

Huber, C. (1994). Needle park: What can we learn from the Zurich experience? *Addiction, 89*, 513–16.

Hughes, J. R. (1995). Applying harm reduction to smoking. *Tobacco Control, 4*, S33–8.

Hurley, S. F., Jolley, D. J., & Kaldor, J. M. (1997). Effectiveness of needle-exchange programmes for prevention of HIV infection. *The Lancet, 349*, 1797–800.

Husak, D. N. (1992). *Drugs and rights*. Cambridge, England: Cambridge University Press.

Institute for Health Policy of Brandeis University. (1993). *Substance abuse: The nation's number one health problem. Key indicators for policy*. Princeton, NJ: The Robert Wood Johnson Foundation.

International Narcotics Control Board (INCB). (1997). *Report of the International Narcotics Control Board for 1997*. Vienna: United Nations.

Italy votes against drug war. (1993). *Drug Policy Action, 11*, 1.

Jacobs, J. B. (1990). Imagining drug legalization. *The Public Interest, 101*, 28–42.

Jahoda, W. (1995, September 29). *Examining the impact of state gambling*. Testimony before the US House of Representatives Committee on the Judiciary.

Jansen, A. C. M. (1991). *Cannabis in Amsterdam: A geography of hashish and marijuana*. Muiderberg, Netherlands: Coutinho.

Jansen, A. C. M. (1994). The development of a "legal" consumer's market for cannabis – The "coffee shop" phenomenon. In E. Leuw & I. H. Marshall (Eds.), *Between prohibition and legalization: The Dutch experiment in drug policy* (pp. 169–82). Amsterdam: Kugler.

Jemmott, J. B., Jemmott, L. S., & Fong, G. T. (1998). Abstinence and safer sex HIV risk-reduction interventions for African American adolescents. *Journal of the American Medical Association, 279*, 1529–36.

Jepsen, J. (1989). Drug policies in Denmark. In H. J. Albrecht & A. Kalmthout (Eds.), *Drug policies in Western Europe* (pp. 107–41). Freiburg: Eigenverlag Max-Planck-Institut.

Johnson, B. (1975). Understanding British addiction statistics. *Bulletin on Narcotics, 27*, 49–66.

Johnson, B. (1977). How much heroin maintenance (containment) in Britain? *The International Journal of the Addictions, 12*, 361–98.

Johnson, B., Goldstein, P., Preble, E., Schmeidler, J., Lipton, D., Spunt, B., & Miller, T. (1985). *Taking care of business: The economics of crime by heroin abusers*. Lexington: D.C. Heath.

Johnston, L. D. (1991). Toward a theory of drug epidemics. In L. Donohew, H. E. Sypher, & W. J. Bukoski (Eds.), *Persuasive communication and drug abuse prevention* (pp. 93–131). Hillsdale, NJ: Lawrence Erlbaum Associates, Inc.

Johnston, L. D., O'Malley, P. M., & Bachman, J. G. (1981). *Marijuana decriminalization: The impact on youth, 1975–1980*. Ann Arbor, MI: Institute for Social Research.

Johnston, L. D., O'Malley, P. M., & Bachman, J. G. (1989). *Drug use, drinking, and smoking: National survey results from high school, college, and young adult populations, 1975–1988*. Rockville, MD: U.S. Department of Health and Human Services.

Johnston, L. D., O'Malley, P. M., & Bachman, J. G. (Annual). *National survey results on drug use from the Monitoring the Future Study*. Rockville, MD: National Institute on Drug Abuse. Estimates for 1991 through 1998 appear at *http://www.isr.umich.edu/src/mtf/*.

Joint Executive-Legislative Task Force to Study Commercial Gaming Activities in Maryland. (1995). *Final Report*. Annapolis, MD: Joint Executive-Legislative Task Force to Study Commercial Gaming Activities in Maryland.

Jones, B. D. (1994). *Reconceiving decision-making in democratic politics*. Chicago: University of Chicago Press.

Jones, J. (1997). *A descriptive exploratory analysis of corrupt drug enforcement agents and their careers in corruption* (dissertation). College Park, MD: University of Maryland, Department of Criminology.

Jones, R. (1987). Drug of abuse profile: Cannabis. *Clinical Chemistry, 33*, 72B–81B.

Jones, R. (1992). What have we learned from nicotine, cocaine and marijuana about addiction? In C. O'Brien & J. Jaffe (Eds.), *Addictive States*. New York: Raven Press.

Jonnes, J. (1996). *Hep-cats, narcs and pipe dreams: A history of America's romance with illegal drugs*. New York: Scribner.

Joy, J. E., Watson, S. J., & Benson, J. A. (Institute of Medicine). (1999). *Marijuana and medicine: Assessing the science base*. Washington, DC: National Academy Press.

Joyce, E. (1998). Cocaine trafficking and British foreign policy. In E. Joyce & C. Malamud (Eds.), *Latin America and the multinational drug trade* (pp. 173–92). London: MacMillan.

Judson, H. (1974). *Heroin addiction in Britain: What Americans can learn from the English experience.* New York: Harcourt, Brace and Jovanovich.

Julien, R. M. (1995). *A primer of drug action: A concise, nontechnical guide to the actions, uses, and side effects of psychoactive drugs* (7th ed.). New York: W. H. Freeman & Co. Publishers.

Kagan, R., & Vogel, D. (1993). The politics of smoking regulation: Canada, France and the United States. In R. Rabin & S. Sugarman (Eds.), *Smoking policy: Law, politics and culture* (pp. 22–48). New York: Oxford University Press.

Kagel, J., Battalio, R., Rachlin, H., & Green, L. (1981). Demand curves for animal consumers. *Quarterly Journal of Economics, 96,* 1–15.

Kahneman, D., & Tversky, A. (1984). Choices, values, and frames. *American Psychologist, 39,* 341–50.

Kahneman, D., Knetsch, J. L., & Thaler, R. H. (1991). Anomalies – The endowment effect, loss aversion, and status quo bias. *Journal of Economic Perspectives, 5,* 193–206.

Kalant, H. (1982). Commentary on the Home Office Report on the effects of cannabis use. *British Journal of the Addictions, 77,* 341–5.

Kallick, M., Suits, D., Dielman, T., & Hybels, J. (1979). *A survey of American gambling behavior and attitudes.* Ann Arbor, MI: Institute of Social Research.

Kandel, D. B. (1980). Drug and drinking behavior among youth. *Annual Review of Sociology, 6,* 235–85.

Kandel, D. B. (1993). The social demography of drug use. *The Milbank Quarterly, 69,* 365–414.

Kandel, D. B., & Chen, K. (1995). The natural history of drug use from adolescence to the mid-thirties in a general population sample. *American Journal of Public Health, 85,* 41–7.

Kandel, D. B., & Davies, M. (1992). Progression to regular marijuana involvement: Phenomenology and risk factors for near-daily use. In M. Glantz & R. Pickens (Eds.), *Vulnerability to drug abuse* (pp. 211–53). Washington, DC: American Psychological Association.

Kandel, D. B., Chen, K., Warner, L. A., Kessler, R. C., & Grant, B. (1997). Prevalence and demographic correlates of symptoms of last year dependence on alcohol, nicotine, marijuana and cocaine in the U.S. population. *Drug and Alcohol Dependence, 44,* 11–29.

Kandel, D. B., Davies, M., Karus, D., & Yamaguchi, K. (1986). The consequences in young adulthood of adolescent drug involvement. *Archives of General Psychiatry, 43,* 746–54.

Kandel, D. B., Yamaguchi, K., & Chen, K. (1992). Stages of progression in drug involvement from adolescence to adulthood: Further evidence for the gateway theory. *Journal of Studies on Alcohol, 53,* 447–57.

Kaplan, J. (1970). *Marijuana: The new prohibition.* New York: Meridian.

Kaplan, J. (1983). *The hardest drug: Heroin and public policy.* Chicago: University of Chicago Press.

Katyal, N. K. (1993). Men who own women: A thirteenth amendment critique of forced prostitution. *Yale Law Journal, 103*, 791–826.

Katz, D., & Schanck, R. L. (1938). *Social psychology.* New York: Wiley.

Kaye, J. (1992, December 10). The corner hash joint. *Los Angeles Times*, pp. E1, E13.

Kelly, J. (1995, May). New light on old casino ghosts. *International Wagering and Gaming Business.*

Kelman, H. C., & Hamilton, V. L. (1989). *Crimes of obedience.* New Haven, CT: Yale University Press.

Kenkel, D. (1996). New estimates of the optimal tax on alcohol. *Economic Inquiry, XXXIV*, 297–319.

Kennedy, D. (1993). Closing the market: Controlling the drug trade in Tampa, Florida. *Program Focus, March.*

Kennedy, D. M., Piehl, A. M., & Braga, A. A. (1996). Youth violence in Boston: Gun markets, serious youth offenders, and a use-reduction strategy. *Law and Contemporary Problems, 59*, 147–96.

Kerr, K. A. (1985). *Organized for prohibition: A new history of the anti-saloon league.* New Haven, CT: Yale University Press.

Kerr, N. L. (1978). Severity of prescribed penalty and mock juror's verdicts. *Journal of Personality and Social Psychology, 36*, 1431–42.

Killias, M., & Uchtenhagen, A. (1996). Does medical prescription reduce delinquency among drug-addicts? On the evaluation of the Swiss heroin prescription projects and its methodology. *Studies on Crime and Crime Prevention, 5*, 245–56.

King, G., Keohane, R. O., & Verba, S. (1994). *Designing social inquiry: Scientific inference in qualitative research.* Princeton, NJ: Princeton University Press.

Kirp, D., & Bayer, R. (Eds.). (1992). *AIDS in the industrialized democracies.* New Brunswick, NJ: Rutgers University Press.

Kirp, D., & Bayer, R. (1993). The politics. In J. Stryker & M. D. Smith (Eds.), *Dimensions of HIV prevention: Needle exchange* (pp. 77–98). Menlo Park, CA: The Henry J. Kaiser Foundation.

Kleber, H. (1994). Our current approach to drug abuse – Progress, problems, proposals. *New England Journal of Medicine, 330*, 361–5.

Kleber, H., Califano, J., & Demers, J. (1997). Clinical and societal implications of drug legalization. In J. Lowinson, P. Ruiz, R. Millman, & J. Langrod (Eds.), *Substance abuse: A comprehensive textbook.* Baltimore: Williams and Wilkins.

Kleiman, M. A. R. (1992a). *Against excess: Drug policy for results.* New York: Basic Books.

Kleiman, M. A. R. (1992b). Neither prohibition nor legalization: Grudging toleration in drug control policy. *Daedalus, 121*, 53–83.

Kleiman, M. A. R. (1997). Coerced abstinence: A neopaternalist drug policy initiative. In L. Mead (Ed.), *The new paternalism: Supervisory approaches to poverty* (pp. 182–219). Washington, DC: Brookings Institution.

Klepper, S., & Nagin, D. (1989). The deterrent effect of perceived certainty and severity of punishment revisited. *Criminology, 27*, 721–46.

Klingemann, H., Goos, C., Hartnoll, R., Jablensky, A., & Rehm, J. (1991). *First European Summary of Drug Abuse 1985–1989/90*. Copenhagen: World Health Organization.

Klingemann, K. K. (1996). Drug treatment in Switzerland: Harm reduction, decentralization and community response. *Addiction, 91*, 723–36.

Knolle, H. (1997). Incidence and prevalence of illegal drug use in Switzerland in the 1980s and early 1990s: An analytic study. *Substance Use and Misuse, 32*, 1349–68.

Kobler, J. (1973). *Ardent spirits: The rise and fall of Prohibition*. New York: Putnam.

Koepp, M. J., Gunn, R. N., Lawrence, A. D., Cunningham, V. J., Dagher, A., Jones, T., Brooks, D. J., Bench, C. J., & Grasby, P. M. (1998). Evidence for striatal dopamine release during a video game. *Nature, 393*, 266–8.

Kondracke, M. (1988). Don't legalize drugs: The costs are still too high. *New Republic, 198*, 16–19.

Korf, D. J. (1988). Twintig jaar softdrug-gebruik in Nederland: Een terugblick vanuit prevalentiestudies. *Tijdschrift voor Alcohol, Drugs en Andere Psychotrope Stoffen, 14*, 81–9.

Korf, D. J. (1994). Drug tourists and drug refugees. In E. Leuw & I. H. (Eds.), *Between prohibition and legalization: The Dutch experiment in drug policy* (pp. 119–43). Amsterdam: Kugler.

Korf, D. J. (1995). *Dutch treat: Formal control and illicit drug use in the Netherlands* (dissertation). Amsterdam: Thesis Dissertation Publishers.

Kornblum, A. (1976). *The moral hazards*. Lexington, MA: D.C. Heath.

Kornblum, W. (1991). Drug legalization and the minority poor. *Milbank Quarterly, 69*, 415–35.

Kozlowski, L., & Pilletteri, J. (1996). Compensation by smokers of lower yield cigarettes. In D. Shopland, *The FTC cigarette test method for determining tar, nicotine and carbon monoxide yields of U.S. cigarettes: Report of the NCI expert committee* (pp. 161–72). Bethesda, MD: National Cancer Institute.

Kraan, D. J. (1994). An economic view on Dutch drugs policy. In E. Leuw & I. H. Marshall (Eds.), *Between prohibition and legalization: The Dutch experiment in drug policy* (pp. 283–310). Amsterdam: Kugler.

Kral, A. H., Bluthenthal, R. N., Booth, R. E., & Watters, J. K. (1998). HIV seroprevalence among street-recruited injection drug and crack cocaine users in 16 US municipalities. *American Journal of Public Health, 88*, 108–13.

Krauss, C. (1993, September 20). Lobbyists of every stripe turning to the grass roots on health care. *New York Times*, p. A20.

Krista. (1992, 1993). *Kriminalstatistic des Kantons Zurich*. Zurich: Zurich City Government.

Kuran, T. (1995). *Private truths, public lies: The social consequences of preference falsification*. Cambridge, MA: Harvard University Press.

Kyvig, D. (1979). *Repealing national Prohibition*. Chicago: University of Chicago Press.

Kyvig, D. (Ed.). (1985). *Law, alcohol and order: Perspectives on national Prohibition*. Westport, CT: Greenwood Press.

Labaton, S. (1993, December 8). Surgeon General suggests study of legalizing drugs. *New York Times*, p. A23.

Lancet. (1995). Editorial: Deglamorising cannabis. *Lancet, 346*, 8985.

Landesco, J. (1929/1968). *Organized crime in Chicago*. Chicago: University of Chicago Press.

Langemeijer, M. P. S. (1997). Prevalence of drug use: A comparison of three Dutch cities. In D. Korf & H. Riper (Eds.), *Illicit drugs in Europe*. Amsterdam: SISWO.

Lasswell, H., & McKenna, J. (1972). *Organized crime in an inner city community*. Springfield, VA: National Technical Information Service.

Laumann, E. O., Gagnon, J. H., Michael, R. T., & Michaels, S. (1994). *The social organization of sexuality*. Chicago: University of Chicago Press.

Lee, R., & Clawson, P. (1996). *The Andean cocaine trade*. New York: St. Martin's Press.

Legal Action Center. (1997). *Making welfare reform work: Tools for confronting alcohol and drug problems among welfare recipients*. Washington: Legal Action Center.

Legislative Analyst's Office (LAO). (1995). The "three strikes and you're out" law – Preliminary assessment. *Status Check. http://www.lao.ca.gov/sc010695. html*.

Leitner, M., Shapland, J., & Wiles, P. (1992). *Drug usage and drugs prevention: The views and habits of the general public*. London: HMSO.

Leroy, B. (1992). The European community of twelve and the drug demand: Excerpt of a comparative study of legislations and judicial practice. *Drug and Alcohol Dependence, 29*, 269–81.

Lester, D. (1994). Access to gambling opportunities and compulsive gambling. *International Journal of the Addictions, 29*, 1611–16.

Leuthardt, B. (1997). Swiss go out on a limb by dispensing heroin to addicts. *Frankfurter Rundschau*, in *AAP Newsfeed*, December 25, 1997.

Leuw, E. (1991). *Dutch penal law and policy: Notes on criminological research from the research and documentation center*. The Hague: Ministry of Justice.

Leuw, E. (1994). Initial construction and development of the official Dutch drug policy. In E. Leuw & I. H. Marshall (Eds.), *Between prohibition and legalization: The Dutch experiment in drug policy* (pp. 23–40). Amsterdam: Kugler.

Leuw, E., & Marshall, I. H. (1994). Introduction. In E. Leuw & I. H. Marshall (Eds.), *Between prohibition and legalization: The Dutch experiment in drug policy* (pp. xiii–xxi). Amsterdam: Kugler.

Lewis, D., Gear, C., Laubli, L. M., & Langenick-Cartwright, D. (Eds.). (1997). *The medical prescription of narcotics: Scientific foundations and practical experiences*. Seattle: Hogrefe and Huber Publishers.

Lewitt, E. (1989). U.S. tobacco taxes: Behavioral effects and policy implications. *British Journal of the Addictions, 84*, 1217–34.

Lindgren, S. A. (1992). A Criticism of Swedish drug policy. *International Journal on Drug Policy, 3*, 100.

LNA Multimedia Report Service. (1995). *Ad summary: January–December 1994.* New York: Competitive Media Reporting.

Loewenstein, G. (1996). Out of control: Visceral influences on behavior. *Organizational Behavior & Human Decision Processes, 65,* 272–92.

Loewenstein, G., & Elster, J. (Eds.). (1992). *Choice over time.* New York: Russell Sage Foundation.

Lopes, L. L. (1987). Between hope and fear: The psychology of risk. *Advances in experimental social psychology, 20,* 255–95. San Diego, CA: Academic Press.

Lord, C. G., Ross, L., & Lepper, M. R. (1979). Biased assimilation and attitude polarization: The effects of prior theories on subsequently considered evidence. *Journal of Personality and Social Psychology, 37,* 2098–109.

Lurie, P., & Drucker, E. (1997). An opportunity lost: HIV infections associated with lack of a national needle-exchange programme in the USA. *The Lancet, 349,* 604–8.

Lurie, P., & Reingold, A. L. (Eds.). (1993). *The public health impact of needle exchange programs in the United States and abroad.* Berkeley, CA: School of Public Health, UC Berkeley; San Francisco: Institute for Health Policy Studies, UC San Francisco.

Lusane, C. (1991). *Pipe dream blues: Racism and the war on drugs.* Boston: South End Press.

Lynch, B., & Bonnie, R. (Eds.). (1994). *Growing up tobacco free: Preventing nicotine addiction in children and youths.* Washington, DC: National Academy Press.

Lynn, M. (Ed.). (1992). The psychology of unavailability: Explaining scarcity and cost effects on value (special issue). *Basic and Applied Social Psychology, 13,* 1–144.

MacCoun, R. (1993). Drugs and the law: A psychological analysis of drug prohibition. *Psychological Bulletin, 113,* 497–512.

MacCoun, R. (1996). Sexual orientation and military cohesion. In G. M. Herek & J. B. Jobe (Eds.), *Out in force: Sexual orientation and the military* (pp. 157–76). Chicago: University of Chicago Press.

MacCoun, R. (1998a). Toward a psychology of harm reduction. *American Psychologist, 53,* 1199–208.

MacCoun, R. (1998b). Biases in the interpretation and use of research results. *Annual Review of Psychology, 49,* 259–87.

MacCoun, R., & Caulkins, J. (1996). Examining the behavioral assumptions of the national drug control strategy. In W. K. Bickel & R. J. DeGrandpre (Eds.), *Drug policy and human nature: Psychological perspectives on the control, prevention, and treatment of illicit drug abuse* (pp. 177–97). New York: Plenum Press.

MacCoun, R., & Reuter, P. (1992). Are the wages of sin $30 an hour? Economic aspects of street-level drug dealing. *Crime and Delinquency, 38,* 477–91.

MacCoun, R., & Reuter, P. (1997). Interpreting Dutch cannabis policy: Reasoning by analogy in the legalization debate. *Science, 278,* 47–52.

MacCoun, R., Kahan, J. P., Gillespie, J., & Rhee, J. (1993). A content analysis of the drug legalization debate. *Journal of Drug Issues, 23,* 615–29.

MacCoun, R. J., Model, K., Phillips-Shockley, H., & Reuter, P. (1995). Comparing drug policies in North America and Western Europe. In G. Estievenart (Ed.), *Policies and strategies to combat drugs in Europe* (pp. 197–220). Dordrecht, The Netherlands: Martinus Nijhoff.

MacCoun, R., Reuter, P., & Schelling, T. (1996). Assessing alternative drug control regimes. *Journal of Policy Analysis and Management, 15,* 1–23.

MacDonald, D., & Atkinson, L. (1995). *Social impacts of the legislative options for cannabis in Australia: Phase I, Research.* Canberra: Australian Government Printing Office.

MacLean's. (1996, June 3). The limits of tolerance: Holland tightens its easygoing approach to drugs. *Maclean's,* pp. 24–25.

Mäkelä, K., Room, R., Single, E., Sulkunen, P., & Walsh, B. (1981). *Alcohol, society and the state 1: A comparative study of alcohol control.* Toronto: Addiction Research Foundation.

Malamuth, N. M. (1981). Rape proclivity among males. *Journal of Social Issues, 37,* 138–57.

Maloff, D. (1981). A review of the effects of the decriminalization of marijuana. *Contemporary Drug Problems, Fall,* 307–22.

Manning, W. G., Keeler, E. B., Newhouse, J. P., Sloss, E. M., & Wasserman, J. (1991). *The costs of poor health habits.* Cambridge, MA: Harvard University Press.

Mansbridge, J. J. (Ed.). (1990). *Beyond self-interest.* Chicago: University of Chicago Press.

Mansfield, E. (1988). *Microeconomics: Theory and application* (6th ed.). New York: W. W. Norton.

Manski, C. F., Pepper, J. V., & Thomas, Y. F. (Eds.). (1999). *Assessment of two cost-effectiveness studies on cocaine control policy.* Washington, DC: National Academy Press.

Marijuana Policy Project. (1995, April). *Possess a joint, lose your license.* http://www.mpp.org.pajlyl.html.

Marlatt, G. A., Baer, J. S., Donovan, D. M., & Kivlahan, D. R. (1988). Addictive behaviors: Etiology and treatment. *Annual Review of Psychology, 39,* 223–52.

Marlatt, G. A., Larimer, M. E., Baer, J. S., & Quigley, L. A. (1993). Harm reduction for alcohol problems: Moving beyond the controlled drinking controversy. *Behavior Therapy, 24,* 461–504.

Mast, B., Benson, B., & Rasmussen, D. (1997). *Entrepreneurial police and drug enforcement policy* (unpublished paper). Tallahassee, FL: Florida State University.

Mathias, R. (1996). Marijuana impairs driving-related skills and workplace performance. *NIDA Notes, January/February,* http://www.nida.nih.gov/NIDA_Notes/NNVol11N1/Marijuana.html.

Mattison, J. B. (1886–7). Cocaine dosage and cocaine addiction. *Peria Medical Monthly, 7,* 572–3.

Mauldon, J., & Luker, K. (1996). Does liberalism cause sex? *The American Prospect, 24,* 80–5.

McCaffrey, B. (1997, May 14). Testimony before the Senate Appropriations Committee, Subcommittee on Treasury, General Government, and Civil Service.

McCaffrey, B. (1998, July 27). Legalization would be the wrong direction. *Los Angeles Times*, p. B5.

McLellan, A. T., & Weisner, C. (1996). Achieving the public health and safety potential of substance abuse treatments. In W. Bickle & R. DeGrandpre (Eds.), *Drug policy and human nature*. New York: Plenum.

McGeorge, J., & Aitken, C. K. (1997). Effects of cannabis decriminalization in the Australian Capital Territory on university students' patterns of use. *Journal of Drug Issues, 27*, 785–93.

McGregor, A. (1998). WHO accused of slowness in evaluating Swiss heroin-addiction treatment. *Lancet, 351*, 891.

McKinnon, C. (1982). Feminism, Marxism, method and the state: An agenda for theory. *Signs, 7*, 515–44.

Meier, K. (1994). *The politics of sin: Drugs, alcohol and public policy*. Armonk, NY: M.E. Sharpe.

Meier, R. F., & Johnson, W. T. (1977). Deterrence as social control: The legal and extralegal production of conformity. *American Sociological Review, 42*, 292–304.

Methadone causes half of drug overdose deaths. (1992, August 28). Copenhagen *Weekendavisen* (Copenhagen). In *JPRS: Narcotics* (1992, October 6, p. 4).

Metz, T. (1989, January 12). Article. *Rotterdam Handelsblad*, p. 2. Cited in FBIS 89-010, p. 31.

Michels, I. (1993). Critical analysis of the drug treatment policy in Germany. In M. Reisinger (Ed.), *Aids and drug addiction in the European Community* (pp. 90–102). Lisbon, Portugal: European Monitoring Centre for Drugs and Drug Addiction.

Mignon, P. (1991). *Drugs and drug policy in France*. Paper presented at International Conference on Drug Policies and Problems. Washington, DC: RAND Drug Policy Research Center.

Mill, J. S. (1859/1947). On liberty. In S. Commins & R. N. Linscott (Eds.), *Man and the state: The political philosophers* (pp. 135–258). New York: Random House.

Miller, D. T., & Prentice, D. A. (1994). Collective errors and errors about the collective. Special issue: The self and the collective. *Personality & Social Psychology Bulletin, 20*, 541–50.

Miller, J. G. (1996). *Search and destroy: African-American males in the criminal justice system*. New York: Cambridge University Press.

Miller, R. L. (1991). *The case for legalizing drugs*. Westport, CT: Praeger.

Miller, S. M. (1980). Why having control reduces stress: If I can stop the roller coaster I don't want to get off. In J. Garber & M. E. P. Seligman (Eds.), *Human helplessness: Theory and applications* (pp. 71–95). New York: Academic Press.

Milman, B. (1980). New rules for the oldest profession: Should we change our prostitution laws? *Harvard Women's Law Journal, 3*, 1–82.

Ministero dell' Interno, Dipartimento Della Pubblica Sicurezza, Direzione Centrale Della Polizia Criminale, Servizio Centrale Antidroga. (1989). *Attivita Antidroga Delle Froze Di Polizia Nel 1989: Dati Nazionali.* p. 9.

Ministry of Foreign Affairs; Ministry of Health, Welfare, and Sport; Ministry of Justice; & Ministry of the Interior. (1995). *Drugs policy in the Netherlands: Continuity and change.* Rijswijk, The Netherlands: Ministry of Foreign Affairs; Ministry of Health, Welfare, and Sport; Ministry of Justice; & Ministry of the Interior. Also see Ministry of Justice fact sheet, *Dutch Drugs Policy*, at *http://www.minjust.nl:8080/a_beleid/fact/cfact7.htm.*

Ministry of Health and Social Affairs. (1992). *Summary of findings from the UNO survey of the extent of drug abuse in Sweden.* Sweden: Ministry of Health and Social Affairs.

Ministry of Health and Social Affairs. (1997). *New Trends in Drug Abuse in Norway. http://odin.dep.no/shd/publ/drugs/drugs.html#1.*

Ministry of Welfare, Health and Cultural Affairs & Ministry of Justice. (1992). *Drugs policy in the Netherlands: Second version.* Rijswijk, The Netherlands: Ministry of Welfare, Health and Cultural Affairs & Ministry of Justice.

Miron, J. A. (1997). The effect of alcohol prohibition on alcohol consumption (unpublished paper). Boston: Boston University.

Miron, J. A. (1998). Violence and the U.S. prohibitions of drugs and alcohol (unpublished paper). Boston: Boston University.

Miron, J. A., & Zwiebel, J. (1991). Alcohol consumption during Prohibition. *American Economic Review, 81,* 242–7.

Miron, J. A., & Zwiebel, J. (1995). The economic case against drug prohibition. *Journal of Economic Perspectives, 9,* 175–92.

Mitcheson, M. (1994). Drug clinics in the 1970s. In J. Strang & M. Gossop (Eds.), *Heroin Addiction and Drug Policy: The British System* (pp. 178–91). Oxford: Oxford University Press.

Model, K. E. (1993). The effect of marijuana decriminalization on hospital emergency room drug episodes: 1975–1978. *Journal of the American Statistical Association, 88,* 737–47.

Mol, R., & Trautmann, F. (1991). The liberal image of Dutch drug policy. *International Journal on Drug Policy, 2,* 16–20.

MMWR. (1992). Public health focus: Effectiveness of smoking-control strategies – United States. *Morbidity Mortality Weekly Report, 41,* 647, 653.

MMWR. (1996). AIDS associated with injecting-drug use – United States, 1995. *Morbidity Mortality Weekly Report, 45,* 392–7.

Moore, M. H. (1976). Anatomy of the heroin problem: An exercise in problem definition. *Policy Analysis, 2,* 639–62.

Moore, M. H. (1990). Supply reduction and drug law enforcement. In M. Tonry & J. Q. Wilson (Eds.), *Drugs and crime* (pp. 109–58). Chicago: University of Chicago Press.

Moore, M. H. (1991). Drugs, the criminal law, and the administration of justice. *The Milbank Quarterly, 69,* 529–60.

Moore, M., & Gerstein, D. (Eds.). (1981). *Alcohol and public policy: Beyond the shadow of Prohibition.* Washington, DC: National Academy Press.

Moore, W. (1974). *The Kefauver Committee and the politics of crime, 1950–1952.* Columbia, MO: University of Missouri Press.

Morais, R. C. (1996, June 17). Just say maybe. *Forbes*, pp. 114–20.

Morgan, H. W. (1981). *Drugs in America: A social history, 1800–1980.* Syracuse, NY: Syracuse University Press.

Morgan, J. P. (1982). The Jamaica ginger paralysis. *Journal of the American Medical Association, 15*, 1864–7.

Morris, N., & Hawkins, G. (1970). *The honest politician's guide to crime control.* Chicago: University of Chicago Press.

Morris, N., & Hawkins, G. (1977). *Letter to the President on crime control.* Chicago: University of Chicago Press.

Mott, J. (1985). Self-reported cannabis use in Great Britain in 1981. *British Journal of Addiction, 80*, 37–43.

Mott, J., & Mirrlees-Black, C. (1995). *Self-reported drug misuse in England and Wales: Findings from the 1992 British Crime Survey.* London: Home Office.

Mugford, S. (1992). Licit and illicit drug use, health costs and the "crime connection" in Australia: Public views and policy implications. *Contemporary Drug Problems, 19*, 351–85.

Mullen, B., Cooper, C., & Driskell, J. E. (1990). Jaywalking as a function of model behavior. *Personality and Social Psychology Bulletin, 16*, 320–30.

Murphy, P. (1994). *Keeping score: The frailty of the national drug control budget.* Santa Monica, CA: RAND.

Musto, D. F. (1971/1987). *The American disease: Origins of narcotic control.* New York: Oxford University Press.

Musto, D. F. (1990). Illicit price of cocaine in two eras: 1908–1914 and 1982–1989. *Connecticut Medicine, 54*, 321–6.

Nadelmann, E. (1989). Drug prohibition in the United States: Costs, consequences, and alternatives. *Science, 245*, 939–47.

Nadelmann, E. (1998). Commonsense drug policy. *Foreign Affairs, 77*, 111–26.

National Center for Health Statistics. (Annual). *Vital statistics of the United States.* Washington, DC: U.S. Government Printing Office.

National Commission on Law Observance and Enforcement (Wickersham Commission). (1931). *Report on the enforcement of the Prohibition laws of the United States.* Washington, DC: U.S. Government Printing Office.

National Commission on Marihuana and Drug Abuse. (1972). *Marihuana: A signal of misunderstanding: The official report of the National Commission on Marihuana and Drug Abuse.* New York: New American Library.

National Council on Compulsive Gambling. (1994). *The need for a national policy on problem and pathological gambling.* New York: National Council on Compulsive Gambling.

National crime victimization survey (Annual). Washington, DC: Bureau of Justice Statistics, U.S. Department of Justice.

National Governor's Conference. (1977). *Marijuana: A study of state policies and penalties.* Washington, DC: U.S. Government Printing Office.

National Highway Transportation Safety Administration (annual). *Traffic Safety Facts.*

National Household Survey on Drug Abuse (annual). Rockville, Maryland. Substance Abuse and Mental Health Services Administration.

National Institute of Justice. (1995, 1997). *Drug use forecasting: Annual report on adult and juvenile arrestees.* Washington, DC: U.S. Department of Justice.

National Institute of Public Health. (1993). *A restrictive drug policy: The Swedish experience* (preliminary edition). Stockholm, Sweden: National Institute of Public Health.

National Institute on Drug Abuse. (1991). *Drug abuse warning network.* Washington, DC: U.S. Department of Health and Human Resources.

National Narcotics Intelligence Consumers Committee. (1996). *The supply of illicit drugs to the United States.* Washington, DC: National Narcotics Intelligence Consumers Committee.

National Opinion Research Center (NORC). (1999). *Gambling Impact and Behavior Study: Report to the National Gambling Impact Study Commission.* Chicago: National Opinion Research Center.

National Research Council. (1982). *An analysis of marijuana policy.* Washington, DC: National Academy Press.

Neave, M. (1988). The failure of prostitution law reform. *Australian and New Zealand Journal of Criminology, 21,* 202–13.

Needle, R. H., & Mills, A. (1993). *Drug procurement practices of the out-of-treatment chronic drug abuser.* Rockville, MD: National Institute on Drug Abuse.

Negro cocaine fiends. (1902, November). *Medical News, 81,* 895.

Newcomb, M. D., & Bentler, P. M. (1988). *Consequences of adolescent drug use: Impact on young adults.* Newbury Park, CA: Sage Publications.

Netherlands Institute for Alcohol and Drugs (NIAD). (1995). *Fact sheet 1: Cannabis policy.* Utrecht, Netherlands: NIAD.

NIAD (1995). *Fact sheet I: Cannabis policy.* Utrecht, The Netherlands: National Institute for Alcohol and Drugs (NIAD).

Nichols, J. L., & Ross, H. L. (1988). The effectiveness of legal sanctions in dealing with drinking drivers. In *Surgeon General's workshop on drunk driving* (pp. 93–112). Rockville, MD: U.S. Department of Health and Human Services.

Nisbett, R., & Ross, L. (1980). *Human inference: Strategies and shortcomings of social judgment.* Englewood Cliffs, NJ: Prentice-Hall.

Noelle-Neumann, E. (1991). *The spiral of silence* (2d ed.). Chicago: University of Chicago Press.

Normand, J., Vlahov, D., & Moses, L. (Eds.). (1995). *Preventing HIV transmission: The role of sterile needles and bleach.* Washington, DC: National Academy Press.

Norwegian Ministry of Health and Social Affairs. (1997). *New trends in drug abuse in Norway. http://odin.dep.no/shd/publ/drugs/drugs.html.*

Nunnally, J. C. (1978). *Psychometric theory* (2d ed.). New York: McGraw-Hill.

Ødegard, E. (1995). Legality and legitimacy: On attitudes to drugs and social sanctions. *British Journal of Criminology, 35,* 525–42.

Offering clean needles. (1997, July 14). *Washington Post,* p. A18.

Office of National Drug Control Policy (ONDCP). (1992). *Price and purity of cocaine: The relationship to emergency room visits and deaths, and to drug use among arrestees.* Washington, DC: U.S. Government Printing Office.

Office of National Drug Control Policy (ONDCP). (1993). *State and local spending on drug control.* Washington, DC: U.S. Government Printing Office.

Office of National Drug Control Policy (ONDCP). (1998). *Drug control: Performance measures of effectiveness.* Washington, DC: U.S. Government Printing Office.

Office of National Drug Control Policy (ONDCP). (Annual). *National drug control strategy.* Washington, DC: U.S. Government Printing Office.

O'Hare, P. A., Newcombe, R., Matthews, A., Buning, E. C., & Drucker, E. (1992). *The reduction of drug-related harm.* London: Routledge.

Opium Research Committee. (1927). *Survey of smoking opium conditions in the Far East.* New York: Foreign Policy Association.

Orcutt, J. (1973). Societal reaction and the response to deviation in small groups. *Social Forces, 52,* 259–67.

Oyserman, D., & Markus, H. (1990). Possible selves in balance: Implications for delinquency. *Journal of Social Issues, 46,* 141–57.

Pacula, R. (1998). Does increasing the beer tax raise marijuana consumption? *Journal of Health Economics, 17,* 557–86.

Parfit, D. (1984). *Reasons and persons.* New York: Oxford University Press.

Parker, H., Bakx, K., & Newcombe, R. (1988). *Living with heroin: The impact of a drugs "epidemic" on an English community.* Philadelphia: Open University Press.

Parker, J., & Grasmick, H. (1979). The effect of actual crimes and arrests on people's perceptions of the certainty of arrest: An exploratory study of an untested proposition in deterrence theory. *Criminology, 17,* 366–79.

Paternoster, R. (1987). The deterrent effect of the perceived certainty and severity of punishment: A review of the evidence and issues. *Justice Quarterly, 4,* 173–217.

Paternoster, R. (1989). Decision to participate in and desist from four types of common delinquency: Deterrence and the rational choice perspective. *Law and Society Review, 23,* 7–40.

Pearl, J. (1987). The highest paying customers: America's cities and the costs of prostitution control. *Hastings Law Journal, 38,* 769–90.

Pearson, G. (1991). Drug-control policies in Britain. In M. Tonry (Ed.), *Crime and justice: An annual review of research, 14* (pp. 167–84). Chicago: University of Chicago Press.

Pearson, G. (1992). Drug problems and criminal justice policy in Britain. *Contemporary Drug Problems, 19,* 279–301.

Perneger, T. V., Giner, F., del Rio, M., & Mno, A. (1998). Randomised trial of heroin maintenance programme for addicts who fail in conventional drug treatments. *British Medical Journal, 317,* 13–18.

Perry, C., Kelder, S. H., Murray, D. M., & Klepp, K. I. (1992). Community-wide smoking prevention: Long-term outcomes of the Minnesota heart health program and the class of 1989 study. *American Journal of Public Health, 82,* 1210–16.

Peters, K. D., Kochanek, K. D., & Murphy, S. L. (1998). Deaths: Final data for 1996. *National Vital Statistics Report, 47.*

Peterson, B. E., Doty, R. M., & Winter, D. G. (1993). Authoritarianism and attitudes toward contemporary social issues. *Personality and Social Psychology Bulletin, 19,* 174–84.

Petry, N. M., & Bickel, W. K. (1998). Polydrug abuse in heroin addicts: A behavioral economic analysis. *Addiction, 93,* 321–35.

The pharmacology of the newer materia medica. (1892). Detroit, MI: George C. Davis.

Phibbs, C. S., Bateman, D. A., & Schwartz, R. M. (1991). The neonatal costs of maternal cocaine use. *Journal American Medical Association, 266,* 1521–6.

Pierre, R. (1996, September 9). Marijuana's violent side. *Washington Post,* p. A1.

Pihl, M. (1989, May 6). Demand for new narcotics debate. *Copenhage Berlingske Tidende, 3.* In *JPRS: Narcotics* (1989, May 23, p. 41).

Piliavin, I., Thornton, C., Gartner, R., & Matsueda, R. L. (1986). Crime, deterrence, and rational choice. *American Sociological Review, 51,* 101–19.

Pincus, W. (1994, July 21). House votes $28 billion for intelligence. *Washington Post,* p. A17.

Pitler, R. M. (1996). Independent state search and seizure constitutionalism: The New York State Court of Appeals' quest for principled decisionmaking. *Brooklyn Law Review, 62,* Spring.

Plasse, T. F. (1991). Clinical use of dronabinol. *Journal of Clinical Oncology, 9,* 2079–80.

Premier's Drug Advisory Council. (1996). *Drugs and our community.* Melbourne, Australia: Victorian Government.

President's Commission on Law Enforcement and the Administration of Justice. (1967). *Task force report: Organized crime.* Washington, DC: U.S. Government Printing Office.

President's Commission on Organized Crime. (1986). *Organized crime and gambling: Record of hearing VII.* Washington, DC: U.S. Government Printing Office.

Prostitution Education Network. (1998). *Prostitution in the United States – The Statistics.* http://www.bayswan.org/stats.html.

Ramsay, M., & Percy, A. (1997). A national household survey of drug misuse in Britain: A decade of development. *Addiction, 92,* 931–7.

RAND Drug Policy Research Center. (2000). *Response to NRC's Assessment of "Controlling Cocaine."* Santa Monica, CA: RAND.

Rasmussen, D. W., & Benson, B. L. (1994). *The economic anatomy of a drug war: Criminal justice in the commons.* Lanham, MD: Rowman and Littlefield.

Rawls, J. (1971). *A theory of justice.* Cambridge, MA: Harvard University Press.

Raz, J. (1986). *The morality of freedom.* Oxford: Clarendon Press.

Recent data on illegal drug abuse and trafficking by National Law Enforcement Monitoring System of the FRG (unpublished manuscript). (1991, November). City of Hamburg, Germany.

Reilly, D., Didcott, P., Swift, W., & Hall, W. (1998). Long-term cannabis use: Characteristics of users in an Australian rural area. *Addiction, 93,* 837–46.

Reinarman, C., & Levine, H. G. (1989). Crack in context: Politics and media in the making of a drug scare. *Contemporary Drug Problems, 16,* 535–77.

Reisinger, M. (1993). Treatment of drug addiction and the epidemiology of Aids. In M. Reisinger (Ed.), *Aids and drug addiction in the European Community* (pp. 15–36). Lisbon, Portugal: European Monitoring Centre for Drugs and Drug Addiction.

Reno, R. (1996). The diceman cometh: Will gambling be a bad bet for your town? *Policy Review, 76*, 40–5.

Rettig, R. A., & Yarmolinsky, A. (Eds.). (1995). *Federal regulation of methadone treatment*. Committee on Federal Regulation of Methadone Treatment, Institute of Medicine. Washington, DC: National Academy Press.

Reuband, K. H. (1990). Research on drug use: A review of problems, needs, and future perspectives. *Drug and Alcohol Dependence, 25*, 149–52.

Reuband, K. H. (1991). *Drug use in Germany and national policy: A review of empirical evidence*. Paper presented at International Conference on Drug Policies and Problems. Washington, DC: RAND Drug Policy Research Center.

Reuband, K. H. (1992a). Drug addiction and crime in West Germany: A review of the empirical evidence. *Contemporary Drug Problems, 19*, 327–49.

Reuband, K. H. (1992b). The epidemiology of drug use in Germany: Basic data and trends. In G. Bühringer & J. J. Platt (Eds.), *Drug Addiction Treatment Research: German and American Perspectives* (pp. 3–16). Malabar, FL: Krieger.

Reuband, K. H. (1995). Drug use and drug policy in Western Europe: Epidemiological findings in a comparative perspective. *European Addiction Research, 1*, 32–41.

Reuter, P. (1983). *Disorganized Crime*. Cambridge, MA: MIT Press.

Reuter, P. (1984a). Police regulation of illegal gambling: Frustrations of symbolic enforcement. *Annals of American Academy of Political and Social Science, 1994*, 36–47.

Reuter, P. (1984b). The (continued) vitality of mythical numbers. *Public Interest, 75*, 135–47.

Reuter, P. (1991). On the consequences of toughness. In E. Lazear & M. Krauss (Eds.), *Searching for alternatives: Drug control policy in the United States* (pp. 138–62). Stanford, CA: Hoover Press.

Reuter, P. (1992). Hawks ascendant: The punitive trend of drug policy. *Daedalus, 121*, 15–52.

Reuter, P. (1994). Setting priorities: Budget and program choices for drug control. *The University of Chicago Legal Forum, 1994*, 145–73.

Reuter, P. (1999). Drug use indicators: What are they really telling us? *National Institute of Justice Journal, April*, 12–19.

Reuter, P., & Kleiman, M. (1986). Risks and prices: An economic analysis of drug enforcement. In N. Morris & M. Tonry (Eds.), *Crime and justice: An annual review of research, 7* (pp. 289–340). Chicago: University of Chicago Press.

Reuter, P., & MacCoun, R. (1992). Street drug markets in inner-city neighborhoods: Matching policy to reality. In J. B. Steinberg, D. W. Lyon, & M. E. Vaiana (Eds.), *Urban America: Policy choices for Los Angeles and the nation* (pp. 227–51). Santa Monica, CA: RAND.

Reuter, P., & MacCoun, R. (1995). Drawing lessons from the absence of harm reduction in American drug policy. *Tobacco Control, 4*, S28–S32.

Reuter, P., & Rubinstein, J. (1982). *Illegal gambling in New York*. Washington, DC: National Institute of Justice.

Reuter, P., Crawford, G., & Cave, J. (1988). *Sealing the borders: The effects of increased military participation in drug interdiction*. Santa Monica, CA: RAND.

Reuter, P., Ebener, P. A., & McCaffrey, D. (1994). Patterns of drug use. In D. J. Besharov (Ed.), *When drug addicts have children: Reorienting child welfare's response*. Washington, DC: Child Welfare League of America and American Enterprise Institute.

Reuter, P., MacCoun, R., & Murphy, P. (1990). *Money from crime*. Santa Monica, CA: RAND.

Rhodes, W., Langenbahn, S., Kling, R., & Scheiman, P. (1997). *What America's users spend on illegal drugs, 1988–1995*. Washington, DC: Office of National Drug Control Policy.

Rhodes W., Layne M., Johnson, P., & Hozik, L. (2000). *What America's users spend on illicit drugs: 1988–1998*. Washington, DC: Office of National Drug Control Policy.

Rhodes, W., Scheiman, P., Pittayathikhun, T., Collins, L., & Tsarfaty, V. (1995). *What America's users spend on illegal drugs, 1988–1993*. Washington, DC: Office of National Drug Control Policy.

Rice, D. (1993). The economic cost of alcohol abuse and dependence: 1990. *Alcohol Health and Research World, 17*, 10–18.

Rice, D., Kelman, S., & Miller, L. (1991). Estimates of economic costs of alcohol and drug abuse and mental illness, 1985 and 1988. *Public Health Reports, 106*, 280–92.

Richards, D. A. J. (1982). *Sex, drugs, death, and the law*. Towata, NJ: Rowman and Littlefield.

Rickets, E., & Sawhill, I. (1988). Defining and measuring the underclass. *Journal of Policy Analysis and Management, 7*, 316–25.

Riley, K. J. (1997). *Crack, powder cocaine, and heroin: Drug purchase and use patterns in six U.S. cities*. Washington, DC: National Institute of Justice and Office of National Drug Control Policy.

Rio, L. M. (1991). Psychological and sociological research and the decriminalization or legalization of prostitution. *Archives of Sexual Behavior, 20*, 205–18.

Rinehart, S. (1993, November 17). Judge rejects anti-pot law, ruling backs earlier decisions. *Anchorage Daily News*, p. A1.

Robins, L., & Regier, D. (1991). *Psychiatric disorders in America*. New York: Free Press.

Robinson, C. E. (1932). *Straw votes*. New York: Columbia University Press.

Robinson, P. H., & Darley, J. M. (1997). The utility of desert. *Northwestern University Law Review, 91*, 453–99.

Rojas, A. (1998, February 26). State top court clears way to shut medical pot clubs. *San Francisco Chronicle*, p. A1.

Ronis, D. L., Yates, J. F., & Kirscht, J. P. (1989). Attitudes, decisions, and habits as determinants of repeated behavior. In A. Pratkanis, S. Breckler, & A. Greenwald (Eds.), *Attitude structure and function*. Hillsdale, NJ: Lawrence Erlbaum Associates.

Rose, G. (1992). *The strategy of preventive medicine*. Oxford: Oxford University Press.

Rosenblatt, A. (1981, July 14). *Miami Herald* (Lexis/Nexis has an abstract of the article but no title).

Rosencrance, J. (1989). Controlled gambling: A promising future. In H. J. Shaffer, S. A. Stein, B. Gambino, & T. N. Cummings (Eds.), *Compulsive Gambling: Theory, Research and Practice*. Lexington, MA: Lexington Books.

Rosenthal, A. M. (1996, October 22). Job for a president: The brightening of America. *New York Times, 145*, A15.

Rosenthal, R. (1990). How are we doing in soft psychology? *American Psychologist, 42*, 775–7.

Ross, H. L. (1976). The neutralization of severe penalties: Some traffic law studies. *Law and Society Review, 10*, 403–13.

Ross, H. L. (1982). *Deterring the drinking driver – Legal policy and social control*. Lexington, MA: Lexington Books, Heath.

Ross, H. L. (1992). *Controlling drunk driving*. New Haven, CT: Yale University Press.

Ross, H. L., & Foley, J. P. (1987). Judicial disobedience of the mandate to imprison drunk drivers. *Law and Society Review, 21*, 315–23.

Ross, H. L., & LaFree, G. D. (1986). Deterrence in criminology and social policy. In N. J. Smelser & D. R. Gerstein (Eds.), *Behavioral and social science: Fifty years of discovery* (pp. 129–52). Washington, DC: National Academy Press.

Ross, L., & Nisbett, R. E. (1991). *The person and the situation: Perspectives of social psychology*. New York: McGraw Hill.

Rossi, P. H., Waite, E., Bose, C. E., & Berk, R. E. (1974). The seriousness of crimes: Normative structure and individual differences. *American Sociological Review, 39*, 224–37.

Rozin, P. (1999). The process of moralization. *Psychological Science, 10*, 218–21.

Rubio, A., & Cerdan, M. (1991, November 18). Drugs: Spain, Europe's courier. *Madrid Cambio*, 11–22. In *JPRS: Narcotics* (1992, January 14, p. 60).

Rudovsky, D. (1994). The impact of the war on drugs on procedural fairness and racial equality. *Chicago Legal Forum, 1994*, 237–74.

Rundall, T., & Bruvold, W. (1988). A meta-analysis of school-based smoking and alcohol use prevention programs. *Health Education Quarterly, 15*, 317–34.

Rutherford, A., & Green, P. (1989). Illegal drugs and British criminal justice policy. In H. J. Albrecht & A. Kalmthout (Eds.), *Drug policies in Western Europe* (pp. 383–407). Frieburg, Germany: Eigenverlag Max-Planck Institut.

Rydell, P., & Everingham, S. (1994). *The costs of cocaine control*. Santa Monica, CA: RAND.

Sack, K. (1995, November 5). There are two sides to every game in town. *New York Times*, p. D4.

Saffer, H. (1996). Studying the effects of alcohol advertising on consumption. *Alcohol Health and Research World*, *20*, 266–72.

Saffer, H., & Chaloupka, F. (1995). *The demand for illicit drugs* (working paper 5238). Cambridge, MA: National Bureau of Economic Research.

Sah, R. K. (1991). Social osmosis and patterns of crime. *Journal of Political Economy*, *99*, 1272–95.

Sandwijk, J. P., Cohen, P. D. A., & Musterd, S. (1991). *Licit and illicit drug use in Amsterdam: Report of a household survey in 1990 on the prevalence of drug use among the population of 12 years and over.* Amsterdam: Department of Human Geography, University of Amsterdam.

Sandwijk, J. P., Cohen, P. D. A., Musterd, S., & Langemeijer, M. P. S. (1995). *Licit and illicit drug use in Amsterdam II: Report of a household survey in 1994 on the prevalence of drug use among the population of 12 years and over.* Amsterdam: Department of Human Geography, University of Amsterdam.

Saner, H., MacCoun, R., & Reuter, P. (1995). On the ubiquity of drug selling among youthful offenders in Washington, DC, 1985–1991: Age, period, or cohort effect? *Journal of Quantitative Criminology*, *11*, 337–62.

San Francisco Task Force on Prostitution. (1996). *Final Report 1996.* http://www.ci.sf.ca.us/reports/sftfp/3sumrec.htm.

Satel, S., Reuter, P., Hartley, D., Rosenheck, R., & Mintz, J. (1997). Influence of retroactive disability payment on recipient compliance with substance abuse treatment. *Psychiatric Services*, *48*, 796–9.

Schaler, J. A. (Ed.) (1998). *Drugs: Should we legalize, decriminalize, or deregulate?* Amherst: NY: Prometheus Books.

Schauffler, H. H. (1993). Health insurance policy and the politics of tobacco. In R. Rabin & S. Sugarman (Eds.), *Smoking policy: Law, politics and culture* (pp. 184–207). New York: Oxford University Press.

Schechter, M. T., Strathdee, S. A., Cornelisse, P. G. A., & Currie, S. (1999). Do needle exchange programmes increase the spread of HIV among injection drug users? An investigation of the Vancouver outbreak. *AIDS*, *13*, F45–F51.

Schelling, T. (1992). Addictive drugs: The cigarette experience. *Science*, *255*, 430–3.

Schlosser, E. (1994). Reefer Madness. *The Atlantic Monthly*, *274*, 45–58.

Schneider, W. (1994, March 4). *The urban front: Scaling back the drug war to reduce crime and disease.* Testimony before the U.S. House of Representatives (no committee listed).

Schroeder, R. C. (1980). *The politics of drugs: An American dilemma* (2nd ed.). Washington, DC: Congressional Quarterly Inc.

Schudson, M. (1993). Symbols and smokers: Advertising, health messages. In R. Rabin & S. Sugarman (Eds.), *Smoking policy: Law, politics and culture* (pp. 208–25). New York: Oxford University Press.

Schultes, R. E., & Hofmann, A. (1992). *Plants of the gods*. Rochester, VT: Healing Arts Press.

Schweizerische Bundesanwaltschaft Zentrapolizeibuero. (1991). *Schweizerische Betaeubungsmittelstatistik 90* [Swiss drug statistics 1990]. Bern: Schweizerische Bundesanwaltschaft Zentrapolizeibuero.

Segal, B. (1990). *Drug taking behavior among school-aged youth: The Alaska experience and comparisons with lower-48 states.* New York: Hayworth Press.

Segalman, R. (1986). Welfare in Switzerland. *Public Interest, 82*, 106–21.

Senay, E., Lewis, D., & Millar, D. (1996). The history and current status of drug substitution therapy for narcotic addiction in the United States. In Swiss Federal Office of Public Health, *The medical prescription of narcotics: Scientific foundation and practical experiences* (pp. 189–200). Seattle, WA: Hogrefe and Huber Publishers.

Shaffer, H., Hall, M., & Bilt, J. (1997). *Estimating the prevalence of disordered gambling behavior in the United States and Canada: A meta-analysis.* Cambridge, MA: Harvard Medical School, Division on Addictions.

Shaffer, H., Stein, S., Gambino, B., & Cummings, T. (Eds.). (1989). *Compulsive gambling: Theory, research, and practice.* Lexington, MA: Lexington Books.

Shalala, D. (1995, August 18). Say "no" to legalization of marijuana. *Wall Street Journal*, p. A10.

Shane, S. (1998, June 10). Test of "heroin maintenance" may be launched in Baltimore. *Baltimore Sun*, p. 1A.

Shane, S., & Shields, G. (1998, June 12). Heroin maintenance quickly stirs outrage. *Baltimore Sun*, p. 1A.

Shedler, J., & Block, J. (1990). Adolescent drug use and psychological health: A longitudinal inquiry. *American Psychologist, 45*, 612–30.

Shweder, R. A., Much, N. C., Mahapatra, M., & Park, L. (1997). The "big three" of morality (autonomy, community, divinity) and the "big three" explanations of suffering (pp. 119–69). In A. M. Brandt & P. Rozin (Eds.), *Morality and health.* New York: Routledge.

Siegel, R. K. (1989). *Intoxication: Life in pursuit of artificial paradise.* New York: Dutton.

Sifaneck, S. J., & Kaplan, C. D. (1995). Keeping off, stepping on and stepping off: The steppingstone theory reevaluated in the context of the Dutch cannabis experience. *Contemporary Drug Problems, 22*, 483–512.

Silverman, L. P., & Spruill, N. L. (1977). Urban crime and the price of heroin. *Journal of Urban Economics, 4*, 80–103.

Silvis, J. (1994). Enforcing drug law in the Netherlands. In E. Leuw & I. H. Marshall (Eds.), *Between prohibition and legalization: The Dutch experiment in drug policy* (pp. 41–58). Amsterdam: Kugler.

Simeone, R., Rhodes, W., Hunt, D., & Truitt, L. (1997). *A plan for estimating the number of "hardcore" drug users in the United States.* Washington, DC: Executive Office of the President, Office of National Drug Control Policy.

Simon, C., & Witte, A. (1982). *Beating the system: The underground economy.* Boston: Auburn House.

Simon, D., & Burns, E. (1997). *The corner: A year in the life of a city neighborhood.* New York: Broadway Books.

Simon, D., Burns, E., & Minton, J. (1998). *The corner: A year in the life of an inner-city neighborhood.* New York: Broadway Books.

Simon, R., Kraus, L., Bauerfeind, R., Bieleman, B., Costes, J., Mariani, F., Olsson, B., & Wiessing, L. (1996). *National prevalence estimates: Improvement of comparability of national estimates of addiction prevalence: Final report* (project CT.96.EP.06). Munich, Germany: Institut für Therapieforschung.

Sinclair, A. (1964). *Era of excess: A social history of the Prohibition movement.* New York: Harper and Row.

Single, E. (1989). The impact of marijuana decriminalization: An update. *Journal of Public Health Policy, 10,* 456–66.

Single, E., Robson, L., Xie, X., Rehm, J., Moore, R., Choi, B., Desjardins, S., & Anderson, J. (1996). *The costs of substance abuse in Canada: Highlights of a major study of the health, social and economic costs associated with the use of alcohol, tobacco and illicit drugs.* Ottawa, Ontario: Canadian Center on Substance Abuse. *http://www.ccsa.ca/costhigh.htm.*

Skitka, L. J., & Tetlock, P. E. (1993). Of ants and grasshoppers: The political psychology of allocating public assistance. In B. Mellers & J. Baron (Eds.), *Psychological perspectives on justice* (pp. 205–33). Cambridge, England: Cambridge University Press.

Skog, O. J. (1993). The tail of the alcohol consumption distribution. *Addiction, 88,* 601–10.

Skolnick, J. (1978). *House of cards: The legalization and control of casino gambling.* Boston: Little Brown.

Skolnick, J. H. (1992). Rethinking the drug problem. *Daedalus, 121,* 133–60.

Smart, R. G. (1989). Is the postwar drinking binge ending? Cross-national trends in per capita alcohol consumption. *British Journal of Addiction, 84,* 743–8.

Smart, R. G., & Murray, G. F. (1985). Narcotic drug abuse in 152 countries: Social and economic conditions as predictors. *International Journal of the Addictions, 20,* 737–49.

Smiley, A. (1986). Marijuana: On-road and driving simulator studies. *Alcohol, Drugs & Driving: Abstracts & Reviews, 2,* 121–34.

Smoking 'em out (1990, September 15). *The Economist,* p. 83.

Solomon, R. (1985). Regulating the regulators: Prohibition enforcement in the seventh circuit. In D. Kyvig (Ed.), *Law, alcohol and order: Perspectives on national Prohibition* (pp. 81–96). Westport, CT: Greenwood Press.

Solivetti, L. (1994). Drug diffusion and social change: The illusion about a formal social control. *The Howard Journal, 33,* 41–61. [Unpublished version from the *International Conference on Drug Use and Drug Policy: A European Perspective* (1994). Cologne, Germany. Includes addiction tables, the published version does not.]

Soros, G. (1997, February 2). It's time to just say no to self-destructive prohibition. *Washington Post,* p. C1.

Sourcebook of criminal justice statistics. (Annual). Washington, DC: Bureau of Justice Statistics, U.S. Department of Justice.

Spence, J. (1975). Opium smoking in Ch'ing China. In F. Wakeman & C. Grant (Eds.), *Conflict and control in late imperial China* (pp. 143–73). Berkeley, CA: University of California Press.

Spillane, J. (1994). *Modern drug, modern menace: The legal use and distribution of cocaine in the United States* (dissertation). Pittsburgh: Carnegie Mellon University.

Spillane, J. (2000). *Cocaine: From modern marvel to modern menace in the United States, 1884–1920.* Baltimore: Johns Hopkins University Press.

Squibb, E. R. (1884). Cocaine. *Pharmaceutical Journal and Transactions, 15,* 465.

Stalans, L. J., Kinsey, K. A., & Smith, K. W. (1991). Listening to different voices: Formation of sanction beliefs and taxpaying norms. *Journal of Applied Social Psychology, 21,* 119–38.

Stares, P. (1996). *Global habit.* Washington, DC: Brookings Institution.

Steadily more narcotics deaths. (1991, May 3). *Oslo Aftenposten,* 48. In *JPRS: Narcotics* (1991, June 4, p. 37).

Stears, A. (1997). The British drug treatment system: Personal perspectives. In D. Lewis, C. Gear, L. M. Laubli, & D. Langenick-Cartwright (Eds.), *The medical prescription of narcotics: Scientific foundations and practical experiences* (pp. 122–9). Seattle: Hogrefe and Huber Publishers.

Steffen, M. (1992). France: Social solidarity and scientific expertise. In D. Kirp & R. Bayer (Eds.), *AIDS in the industrialized democracies* (pp. 221–52). New Brunswick, NJ: Rutgers University Press.

Stelzle, C. (1918). *Why prohibition!* New York: George Duran.

Sterngold, J. (1996, July 14). Muting the lotteries' perfect pitch. *New York Times,* p. 1.

Stetzer, A., & Hofman, D. A. (1996). Risk compensation: Implications for safety interventions. *Organizational Behavior and Human Decision Processes, 66,* 73–88.

Stimson, G. (1994, July 14). *AIDS and injecting drug use in the United Kingdom, 1988 to 1993: The policy response and the prevention of the epidemic* (draft, unpublished manuscript). London: University of London.

Stimson, G. (1996). Has the United Kingdom averted an epidemic of HIV-1 infection among drug injectors? *Addiction, 91,* 1085–88.

Strang, J. (1989). "The British system": Past, present and future. *International Review of Psychiatry, 1,* 109–20.

Strang, J., & Gossop, M. (Eds.). (1994). *Heroin addiction and drug policy: The British system.* Oxford: Oxford University Press.

Strang, J., Ruben, S., Farrell, M., & Gossop, M. (1994). Prescribing heroin and other injectable drugs. In J. Strang & M. Gossop (Eds.), *Heroin addiction and drug policy: The British system* (pp. 192–206). Oxford: Oxford University Press.

Strassman, R. J. (1995). Hallucinogenic drugs in psychiatric research and treatment: Perspectives and prospects. *Journal of Nervous & Mental Disease, 183,* 127–38.

Strathdee, S. A., Patrick, D. M., Currie, S. L., Cornelisse, P. G. A., Rekart, M. L., Montaner, J. S. G., Schechter, M. T., & O'Shaughnessy, M. V. (1997). Needle exchange is not enough: Lessons from the Vancouver injecting drug use study. *AIDS, 11,* F59–F65.

Strausbaugh, J., & Blaise, D. (Eds.). (1991). *The drug user: Documents 1840–1960.* New York: Blast Books.

Substance Abuse and Mental Health Services Administration (SAMHSA). (1995). *National drug and alcohol treatment utilization survey*. Rockville, MD: U.S. Department of Health and Human Services.

Substance Abuse and Mental Health Services Administration (SAMHSA). (1997a). *Drug abuse warning network series: D-3 Year-end preliminary estimates from the 1996 Drug abuse warning network. http://www.samhsa.gov/oas/dawn/dwn96.htm*.

Substance Abuse and Mental Health Services Administration (SAMHSA). (1997b). *National admissions to substance abuse treatment services: The treatment episode data set (TEDS) 1992–1995*. Rockville, MD: U.S. Department of Health and Human Services.

Substance Abuse and Mental Health Services Administration (SAMHSA), Office of Applied Studies. (Annual). *Year-end preliminary estimates from the drug abuse warning network: Medical examiner*. Rockville, MD: U.S. Department of Health and Human Services.

Substance Abuse and Mental Health Services Administration (SAMHSA). (Various years). *National household survey on drug abuse*. Rockville, MD: U.S. Department of Health and Human Services. *http://www.health.org/pubs/95hhs/app5.htm*.

Swedish Council for Information on Alcohol and Other Drugs. (1993). *Trends in alcohol and drug use in Sweden*. Stockholm: Swedish Council for Information on Alcohol and Other Drugs.

Swedish National Institute of Public Health (1993). *A restrictive drug policy: The Swedish experience*. Stockholm.

Sweet, R. W., & Harris, E. A. (1998). Moral and constitutional considerations in support of the decriminalization of drugs. In J. M. Fish (Ed.), *How to legalize drugs* (pp. 430–84). Northvale, NJ: Jason Aronson, Inc.

Swierstra K. (1994). The development of contemporary drug problems. In E. Leuw & I. H. Marshall (Eds.), *Between prohibition and legalization: The Dutch experiment in drug policy* (pp. 97–117). Amsterdam: Kugler.

Swift, W., Hall, W., & Copeland, J. (1997). *Cannabis dependence among long-term users in Sydney, Australia*. Sydney, Australia: National Drug and Alcohol Research Center.

Swiss Health Department. (1995). Principles for the Future of Swiss Drug Policy. *Spectra, 1*.

Swiss Health Department. (1997). *Spectra*.

Szasz, T. S. (1974). *Ceremonial chemistry: The ritual persecution of drugs, addicts, and pushers*. Garden City, NY: Doubleday.

Szasz, T. S. (1987). The morality of drug controls. In R. Hamowy (Ed.), *Dealing with drugs: Consequences of government control* (pp. 327–51). San Francisco: Pacific Research Institute for Public Policy.

Tapp, J. L., & Kohlberg, L. (1971). Developing senses of law and legal justice. *Journal of Social Issues, 27*, 65–91.

Tempesta, E. (1991). *Drug dependence in Italy: Past, present, and future*. Presented at the International Conference on Drug Policies and Problems. Washington, DC: RAND Drug Policy Research Center.

Terry, C., & Pellens, M. (1928/1970). *The opium problem.* New York: The Committee on Drug Addictions, Bureau of Social Hygiene. Reprint: Montclair, NJ: Pattern Smith Publishing Company.

Tetlock, P. E. (1983). Accountability and complexity of thought. *Journal of Personality and Social Psychology, 45*, 74–83.

Tetlock, P. E. (1989). Structure and function in political belief systems. In A. R. Pratkanis, S. J. Breckler, & A. G. Greenwald (Eds.), *Attitude structure and function.* Hillsdale, NJ: Lawrence Erlbaum Associates.

Tetlock, P. E. (1993). Cognitive structural analysis of political rhetoric: Methodological and theoretical issues. In S. Iyengar & W. J. McGuire (Eds.), *Explorations in political psychology. Duke studies in political psychology* (pp. 380–405). Durham, NC: Duke University Press.

Tetlock, P. E., Peterson, R. S., & Lerner, J. S. (1996). Revising the value pluralism model: Incorporating social content and context postulates. In C. Seligman, J. M. Olson, & M. P. Zanna (Eds.), *The psychology of values: The Ontario symposium* (pp. 25–51). Mahwah, NJ: Lawrence Erlbaum Associates.

Thies, C. F., & Register, C. A. (1993). Decriminalization of marijuana and the demand for alcohol, marijuana and cocaine. *Social Science Journal, 30*, 385–400.

Thomas, C. (1995). *Marijuana arrests and incarceration in the United States: Preliminary report. http://www.mpp.org/arrest94.html.*

Thompson, S. P. (Ed.). (1998). *The war on drugs: Opposing viewpoints.* San Diego, CA: Greenhaven Press.

Thornton, M. (1991). *The economics of prohibition.* Salt Lake City: University of Utah Press.

Tobacco Institute. (1994). *The tax burden on tobacco.* Washington, DC: Tobacco Institute.

Tobler, N. S. (1992). Drug prevention programs can work: Research findings. *Journal of Addictive Diseases, 11*, 1–28.

Tonry, M. (1995). *Malign neglect.* New York: Oxford University Press.

Torry, S. (1998, May 19). Fearing gain for trial lawyers, business groups fight tobacco bill harder. *Washington Post*, p. A5.

Torry, S., & Dewar, H. (1998, June 17). Big tobacco's ad blitz. *Washington Post*, p. A1.

Towns, C. B. (1917, January 17). Clean-up day in the narcotic situation. *Pharmaceutical Era*, p. 14.

Toxic Substances Board. (1989). *Health or tobacco: An end to tobacco advertising and promotion.* Wellington, New Zealand: Department of Health.

Trachtenberg, A. I. (1994). Opiates for pain: Patients' tolerance and society's intolerance (letter). *Journal of the American Medical Association, 271*, 427.

Trautmann, C. (1990). Lutte contre la toxicomanie et le trafic des stupéfiants: Raport au Premier Ministre. *La mission interministérielle de lutte contre la toxicomanie.* Paris: La Documentation Française.

Trimbos Institute. (1997, April, 1). *Fact sheet 7: Cannabis policy.* Utrecht, The Netherlands: The Trimbos Institute (formerly NIAD).

Troyer, R. J., & Markle, G. (1983). *Cigarettes: The battle over smoking.* New Brunswick, NJ: Rutgers University Press.

Tsebelis, G. (1990). Penalty has no impact on crime: A game theoretic analysis. *Rationality and Society, 2,* 255–86.

Turin La Stampa (Italy). (1992, March 31). Article. Cited in FBIS, 92–017, p. 50.

Turrisi, R., & Jaccard, J. (1991). Judgment processes relevant to drunk driving. *Journal of Applied Social Psychology, 21,* 89–118.

Tversky, A., & Kahneman, D. (1974). Judgment under uncertainty: Heuristics and biases. *Science, 185,* 1124–31.

Tyler, T. R. (1990). *Why people obey the law.* New Haven, CT: Yale University Press.

Tyler, T. R., & Lind, E. A. (1992). A relational model of authority in groups. *Advances in experimental social psychology, 25,* 115–92.

Uchtenhagen, A., Gutzwiller, F., & Dobler-Mikola, A. (1997). *Programme for a medical prescription of narcotics: Final Report of the Research Representatives. Summary of the synthesis report.* Zurich: University of Zurich.

Udsendt af Rigspoliticehfen. (1991). Copenhagen: Politets Årsberetning.

Uleman, J. S., & Bargh, J. (Eds.). (1990). *Unintended thought.* New York: Guilford Press.

Ulrich-Vogtlin, U. (1997). An overview of the projects. In D. Lewis, C. Gear, L. M. Laubli, & D. Langenick-Cartwright (Eds.), *The medical prescription of narcotics: Scientific foundations and practical experiences* (pp. 76–9). Seattle: Hogrefe and Huber Publishers.

U.S. Department of Health and Human Services. (1987). *Sixth special report to Congress of alcohol and health.* Washington, DC: U.S. Department of Health and Human Services.

U.S. Department of Health and Human Services. (1993). *Eighth special report to Congress of alcohol and health.* Washington, DC: U.S. Department of Health and Human Services.

U.S. Department of Justice. (1995). *Audit report: Asset forfeiture program – Annual financial statement.* Washington, DC: U.S. Department of Justice.

U.S. Department of Treasury. (1930). *Statistics concerning intoxicating liquors.* Washington, DC: U.S. Government Printing Office.

U.S. House of Representatives. (1997, September 17). *Hearing on Needle Exchange Programs.* Washington, DC: The National Security, International Affairs and Criminal Justice Subcommittee of the House Government Reform and Oversight Committee.

U.S. Public Health Service. (1964). *Smoking and health: Report of the advisory to the Surgeon General.* Washington, DC: U.S. Public Health Service.

U.S. threat over drug is lifted in California (1997, May 1). *New York Times,* p. A19.

Vaillant, G. E. (1995). *The natural history of alcoholism revisited.* Cambridge, MA: Harvard University Press.

van Luijk, H. J. L. (1991, June 26–29). *A lesson from history on the issue of drug legalisation: The case of the opiumregie in the Dutch East Indies (1890–1940).*

Presented at the International Conference of Law and Society, University of Amsterdam.

van Ours, J. C. (1995). The price elasticity of hard drugs: The case of opium in the Dutch East Indies, 1923–1938. *Journal of Political Economy*, *103*, 261–79.

Veenman, J. (1995). Ethnic minorities in the Netherlands. In K. McFate, R. Lawson, & W. J. Wilson (Eds.), *Poverty, inequality and the future of social policy: Western states in the new world order* (pp. 607–28). New York: Russell Sage Foundation.

Volberg, R. (1994). *Gambling and problem gambling in Iowa: A replication survey*. Ames, IA: Iowa Department of Human Services.

Vorenberg, E., & Vorenberg, J. (1977). The biggest pimp of all: Prostitution and some facts of life. *Atlantic Monthly*, *239*, 27–38.

Votey, H. L., & Phillips, L. (1976). Minimizing the social cost of drug abuse: An economic analysis of alternatives for policy. *Policy Sciences*, *7*, 315–36.

Waldo, G. P., & Chiricos, T. G. (1972). Perceived penal sanction and self-reported criminality: A neglected approach to deterrence research. *Social Problems*, *19*, 522–40.

Walsh, E. (1989, December 7). Edmund convicted on all counts in drug conspiracy case. *Washington Post*, p. A1.

Warburton, C. (1932). *The economic results of Prohibition*. New York: Columbia University Press.

Ward, J., Mattick, R., & Hall, W. (1992). *Methadone maintenance treatment*. Sydney, Australia: University of New South Wales Press.

Warner, K. E. (1979). Clearing the airwaves: The cigarette ban revisited. *Policy Analysis*, *5*, 435–50.

Warner, K. E. (1991). Legalizing drugs: Lessons from (and about) economics. *The Milbank Quarterly*, *69*, 641–61.

Warner, K. E., Slade, J., & Sweanor, D. (1997). The emerging market for long-term nicotine maintenance. *Journal of the American Medical Association*, *278*, 1087–92.

Watters, J. K., Estilo, M. J., Clark, G. L., & Lorvick, J. (1994). Syringe and needle exchange as HIV/AIDS prevention for injection drug users. *Journal of the American Medical Association*, *271*, 115–20.

Weaver, F. M., & Carroll, J. S. (1985). Crime perceptions in a natural setting by expert and novice shoplifters. *Social Psychology Quarterly*, *48*, 349–59.

Weil, A. (1972). *The natural mind*. Boston, MA: Houghton Mifflin Co.

Weiner, B., Perry, R. B., & Magnusson, J. (1988). An attributional analysis of reactions to stigma. *Journal of Personality and Social Psychology*, *55*, 738–48.

Weinstein, N. D., & Klein, W. M. (1995). Resistance of personal risk perceptions to debiasing interventions. *Health Psychology*, *14*, 132–40.

Weitzer, R. (1991). Prostitutes' rights in the United States: The failure of a movement. *The Sociological Quarterly*, *32*, 23–41.

Weitzer, R. (1997). *Rethinking American prostitution policy* (unpublished paper). Washington, DC: Department of Sociology, George Washington University.

West, S. G., Hepworth, J. T., McCall, M. A., & Reich, J. W. (1989). An evaluation of Arizona's July 1982 drunk driving law: Effects on the city of Phoenix. *Journal of Applied Social Psychology, 19*, 1212–37.

White, G. L., & Zimbardo, P. G. (1980). The effects of surveillance and actual surveillance on expressed opinions toward marijuana. *Journal of Social Psychology, 111*, 49–61.

Whiteside, H. O. (1978). The drug habit in nineteenth century Colorado. *Colorado Magazine, 55*, 47–68.

Wickelgren, I. (1997). Marijuana: Harder than thought? *Science, 276*, 1967–8.

Wilde, G. J. S. (1982). The theory of risk homeostasis: Implications for safety and health. *Risk Analysis, 2*, 209–55.

Wille, R. (1987). Drug addiction in the Federal Republic of Germany: Problems and responses. *British Journal of Addiction, 82*, 849–56.

Williams, A. F., & Lund, A. K. (1984). Deterrent effect of roadblocks on drinking and driving. *Traffic Safety Evaluation Research Review, 3*, 7–18.

Williams, F. V. (1920). *The hop-heads: Personal experiences among the users of "dope" in the San Francisco underworld*. San Francisco: Walter N. Brunt.

Williams, K. R., & Hawkins, R. (1986). Perceptual research on general deterrence: A critical review. *Law & Society Review, 20*, 545–72.

Williams, K. R., & Hawkins, R. (1989). The meaning of arrest for wife assault. *Criminology, 27*, 163–81.

Wilson, J. Q. (1990). Against the legalization of drugs. *Commentary, 89*, 21–8.

Wilson, J. Q. (1993). *The moral sense*. New York: Free Press.

Wilson, J. Q. (1997). What, if anything, can the federal government do to reduce crime? *Perspectives on Crime and Justice* (pp. 1–22). Washington, DC: National Institute of Justice.

Wilson, J. Q., & Herrnstein, R. J. (1985). *Crime and human nature*. New York: Simon and Schuster.

Wilson, W. J. (1996). *When work disappears: The world of the new urban poor*. New York: Alfred A. Knopf.

Wish, E. (1990–91). U.S. drug policy in the 1990s: Insights from new data from arrestees. *International Journal of Addictions, 25*, 377–409.

Wisotsky, S. (1986). *Breaking the impasse in the war on drugs*. New York: Greenwood Press.

Wodak, A. (1997). Injecting nation: Achieving control of hepatitis C in Australia. *Drug and Alcohol Review, 16*, 275–84.

Wodak, A., & Crofts, N. (1996). Once more unto the breach: Controlling hepatitis C in injecting drug users. *Addiction, 91*, 181–4.

Wolfgang, M. E., Figlio, R. M., Tracy, P. E., & Singer, S. I. (1985). *The national crime survey index of crime severity*. Washington, DC: U.S. Department of Justice, Bureau of Justice Statistics.

Woodcock, J. (1995). Commissions (Royal and otherwise) on drug misuse: Who needs them? *Addiction, 90*, 1297–308.

Woodhouse, D. E., Potterat, J. J., Muth, J. B., Reynolds, J. U., Douglas, J., & Judson, F. N. (1992). Street outreach for STD/HIV prevention – Colorado Springs, Colorado, 1987–1991. *Morbidity and Mortality Weekly Review, 41*, 94–5, 101.

Woodman, W. (1885). Cocaine for sleeplessness. *Boston Medical and Surgical Journal, 112,* 287.

Woodiwiss, M. (1988). *Crime, crusades, and corruption: Prohibitions in the United States, 1900–1987.* London: Pinter Publishers.

Worchel, S., & Arnold, S. E. (1973). The effects of censorship and the attractiveness of the censor on attitude change. *Journal of Experimental Social Psychology, 9,* 365–77.

Workshop on the medical utility of marijuana: Report to the director of the National Institutes of Health. (1997). Ad Hoc Group of Experts, Rockville, MD.

World Health Organization. (1996). Smoking prevalence. *The tobacco epidemic.* http://www.who.ch/programmes/psa/toh/Alert/apr96/intro.html.

Wren, C. (1997, July 22). Reno and top drug official urge smaller gap in cocaine sentences. *New York Times,* p. A1.

Wren, C. (1999, May 9). For heroin's new users, a long, hard fall; Couple's addiction reflects lure of a purer, more potent drug. *New York Times,* p. A29.

Wyer, R. S., & Gruenfeld, D. H. (1995). Information processing in interpersonal communication. In D. E. Hewes (Ed.), *The cognitive bases of interpersonal communication* (pp. 7–47). Hillsdale, NJ: Lawrence Erlbaum Associates, Inc.

Yondorf, B. (1979). Prostitution as a legal activity: The West German experience. *Policy Analysis, 5,* 417–33.

Zamichow, N. (1990, December 3). New 0.8% law spurs surge in drunk driving arrests. *Los Angeles Times,* pp. A3, A29, A30.

Zellinger, D. A., Fromkin, H. L., Speller, D. E., & Kohn, C. A. (1975). A commodity theory analysis of the effects of age restrictions upon pornographic materials. *Journal of Applied Psychology, 60,* 94–9.

Zimmer, L., & Morgan, J. (1997). *Marijuana: Myths and facts.* New York: The Lindesmith Center.

Zimring, F. (1993). Comparing cigarette policy and illicit drug and alcohol control. In R. Rabin & S. Sugarman (Eds.), *Smoking policy: Law, politics and culture* (pp. 95–109). New York: Oxford University Press.

Zimring, F. E., & Hawkins, G. J. (1973). *Deterrence: The legal threat in crime control.* Chicago: University of Chicago Press.

Zimring, F. E., & Hawkins, G. J. (1992). *The search for rational drug control.* New York: Cambridge University Press.

Zinberg, N. (1984). *Drug, set and setting: The basis for controlled toxicant use.* New Haven, CT: Yale University Press.

Zorrilla, G. (1993). Drugs and criminal policy in Spain (1982–1992). *European Journal on Criminal Policy and Research, 1–2,* 76–95.

Zuckerman, M. (1994). Behavioral expressions and biosocial bases of sensation seeking. New York: Cambridge University Press.

Data Sources for Figures

CHAPTER 10

Figures 10.3, 10.4, 10.5

Multinational Sources: EMCDDA (1996; 1997)
Norway: Ministry of Health and Social Affairs (1997)
United States: Bureau of Justice Statistics, *Sourcebook of Criminal Justice Statistics* (1996), Tables 4.34, 4.35, and 4.40

Figure 10.6

France: *1980–1986* Trautmann (1990); *1986–1994* EMCDDA (1997)
Germany: *1980* Wille (1987); *1981–1989* Albrecht (1989); *1986–1994* EMCDDA (1997)
Italy: *1980–1989* Solivetti (1994); *1980–1990* Savona (1990, Unpublished data); *1990–1996* EMCDDA (1997)
Netherlands: *1986–1995* EMCDDA (1997)
Spain: *1980–1983* Cami & Barrio (1991); *1984–1990* Delegatión del Gobernio para el Plan Nacional Sobre Drogas (1990); *1989–1996* EMCDDA (1997)
Sweden: *1980–1986* Swedish Council for Information on Alcohol and Other Drugs (1993); *1986–1994* EMCDDA (1997)
Switzerland: *1980–1989* Bundesamt für Statistik (1991); *1990* Schweizerische Bundesanwaltschaft
Zentrapolizeibuero (1991); *1991–1994* Klingemann (1996)
United Kingdom: *1980* Rutherford & Green (1989); *1980–1990* Home Office (1992); *1986–1995* Personal communication with J. Corkery, Crime & Criminal Justice Unit, Home Office (25 July 1997); *1986–1994* EMCDDA (1997)
United States: FBI, *Uniform Crime Reports* (Annual)

Figure 10.8

Multinational Sources: Bensinger & Reuter (1992); Bless et al. (1993); Brenner et al. (1991); EMCDDA (1996); Farrell (1996); Klingemann et al. (1991); Methadone causes half of drug overdose deaths (1992); Ministry of Foreign Affairs et al. (1995); Reisinger (1993); Reuband (1995)
Denmark: Pihl (1989); *Udsendt af Rigspoliticehfen* (1991)
France: French Observatory of Drugs and Drug Addiction (1996)
Italy: Savona (1990); Solivetti (1994)
Netherlands: Grund (1993); Leuw (1991)
Norway: Hansen (1990)
Spain: 1988 heroin addiction, treatment statistics (1988); Almost all heroin seized (1991); Beaumont (1989); Rubio & Cerdan (1991)
Sweden: Lindgren (1992); Ministry of Health and Social Affairs (1992)
Switzerland: Bundesamtes fur Gesundheitswesen (1990); Grob (1992); Riis-Middel (1993, Personal correspondence)
United Kingdom: Stimson (1994, 1996)
United States: SAMHSA, *National Household Survey on Drug Abuse* (Various years)
West Germany: Degkwitz et al. (1993); Michels (1993); Reuband (1991)

Figure 10.9

Italy: *Through 1989* Solivetti (1994); *1990–1995* EMCDDA (1997)

Figure 10.10

Italy: Simon et al. (1996)

CHAPTER 11

Figure 11.1

Netherlands: Cohen (1995); de Zwart et al. (1997)
Norway: Norwegian Ministry of Health and Social Affairs (1997)
United States: Johnston, O'Malley, & Bachman (Annual)

CHAPTER 12

Figure 12.1

Multinational Sources: Bless et al. (1993); Brenner et al. (1991); Des Jarlais & Friedman (1994); Des Jarlais et al. (1996); Farrell (1996); Hartnoll (1994); Kral et al. (1998); Stimson (1994)

Figure 12.2

European Sources: EMCDDA (1997)
United States: Centers for Disease Control and Prevention (1997)

Figure 12.3

Multinational Sources: Farrell (1996); Ministry of Welfare, Health and Cultural
   Affairs & Ministry of Justice (1995)
Sweden: EMCDDA (1997)
United States: Rettig & Yarmolinsky (1995)

Figure 12.4

Multinational Sources: EMCDDA (1996; 1997). This source includes new data
   series for the Netherlands and the UK that differ from earlier data series
   produced by their respective governments; see below
Denmark: *1980–1984* Jergen (1989)
France: *1980–1984* Mignon (1989)
Germany: *1980–1982* Reuband (1992b); *1983–1984* Recent data on illegal drug
   abuse (1991)
Italy: *1980* Tempesta (1991); *1981–1984* Ministero dell'Interno (1989)
Netherlands (old series): *1980–1984* Bundesamtes fur Gesundheitswesen (1990)
Norway: *1980–1989* Hauge (1991); *1981–1996* Ministry of Health and Social
   Affairs (1997)
Spain: *1981* Cami & Barrio (1991)
United Kingdom (old series): *1980–1989* Home Office (1991)
United States (Drug Abuse Warning Network [DAWN]): *1980–1994* SAMHSA
   (1997b)
United States (Vital Statistics [VS]): *1980–1994* National Center for Health
   Statistics (Annual)

Author/Name Index

Subject Index